A Day
in the Night
of America

A Day
in the Night
of America

KEVIN COYNE

Random House   New York

Grateful acknowledgment is made to the following for permission to reprint previously
published material:
BMG-MUSIC PUBLISHING, FRANNE GOLDE MUSIC, DENNIS LAMBERT, WALTER ORANGE MUSIC,
AND WARNER/CHAPPELL MUSIC, INC.: Six lines from "Nightshift" by Franne Golde,
Dennis Lambert, and Walter Orange. Copyright © 1985 by Tuneworks Music
Company, Rightsong Music, Inc., Franne Golde Music, Inc., and Walter Orange Music.
All rights on behalf of Franne Golde Music, Inc., are administered by Rightsong Music,
Inc. All rights reserved. Reprinted by permission.
FRANCO-LONDON MUSIC PUBLISHING CORPORATION: Three lines from "Here Comes the
Night" by Bert Berns. Copyright © 1964 by Keetch, Caesar & Dino Music, Inc.
Copyright transferred © 1984 to Franco-London Music Publishing Corporation.
Reprinted by permission.
HARWIN MUSIC COMPANY: Excerpt from "One for My Baby (And One More for the
Road)," lyrics by Johnny Mercer and music by Harold Arlen. Copyright © 1943
(renewed) by Harwin Music Co. All rights reserved. Reprinted by permission.
JERRY LEIBER MUSIC AND MIKE STOLLER MUSIC: Excerpt from "Poison Ivy" by Jerry
Leiber and Mike Stoller. Copyright © 1959 by Jerry Leiber Music and Mike Stoller
Music. All rights reserved. Reprinted by permission.
HAROLD OBER ASSOCIATES: Excerpt from "Morning Has Broken" from *Children's Bells*
by Eleanor Farjeon, published by Oxford University Press. Copyright © 1957 by
Eleanor Farjeon. Reprinted by permission of Harold Ober Associates.

Coyne, Kevin.
A day in the night of America / Kevin Coyne.
p. cm.
ISBN 0-394-57640-3
1. Night work—United States. 2. White collar workers—United
States. 3. Night people—United States. I. Title.
HD5113.2.U6C69 1992
331.25′74—dc20   90-53139

FOR JANE

What hath night to do with sleep?

—JOHN MILTON

Well, here it comes,
Here comes the night,
Here comes the night.

—VAN MORRISON

INTRODUCTION

JOINING THE 10 MILLION

If you read any part of this book in bed at night, in the small island of light cast by a nightstand lamp—and I hope that you do—I'd like to ask a favor of you. I'd like to ask you to set the book aside for a moment. At some point in your reading, while your mind is still at the top of the stairs and hasn't yet started its balmy descent into the alternate landscape of sleep and dreams, close the book and look around. Follow the dying beam of your lamp into the corner of the room, where it surrenders its power to illuminate to an indistinct web of accumulating shadows. Reach over then and switch the lamp off. Sit silently for a few minutes, eyes open, and fit your vision to the dark. When the black fades to gray, and the rough outlines of your room warily emerge again, get up and go to the window and look out into the night, out toward the warm yellow lights in the wakeful rooms of your neighbors and across the pale pools of light that lap the pilings of the streetlamps and past the twin tunneling headlights of the passing cars and beyond whatever frail light stumbles down onto Earth from the moon and the stars, out until, finally, the gray deepens to black and your eyes reach the place where all light is swallowed and you can discern no evidence of the houses and the trees and the school and the apartment building and the streets and the stores and the church and the fields that you know, by experience and faith, lie hidden somewhere beneath this dark shroud. Look out from your window into a world that seems to have been erased by the coming of night.

Try to picture then what is out there. If you are, as most Americans are, a diurnal creature who works in the day and sleeps in the night, your vision of the nighttime world is probably compiled from a miscellany of isolated past experiences—a string of sleepless hours comforting a sick child; a bachelor party that careened until dawn; a project due at work or school the next day; eggs in a diner at 3 A.M. after a round of nightclubbing; an insomniac blur of TV commercials for cubic-zirconium earrings; a fearsome, moonlit gallery of bad horror movies; maybe even a few months sleepwalking through a night-shift job. So when you look from the window into that featureless, impenetrable black void, you are actually looking at a blank screen, ready to reflect whatever stories and images you choose to project onto it. You can see on it an empty Edward Hopper world of thick white coffee cups in all-night cafés and lonely pockets of wan yellow light. You can see the stalking army of flesh-eating zombies from *Night of the Living Dead*. You can see Fred Astaire and Ginger Rogers dancing to "Top Hat, White Tie, and Tails," or Burt Lancaster and Deborah Kerr intertwined and rolling in the moonlit surf in *From Here to Eternity*. You can see a knife flash before your face as a thief demands your wallet on a dark city street. Or you can see countless other things that illustrate any of the wildly diverse words that the word *night* itself can modify, or even replace—*evil, romance, lust, mystery, magic, sin, freedom, imprisonment, death, disease, failure, possibility, tranquillity, silence, fear, ignorance, despair, peace, emptiness, winter, stealth, security, creation, apocalypse.*

But how many of the pictures you see as you stand there are true? If you were to pull on your shoes and venture out to explore the night, how would what you imagined from inside your bedroom square with what you find in the dark world outside it? Who would you meet out there, and what would they be doing? If you started your night visit just after midnight, when the evening gives way to the true night, you wouldn't have to walk too far before finding a companion, because twenty-nine million other Americans are still awake then. And if you were still out between 3 A.M. and 4 A.M., the darkest and farthest part of the night, you wouldn't be alone: ten million Americans are up and about at that hour, a number equal to the combined populations of Ireland, Israel and Nicaragua. Many of these inhabitants of night would be familiar to you—the two cops patrolling the streets of midtown Manhattan; the two Chicago nurses patching up the young victim of a gang shooting; the steelworker tending the fires of a Cleveland mill; the trucker hauling a load of beef from Nebraska to Philadelphia; the telephone operator connecting long-distance calls in Florida; the 7-Eleven clerk in Colorado selling a pack of cigarettes. But many others would be strangers—the Wall Street traders calling Tokyo to buy and sell millions of dollars worth of yen; the Boston bank workers processing the day's checks; the movie crew shooting a location scene in downtown Los Angeles; the operator taking phone orders at a catalog sales center in Wisconsin; the railroad engineer blowing the whistle at a remote Nebraska crossing; the air force general in a hollowed-out mountain in the Rockies watching for incoming missiles; the park ranger watching for errant grizzly bears around an Alaska campsite. You would find that the color of night comprises a multitude of shades beyond just monolithic black.

You can turn from the window now and climb back into your bed. Switch the lamp back on and pick the book back up, and as you read the pages that follow, which will introduce you to these people and many others of the ten million, glance up occasionally back to your dark window. And each new time you see the night outside, I hope, it will look slightly different, its face gradually illuminated by your gathering knowledge of what is actually going on out there—what is going on now, as you read, and in an hour, after you have slipped into the sleep that falls over most of the populace as a living darkness falls over the rest.

Night is a time, not a place. It is not a dark place you visit, like Siberia or a coal mine, but a dark time that daily visits you, wherever you are. It occupies the same geographic space as the day, but its defining feature—the absence of light—so dramatically alters the familiar daylit world that the night is often thought of as a separate territory, a sovereign nation even, deserving of its own page in the atlas. The night is not an easy nation to map, because the landscape is hidden under darkness and its borders shift as often as those of a nineteenth-century European state. But this book aims to chart at least a portion of it, to show what the night—the time and the place—has come to look like in America today.

For most of the forty thousand years of human history, the rhythm of life was regulated by the rhythm of light. You worked during the day, and when night fell you slept—because your body demanded it, because you couldn't till the fields in the dark, and because fear and superstition kept you from venturing into a world populated mainly by highwaymen, adulterers, spirits and monsters. Darkness is what preceded life in many creation stories— Genesis, Greek mythology, the Big Bang theory in modern cosmology—

and night was a daily remnant of that immemorial world, marked by all its violence, disorder and emptiness. As your body lay in bed at night, safe amid the collective unconsciousness of humanity, your soul flew out and traveled the world, and the dreams you had were the record of its adventures.

The night stayed mostly dark until the nineteenth century—when technology provided a means for its conquest, and economics provided an incentive. Gaslight first, and then the more reliable light of electricity—courtesy of Thomas Edison, the Columbus of the night—allowed humans to do more than just tiptoe into the evening with candles, and the concurrent rise of the factories of the Industrial Revolution gave them a reason to challenge the schedules set by biology and tradition. The longer the new machines ran, the more goods, and profits, they made. Since World War II—when the war effort enlisted more factories than ever before in round-the-clock production, and in the process illustrated the benefits of cheating sleep—the number of shiftworkers worldwide has doubled. About 20 percent of all American workers now work something other than the standard daytime schedule, whether evenings or nights or rotating shifts. Manufacturing still accounts for a third of the nation's shiftworkers, but the most growth now is in the computer-heavy service economy, which has learned the same lesson about incessancy that factories learned long ago. "This sweaty haste," Shakespeare wrote, as if anticipating our century, "doth make the night joint-laborer with the day."

The traffic through the night—the souls joined by bodies now—is heavier in America than in almost any other nation, except perhaps Japan. If you could perch in one of the satellites hovering in the dark sky over America, you would see a nation aflame, burning like a forest, the restless pattern of lights depicting the restless pattern of human settlement as accurately as a census map. The fire burns uncontrolled because we keep stoking it—by staying up later and sleeping less: The average night's sleep, nine and a half hours in the nineteenth century, had dipped to under eight hours by the 1950s, and is closing in on seven hours now. We have moved so quickly into the night because it offers pleasures, possibilities, jobs, money (10 percent is a common night-shift pay differential) and child-care choices (in a third of all families where both parents work full-time, at least one spouse works a nonday shift, leaving the other at home to watch the kids) unavailable in the day; and because, as sociologist Murray Melbin has written, we are heeding a deep impulse in our national character. The night, Melbin contends, is a new frontier, opened by electricity in the same decade

Introduction

that the Census Bureau declared our land frontier closed, and America is an expansive, insatiable nation hungry for new frontiers. The night is a place that offers economic opportunity and social escape—just as the American West, our original frontier, did—so we have started to devour it much as we once devoured forests to build new towns. We have run out of geographic frontiers to colonize, so we are colonizing a new frontier of time. And like the early western settlers, we have endured certain hardships along the way.

When you stay up past midnight, you defy your body's commands. You have, as even one-celled creatures have, a biological clock—a tiny cluster of nerve cells in your brain's hypothalmus, hooked up to your eyes and set by light and darkness—that regulates the daily rhythm of everything from your heartbeat and body temperature to the secretion of the hormone that makes you drowsy; and when you upend these normal circadian rhythms, your body makes you pay for it. You sleep poorly: Night workers lose on average a full night's sleep each week, and with it goes some of their concentration, creativity, short-term memory and decision-making ability. Your health suffers: You are more susceptible to heart disease, depression, reproductive disorders, ulcers, high cholesterol, constipation, gastrointestinal ailments and obesity. Your job performance slips, especially between 4:00 A.M. and 6:00 P.M., the black hole of the night, when your circadian rhythms drop into their lowest valley: The nuclear accidents at Three Mile Island and Chernobyl happened at, respectively, 4:00 A.M. and 1:23 A.M. You become a danger to others: The Department of Transportation reports that as many as 200,000 traffic accidents a year may be sleep related.

The costs of the national sleep deficit are so high that Congress recently asked a panel of scientists to study it and then to suggest how the government might help ease America's fatigue: regulate night-shift work hours, they said; run sleep-awareness workshops in schools and workplaces; establish a "national center for research and education on sleep and sleep disorders." Individually you can, without federal help, darken your daylit bedroom with heavy curtains and unplug the phone. You can, as Winston Churchill did, nap frequently: In Japan many factories provide cots for late-shift sleep breaks. You can eat an after-dark diet high in protein and low in hard-to-digest foods. Adjustments to standard shift schedules help—a clockwise day-evening-night rotation that takes advantage of the body's natural inclination to stay up later on successive days, rather than the usual counterclockwise day-night-evening; longer shifts, shorter workweeks and more days off, which concentrates the discomfort rather than spreading it out; longer blocks in each shift, maybe several weeks at a time rather than one, which slows the carousel and lets the body adjust. You can also trick your body with false suns: Medical researchers have recently discovered that precisely timed doses of bright light can alter your circadian rhythms to better fit a nocturnal life-style. All our effort may yet make the night look something like the day.

The new American night is a territory with its own rituals, routines, rules, habits, folkways and politics, its own economy, ecology, biology, psychology, sociology and mythology, and like most new territories it is still spottily explored and incompletely mapped. Through the passports issued by television and the *National Geographic,* we can easily become acquainted with Tibet or Zaire, yet the night remains a largely unfamiliar province, probably only as well known as, say, Montana was in the first part of this century. That seemed inequitable, so I went out to visit the neighboring world that breathes around us in America, all night every night, but out of our sight.

You can't see the night too well by looking out the window of a lighted room; the interior light makes the window more a mirror reflecting what's inside than an opening revealing what's outside. You have to go out and let the darkness surround you. To see the night, I got in my car, a 1980 Chevy Citation, in Massachusetts one March, zigzagged through forty-one states for 18,028 miles interviewing 429 people, and by the time I came home in July, my eyes found the summer sun so bright that I bought the first pair of sunglasses I have ever owned. I joined the ten million colonists for those months and, like them, I slept poorly, ate poorly, lost all sense of date and time, felt out of sync with the rest of humanity and endured the phone calls, doorbells and other daytime intrusions of people so fixed in the diurnal world as to be almost incapable of conceiving that there might be other people who are not. There were times when I loved the night, and times when I hated it. I loved the solitude, and hated the isolation. I loved the freedom, and hated the claustrophobia. I loved the tranquillity, and missed the commotion. I liked listening to Larry King, and tired of listening to nothing but Larry King. I enjoyed the free passage on normally clogged streets, but at 7 one Sunday morning, craving a chocolate milk shake in what felt to me like early afternoon, I longed vainly for an open Dairy Queen. And in the end I rejoined, gladly and without regret, the mass of Americans who time their lives to the arc of the sun; and only once in a great

Introduction

while now do I look out toward the night, before yielding to sleep, and wish to return to the smaller nation that lives under the more irregular arc of the moon.

The intent of this book is to depict a typical day in the night of America, to chronicle what happens in the real world that emerges when most of us retreat into the illusory worlds of our private dreams. It is a big subject, and a big country, both easy to get lost in, so before starting my trip I decided on a few guiding principles. Because work is what spurred the settlement of night, and work is what sustains the permanent community there, I spent my time mainly with people who work through the night, not with those who idle or play through it. Night workers are the taxpaying, bedrock citizens of the dark hours; the moonlighting day people who visit for an occasional dose of entertainment are just tourists. I tried to strike a balance between familiar people and places and unfamiliar ones, between people who choose the night and people who are chosen for it, between intense jobs and soporific jobs, solitary jobs and team jobs. I included representatives of each distinct category of night workers—protectors, suppliers, communicators, movers, makers, watchers, preparers, finishers and the rest. I treated the night not as an extension of evening or a preview of morning but as a discrete unit—the period that spans the gap between the end of Johnny Carson's monologue and the start of the radio traffic reports. (I also dispensed with the semantic question of what is night and what is morning: In these pages 3 A.M. on the fifth is late in the night of the fourth, not early in the morning of the fifth; a new day doesn't start until the sun returns.) I traveled generally westward, the same direction as the lengthening shadow of night that daily falls over the continent, and I visited each major region of America—New England, the Mid-Atlantic, the Deep South, the Middle South, the industrial Midwest, the agricultural Heartland, the Southwest, the Rockies, California, the Pacific Northwest, even Alaska. And the resulting book follows here as the trip did—starting at midnight in the East and ending at dawn in the West.

As a nation, I discovered, the American night more resembles Canada than it does the movie version of Dracula's Transylvania. Like Canada it is a largely benign place, its sparse population scattered widely over a huge landmass. Parts of it are violent and frightening and oppressive, but other parts are more civilized and welcoming than I had expected. I found that night people often do embody many of the frontier characteristics ascribed to them by Murray Melbin—a healthy disdain for authority and status distinctions, a willingness to endure adversity, the ability to form friendships quickly, an open and generous disposition to strangers and a tendency toward unconstrained, even quirky, individualism. It didn't take long in their company before I started seeing daytimers the way they often do, which is much the way the military often sees civilians—pampered, undisciplined, ignorant of life's harsher truths.

But maybe what the American night most resembles, I learned, is the body of one of its sleeping citizens. Like the body it can't shut down completely or it would die, but it does shut down all but the most essential functions. Its organs continue to produce necessary goods: bakeries bake bread, steel mills make steel. Its immune system stands guard against invaders: police cruisers patrol, missiles crouch in silos, hospitals aid the sick. Messages travel through its nervous system: telephones ring, TVs broadcast pictures, radios send voices. Traffic circulates through its veins and arteries: trucks, trains, buses, cars, ships and planes all keep moving. It even dreams: roulette wheels spin, prostitutes offer their bodies, astronomers survey the stars, Wall Street traders bet on the international market. And when the body slows to its most nearly comatose state, between 3 A.M. and 5 A.M., so, too, does the night enter its stillest hours then, and reach the lowest ebb of national consciousness. The deepest night reveals what is most necessary to the continued life of the body, and the nation. It is not a time of chaos, but instead a time that offers the clearest view of just those hidden forces that prevent the body, and the nation, from reverting to Chaos—the dark, formless, lifeless void that the ancient Greeks believed preceded creation. The night reveals the outline of life on earth.

It also reveals an even larger picture, one that early and dramatically altered my view of the night: It reveals the outline of the universe. When I started my trip, I thought of the night, as I guess most people do, as a roof dropping on the earth, an obstacle that severely restricted how far you could see. But I soon came to understand that it is precisely the opposite: It is instead the opening of a window that immeasurably extends how far you can see. During the day, when the ground you stand on faces the sun, the atmosphere traps the light, holding it so that you can see the world immediately around you but also blocking your view of the world beyond the earth. When night comes, and the ground you stand on turns away from the sun, the light hisses out of the atmosphere like air from a balloon, obscuring your neighborhood but exposing the skeleton of the heavens. You can see the stars then, a nightly theater of eternity and infinity, and try to fix your place in the universe. It is a time, naturally, of big thoughts and revelations, when the light of your mind, as you lie in bed in the gracious moments before sleep, might shine on places it shies from during the day and flash on insights that, even if they're erased by the coming of dawn, leave you with the restorative sense of having wrestled with the ineffable. Hassidism, I have read, teaches that if you stay awake for one hundred nights, you will receive a vision of Elijah, the biblical prophet who ascended into heaven in a chariot of fire and who now shuttles as a messenger between heaven and earth. I stayed awake for one hundred nights and more, and while I didn't see Elijah, I did see many things I would not have seen had I slept through those one hundred nights—things that showed that, despite all its earnest business routines in America today, the night is not just a darker version of the day. I saw Pluto, the farthest planet in the solar system, through a telescope perched high on a California mountain. I saw several couples united in matrimony at the same Las Vegas wedding chapel where Joan Collins once said her vows. I watched scores of homeless men fill the tight rows of cots in a Chicago shelter and enjoy the rare peace of undisturbed sleep. I stood on the shore of the Arctic Ocean in Alaska, 250 miles above the Arctic Circle, in the 3 A.M. daylight of a summer sun that just circled the sky, never setting. I watched white-robed Trappist monks, hours before dawn, file into a chapel on a mile-high alpine meadow ringed by the snow-capped Rockies; and I listened as they sang the Psalms in the haunting rhythm of a Gregorian chant. They sing at that hour because their voices, they believe, carry farther in the deep, clear silence. The darkest night, they believe, is when God hears them best.

A Day
in the Night
of America

At MIDNIGHT, off the MASSACHUSETTS coast, eight
herring fishermen sat on the rear deck of a purse
seiner, drifting in the moonlit sea, lacing a torn
net.

The *Barnegat,* plowing south at ten knots along the outskirts of Massachusetts Bay, was just past Boston when the horizon, like a drowning swimmer,
finally went under for the last time. Off the boat's starboard side you could
see the city lights, tracing the skyline and marking the border between the
land and the sea; but off the port side you could see nothing but shadowy
gray. Just a couple of hours before, when the *Barnegat* left its home port
of Gloucester, the horizon had been a knife edge—a surgical incision
separating the deep-blue ocean from the incandescent blue sky of a late-
winter day that was a rare premonition of spring. But as the boat had
traveled south toward its fishing grounds, the sun had traveled west, toward
the ocean on the other side of the continent. The farther the boat pulled
from the harbor and the lighthouse and the clapboard houses washed by the
oblique late-afternoon light, the more color drained from the day. The
darkening sky came down to meet the sea, first dulling the horizon's edge
and then erasing it entirely, until the two merged into a single, shrouded
mass, where the difference between the air and the water was tactile only.

Jerry Curcuru sat in one of the two dusty, sprung-seat barber chairs that
gave the *Barnegat*'s pilothouse the look of an abandoned Main Street
storefront, leaning forward occasionally to turn the wheel and keep the boat
straight on course for the waters south of Boston that lately had been thick
with herring. The only light against the gathering darkness was a dim glow
from the floating compass above the wheel. His father, Joe, was asleep in

the tiny captain's room behind him—a dark cell, not much bigger than a trucker's cab, adorned with a small TV and a portrait of the Sacred Heart of Jesus. Six other crew members, including his brother and his uncle, were asleep in the cramped bunks below the galley on the forward deck, like commuters sleeping on the bus on their way to work. A small-craft advisory was in effect, but the *Barnegat*, at 125 feet, was no small craft, and the light swell was just a gentle rocking chair that could set you to dozing. "They take a nap now, because if we see fish, we'll be up all night," Jerry said. He had the radio tuned to a Boston rock station that gave periodic traffic reports to homeward-bound drivers. "I'd like to get a northeaster for a couple of days. I'd love to get eight hours' sleep."

A good night's, even a good day's, sleep, in a real bed on solid ground, had been a rare catch for the *Barnegat* crew lately, and the way things were going, it would probably take a storm to keep the boat, and them, in port for a night. A fisherman's schedule is determined by forces beyond his control—marine biology, meterology, economics—and it was the last of these that now told the *Barnegat* to fish every night. The problem for most Gloucester fishing boats in recent years had been supply: The stocks of cod, haddock and the other fish the market craved had dwindled. But the problem for the *Barnegat* had been demand: Herring were generally plentiful, but the market mostly turned up its nose at them. Americans didn't eat sardines like they once did, so much of the *Barnegat*'s herring wound up as lobster bait, or in cat food, or in the dinner pails of zookeepers who tossed them to the seals. Lately, though, the *Barnegat* had been fishing for a more appreciative audience—the Russians, the world's most prodigious herring eaters. Two giant Russian factory ships were now anchored off Gloucester, in a pioneering experiment in piscatory glasnost, and they were buying as much herring as the local fishermen could catch. They planned to stay until their holds were filled, and the *Barnegat* planned to do its part to ensure that no Russians went hungry for herring. They did, after all, pay in dollars—eighty-seven dollars a ton this week—not rubles.

The gray faded to black, and Jerry's gaze fixed on a small TV screen that displayed, like a video game, an abstract array of bright colors. He was waiting for a red splotch to bleed across the center of the screen and tell him where the fish were. Fishermen inhabit, in the day and the night both, a world of few guideposts. To get around on the roadless ocean, they rely on compass headings, the navigational numbers of the loran radio signal system (which have made the nighttime stars mainly a decorative accessory) and, if they plied mostly inshore waters, as the *Barnegat* did, coastal landmarks. Finding the fish is harder, because water that is transparent in a glass is instead, when collected into an ocean, as solid and concealing as the earth that separates a driller from oil. They do not, as farmers do, fertilize their fields, so they don't know where their crop will be when they set out to harvest it. History and memory and experience point the way toward the herring, as do some of the other creatures that hunt them—the whales that troll through schools of them, the garnets that dive-bomb for them. Mostly, though, they rely on the sonar screen—an X ray of the unseen world below. A red spot appeared on the screen, drawing Jerry in for a closer look as it slowly grew, like blood soaking into a shirt, and making him think about whether he should wake his father and the rest of the crew to set the net out and capture the school of herring the spot depicted. He decided not to, because the screen also showed a shallow, rocky ocean bottom here, the kind that devours fishing nets, and the school wasn't big enough to justify the risk. "You can go through fish for forty or fifty miles, you can go over billions and billions of pounds of fish, but then you can set all night long and get nothing," he said.

Herring do not behave with any thought to the convenience of the *Barnegat*'s crew. They are low enough on the aquatic food chain to be more prey than predator, so they have devised certain survival strategies—traveling in packs, like teenage boys, and staying out of sight during the day, when the bigger fish are looking for smaller fish to eat. They generally start showing up on sonar screens around suppertime, and are gone by breakfast the next morning. Jerry was just twenty-eight, but he had been on herring time for almost half his life. "When I first started, I used to pray for the sun. The first time we set in the day, I said to myself, 'This ain't right, we ain't supposed to be working now,' " he said. He tucked his hands in the pockets of his black corduroy pants against the evening chill. He hadn't slept for more than a few hours at a stretch in over a week. "After you do it for so long, you don't think about it, I guess. You don't really get used to it. You gotta do it, that's all." But when he first started, during his high school summers, he wasn't convinced of how much he wanted to do it, because the net came up empty on each of his first forty nights on the water. "I wanted to quit right then." He didn't, but the fickle herring hadn't since endeared themselves to him. The only fish he wanted to see on his plate when he was home on land was tuna, out of a can.

Jerry slowed the boat and woke his father when it was just north of

Plymouth, in an area the fish had been frequenting lately. Five other herring boats had been fishing out of Gloucester since the Russians had arrived, and several of them were parked here now—solitary outposts of light that gave this corner of ocean the look of a dark prairie dotted with farmhouses. Jerry gave way as his father took the wheel and switched the radio back to his easy listening station. The son had a round, smooth face, not yet weathered by the sea, and a halo of dark, curly hair; the father had fished for forty-five of his sixty years, and his face had become a granite breakwater, scoured and hard. His dusty black hair was like a wire brush, pushed straight back as if he perpetually faced into a gale. Joe—who was better known by his child-hood nickname, Cheeks—took the radio microphone to talk to one of the neighboring boats. His voice was low, and tended to drop into a mumble when he was tired. "How's the bottom look there, Bobby?" he asked.

"Joe, you sound like you just woke up," Bobby answered, in the sharp Down East Yankee accent of Maine, the permanent home of the four boats that had migrated to Gloucester for the Russian buying spree. "Put some cold water on your face and say it over again."

"How's the bottom look there?" he repeated.

"Flat, it shows flat. But we haven't set yet. We'll look around awhile, see if we can find some fish."

The captains were remarkably generous among themselves, sharing infor-mation and even fish, if they caught more than they could carry. But nobody had caught anything yet tonight; one boat had set its net out, only to have it hang up on the rocky bottom. Joe steered the boat on an erratic bumper-car course, seeking the elusive red sonar spot that his mind could translate into an enticing image of a darting, almost solid, mass of slender, iridescent, foot-long fish, just waiting to be scooped out of the dark ocean below into the dark night above. To get a second angle, he switched on the sounder, which scratched a polygraphlike line that would jump wildly when the boat passed over a school of herring. The *Barnegat*'s 600-horsepower engine sounded like a jackhammer, digging to uncover the buried fish.

The other crew members were out of their bunks, into their oilskins and on the deck, looking up toward the wheelhouse where Joe, like a bomber pilot deciding where and when to drop his bombs, was deciding where and when to drop his net. The wrong decision could mean a ruined trip, a payless night. The net is a precious and vulnerable piece of equipment—a giant, spidery fish prison, 250 fathoms long by 25 fathoms deep, worth upward of $200,000 when new—and you must be careful where you deploy it. In deep waters it drifts like a sheet on a clothesline in the breeze; in shallow waters, like these, it can snag on a rock, and tear like a stocking when you try to pull it free. The sonar revealed a school of herring, and Joe closed in on them. The sounder scratched a mountain range of sharply peaked spears, as if it were wired to somebody telling a whopping lie. Joe's younger son, Phil, stood at the wheel of the skiff that bobbed along behind the *Barnegat,* awaiting the signal to haul the net out and set it. Joe lined the fish up in the boat's crosshairs. The bottom looked like it could be a problem, but the school was too big to be granted immunity.

"Let her go," he said.

Phil gunned the skiff off into the darkness, pulling the net behind him and trying to corral the fish before they could sense their dim fate and try to flee.

"Fifteen," the call came back to the wheelhouse, indicating that a quarter of the net had unraveled off the rear deck where it was piled and dropped into the water behind the skiff. Phil was a speck of red light in the distance, turning now to race parallel with the boat.

"Half a seine," the call came. The *Barnegat*'s net was of a type known as a purse seine, and half of it was in the water now.

"Last fifteen." Phil made a wide turn and headed for the right side of the boat. Trawlers tow their nets behind, scooping up whatever crosses their path; gill netters stretch their nets between buoys and then leave them, returning to collect the fish that get snared in the mesh. But a purse seiner like the *Barnegat* ladles the fish out of the ocean. It is something like one of those carnival games where you maneuver a claw inside a prize-filled glass case and try to snatch yourself a watch.

The skiff pulled up to the *Barnegat*'s right side, closing the huge circle it had inscribed in the water, and Phil handed off the end of the net to the crew on deck. He sped clear of the boat as they attached the end to a winch. A purse seine is so named because it works just like a drawstring purse, and the winch started to draw the string tight. The net formed a deadly pool, swimming with what seemed a good catch, maybe even good enough to make a trip and send the *Barnegat* home early. Then the winch stopped, and in an instant they knew they would not sleep in Gloucester tonight. "We're hung up on the bottom," Joe said.

It was 11:30, almost three hours later, before the net was back on board. They had strained and pulled and tugged and finally wrenched the net free, but they knew, as they were hauling it up, that tons of fish were pouring out through the holes they had torn in it. They managed to get 50,000 pounds of herring into the boat, but probably another 100,000 pounds had escaped, like coins spilling through a hole in a purse. On a boat that could hold 350,000 pounds, 50,000 pounds was not a trip.

As wispy clouds slid over the face of the half moon, the crew gathered on the rear deck, needles in hand, to try to salvage the night. They fanned out across the gentle black hills of the piled net and, like a quilting bee in a parlor, set to lacing the holes in the fine mesh. It was as pleasant a night as winter could offer. The wind was still, and the water was pond-calm. The cold air soaked into their bare sewing hands, but it didn't encase them in ice. The ocean at night may be fearsome at times, but it can also be a placid, welcoming place, a theater of the sublime, as Jerry could testify. "When I was the skiff man and had nothing to do out there for an hour, sometimes I'd lie back in it and see seven or eight shooting stars," he recalled. "I saw the space shuttle once. It looked like a shooting star, a little bright light moving across the sky. And at night you can hear porpoises pop up by the skiff. You can't see them, but you can hear them come up and breathe. You hear them puff. They're smart as hell. We caught one once, and this other one, I don't know if it was its mate or not, stayed and waited for it. It was out there crying and wheezing, waiting for it. We rolled it off and they both went down together, then they both jumped and swam off." Tonight, as the *Barnegat* drifted in the silent moonlight, the ocean was like a womb.

Midnight passed, and left no sign of the new date it brought. The crew sewed on, stopping now and then to warm their hands over the stove in the galley and maybe grab a sandwich and watch a few minutes of the basketball game on the snowy TV. By 2 A.M., as the bars were closing in Boston, the net was whole again. By 2:15 Joe had found another school of herring, even bigger than the first, and the net was back in the water. "There's fish ganged up top to bottom," he said. "It looks like a real good set. Now you gotta save 'em, that's the thing."

The net came up cleanly this time. The purse rose heavily through the water, and the circle of orange floats tightened around what looked like a fish-farm tank at feeding time—a ghostly swarm of herring swimming frantically through the shadows beneath the surface. The net hefted them far enough up so that they were solid inside it, packed tight as a sardine can, and they finally broke the surface. They were a vat of boiling mercury. There were so many herring, it seemed possible the *Barnegat* had captured the entire species. When the light caught them, there were flashes of blue and green and copper, but the dominant color was silver, and what they most resembled was what they represented to the crew—money. You almost expected to hear the prosperous jingle of coins emanating from the undulating herringbone pattern of silver and gray in the net, not the soft flaps of the writhing fish.

The haul was big enough to slice the age of the crew in half. The *Barnegat*'s crew, most of whom were past fifty, was older than most in Gloucester, and while fishing does keep a man fit beyond his years, a catch like this can make him younger still. They were agile as boys as they maneuvered around the slippery deck, consumed by the strenuous, delicate, physics-challenging job of transferring from the net to the boat a load of fish weighing several times more than the boat itself. A laden purse seine must stay in the water, because lifting it would tip the boat over, so they dropped a long, thick hose like an elephant trunk into it. The fish were sucked up through the hose, through the descaling box—fish scales help make nail polish shiny—and then disgorged into the belly of the boat. The net was hoisted incrementally, just enough to keep the water bubbling with fish. The *Barnegat* was overrun with a plague of herring. They poured into the hold, wide-eyed and unblinking, voluminous as corn in a silo. They rained down on the bright orange and yellow oilskins of the crew members who pulled the net back down onto the rear deck. They were a floating, floodlit dinner table for the squawking, scavenging gulls. They littered the deck, slick as sitcom banana peels, but far more treacherous ("I slipped on a fish and went overboard once," Jerry said. "It's a good thing I was able to grab the top rail, because no one would've seen me and that would've probably been it"). Scales sparkled like sequins fallen from an evening gown after the ball. When the net was finally empty, it had given the *Barnegat* 225,000 pounds of herring, short of their record—the million-pound haul they had once shared with several other boats—but when added to the 50,000 pounds from the first set, it was more than enough to send them home.

"You did all right, did you, Joe?" one of the Maine captains asked over the radio when Joe returned to the wheelhouse.

"We did all right."

"Ay-uh, we did, too. Finest kind, finest kind."

It was a night that made up for the other nights when the crew share was no percent of nothing, and by 4:15 they were back in their bunks, sleeping easy. Yet another Curcuru—Joe's older brother, Nick—was the designated driver for the ride home. Curcuru was almost as common a name in

Gloucester as Smith: Joe and Nick had thirteen brothers and sisters. Their grandfathers were fishermen in Italy, and their father had a mackerel seiner in Gloucester, the boat that Nick started fishing on when he was thirteen. "You'd stand up there at night with a five-battery flashlight, and you'd see a school of mackerel like phosphorus," he remembered. "If you hit a school, you'd see fire in the water. That was the only way to find them. There were no sounding machines then." He was sixty-nine now, although he looked and moved like fifty, and he had worked on many boats since then, including a PT boat in the South Pacific during World War II. His experience was welcome now, because a bowful of herring made the *Barnegat* hard to steer, like a shopping cart with a dead wheel.

The black started leaking out of the night just after five. Nick was broad and solid and looked a little like Spencer Tracy, and he held the boat straight as it rode low in the water, the wake rushing through the gunwales. He had switched the radio to a country-music station. The nearing morning light brought nothing but gray—gray sea, gray sky, gray drizzle, and a gray haze that obscured the coast and made it seem that the boat was bouncing through a rain cloud. "Last night was beautiful, an ideal night," he said. "Now it's starting to look like wintertime again." He caught sight of the Gloucester lighthouse just before 6:30, and soon he was sliding past the Russian ships that, later this afternoon, would pump the herring from the *Barnegat*'s hold—and then can it, pickle it or freeze it, and ensure that each *Barnegat* crew member would probably earn more this year than the $18,000 they had averaged last year. It was Saturday morning now, and the dawn had resurrected the horizon. The harbor was silent and gray. In the condominiums that had spawned along the Gloucester waterfront in recent years, elbowing aside the fishing industry, most people were still asleep—unaware the *Barnegat* had returned, or even that it had left at all.

Gloucester has been a fishing port for 350 years now, so the Gloucester fishermen, and the lumpers who helped unload their catch, may have been the first regular night workers in the American colonies. But they worked at night because nature told them to; the first American colonists to work at night because a boss told them to were twenty-five miles south of Gloucester, at the Saugus Iron Works, the first American factory. The boss was John Winthrop, Jr., son of the governor of the Massachusetts Bay

Colony, who saw how imprudent it was for the colony to continue importing costly tools, nails and other necessary iron goods from England when it had abundant supplies of the raw materials needed to make these same goods locally. Winthrop went to England to get the investment capital and skilled workers Massachusetts didn't have, and in 1646, on the banks of the Saugus River north of Boston, the blast furnace was first fired up. Because the heat required to smelt iron is so intense, the furnace burned constantly, tended round-the-clock by shifts of ironworkers. The ironworkers were gone by 1668, when the furnace went cold for the last time, but they dispersed through the colonies to establish other forges—which is why the National Park Service sign at the Saugus site called it the "birthplace of American industry." It was just a reconstruction now, staffed only by rangers, but the modern counterparts of these first factory workers were not far down the river at a giant General Electric plant that, three shifts a day, made aircraft engines; and a couple of towns over at another plant, also on three shifts, that made a product instrumental to the conquest of night—light bulbs. The population of the American night has multiplied prolifically since seventeenth-century Massachusetts, and while it still includes those called into the night by the demands of nature and industry—as the first fishermen and ironworkers were—it also now includes a swelling number of people called there by the demands of a nation so busy it can no longer afford to rest.

"If I tell people I work nights, they assume I'm a nurse," said Judy Brawley, who wasn't, as she stacked checks into a bank computer at 4:05 A.M. "I tell them to ride by Boston and see the lights on on two or three floors in some of the big buildings. I tell them there's people in there working. They think someone just left the lights on." The lights she worked under were on the seventh floor of a thirty-eight-story downtown office building that was headquarters to Shawmut National, one of the largest banks in Boston. On the outside the lights contributed to the festive tracery of the skyline the *Barnegat* could see when it passed the harbor; on the inside they illuminated a fluorescent ghost town. An office is an archetype of a daytime workplace. It fills by 9 A.M. with secretaries and middle managers, thrums for eight hours with phone calls, meetings, football pools and water-cooler gossip, and then retreats like the tide, bequeathing to the cleaning crew a sea of vacant desks awash in nauseous, liquid light. It is such a familiar place in the daylight that it becomes doubly, eerily unfamiliar when viewed from a darker angle—and maybe the most striking evidence of the changing face of night work is that it has even infiltrated these bastions of the 9-to-5 world.

On the ground floor at Shawmut headquarters the tellers' windows were open from 8:30 A.M. to 4 P.M.; on the seventh floor Judy Brawley worked from midnight to 8 A.M., a schedule that inverted the genteel notion of traditional bankers' hours. Her domain was a windowless, antiseptically bright room that was always kept cooler than the rest of the floor, not for her benefit but for the benefit of the giant IBM high-speed computer sorters she operated. The sorters were long enough to make her job an aerobic exercise. In the middle of her shift on a Thursday night, at an hour when the body wants to do nothing but sleep, she sprinted along the whirring machine and kept the checks flowing through it like a stream. She punched in instructions on how to sort each batch of checks, and when they had fallen like shuffled cards into the right pockets, she retrieved them and set them in trays. By 4 A.M. she had shepherded 82,316 checks through this massive filing system. She plucked out one check made out for $247,000. "There's money out there, but most of us never see it," she said.

Brawley had been divorced six years, and she had worked nights at Shawmut six years, and in that time she had seen far larger checks than that, and checks made out to neighbors of hers, to Red Sox players, to Linda Ronstadt ("Maybe it wasn't her, but how many Linda Ronstadts can there be?"). She chose to work nights because it allowed her to wring some extra time from her too-short days. She had five children and she cared for her ninety-year-old father, so it seemed logical for her to work when they were asleep and needed her least. She was red-haired and fueled by more energy than you would rightly expect in someone who generally sleeps only from 10 A.M. to 3 P.M. each day; working women, studies have shown, sleep twenty-five minutes less each day than men. "Eventually I'm not gonna have my dad to take care of, and I don't know if I'll go on days or not," she said, pulling a batch of checks from the sorter. "There's less pressure at night. Your guard is down then. I'm friendly with people who work the day shift, but I care about the people who work nights. You do a lot of laughing, a lot of fooling around. You don't have to worry about a lot of customers getting mad at you. People might be here for six or nine months and then leave. I miss them and I call them to see how they're doing." She hoisted two trays of checks and carried them out to the sending area, where they would be packaged for their trip to the Federal Reserve Bank.

Shawmut, and most other large commercial banks like it, employs a night shift because time, to a bank, really is money. When the tellers downstairs cash a check for you—a birthday check, say, from your mother in California—they are giving you money that doesn't quite belong to Shawmut yet. Your mother's bank will hold on to the money until Shawmut lays claim to it, which can't happen until they process the check up on the seventh floor and get it over to the Federal Reserve Bank. The night shift in effect tries to keep Shawmut's immense checkbook balanced, and they are guided by one unchanging rule: The faster the checks move, the better it is for Shawmut.

The rhythm of work on the seventh floor was set by the regular deadlines at the Fed. The big deadline was at 11, so evenings were the busiest time, and also the only time when there was somebody around who was wearing a tie. As the assistant vice president who managed the shift, Dan Synan was the designated tie-wearer. "I used to wear jeans, but then they told me I'd have to wear a tie so that people would know who's in charge," he said. The night fit him well. Almost twenty-two of his twenty-four years at Shawmut had been spent on after-hours shifts, and his dream retirement job would be to host an all-night oldies request show on the radio. The deadlines he faced were not just suggestions. If the checks arrived at the Fed at 11:01, it was as if they didn't arrive at all, and Shawmut was out several hundred dollars in interest costs for each $1 million the checks represented. The checks usually made the half-mile journey in a bank van, but they had also traveled in hastily summoned cabs and even, when snow blocked the streets, in bags slung over the shoulders of Shawmut workers, who carried them to the Fed like mailmen. Synan cleared a path for the checks like a blocking fullback. "I have preference, but sometimes I have to fight the cleaning people for the freight elevator. I tell them 'I want a goddamn elevator. I've got sixty million dollars in here and if I miss the Fed it's your fault, that I couldn't get an elevator.' "

Synan left at midnight—in time to catch the last train home to his wife and four kids, the David Letterman show, and the repeats of the local news that followed it—but the deadlines continued straight through till dawn, when the trains started running again. More checks went out at 1 A.M., and again at 1:30, 2:30, 5 and 7, and the couple of dozen people who got these checks out were maybe the most invisible of all Shawmut workers. When their lunch hour arrived, around 3 A.M., they couldn't visit the smorgasbord of food stalls down the street at Quincy Market, as the evening shift could; they settled instead for the empty steam tables of the darkened eighth-floor cafeteria, where they might get the lone cook on duty to make them a hamburger. "You get the feeling they don't even know you're here, that they don't give a shit as long as the work gets done," George Biagiotti, the night manager, said of the day staff. "I think we all feel a little superior, we feel we're a little better than all those people who whine about having to get up and come to work in the morning, when we've been up working all night. I try to get out of here before I see the day people coming in. I feel uncomfortable if I'm still around when they're here." Biagiotti had worked evenings or nights for twenty-six of his thirty-one Shawmut years, but he had spent his off hours in a pursuit unique among his compatriots: He examined feet. When he woke from his day's sleep, which usually lasted from noon to 6, he went to the podiatry office he maintained at his house and attended to his unshod patients. He planned to flip his sleep schedule soon, though; tonight was just a few weeks short of his retirement date.

Well more than a million checks, worth hundreds of millions of dollars, passed through Shawmut's seventh floor on a busy night—the largest I saw was made out for $1,186,086.82 to Bank of America, and the smallest was for $6.99 to the Gap—but for all the speed-of-light processors, each of these checks still had to ride in Jamie Paz's canvas mail hamper. It was just an unassuming cart, scuffed with wear, of the same type hospitals use to transfer soiled sheets down to the laundry. At 4:30 A.M. it yawned beside Paz, slowly filling with clear plastic bags of checks. Paz stood at a table that held the checks Judy Brawley had brought out from the computer room, and he worked on them like a newspaper carrier readying his route. He, along with several other people, wrapped the bunches of checks in their corresponding sheets of green-and-white computer paper, secured them with rubber bands, deposited them in bags and then tossed the bags in the cart. At 4:45 Paz topped off the load, which had risen above the cart's lip, with the early edition of the *Boston Herald,* and he started pushing. "I don't have time to fall asleep, because there's so much to do," he said. His body was well acquainted with the night shift: He had worked it for almost fifteen of his sixteen years at Shawmut, and before that he worked it at a B. F. Goodrich plant in his native Philippines.

The 5 A.M. load, crammed with checks Shawmut would swap with other Boston banks, was generally the heaviest of Paz's 11-to-7 shift. It had taken a running start to get the cart, all 1,500 pounds of it, up the ramp into the rear of Shawmut's white Ford Econoline van, and now it rattled around back there like a chained dog. The flashing traffic signals gave Paz free passage through the empty streets. He drove the van not quite seven miles a night, the distance of six round trips between Shawmut's basement garage and the Fed, each so short he barely had a chance to get out of second gear. He wheeled the van down the ramp into the Fed's basement. "Shawmut Bank," he said to the security guard. The steel door opened for him as if he had uttered the secret password.

The Federal Reserve Bank is a gleaming washboard tower, encased in shiny aluminum panels that catch the light and punctuate the downtown skyline like chrome on a new car, but the Consolidated Check Receiving Unit in its basement was just another loading dock. Pax deposited his bags at a window that looked like a betting window at a racetrack. He also deposited his *Herald* there, as thanks for the cup of coffee the window clerk had given him on an earlier trip. He then joined six other drivers from six other Boston banks in a ritual of banking in its most elemental form. "Let's see, here, BayBanks, these are yours," he said, handing over to the Bay-Banks driver a load of checks written on BayBanks accounts that had been deposited in Shawmut the previous day; and in return the BayBanks driver gave him Shawmut's checks. The drivers traded among themselves like kids trading baseball cards. Paz left with enough work in the back of the van to keep the seventh floor busy for the rest of the shift.

On the street outside Shawmut the van passed a seventh-floor worker who had come down to move his car; the meter maids would be out soon, ending the grace period of free night parking.

The campus of Dunkin' Donuts University, just south of Boston on a suburban strip in Braintree, consists mainly of a single building that more resembles an industrial-park warehouse than a school, but it does have Harvard beat on at least one count: It is the best-smelling school in America. The sugary perfume originates in the kitchens where students hone their jelly doughnut technique, and it drifts out toward the road, leading my nose to find the school before my eyes did. It settled, too, in the classroom where the students had started their schoolday. Printed neatly on the board was the lesson plan: Yeast Theory, Introduction to Yeast Troubleshooting. A quiz on cake doughnuts was imminent.

Dunkin' Donuts University is not counted among the one hundred or so outposts of higher education that make the Boston area America's

Kevin Coyne

college capital. Matriculation is restricted to members of the Dunkin' Donuts family. The course of study lasts six weeks and awards a degree recognized only within the Dunkin' Donuts world. But DDU is vital to the continued health and well-being of millions of nocturnal Americans, because in training Dunkin' Donuts' franchise owners and managers, it serves as a sort of boot camp for night workers.

Dunkin' Donuts started with a single shop in neighboring Quincy in 1950 and has since built an empire of 2,500 outlets, most of them open all night, every night. They have become an indispensable part of America's nocturnal infrastructure, because the sugar-and-caffeine rush they offer is one of the most effective legal ways to speed your body up. They are the gastronomic equivalent of twenty-four-hour gas stations. It is the nation's largest doughnut chain, and DDU is one way it tries to answer the challenge that title brings: how to ensure that the Boston Kreme doughnuts taste the same in Alaska as they do in Boston. Every Dunkin' Donuts is a franchise, and whenever one is sold, whether it's new or used, DDU enrolls two more students; all new owners are required, as part of the franchise agreement, to attend the school, and to bring with them their designated managers. There is no tuition, but the six hundred annual attendees must pay their own travel and expenses. "When people ask me what I do, the easiest way to explain it is to say that I'm principal of a school," said Vern Schellenger, manager of training at DDU. He had spent fifteen years with Dunkin' Donuts—which meant he had, as they said of company stalwarts, "jelly in the veins"—starting as a baker when he was an MBA student in Albany. His student body now included fellow MBAs, along with recent immigrants marginally conversant in English and assorted other people who, as he said, "don't know the difference between a yeast doughnut and a cake doughnut." "That's probably our most difficult obstacle," he added. "In almost every other educational system there are at least some prerequisites, some commonalities. Everybody has to go to kindergarten before first grade."

The only prerequisites for DDU are the price of a franchise and a willingness to come to Braintree, to the classrooms and the five surgically clean kitchens and the facsimile storefront, and learn the difference between cake doughnuts (the denser, old-fashioned kind) and yeast doughnuts (the lighter, often filled, ones)—and then make about 1,000 dozen of them. Students spend the first four weeks in the kitchens, dusted with flour. They mix and loaf and knead and cut and fry and inject and top until their doughnuts are consistently of display-case quality. They learn how to make the famed Dunkin' Donuts coffee, but not the formula for its trade-secret blend of beans. They learn of geographical variations in doughnut tastes: New England likes jelly sticks, the Midwest likes long johns, which are, inexplicably, chocolate eclairs stripped of their best feature, the filling. For their final exam they have to make 140 dozen doughnuts in eight hours, an under-fire baptism that proves they have the mettle to leave their beds on a dark night when everybody calls in sick and then gird their shop for the morning rush that can account for as much as half the day's total business. "That would fill a doughnut case, and you'd still be in business," Schellenger said. "Most of them know it's a twenty-four-hour business, and most know they're gonna have to work nights at some point in time. They know it's time to make the doughnuts." The final two weeks are spent in the classroom, where the lessons are in how to manage a business that employs between twenty and thirty people and takes in close to $500,000 a year—and can earn for its owner between $50,000 and $100,000 a year. "Because the business is so demanding, and because for whatever socioeconomic reasons many people find Dunkin' Donuts too hard a way to make a living, we get a lot of immigrants—Asians, Koreans, Indians, Pakistanis. Here's the American Dream for them—a chance to own their own business, something they could never hope to do where they came from."

The school is a fitting preview of the life that awaits the students as franchisees. The kitchens can't hold everybody at once, so time must be parceled out in shifts—day, evening, sometimes even nights, a 1 A.M. to 9 A.M. stretch that has the students making practice doughnuts at the same time their professional counterparts are making real ones. The class I visited was in its second week and back on day shifts, gratefully, having spent its first week on nights. "I'm a housewife with three kids. I don't know about working nights," Pat Oliveira said as she kneaded a big pillow of yeast dough that moved like a living creature. Her brother-in-law had bought a Dunkin' Donuts near Cleveland and, like many other Portuguese franchisees, decided family makes the best managers. "I'll get used to it, I guess." Her classmates came in as many varieties as the doughnuts in the company's repertoire. They came from, among other places, Brazil, Indiana, Quebec, New Jersey, Alaska and Virginia, and they included a government systems analyst from Washington State ("I wanted more money and less stress") and a Vietnamese chemical engineer from Cincinnati ("McDonald's required a little more money to get into"). An Indian student was cutting cake doughnuts when Schellenger, like a principal slipping into the back of a classroom, stopped to sample one from his earlier batch. "Is okay?" the student asked warily. His concern was legitimate, because some students do fail, and must repeat the class; right on the corner outside DU was a reminder to them that the doughnut business isn't all sugar and frosting—a Mister Donut shop, part of a competing chain started by the brother-in-law of Dunkin' Donuts' founder, and recently gobbled back up by its longtime rival. Schellenger took a bite, then nodded his approval. The student looked relieved.

A light snow fell on Chelsea, north across the Mystic River from Boston, and dusted its barren streets white. A lone eighteen-wheeler trundled past the dark warehouses and gas storage tanks toward the New England Produce Center, a fenced forty-acre compound that briefly shelters the bulk of the fruits and vegetables eaten in New England. People who pass here in the middle of the afternoon, when the market is empty and still, wonder whether it is an abandoned relic. They are accustomed to buying their produce in supermarkets at civilized hours, and they read the sign at the gate—HOURS MON–FRI 5AM—as a non sequitur. Were they to pass instead in the middle of the night, they would find a bustling cornucopia. Trucks lined the loading docks of the long warehouses, disgorging a harvest of Florida oranges, California broccoli, Chilean grapes and assorted other produce from places where snow doesn't fall in March. Crate-laden hand-trucks and forklifts scuttled in and out of the warehouse bays. Fresh produce, like a doughnut, has a short life span, and since we are no longer a nation of farmers, each growing our own crops for our own tables, somebody else must work through the night to ensure it reaches us before it rots.

Inside the warehouse of Bay State Produce, one of forty-five or so produce dealers in the complex, it is always March, even in July; the temperature is kept between 40 and 45 degrees year-round. John Grant wore a thin, quilted blue smock against the chill. He stood like a professor at a scuffed wooden lectern, surrounded by two stories of crates packed with avocados, mushrooms, grapes, pineapples, tomatoes, strawberries, plums, rhubarb, limes, peas, asparagus, mangoes, Belgian endive, apples, kiwi, radicchio and New Zealand passion fruit. It was an enviable larder, but it wasn't quite complete. "Seen any sign of those raspberries yet?" he asked one of the warehousemen; the answer was, to his disappointment, no. It was 2:30 already on a Sunday night, the first night of the produce week, and the raspberries should have arrived hours ago on their flight from Miami. Grant bent back over his lectern and worked on a column of figures, setting his price list—a complex, partly instinctive exercise that required him to consider a bushel of variables, from the size of his inventory to the weather report in Florida, and that would be felt over the next few days in the food bills of millions of New Englanders. He stood on a worn doormat-sized rug to cushion his legs against the cold concrete floor. "When the alarm clock goes off at 1 A.M., I don't care how many years you've been doing it, I think you feel a trifle melancholy," he said. "But once you're here, the comrade-ship takes over. Everybody is in it together, and I think a part of it is because it's night."

Grant and his fellow produce workers were a hidden link in the commercial food chain, isolated by geography as well as by darkness. The wholesale market's original home was at Faneuil Hall in downtown Boston, but it was displaced twenty years ago by the redevelopment that swept away the wilted cabbage leaves and transformed the old warehouses into an upscale tourist mecca of souvenir T-shirt stalls and gourmet ice cream. Its present Chelsea home is in little danger of tourist encroachment, but it does offer a rail link for produce-packed boxcars and easy access to Boston's highways, the route the hydroponic lettuce had just taken. It came from Bill Whitney's farm in Hubbardston, in the rural middle of the state, having traveled in the back of Bill Whitney's truck. Whitney was among the few produce deliverers with earth—or in his case, water—on his hands. He had started picking the lettuce in his greenhouse at 5 the previous evening, and now, his breath fogging in the cold night air, he unloaded boxes of it onto a pallet. "These guys here go to sleep, then come to work," he said of the Bay State workers. "I get up Sunday morning and have to work straight through." And in just about twelve hours he was due at his regular job, as a second-shift process engineer supervising the manufacture of semiconductors at Digital, the computer company. A warehouseman forklifted Whitney's lettuce off the loading dock and added it to the stockpile inside. A salesman selected a few choice samples and added them to the display that was rising at Bay State's entrance. The other salesmen, all in their blue butcher-length smocks, were also busy assembling a produce display meant to entice consumers far more discriminating than the average supermarket shopper. They pried open the pale, splintery crates with their crate hammers, and they sliced the fruits with their knives to gauge their ripeness. Occasionally they slipped into the small glass office on the warehouse floor, an island of warmth, where they found brief refuge from the constant chill. "It's like we're in an isolated little world here where everybody's going a hundred miles an hour," said salesman Fred Boudreau, who had sped through this night world for twelve of his thirty years, "but everyone else is asleep."

Unlike many dealers, Bay State didn't specialize—handling only citrus fruits, say, or potatoes—so its display was a multihued bounty. Joe Novellini, the company's owner, surveyed the strawberries that glowed against the office's exterior. "These are the girls I had dates with in high school," he said, pointing to the paler, more languid Parkers, "and these," pointing to the juicier Chandlers, "look like the girls all the other guys had dates with." He was a tall, forceful man, an engineer by training, and he worked for a time on a nuclear power plant; but genetics—his father started Bay State sixty years ago—proved a stronger pull. Produce is a fluid, seat-of-the-pants business, resistant to the long-range planning nuclear engineering requires, but it does demand a similar attention to detail and the ability to confront "round-the-clock problems, like a container of papayas from Hawaii that might be stuck in Chicago." It also leaves little room for error; produce can't be held in inventory like toasters, and a wrong decision could wake you every morning with the acrid smell of decaying fruit, and the even worse smell of burning money that accompanies it. The produce business, though, is generally as stable as a nucleus in fission is not. "People are gonna eat for a long time."

To see Novellini was right, and that New England was hungry again, you only had to look at the dark street outside the market fence. A long line of trucks waited there, engines idling like growling stomachs, ready to dash through the gate when it opened at the stroke of five. Bay State was poised for the rush. At least some of the raspberries had finally arrived; they had been flown to New York and trucked the rest of the way, and now were the final topping on the display. It was 4:45, and one job remained: the final intelligence-gathering reconnaissance mission. Bay State's newest salesman, Shawn Grant, walked along the loading docks like a window-shopper, seeing how the competition's produce stacked up. He, too, came into the produce business as a legacy; John Grant was his father. "I probably would've been more afraid of the hours if it hadn't been for my father," he said. "Your wife has to be willing to sneak around with a flashlight at eight at night." He had earned an MBA and worked as an agricultural loan officer in Maine, and now here he had landed in a more elemental arena of capitalism—the predawn produce market, with its often intoxicating brew of instant dealmaking, locker room banter, weekend wardrobes, fast and heavy food traffic, plus the more intangible lure cited by a veteran produce man Shawn met on his rounds: "Once you get the smell of apples," he said, "you don't care about the hours."

When the gates opened at 5, the dealers were conveniently lined up like storefronts at a mall, and the buyers browsed accordingly. Some who stopped at Bay State wore jackets emblazoned with the names of the supermarket chains they represented; others came straight from their own small groceries and restaurants, wielding cash and their own handtrucks. Some were still bleary and bed-rumpled; others were fresh-pressed and noon-sharp. All were looking for a good price and were eager to speed their purchases out of the market in time to grace the day's supper tables.

Novellini pulled a receipt book from his back pocket like a waiter. "No waiting today, three barbers," he said, scrawling out a buyer's order. Produce is an informal business with little room for titles or pretensions; even the owner makes sales. The price a salesman quotes, and the buyer agrees to, constitutes a verbal contract, and the only record of it is on the order pad. One copy goes to the buyer, one goes to the warehouse crew so that they can fill the order, and no copy goes into a computer down here.

"Now the magic question—what are you getting for lime forty-eights? Ten dollars? Give me five."

"Those mangoes, they got any blush on 'em?"

"Five bucks? That's cheap."

"Danny, show him the twenty-eight Bacons."

"Three avocados, the cheapest you got."

"The kumquats are small but nice today."

"What are you charging him? That doesn't sound right."

"What do you got in raspberries I can afford?"

Raspberries were in short supply, and John Grant had started the morning asking $2.50 for each half-pint of them. When they didn't move, he dropped the price to $2, which still wasn't low enough for this shopper, who passed on them, despite Grant's parting pitch: "Why don't you put them on your Cheerios?" he suggested. Grant was once on the other side of these transactions, as vice president of produce sales and procurement for Stop & Shop. He was still a vice president, and general manager, at Bay State, but he rarely told anyone. He stood at his sales lectern in work boots and corduroys. "I haven't written a memo since I left Stop & Shop. I wouldn't know how to now." Somebody was asking after the strawberries now.

"These Chandlers? I was asking a buck and a half. They say they're gonna be tight." The buyer was hesitant, claiming he had seen them elsewhere priced as low as $1.15. Grant wasn't budging. "No, I'm gonna hang in there. They're gonna be short. If you get stuck, call, because I think the market will be good."

The discourse was not always this civil. "If you worked at a bank and yelled and screamed at a customer the way we sometimes do, they'd take you out in a straitjacket," Grant said. "I was telling my wife once about an argument here at work, and she said to me, 'You mean, you men fight over vegetables?' " Today, though, was relatively calm, and tempers were even. The gray, snowy weekend weather had kept shoppers away from the stores, so the stores had less need to replenish their stocks, so the usually busy Monday wholesale trade was slack. Somebody was interested in blueberries.

"Blues? No blues until Wednesday or Thursday. Raspberries?" Grant paused to calculate his options. Was a competitor selling raspberries cheaper, and if so, were theirs as good as his? Would sticking to his price leave him stuck with too many berries? He was forty-seven, with straight, graying hair and sharp, handsome features. His relationship with the products of nature was not just vocational: He was an avid horticulturalist who went home to orchids, fruit trees and pheasants, and he sat on his town's conservation commission. He shared the same strong, set jaw as his son. He stood fast. "Two dollars." No sale.

It was definitely Monday morning now. The displays had been pawed over, and receipt carbons littered the floor like a stock exchange trading pit. Sometimes Bay State gets a double sunrise—when the new sun itself is framed in the east loading dock bay while the west bay frames its blinding reflection off the glass façade of the John Hancock tower in Boston. Today a truck blocked the view, but the early sun did reveal the Boston skyline and the river of commuters rolling over the bridge toward it. The snow was mostly gone, and outside, the market smelled of diesel fuel and tomatoes. At 8:30 John Grant cut three strawberries into a bowl of oat bran cereal in his upstairs office. "I know I'm gonna be right on the berries," he said. "I'll sell them tomorrow."

2

At 12:30, in a MANHATTAN *office tower, a currency trader spoke by phone to Hong Kong, discussing, in Chinese, the behavior of the Japanese yen.*

Citibank's main trading room stretches across the forty-seventh floor of an office tower on the southernmost tip of Manhattan, so when the lights are burning there, and they almost always are, they accent the foreground of maybe the most electrifying vista in the American nightscape: the New York City skyline. Night becomes this building, as it does the whole city. By day the bank traders' home is just another anonymous box in a long wall of boxes, but at night its façade fades to black, leaving only a skeleton of lights, like a constellation in a galaxy of stars fallen to earth. The lights have grown so tall here because they were planted so long ago (America's first central electricity station lit up a web of city blocks around Wall Street in 1882), but their height and brightness is an illusory measure of the activity within. The city's nocturnal life tends to concentrate in pockets—of glamour, of danger, of both at once—and Wall Street, as luminous as it is from the outside, is not one of them. Soon after dark the financial district, where many people work but almost nobody lives, reverts to a backlot set for one of those *Twilight Zone* episodes about the after-the-Bomb world, the hollow wind riding through lifeless urban canyons. It isn't nuclear fallout that daily vanquishes Wall Street, though, just the 6:07 to Scarsdale.

The trading room echoed the emptiness of the streets below. The vacant desks reached almost from window to window, half a football field in length, attached to each other in a straight line like rowhouses and equipped with an array of computer screens and telephones. All the desk rows faced in the same direction and gave the room the look of NASA mission control. It was 10:30 in the evening and the traders had been replaced by cleaning women, who moved along the narrow, furrow-straight aisles like farm workers at harvest time, vacuuming and dusting and emptying wastebaskets of the detritus of the day just past. But they weren't entirely alone. At the far end of the room was a knot of a dozen or so young men in shirtsleeves and ties, Citibank's night traders, buying and selling vast amounts of dollars, yen and German marks. The traders scanned the blinking green numbers on their screens, in type as tiny as a racing form, and talked by phone to colleagues on the other side of the globe, trying to gauge the shifting contours of the world financial market.

"Ninety-one bid, looking for an offer."

"Sixty was paid thirty seconds before you asked for a price."

"Forty-three given."

"I think the dollar goes higher, but it doesn't seem like the market agrees."

"Singapore pushed it up fifteen points, but it's back down where it was."

"I didn't get any at forty-eight, so I didn't get my position."

"I'm more inclined to buy, but it looks kinda soft. I think we've seen the high."

"The yen tested high at forty-five. It doesn't want to break out."

Each step the cleaning women took toward the traders moved them closer to an encounter that embodied, better than any other I saw in my travels, the tensions between the old and the new versions of the American night. Currency trading is a high-stakes, trip-wire game where the distance between winning and losing can sometimes be measured in seconds. When the market is moving fast, prices broadcast from the squawk boxes on each desk as fast as the call of the final lengths of a tight horse race; and traders must process this dizzying blur of information as fast as they hear it, making instant decisions about the fate of tens of millions of dollars. The drone of a vacuum cleaner doesn't help. "We hate it, absolutely hate it," one trader said. "We have to shout at the top of our voices, 'Please turn down that machine,' and they say, 'What? What?' They don't like us. 'Why do you work nights?' they ask us. We are just in their way."

Their mutual antipathy is understandable: They are two parties with opposing interests vying to occupy the same space at the same time. Until just a few years ago the cleaning crew held unchallenged dominion over the forty-seventh floor. To the traders who worked here during the day, they were a mysterious, invisible force, like gravity—the unseen hand that kept the trading room from collapsing under the weight of the crumpled papers and stained coffee cups it generated each day. They could play their radios and clean the bathrooms without knocking first. It was only the advent of night trading that rendered gravity visible.

The forty-seventh floor had taught Ruby Williams a basic principle of entropy—that a place in constant motion can never truly be put in order. She had started cleaning offices fifteen years ago and now supervised the crew that counted the forty-seventh as its most troublesome. "All cleaning people know you can do a much better job if you're cleaning by yourself. You can do everything you need to do without saying 'Excuse me, excuse me,' " Williams said, her voice still carrying a hint of her native Jamaica. "When these people are on the phone, they don't want to be disturbed. You have to clean out the garbage cans and clean the ashtrays, but if they're on the telephone, you can't do that. You can't vacuum there. You don't want to trouble with their papers. The girls are told not to touch any papers. They're doing business. Sometimes you just have to leave it." The cleaning people could no longer listen to radios, even through earphones, while they worked, and they had to put a sign on the door when they cleaned the bathroom. "Before when you cleaned it, it stayed clean. Before you could do a perfect job, a good job. Now it's different. They want it to be the same, to be perfect, but it cannot be."

Tonight, though, was exceptionally quiet for the traders; the vacuums moved much more briskly than the yen. When a cleaning woman reached the night desk, there were no deals to interrupt, and the traders parted to let her pass. She squeezed by with her vacuum like a moviegoer slipping out to get popcorn, and was quickly gone. Yet even this mild intrusion was enough that one trader turned to me and, unprompted, said, "That's the worst part of the job." Not five minutes after she left, somebody deposited a Diet Coke can in a wastebasket she had just emptied, where it would sit for another twenty-four hours now, more evidence of the accelerating entropy of the night.

Five nights a week Richard Chen drove fifty miles from his Westchester County home to the Citibank trading room, where he was paid to do as a profession what many other American men spent their nights doing as a recreation: He played a kind of poker here. In his game the players did not sit around a green felt table, since many of them were half a world away, and when they said "a buck" or "a dollar," it was shorthand for a million. The basic principles, though, were the same. Each Citibank player dealt and raised and called and bluffed and stood and folded and cashed in and generally tried, just as their nickel-and-dime cousins did, to make a profit out of nothing but knowledge, instinct and luck. "The way I explain it to my father is that I gamble for a living and get paid for it," Chen said.

The foreign-exchange market is based on the principle that money is not just a means for buying commodities, but is also itself a commodity that can be bought and sold, just like a crate of fresh raspberries. The dollar folded in your wallet—wrinkled, green, solid, earmarked for groceries—is actually as liquid as the milk you plan to buy with it. The same is true of the Japanese yen, the German mark and all the other currencies folded safely in the wallets of the world. Their relative worth is in perpetual motion, measured not only by what they can buy within their own borders (how much milk, say) but also by what they can buy around the world (how many Toyotas). Today the dollar might be worth 143.79 yen, tomorrow it might only be worth 143.65 yen, and in this motion is the opportunity to make money. What makes the market a poker game is that every day the traders bet against each other on the direction they think the currencies will move. If they think the value of the dollar, for instance, is headed up, they buy dollars. If they're right, the dollar will rise, and they'll then sell their dollars at a profit; if they're wrong, the dollar will fall, forcing them to sell at a loss. Currencies generally tend to move in small increments, so traders must wager huge sums in order to make real profits: The standard transaction is $5 million. Citibank—the largest bank in the nation, and the biggest player in this game—does $200 billion in foreign-currency transactions per day; foreign-exchange dealings would net Citibank $471 million this year.

The foreign-exchange market is global by definition, and since a global market never sleeps, neither can its players. Richard Chen was Citibank's lead American hand on this shift, a position that required him always to hold in his mind a picture of one of those old TV newsroom walls covered with clocks showing the time in cities around the world; he well knew that midnight in his silent Manhattan trading room was two the next afternoon in a busy Tokyo trading room. The night trading desk he headed was Citibank's way of capitalizing on the effect of the earth's rotation.

Chen's job was a new and exotic entry to the night work force, but Ignatius Donnelly had seen it coming from a century away. In *Caesar's Column,* his hugely popular 1891 novel, Donnelly outlined a vision of New

York as he thought it might look in 1988—a city lit so brightly that "night and day are all one," and where "the business parts of the city swarm as much at midnight as at high noon." His scale was off—not even Las Vegas swarms all night long—but he was prescient in imagining the incessancy of the modern business world. In the last decade the number of night office workers rose several times faster than the number of all other night workers, to more than four million people. Busy tonight in offices all over New York—a city with a sturdy all-night infrastructure that included greengrocers, clothing stores, Italian restaurants, car washes, copy shops, poolhalls and even, not far from Citibank, a Human Resources Administration office that took in an average of thirty abused or abandoned children each night—were proofreaders, data entry clerks, word processors, computer jockeys and deadline-bound corporate lawyers.

The next century's offices will likely glow even brighter at night, especially on Wall Street, as other financial institutions try to appease the gnawing feeling that, while they doze, someone, somewhere, is making money that could be theirs. The eyes awake at night on Wall Street now were focused mainly overseas—the currency traders; the stockbrokers who, either at the office or on home monitors, watched the overseas securities markets. But they were slowly turning to focus on something closer. Spurred by a globalizing economy—where the sun is always shining on somebody with money to invest, where technology has brought Kuala Lumpur as close to Manhattan as Brooklyn, where Tokyo and London have taken business that was once New York's—America's markets are stretching the trading day, moving toward a time when the closing bell will be silenced. Nasdaq now starts trading in over-the-counter stocks at 3:30 A.M. The American Stock Exchange, the Cincinnati Stock Exchange and the Chicago Board Options Exchange have plans for a worldwide, after-hours system for trading stocks and options. The Philadelphia Stock Exchange trades foreign-currency options twenty and a half hours a day. The New York Mercantile Exchange plans to start computerized round-the-clock trading in oil-futures contracts. The Chicago Board of Trade and the Chicago Mercantile Exchange have just opened a twenty-four-hour futures and options trading system called Globex. Finex, a division of the New York Cotton Exchange, offers near round-the-clock trading in financial futures. Off-exchange networks (Instinet, the Crossing Network, Posit and others) match buyers and sellers electronically at almost any hour. And the New York Stock Exchange, the biggest and most important of all, announced a long-term plan to extend trading to twenty-four hours by the turn of the century; but opposition to two early steps (an earlier opening, at 9 A.M., and three brief night sessions, at 8 P.M., midnight and 5 A.M.) forced an indefinite postponement. Not everyone was convinced yet that longer trading would actually mean more trading.

Tonight, as usual, Richard Chen, crisply dressed in a daylight-suitable white shirt and red tie and gray pants, sat at his trading desk surrounded by a bank of electronic wizardry that allowed him to monitor the market as closely as a night nurse monitors the vital signs of a critical patient. He mainly watched the patient sleep. "You can't make any money tonight," he said. "It's not worth it." The dollar had been sluggish all day and, for a couple of reasons, wasn't likely to take off anywhere now: The Consumer Price Index was due tomorrow, and nobody was venturing out until they heard this key economic weather report; and it was a holiday for the Japanese, who have the good sense to celebrate the spring equinox, the start of the warm half of the year, when the days last longer than the nights. Still, an occasional bid-and-offer came over the squawk box in a forlorn, any-body-out-there voice: "Thirty-five, thirty-eight yen." Translated, that meant the disembodied trader would pay 131.35 yen for each dollar Citi-bank wanted to sell, and would sell the dollars he held for 131.38 yen apiece; traders always dropped the first part of the price, saving their breath for the part that mattered. Also translated, Chen's silence meant there were no takers.

A night like this demanded of a trader a quality not always apparent in the breed: the ability to sit patiently on the bench. "Night in our industry is slower, less profitable, given the nature of the business," Chen said. "The night crew is less cowboyish. If you were young and aggressive, you might prefer the craziness during the days. Nights are a little more conservative, a little more subdued. If you lose money at night, it's harder to make it back." He had earned a degree in electrical engineering before getting an MBA and joining Citibank, where he worked as a financial analyst before he started trading. "I'm really an engineer at heart. I like to understand how things work. I don't fit in with the personality of some of the traders. I don't like prima donnas. I don't need a crowd to play to. I'm content to chug along, take small positions and make my money. It will always add up. I can keep control. I know when to raise the flag. But it's difficult to find the same kind of person to work this shift."

At 12:30 the yen still wasn't going anywhere, and neither, it seemed, was

Chen. The other traders had left. "I made a few thousand here, a few thousand there," one said on his way out, "nothing to write home about." The market was so stagnant that their stop-loss orders—the directions they left to sell their currency holdings if the price dipped below a certain level—were mainly earthquake insurance. "The longer it stays here and does nothing, the harder it is to do anything, and the more entrenched the market is," Chen said. Yet he was reluctant to leave. The TV that hung beside the trading desk was on, as it always was, because any minute could bring a calamitous news bulletin that left the market reeling; what it brought now was David Letterman, who was bemusedly watching a quick-draw performance by "the world's fastest gun." A call came in from Hong Kong, and Chen pounced on it like a cat. He spoke in Chinese. Though he had, when the market demanded it, traded straight through till the next noon, he didn't learn anything from this call that would lead him to stay. Tonight the market sent him home at 12:45, with plenty of time to stop for one of the late snacks he favored in Chinatown. He did not switch off the lights when he left.

"What did Frankfurt say about the dollar?"
"I was asking for a price for ten dollars."
"Try to see what price Lloyds gives you."
At 2 A.M. Citibank's New York hand in the poker game had passed to the last four traders left on the forty-seventh floor, which dwarfed them the way Yankee Stadium dwarfs the players at morning batting practice. Daylight had traversed the capitalist black hole of the Soviet Union and now fell on Western Europe, opening the markets there. Frankie Sevilla, chief of the overnight traders, typed a message and delivered it across the ocean via computer: Is that U Guy? *Oui Oui,* the reply came, *Just Stepped In.* U Think They're going to do anything w/ this buck in Europe? *Don't Think so Pal. The Only Movement I see is in Kiwi & Oz* (trader shorthand for the New Zealand and the Australian dollars).

The third shift was the foreign-exchange department's overnight information directory, sales desk, alarm clock, communications switchboard, respite care service and smoke detector. They monitored the ceaseless parade of market information that marched across their computer screens, and they executed currency orders for Citibank's corporate customers. They answered the calls of anxious traders, who tossed and turned in their beds with visions of wild market swings. They prevented the liquid currency from becoming vapor and vanishing in a cloud of smoke. They also searched for delis that would deliver middle-of-the-night lunches. "No, that deli closes early," one trader said to one suggestion. "At twelve or so."

Sevilla picked up a phone and dialed Switzerland. "Hans, this is Frankie. What do you think about this dollar-yen today?" Hans was at a Zurich bank. "How about the dollar-mark? You anticipate that to happen before the CPI number comes out?" For the past four days Sevilla had been holding dollars he had bought against yen, and now he was looking for clues as to whether he should continue to hold them. He gleaned an almanac assortment of infobits. He scanned the shifting prices. He read the news headlines that flashed in a string of seeming non sequiturs: SUGAR RECOVERS FROM DEEP LOWS TO END HIGHER; TAKEOVER STOCKS WERE BIG MOVERS IN SESSION; FINNISH REVALUATION MAY NOT BE ENOUGH, ANALYSTS SAY. He studied a chart faxed from a Swiss bank that showed the dollar's hourly price range since yesterday. "I'm looking for 131.5 yen. If the dollar goes up and breaks through 131.5 during London, I'll hold on. If it doesn't get above that during London, I'd probably get out of my position and hold off before taking another position." London trading would open at 3 A.M. Though Sevilla would have preferred to wear a T-shirt and jeans to work, his job overlapped with the day shift, and such casual attire was considered unprofessional; like Chen, he wore gray pants, white shirt and a tie. A native of the Philippines, he was the only third-shift trader to take speculative positions in the market. Citibank would have preferred more, but experienced traders were in short supply and were reluctant to work nights. Their reasons were financial as well as biological: Traders, whose annual base salaries ranged roughly between $25,000 and $125,000, made their real money in bonuses, which were tied to what they earned for the bank in the market; since the slower overnight market meant less bonus potential, there was less incentive to push their bodies into an unnatural schedule. It didn't pay to put less experienced traders on the shift, because the opportunity to make money in the market at night was also the opportunity to lose money. "There's no gray area," Sevilla said. "You beat him or he beats you."

Alex Park's eyes were on the escudo, the Portuguese currency he had an order for. He sat alone, a few desk rows south of the other traders, separated from them in much the way the currency he handled was separated from theirs. The main foreign-exchange desk handled what are considered the world's major currencies, the mark and the yen chief among them; the exotics desk, where Park worked, handled 120 currencies that are considered minor. All night long he was immersed in a numismatist's dream of wons, bahts, dinars, riyals, rands, markkas, drachmas and kronas. "It's a job just knowing where all these countries are," he said. The exotics desk mainly stayed away from speculation and concentrated instead on obtaining foreign currency for customers who needed to buy goods from foreign countries, the more traditional role of a bank's foreign-exchange department. Park had already done deals with Indonesia, India and Bahrain. He still had to buy escudos and Egyptian pounds.

By 4 A.M. the flurry triggered by the opening of Europe had passed. Sevilla had sold his dollars against yen, reversing his position from long to short and making a $6,000 profit. "It seems to have difficulty breaking above .50," he said of the yen. "I'm gambling it won't. Even if it did, I think it'd only be temporary. It's a tricky gamble, but I have a feeling we'll see a downswing before the [CPI] number comes out." The leading edge of the morning daylight was racing west along the equator now at seventeen miles per minute, and it would open no new markets until it hit New York. The TV was still on, playing a game show now: "We're ready to play round three of *Liar's Club*." The phone calls, both in and out, continued.

"Your order at 131.50 to buy one hundred million has been done."

"Richard Chen's on the phone. He wants to be called if it hits 131.55."

"What happened to that Ozzie one million? Was it done?"

It was the deepest part of the night, and they were facing the hardest part of the job: trying to stay awake. Napping here could be quite expensive. "You might close your eyes, and in a matter of seconds the market has moved, there's been an announcement or something, and you have all these orders you have to execute then," Sevilla said. "But when the market starts moving, you'd be surprised how your adrenaline gets you wide awake. When the market starts moving, I don't know how your body system does it, but you're going. Your body clock adjusts to the market."

The day slowly revealed the forty-seventh floor's panoramic view—the Brooklyn Bridge, the Verrazano Narrows Bridge, the confluence of the Hudson and East rivers, the Staten Island Ferry plowing past the Statue of Liberty toward Manhattan—that had been obscured all night, both by the darkness outside and by the reflective interior of the windows. It was raining out, and the gray morning matched the gray carpets and chairs and desktops inside. Soon Sevilla would relinquish his desk to its third occupant and drive home to his wife and four children in New Jersey; the Holland Tunnel was where the accumulated weariness usually hit him. By 6:30 the first of the two hundred daytime traders were filling the room like time-lapse photography. Every time I looked up, another desk was occupied. They shed their jackets quickly, drank in the screens, picked up the phones. Boxes, copy machines, tables, desks and assorted other office paraphernalia lined the windows as if it were just another wall, and the traders mostly ignored the view. They fixed on their screens, on the prices and headlines streaming by: RECESSION MIGHT BENEFIT LOWER-PRICED HOTELIERS; STUDY SAYS GAP BETWEEN RICH AND POOR WIDENING IN U.S.

Officers Bob Wheat and Greg Angotti were cruising slowly in an unmarked police car along Forty-second Street, broad and traffickless at 2 A.M., past the jittery small-time crackheads, the jut-hipped whores in microskirts wrapped tight as Ace bandages, the homeless people shopping through fast-food trashbags, past the peep shows and the mossy old movie palaces that now screened such gynecological classics as *Erotic Sex Goddess* and *Trashy Girls in Heat,* through the heart of a world whose population the night had stripped of all but the hunters and the hunted, when a message over the radio, unintelligible to me in the backseat, caused Wheat, who was driving, to turn to his partner and say, "Let's go see the circus." In this precinct, at this hour of the night, going to see the circus could, I thought, mean a hundred different things, and none of them seemed too pretty. Wheat wheeled the car south. I expected they were headed toward a knifing over a vial of crack, maybe a corner turf battle among some prostitutes. When they got to Thirty-fourth Street, several other police cruisers had already arrived at what turned out to be the most obvious, benign and, to me anyway, unexpected meaning of all. An elephant trundled up Thirty-fourth Street, followed by another elephant and another and another, maybe twenty in all. Behind them was a menagerie of strolling camels, llamas, horses and spangled circus performers. Wheat was slightly disappointed. "They used to have big cages with the big cats in them," he said.

The animals belonged to the Ringling Brothers and Barnum & Bailey Circus, and they were nearing the end of the annual postmidnight march to their engagement at Madison Square Garden. They had journeyed by circus train to the Queens rail yards and then walked the rest of the way; one tube of the Midtown Tunnel had been closed to give them clear passage. "It breaks the monotony of the night," Wheat said. He and Angotti watched for a few minutes before resuming their laps around the precinct.

The precinct Wheat and Angotti patrolled night after night, Midtown South, is enormous from every angle save one. It is home to a grove of some of the world's tallest buildings, including the Empire State Building. It is the city's transportation hub; Grand Central and Penn Station are here, as is Port Authority, which is where you end up if you board a New York–bound bus in some small Ohio town. It comprises a souvenir album of trademark New York landmarks: the New York Public Library, Times Square, Madison Square Garden, the Broadway theaters, the garment district. Upward of three million people pass through Midtown South each day, leading it to claim the title of busiest precinct in New York and, by extension, maybe the world, too. In real estate square footage, though, it is remarkably small—a .67-square-mile box bounded by Forty-fifth Street on the north, Twenty-ninth Street on the south, Ninth Avenue on the west and Lexington Avenue on the east—so the scenery in the windshield of Wheat and Angotti's patrolling car unreeled all night in a continuous, repeating loop. The sculpted lions that guard the library steps reappeared at regular intervals like ornaments on a spinning carousel.

"You're looking for something unusual," Wheat said, as they pulled away from the station house on Thirty-fifth Street shortly after midnight, under a full moon, to start their tour. To me, something unusual was almost everything I saw. Wheat, after twenty-three years as a cop and more than a decade on nights, had a different threshold. "It's hard to explain it to someone. You drive these streets hundreds of times, and then when you don't see something you always see, you stop and notice. There might be a door piled with boxes and the pile's too high, or a street trash can is by a window. Maybe a guy was gonna break in and he got nervous. But maybe he'll come back when he gets enough balls to break a window and grab a radio and run off with it."

The two young women standing at the corner of Forty-fifth Street and Eighth Avenue, poured into outfits that exposed to the elements more flesh than was medically advisable in March, did not rank among the unusual. Wheat recognized one from half a block away. "I haven't seen her in a dog's age. We must've locked her up six years ago." He and Angotti were equally recognizable. They wore plainclothes, jeans and sweaters, and drove a plain car, a new blue Chevy Caprice, but it wasn't hard for the street regulars to see that two men, in this neighborhood at this hour, in a generic late-model four-door American sedan, were not coming home from a Knicks game. "See how long it takes them to figure out who we are," Angotti said. As soon as the women spotted the car, they turned on their stiletto heels and, with a casual who-me? air, sauntered down the street.

The relative criminality of prostitution in Midtown South is, unlike murder, subject to change. It is always illegal here, but how tightly that law is enforced is determined by the shifting winds of public morality, neighborhood tolerance and political rhetoric. Tonight the winds were permissive. A string of burglaries in the garment district meant that Wheat and Angotti, normally with the prostitution-control unit, were assigned instead to the precinct's anticrime unit, a plainclothes outfit whose mission was preemptive rather than just reactive. Tonight they were trolling for fur thieves, not prostitutes, so the pair with the Forty-fifth Street franchise didn't warrant much attention.

"Whatever happened to Speedy?" Wheat asked.

"She hung up her spurs," answered Angotti, who then filled me in on the professional demise of a skinny runaway who once worked these streets. "A guy had a heart attack and died on top of her. He was a real heavy man, and she couldn't get him off of her. She was screaming and screaming. The hotel guy tried to get him off, but couldn't. When the cops got there, she was still underneath this guy. She was so overwhelmed by it that it ended her career as a prostitute. She said, 'When I start killing them, that's when I stop.' "

Wheat spotted another recidivist among the trio of prostitutes that accented the corner of Forty-second Street and Eighth Avenue. "I locked her, uh, him up. See, I even call them 'her.' " I would have, too, since she, uh, he was a tall blonde in a short skirt, but I would have been wrong, since she, uh, he was actually somewhere in between—one of the many transvestites who work these streets. Some he-shes, as the police often called them, just dress as shes, while others, like the one Angotti remembered now, try to eliminate their he-parts altogether. "She used to be a football player, I think, but fourteen years ago she had the operation," he said, referring to the surgical procedure that causes men to wince and cross their legs together tightly, protectively. "A few of them fool me. We took one out of a hotel for burglary once and took her as a girl to be searched by a female. We heard a shout and she brought her out and said, 'You ain't got a girl here.' He had slender hands and was slender through the waist. The Adam's apple is usually a dead giveaway, but he had done that. But he didn't have the organ done yet." If you still have the organ, you go in with the men.

Wheat took the corner slowly around Grand Central, which sits like a river island in the middle of Park Avenue, and headed south into the sector of the precinct where the prostitutes, like the real estate, were a little higher-rent. "You don't get 'em with track marks up and down their arms here," he said. Most of the streets of Midtown South are the sex industry's discount basement, populated largely by runaways, addicts, women too old or new or dirty to get better work, as a topless dancer, say, or a call girl. They do most of their work in their customers' cars, dispensing twenty-five-dollar blow jobs, the erotic equivalent of fast food. Their lives are sometimes as cheap as their prices. "One of the girls got shot in this hotel," Angotti said, pointing out a hotel of the type not generally rated by the Mobil Travel Guide. "Her trick shot her. She went up there with him, and when he finished, he took out a gun and shot her. No motive. Most people who kill people know each other, but there are some people who off people just for the hell of it, especially in that kind of world, where nobody keeps track of nothing."

Greek mythology explained the night as the creation of the goddess Nyx, the daughter of Chaos, who soared across the sky at the close of each day, trailing behind her a black veil studded with stars. She was not a benevolent goddess. Among her children were doom, disease, pain, strife, sorrow, old age and death, earning her a place in the long tradition, reaching across time and the globe, that considers night an accomplice of evil. The evil freed by darkness can be supernatural—the spirits and monsters of legend—but it can also be human, as was clear to Euripides, author of a line that holds as true in Manhattan today as it did in Athens in the fifth century B.C.: "The night is the safe time for robbers, as the light for just men." Protecting the just against the evil has taken many forms. The gates of medieval cities were closed after sunset, and individual houses were required by law to be locked. Curfews were standard policy, not, as they are today, extraordinary measures imposed only in times of civil unrest. "And no man walke after IX of the belle streken in the nyght withoute lyght or withoute cause reasonable in payne of empresonment," ruled a 1467 English decree. Paris started installing streetlamps in 1667, by order of Louis XIV, the "Sun King," and within a century they had become both a costly line item in the police budget, consuming 15 percent of it, and a resented symbol of an authoritarian government. When the Revolution came, its first victims were hanged from the lampposts.

A wall around Manhattan would only fence the bad in with the good, and lamps have long since been lit, so the city relies now on the police department's late tour to protect it through the hours when, according to modern mythology, anarchy rules. But the new myth, when examined from Wheat and Angotti's patrol car, proved only slightly more credible than the old. Their average shift was relatively—and *relatively* is an important word in Midtown South—peaceful. Crime does prefer to use darkness as a shield, but it also requires a ready pool of victims, which means that the evening, when the absence of light coincides with the presence of wakeful people, is actually the precinct's most dangerous time. Statistics reflect this nationally: According to the Justice Department's National Crime Survey, 47.4 percent of all crimes of violence occur between 6 A.M. and 6 P.M., 38.3 percent between 6 P.M. and midnight and just 13.4 percent between midnight and 6 A.M. Even the bad guys have to sleep sometime.

Wheat wheeled slowly through streets so empty it was hard to believe that, in just a few hours, they would be crippled by gridlock. The other traffic now was mostly garbage trucks and cabs. New York, despite its affinity for darkness, is less a city of the night than it is a city of the evening; these smallest hours are when rats and cockroaches, the two species best adapted to urban life, emerge to forage. He passed again through Times Square, where a quarter-million people, plus Dick Clark, gather on New Year's Eve to watch the ball drop; the few score scattered here now seemed to be watching their hopes drop. "Everybody's a suspect," he said. "Who else has a legitimate reason for being around at 3 A.M.? If you get robbed here, the D.A. asks you what you were doing out at 3 A.M."

At 3 A.M. on Madison Avenue it wasn't who got robbed, but what. They stopped to talk to some uniformed officers from one of the blue-and-white patrol cars that answered radio calls, who were at the scene of a fresh burglary—a shoe store whose display window had just been smashed by a garbage can. Two shoes were missing, taken by a thief apparently unaware that the store displayed only left shoes, not matching pairs.

"Maybe it's a one-legged man," Angotti said.

"He broke a five-hundred-dollar window for one black shoe and one brown shoe," Wheat said.

"He doesn't care, as long as they're size nine."

A Day in the Night of America

"Maybe he's smarter than we think. Maybe he'll wait two weeks, then go back and get a matching set."

At 4 A.M., the hour when New York's bars finally close, the radio brought word of the night's first blood. "Male shot in the head" was all I could make out, then a location on Eighth Avenue. "Did she say 'shot'?" Angotti asked.

"He probably got bopped in the head, and they saw all that blood and thought he must be shot," Wheat said. He sped across to Eighth. The crime the late tour does see tends to be more serious, often bloodier; statistics show that murders peak around midnight. Two people had been stabbed on the precinct's streets the night before, one of them, in Angotti's words, "flayed like a mackerel." He was accustomed to such sights now, after eighteen years on the force, but he wasn't always. His first murder scene was in a bakery, where in the heat of an argument, one baker had killed another, spewing blood all over the white, flour-dusted kitchen. "These older cops were eating doughnuts right out of the oven, while I'm turning green. To them it was no big fucking deal."

Several other police cars and an ambulance were already at the scene—a small, all-night Korean grocery—when Wheat arrived. A young uniformed cop approached the car to fill them in: The night clerk had apparently attacked someone he had caught stealing. "I think somebody split the motherfucker's head open, I don't think he's shot," the cop said, confirming Wheat's instinct. Wheat and Angotti weren't needed here, so they continued on their circuit. "Did you see that young cop?" Angotti asked as they pulled away. "He had the same green face I had in that bakery."

Wheat and Angotti averaged one arrest each week, but tonight, it now appeared, wasn't going to be the night they got it. The furs and their thieving predators seemed to be hibernating. No burglar alarms had sounded in the garment district, and no unusual activity had been spotted there—which didn't surprise the partners, who suspected the thefts were inside insurance-fraud jobs. "We're convinced the stuff never leaves the buildings," Wheat said. A tentative, milky-blue light bathed the streets now, and when I looked up, I saw, in a few scattered crevices, the sky I hadn't seen all night. The unnatural height of the buildings here, combined with the squat view from the patrol car, had created in the darkness the illusion that the precinct was an enclosed, interior space; but the dawn was slowly revealing that the city was still outdoors after all. Daylight seeped into the gaps in the skyline, and into the wedges of sky that hovered over the

Hudson River at the far end of the cross-street corridors, ushering in Manhattan's eeriest, most placid time—the hour when the day first exposes the night-empty city. A group of homeless people were bunched at the entrance of Grand Central like commuters pressing toward a rush-hour train; the terminal had closed at 1:30 and they were waiting to claim a warm space inside when it reopened at 5:30.

The radio beckoned one last time: Somebody was doing some early shopping in the Woolworth's at Forty-first and Third. Wheat and Angotti sprang from the car when they arrived to assist several uniformed cops who had already corralled three suspects. The glass in the front door was smashed, and the three men kneeled against the store's outside wall, hands behind their backs.

"Man, I didn't do nothing, I was just walking by," one suspect protested loudly, repeatedly.

"Shut the fuck up," a cop told him.

The other cops made the arrest—only the third of a slow night, in a precinct that often saw a dozen or more on this shift, and that would see 27,000 felony arrests before the year was out. It was the sort of crime that wouldn't make the papers, much less the headlines that flashed across the traders' screens at Citibank. "What are you gonna get out of Woolworth's?" Angotti wondered as they left. "We deal with so much shit here that to other people is a big deal. We're more complacent. We know that this, too, shall pass."

The first joggers and delivery trucks were bouncing along by 6, and deep in the outer boroughs and New Jersey and Long Island and Westchester groggy commuters were stirring, readying for their trek to this precinct. The homeless men were still asleep in the porn theaters on Forty-second Street, de facto flophouses where, for a few bucks, they can sit in a darkened room and dream in the flickering light. Wheat and Angotti were headed back to the station house—for their lunch hour; they generally waited for the light to arrive before coming in from patrol. Not long after, Wheat would start home to Long Island, Angotti to Staten Island, both far from the circus of Midtown South, passing, on their way out, many of the three million day people on their way in. Each earned about thirty dollars more than their daytime colleagues for working midnights, and neither had any inclination to switch. "I hate this place in the daytime," Angotti said.

They passed a florist shop whose window was grateless but unlit. "They don't light the flowers up," Wheat said, "because they figure nobody's around to look at them but cops. No real people."

A Day in the Night of America

●

The defendant stood before the bar of justice, eyes cast down toward the worn linoleum floor, his case giving pause to Judge Robert Haft. All night long the judge, posted behind a scuffed wooden bench in the Manhattan Criminal Courts Building, had presided over the arraignment of accused thieves, muggers, drug dealers, prostitutes, unlicensed vendors, subway-token suckers and assorted other miscreants, swiftly fixing bail or passing sentence or setting future court dates, but now he faced a crime unfamiliar enough that he wasn't quite sure of the penalty for it. He flipped through an outdated, dog-eared paperback copy of the Criminal Law book. The courtroom's tall windows opened onto fragments of a dim gray sky, and the plain classroom clock that hung on the far wall, over the empty pews of spectators' seats, marked the time as 5:30. When I looked at the sky and the clock, and then at the full complement of court officers and public defenders and assistant district attorneys and waiting defendants and a judge in a long black robe, my first instinct, even after sitting here through the night, was to think it was late in the afternoon, not early in the morning. The judge solicited some help. "Why can't we have an updated book on the bench?" he asked. "What's the minimum on impaired?"

The defendant, a tall and burly construction worker from Connecticut with a red face and a dirty-blond beard, had been caught driving on 165th Street with enough alcohol in his system to warrant a charge of driving while impaired, a lesser charge than driving while intoxicated. Drunken driving is certainly a serious offense, and it may be alarmingly common in the court-rooms of suburban New York, but the Manhattan courts generally host a different sort of criminal. A court officer found the answer—"It was just amended, two hundred fifty dollars for impaired, three-fifty for intox-icated"—and the defendant was soon on his way out into the dawn.

In the daytime this building is a criminal-justice bazaar. It is an imposing art-deco block, one of the many government buildings clustered around Foley Square and City Hall at the Manhattan end of the Brooklyn Bridge, distinguished by a granite base, a limestone ziggurat crown and severe, straight lines of windows running down its facade like bars on a jail cell. An inscription at the entrance warns, WHERE LAW ENDS THERE TYRANNY BEGINS. Its courtrooms are crowded then with judges, lawyers, juries, defendants, reporters and the court buffs who compete for seats at the headline trials. TV camera crews are parked outside and cops are sprawled across the

benches of a room across from the D.A.'s complaint room, earning hours
of overtime as they wait to be interviewed by the D.A.'s processing their
arrests.

After midnight all the building's activity, and therefore all the activity of
the Manhattan criminal justice system, was concentrated in Room 129, a
ground-floor arraignment courtroom that looked less like the civics-class
image of a courtroom than it did the waiting room of a bus station in some
forlorn, dying town. It had the resigned demeanor of a place so heavily
trafficked that any efforts at lasting cosmetic rehabilitations are futile. The
weighty brass doors opening into the courtroom were decorated with a
bas-relief of the scales of justice, eroded by the touch of too many hands;
cardboard covered one door's small broken window. Battered wainscoting
rose halfway up the dingy white walls. Flat rectangular fixtures dangled low
from the high ceiling, casting a sickly greenish light over the room, and
when you looked up at their white plastic bottoms, you could see the
shadows of the rubber bands shot into them by bored observers, interlock-
ing now like a diagram of dividing cells multiplying themselves over and
over and over again.

The overnight session here exists because a vast population of accused
criminals—the drunken driver, the Woolworth's burglars and the 164,000
other arrests in Manhattan this year—exists. Arraignment court is the
funnel of the criminal justice system, the common ground where celebrity
mobsters and petty thieves alike have their first audience with a judge, and
the overnight session is the narrowest part of the funnel's neck. To plug,
or even slow, the funnel is to risk deluge (the courts later ruled that the
average arrest-to-arraignment time, forty hours in Manhattan this year, was
too long, and imposed instead a twenty-four-hour limit), so the stream of
prisoners keeps flowing through all night long. "You can do a good day's
work and then come back the next day and it's the same thing all over
again," said Steve Kufs, deputy chief clerk of arraignments for New York
County, the formal name for the borough of Manhattan. He arrived early
each morning to find night court still in session and the looming backlog
of cases still intact. "It's like shoveling a load of shit against the tide."

The young prosecutor faced Judge Haft and read from the statement of
the arresting officer in the case. " 'When he was found sleeping in the car,
he said, "It's not my car, I'm working for Lopez. Lopez told us to wait here
and he'd come back soon." ' "

A Day in the Night of America

"You want to say anything?" Haft asked the defendant, the man who had been waiting for Lopez and who now stood charged with breaking into a parked car.

The public defender who stood beside the defendant prompted him with a whisper from the side of his mouth, "No, sir."

"No, sir," the defendant answered, shaking his head.

Haft leaned forward in his high-backed swivel chair, perched several steps above the courtroom floor, to calculate what the crime was worth to New York County. Behind him hung an American flag and in front of him, on the face of the bench, hung a calendar the lawyers referred to when setting future court dates; the calendar bore a slogan from the credit union that supplied it, WE HAVE WHAT YOU WANT. He scanned the package of papers that chronicled the case, including the long list of previous offenses on the defendant's rap sheet, and he factored into the equation the judicial instincts acquired from his seventeen years on the bench. Since the crime was a misdemeanor, he could accept a guilty plea here and pass sentence immediately, thereby expelling one more case from a swamped judicial system.

"I'll give him six months."

The defendant was noncommittal as word of the judge's offer passed to him through the public defender and the translator, who rendered it into Spanish. "Would you knock it down to four months, Your Honor?" the public defender asked.

"No, he's a bad guy. They were in the car. The window was broken."

The defendant stroked his beard like a car dealer pondering an offer on a used Chevy. Justice here is sometimes a negotiable commodity, like the currency traded not even a mile away at Citibank, and its price, like the price of the dollar, can be subject to change. The defendant wasn't buying tonight. "We do not have a deal, Your Honor," the public defender said. "He'll take his chances." The defendant was led back through a door with the sign NO FIREARMS BEYOND THIS POINT. He was headed to jail to await his next court date, where he hoped to hear a better offer.

Officially this night court, designated as Part AR-5 and occupying Room 129 between 1 A.M. and 9 A.M., wasn't called night court at all. It was more familiarly known as the lobster shift, echoing a term often used at newspapers, and it was the only one in the city; *night court* here referred instead to the session that met from 5 P.M. to 1 A.M., and that had gained notoriety from the TV sitcom that ascribed far more humor to it than any real observer would. The lobster shift was not considered a delicacy by the city's judges, who shared it in a weekly rotation and whose complaints were loud enough to reduce it to four nights a week, Wednesday through Saturday, from its original seven. In the week before Easter lobster duty fell to Haft, a state supreme court judge, who did find one consolation in it: The shortened work week had allowed him a long weekend in New Orleans. "I'm a marathoner, so I can probably do with a little less sleep than some of the others." But the lobster shift was more like a long series of wind sprints—dozens of distinct cases passing in review, demanding quick, concentrated bursts of decision making.

"Miss Jones, is there anything you wish to say before sentence is imposed?" he asked a woman who had just pleaded guilty to a charge she had announced with her attire—a fur-trimmed purple jacket and a tight black dress that fell about as far as a T-shirt—long before the prosecutor had.

"No, Your Honor."

"One hundred dollars or fifteen days." She took the one hundred dollars and then joined some business associates waiting for her at the courtroom door.

Up stepped a young man who had broken into a subway-token box. His long record led the prosecutor to ask for sixty days.

"That's ridiculous," the public defender countered. "The most he's ever taken in his life is ten days."

Haft corrected him. "He got fifteen days last time for the exact same thing. We don't want him to perpetuate his mistakes over and over again." He offered thirty days.

"That's too much."

"Not for a guy who makes a career out of it."

The judge held, and the offer was accepted. "Thirty days," the public defender shrugged. "This guy, he'll do it on one finger."

The cases passed before Haft like a mural illustrating all the offenses in the criminal code.

"I'm not gonna hold that against him," he told a public defender who was explaining why a defendant had only been at his present address for two months. "It's all the other things I'm gonna hold against him."

"If you have a thousand dollars, you can go home. If you don't you can't," he told one prisoner as he fixed bail, and the prisoner replied with a weary, frustrated "Sheeit."

He listened to the defense argue that a prisoner, because he lived with his girlfriend, demonstrated sufficient "community ties" to be released without bail. "Everybody lives somewhere. That's not community ties." He fixed $2,500 bail.

"Well, that's a start—he knows who his probation officer is."

"He's apparently an addict. There could be nobody less reliable than your client."

"You're to stay away from her, is that clear?"

"How can we determine if he suffered any pain?"

"Did you have crack on you? Did you have a pipe?"

"Mr. White, Mr. White," he called toward a waiting suspect, slumped asleep on the prisoners' bench. I was surprised to hear Haft say "Mr. White" because I had assumed, as I had about the transvestite I had seen from the patrol car, that Mr. White, who wore a black miniskirt, was really Ms. White. "Your case is up. You've got to get up now."

"Shhh," he admonished the prisoners' bench when a joke apparently got loose there and triggered a wave of snickering. He didn't have a gavel, so, to punctuate his order, he rapped a rubber stamp against the bench.

"I wouldn't mind it so much if it weren't so boring, so mechanical," he said later.

To sit here in arraignment court was to witness the final acts of tawdry, violent stories that had started in small, airless tenement rooms uptown, on the broad, open avenues of midtown and in every other corner of Manhattan Island. In addition to the common stage set, many of the stories also shared a common plot device: drugs. Drug arrests had risen dramatically in New York in recent years, sparked in large part by the spread of crack, and they now accounted for almost a third of all the city's arrests. A new addition to the collection of rubber stamps on the bench was the one that emblazoned CRACK in red ink on the papers of all the crack cases. "It is more violent now," Haft said. "Even I get shocked sometimes, and I'm not easily shockable. The gratuitous violence, where the victim gives up the money and then still gets shot—that's different from years ago. It seems crack has apparently released inhibitions in people who are already violent to begin with."

The present defendant had been caught in one of those small rooms, along with a loaded .38, four ounces of cocaine, equipment to weigh and package it, and $100,000 in cash—a sum that caused the prisoners waiting on the on-deck bench to utter a collective "Oooooh" and lean forward for a better look. The money also meant the defendant had a private lawyer at his side, an unusual sight here. "I realize the charges are serious," the lawyer said. "All I ask you to do is set a lot more reasonable bail than twenty-five thousand dollars."

"He's used a different name. He has no family, so he'd be likely to flee, and now he has two charges against him," Haft said before fixing bail at ten thousand dollars, less than that recommended by the prosecutors, who tend to aim high, but still the highest of the night.

The next dealer was farther down the corporate ladder, and had been caught on an open avenue holding considerably less capital. He was also apparently guilty of consumer fraud—trying to pass off tea leaves as marijuana and bread crumbs as cocaine—although no customers had registered complaints. "He smokes the good stuff and sells the rest," the public defender said. "The only thing real is the residue in the pipe."

"I'll give him fifteen days."

"I gotta go into a drug program Monday morning," the defendant said, which sounded to Haft like another battlefield conversion.

"They're always going into a drug program the next day," he said. "He got thirty last time. He deserves sixty. If he wants to try the program, let him try it."

Another man, accused of running a more substantial retail operation, stood flanked by his wife and son, who were there not to lend moral support but to answer charges that they helped him make their Lower East Side bodega the kind of family business the law doesn't approve of. On four separate occasions, the prosecutor said, undercover cops spent a total of $6,500 there on cocaine.

"He came from Santo Domingo in the Dominican Republic eight years ago and he has three other kids," the public defender said of the father. "He's had four different stores. The family has never been on welfare. He has no prior record."

Haft stood from his seat and leaned against the bench to think, towering over the courtroom like a basketball center. He was a small, wiry man, his short black hair flecked with gray, who looked much younger than his fifty-eight years. His runner's energy had carried him across the biological valley of the deepest night, and he seemed not to notice that the windows were still black. Under his robe he wore gray pants, a blue shirt and a red tie. His collar button was still buttoned. "What perplexes me is that there's no lab report," he said. "Were the undercover negotiations in Spanish?"

Yes, they were. The father was a short, pudgy man whose face betrayed a sense of fear, an emotion not often seen here. His eyes darted nervously around the room and his mouth hung slightly open, never quite shutting. "If they have passports, we'll surrender them," the defense offered. Haft sat down again, his decision made. He released the son without bail and fixed bail at five thousand dollars for the father and one thousand dollars for the mother.

A young New Jersey couple, still in their teens, came before Haft dressed in black and wearing hairstyles that suggested they would have preferred, at this hour, to be dancing at one of the clubs that bloom in the city's darkness. They had crossed the George Washington Bridge from their Fort Lee homes to shop in the Washington Heights street supermarket in upper Manhattan that caters to the vast suburban drug appetite. They were arrested there after buying cocaine.

"They all come in here and partake of our goodies," Haft said. He allowed them to plead guilty to a reduced charge and let them go with a warning lecture. "If you should come over here again to buy coke or crack, you'll end up with a criminal record. You'd better stay on the other side of the bridge."

"Don't come back," the public defender added as they left.

The prisoners' bench was still full, its eternal condition, but the audience pews were almost empty. A public defender talked with a defendant in the wood-and-glass interview booth that hugged the wall like a confessional. A young mother nudged awake her small son, who looked no more than four or five. "Wake up," she said to him. "We're gonna go now." He clung to her with a pout. The floor plan of Room 129 is an architectural illustration of the changing sociology of crime: When it was built, waiting families and friends outnumbered the prisoners, but now, fifty years later, the equation has been reversed.

"I feel bad for the kids waiting in the audience for their fathers," Angelo Melillo said. He was the bridge man tonight, the court officer who called up the prisoners and handed the case papers to the judge and generally, like a conductor, kept the action moving. When he called up a young man in dark glasses, it immediately made clear the identity of the heavyset, fiftyish couple who had been waiting in the audience all night with worried, rosary-bead faces. The defendant's father leaned forward, arms draped over the pew in front of him, as if kneeling in church; the mother alternately looked at the bench and up toward the ceiling. Their son stood charged with drug possession.

"I wanna go to sleep," the defendant said, wearily holding his head in his hands. He looked to his parents, who shushed him. He wore blue jeans, a yellow shirt and a tie under a fleece-lined denim jacket. It was his first visit with the law, and his denials were emphatic.

"This is a setup," he insisted. "I never used the stuff." Haft let him free with a guilty plea to a simple disorderly conduct charge and he sealed the record. The man bounded past the bar, out of the gravitational reach of the court and, in the only moment all night that resembled even vaguely a victory for anybody, was greeted with an embrace from his father. Morning had arrived, bringing Good Friday with it.

"Thirty days, Your Honor? Thirty days?" Steve Mechanic, the Legal Aid supervisor on the lobster shift, was incredulous at the sentence the prosecutor was recommending for his client. It was late Friday night, and the curtain had fallen on Broadway—and on the symphony, the opera, the rock concerts and much of the rest of the city's evening entertainments—but it was just rising again on another session of night court. "Thirty days? For sucking a token?"

Token sucking, a common scam in the city subway system, is one of those phenomena that cause non–New Yorkers to roll their eyes and say, "Only in New York." A token sucker jams a turnstile slot, usually with a piece of paper, and then waits nearby like a hunter over a baited trap; when an unsuspecting rider drops a token in, it gets stuck, and the sucker swoops in to put his mouth over the slot and, hence the name, suck it out. Thirty days, as Mechanic knew, was high for token sucking, but this particular token sucker had previously diversified into other enterprises—his rap sheet included arrests for robbery and marijuana possession—and the D.A.'s office wanted to teach him a little lesson.

"He's just a creep," Judge Haft said to Mechanic.

"So he's turned from marijuana to token sucking in his old age," Mechanic answered. He had been a public defender for almost twenty years and was sufficiently at home within the system to appear in court wearing a sweater in place of a jacket and tie, looking more like a rumpled history teacher than a lawyer. His discourse was similarly informal. He peered at the judge from over the top rim of his thick glasses, which had a tendency to slip down his nose, and drew an analogy to illustrate how unfair he thought the proposed sentence was when compared with the sentence commonly imposed on prostitutes. It was not the kind of analogy they teach in law school. "But thirty days for sucking a token? Come on," he said. "You only give time served for sucking a person."

The judge couldn't help but laugh, but he still resisted Mechanic's suggested sentence of five days. "I don't want him walking out of here today," he said. He gave him seven days.

Five teenage boys, lined up before Haft as if he were a high school principal, were charged with a transgression far more serious than skipping math class: a wolfpack robbery. While riding the subway, the prosecution alleged, they had assaulted several passengers, stealing a gold chain and a set of stereo headphones. Four were accompanied by public defenders; one had a private lawyer, still well pressed at 3:30 in a sharp double-breasted suit and arguing strenuously that his client was actually a sheep wrongly rounded up with the wolves. "My client was coming home from school and he says there was a melee he got caught up in," the lawyer said. "I've known his family personally for fifteen years. His whole family has maintained a vigil outside the courtroom for twenty-four hours."

The five-hundred-dollar bail Haft suggested wasn't low enough to end the family vigil. There were no bail bondsmen to turn to, because bail bondsmen work at courts where the defendants are likely to have some collateral, a standard that generally rules out this court. The lawyer offered other evidence of his client's good faith. "His father brought his passport, which he will surrender—that's how seriously he takes this matter," he said. "I can personally guarantee he will return. Can I show you his grade-point card?"

The judge examined the school record, which showed an 83 average. "What instrument did he play that he got a ninety-eight in band?" he asked.

"Drums," the defendant answered, his only word of the whole proceeding. Haft released him without bail.

The prosecutor handed Haft a Polaroid illustrating the result of another youthful crime: the bandaged face of a pretzel vendor allegedly robbed and beaten by the two defendants. It had taken thirty stitches to close the wounds. The good-student defense wouldn't work for this pair, one of whom was twenty and claimed to be in the eighth grade. "My understanding is that the pretzel vendor beat up the boys first," the public defender said.

Haft was skeptical. "Knives usually beat pretzels."

"Maybe these were hard pretzels, not soft ones," the defender tried. Five thousand dollars bail.

Mechanic appeared again, this time with a client who demonstrated that sleep deprivation wasn't the only health hazard on the lobster shift. The defendant had been arrested for smoking crack on 119th Street, an action that surely didn't help the medical condition he informed Haft, and Mechanic, of in the middle of the arraignment. "I have TB," he said. His age was listed as thirty-three, but he looked fifty-three.

"Is it active?" Mechanic asked.

"Yeah. Sorry I breathed in your face."

"Don't worry, I had an uncle who had it. I lived."

Haft decided on ten days and went through the ritual for accepting a guilty plea: "You're doing so of your own free will? You understand you're waiving your right to a jury trial?" Like most defendants here, the tubercular crack smoker stood blankly through all this, detached and emotionless, as if the judge and the lawyers were discussing someone else, not him. His visit to Room 129, his demeanor suggested, was just a routine encounter between a citizen and the government, no more significant than buying stamps at the post office. The unlicensed flower vendor was less certain of his footing.

"Come on, step up," Haft urged him. "Don't be shy."

The vendor spoke little English and looked thoroughly bewildered, as if he had awakened on a strange new planet. "It's an overtime arrest," the defender explained to Haft, meaning it had been made by a cop who needed the overtime pay that accrued when you accompanied a new case into the system. Haft released him on time served. He left tentatively, looking like he still hadn't quite figured out where he was, or how he had gotten here, or why.

The chocolate thief knew why he was here—for the eight boxes he had shoplifted. "You're gonna get pimples," Haft advised him.

The defendant assured Haft that the theft was not gluttonous, and that he wasn't a crazed chocolate addict, driven to crime by his cravings for a sugar rush. "I stole them to give some to my family and to sell some," he explained.

"Eight boxes of chocolate—it's not the end of the world," the defender added.

"Eight days," Haft suggested. "What could be more appropriate?"

As the night shortened, the line of case papers on the prosecutors' table seemed only to lengthen—blue sheets covering the misdemeanors, yellow on the felonies. They had gotten through seventy-four the night before, close to the lobster-shift average of seventy-seven, but tonight there was a lot of yellow on the table. "It's a lot more gloomy, it's dark out, and you're the one person representing all of Manhattan, representing the whole state of New York really, against crime," Assistant D.A. Robert Seiden said. He was not long out of law school, saddled with a rite-of-passage week on nights, and he had to get up early for a trial on Monday morning. He wore sneakers with his gray suit. "You learn more about people, about social interaction, in one night here than you do in a year of law school."

His partner was Francine James, a Manhattan native now protecting her hometown. "I made a pledge to myself that I'd look up at the defendants," she said. "You can do this whole job always looking down. I make sure to look up—just to see." She kept her pledge when she read the judge the defendants' statements as reported by the police. " 'Me and you gonna go at it—you fucked me up,' " she read at one point, which sounded less menacing coming from her, a calm lawyer in an olive dress, than it probably had coming from the defendant, a tall man in a Pittsburgh Steelers' sweatshirt, but which got the message across anyway.

James looked up again at a man accused of snatching a ten-dollar bill from a woman's hand and then sprinting away with it through the noon crowds at Forty-second Street and Seventh Avenue.

"He's a crack dealer," Mechanic told the judge. "She paid ten dollars and got beat."

"My facts are that she had the ten dollars in her hand to buy lunch," James countered.

"Bullshit—unless she was having crack for lunch. I don't say he's a nice person, but this is not a case."

"I was thinking fifteen days," Haft said. He didn't like to free the guilty until they had spent at least some time, even if just a few nights, behind bars. "If they just walk in and walk out," he had said earlier, "they haven't been exposed to the system at all."

"How about seven to ten so I can sell it?"

Haft agreed to ten days, but the dealer was reluctant to make the deal. "No, no, listen to me," Mechanic said to him. "You smarter than I am? The most you'll do is four days. You fool around with this and you'll get sixty days."

The dealer finally, grudgingly, relented. "Next time you come up here, I'll let you take care of yourself, you're so smart," Mechanic said to him as he was led back toward jail.

At 6 the shift broke for breakfast, and the opposing parties went their separate ways. The prisoners stayed in the holding pens on the other side of the courtroom's rear wall. Haft took an elevator up to his chambers.

James and Seiden surveyed the cases they hadn't gotten to yet. "It definitely shatters all illusions you have of justice," Seiden said. "You read these cases and everything is very serious. But this is a different ballpark, this is New York. The same offense that might get you six months in Seattle gets you time served here."

Mechanic and several other public defenders headed to a restaurant in nearby Chinatown for the kind of morning meal only night people could stomach. Because it was Saturday now, and he was a cantor at a synagogue near his New Jersey home, he would leave at shift's end carrying the black robe he had hung for the night alongside the judges' black robes. He was due to sing at morning services. "It makes your voice better when you've been up all night," he said. "Your cords haven't dropped."

The rain that had fallen lightly through the night had stopped, and the empty streets glistened, freshly cleansed, in the pale dawn sun. The police, as ever, were still out trawling, and the court, as ever, would meet again tonight—the night before Easter, the last lobster shift of the week—to sort through whatever came up in their nets. It wouldn't finish until Sunday morning, just about the time when worshipers, done up in spring finery and hope, would be on their way to church to praise the light.

3

At 1:00, in a government building outside WASHINGTON, technicians watched a portrait of Earth, snapped by an orbiting satellite, emerge on a video screen.

Driving west down from the Capitol, long past a midnight in cherry blossom week, I could see the Washington Monument at the far end of the Mall, radiant white against the dark sky like democracy's exclamation point. Floodlights climbed straight to its pyramid peak, slicing the night like a Hollywood premiere, but when I got to its base, I was alone at the show. The whole of official Washington surrounded me like a postcard dream. I had conquered the capital as easily as the British had in the War of 1812, and I circled again unchallenged through this archetypal American history-scape, past the familiar landmarks whose symbolic weight seemed even heavier in the darkness, now that they stood empty of bureaucrats and tourists, their classical façades pristine as new ivory. The decorative icing of the Capitol dome floated over the blocky museums and federal offices that lined the broad, dark Mall. The cherry blossoms, their briefly explosive daytime pink now dimmed, were pale and translucent, almost ghostly, in the sparse reflected light. The exterior lights at both the Jefferson and Lincoln memorials had been extinguished, but I could see, between the columns, the inside lights still shining on the statues of the two presidents, wide-eyed and awake. On the south lawn of the White House spotlights played over the spouting fountain, but the lights that had earlier shone on the house itself were off now. There was, after all, a president asleep in that monument at this hour.

The Constitution invests great powers in the executive branch of the federal government, but among them is not the power to forgo sleep. A time comes each day—for Ronald Reagan it often came more than once each day—when the president's body, like every other citizen's body, demands to be shut down, forcing him to leave behind the cabinet meetings and the briefing papers and the Moscow hotline and even the Football, the ever-present briefcase that holds the codes for a nuclear launch, and then slip out of consciousness into a world of dreams the Secret Service can't protect him from. When he does sleep, most of Washington sleeps along with him, leaving me alone out here amid the marble columns of power, wondering if the nation was as vulnerable now as its capital seemed.

It wasn't, of course, because the president's surrogates were fanned out all across the world, awake and watching, evidence that the power you see least is maybe the power you should fear most. Aloft somewhere over the Midwest now was a plane carrying an air force general, ready to serve as an airborne nuclear command post in the event that the main nuclear command post, an underground bunker in Nebraska where military officers were also on duty, was incapacitated or destroyed by an enemy attack. Inside a Colorado mountain other officers scanned the data collected by satellites and radar stations, watching for enemy invaders. Bomber pilots stood at alert, and two-man crews sat in underground launch capsules, prepared to turn the keys that would send the missiles flying. Missile-loaded submarines patrolled the oceans. It was anyone's guess where the CIA was. I drove another lap around the Mall, under a low cloud cover that hovered over the city like a dome, shielding it from the stars.

Washington doesn't always sleep this soundly. Congress often works late into the night when it approaches the end of a legislative session, rushing through last-minute business in a frenzy of fast votes, and the traditional phone call to tell the White House of its formal adjournment sometimes wakes a sleeping president. Strom Thurmond, South Carolina's senator-for-life, once held the Senate floor for twenty-four hours and nineteen minutes, the nation's longest filibuster, speaking all through a day and a night in an attempt to block the Civil Rights Act of 1957. The Supreme Court sometimes considers last-hope stay-of-execution requests, and after they issue a denial, as they usually do, a condemned man walks to his death in a prison somewhere in America. When the military launched surprise night attacks—of Panama (1 A.M.), of Iraq by air (3 A.M.) and then by land (4 A.M.)—the president and his aides monitored the fighting from the White House through the night. Invasion or not, officers are always on duty in the

National Military Command Center, across the Potomac at the Pentagon, and at the State Department the operations center constantly monitors the state of the world.

Most nights, though, are more like this night—vacant and silent and respectful of the 9-to-5 work force that rules here. Washington's schedule is largely set by the government, and the government here is a giant, many-tentacled beast whose natural habitat is the city's daylit offices. About the only activity I saw on the postmidnight streets was far from the Mall, at Fourth and Rhode Island at 3 A.M., where the police held guns on a carload of young men they had just chased to a stop.

An early spring warm front was resting over Washington, a premonition of June and a climatic reminder that I was now south of the Mason-Dixon Line, so Adrian McCrae had left up the firehouse's red front doors to let in the soft night air. He sat just inside at the watch desk, studying a copy of *Essentials of Firefighting*. It was past a midnight in March, but the open doors gave the station the front-porch feel of a summer evening. Behind him the firetrucks were parked in the weak fluorescent shadows. Above him nine other firefighters were asleep in the second-floor bunkroom; his job was to wake them when an alarm came in. "Truck Sixteen," the dispatcher's voice called through the radio, snatching McCrae's attention from his studies. "Truck Sixteen, Peoples Drug Store," the radio continued, and McCrae relaxed. The "16" in the radio message was one of the numbers he was listening for—since this station was home to Engine 16, Truck 3, and the Sixth Battalion Headquarters of the city's Fire Department—so it had caused his heart to race in the brief second before he realized the dispatcher was calling a 16 from a different station. "A lot of guys do their watch back there," he said, gesturing toward the back room, where a television was tuned to MTV. "They can hear it in the dead of sleep, then run out here and turn the company out, no problem. I'm not that good yet."

The redbrick firehouse was just a few blocks from the White House—its trucks were the first due there in a fire, and they stood by at helicopter landings—but it was already part of the other Washington, the one known less as the nation's political capital than as its murder capital. It covered a dense collection of high rises, offices, apartment buildings, rowhouses, detached houses, even crackhouses, several of which had been torched lately by a vigilante arsonist overeager to rid the neighborhood of drug dealers. "It's a live place, I found out fast," McCrae said. "You've got whores out there, you've got drug traffic. At some stations you'd get bored. You're stuck in an alley, and once the sun goes down nothing goes on."

McCrae returned to his book and yawned—from fatigue, not boredom: He had been up since 4:30 the previous morning. He was new to the job, recently out of the academy and still in his probationary period, but he well knew that one of the most essential of the essentials of firefighting was the ability to sleep lightly, and sometimes not at all. "You never really sleep here. It's just like"—he knocked lightly on the desk—"if you hear just a tap, you're awake. I imagine I'll be a nervous wreck after twenty years. Even if you're in a deep sleep, your subconscious is wide awake, listening. Usually something's gonna happen at least one time a night. Even if your piece doesn't leave the house, the bell wakes you up. You're in a dead sleep and then"—he snapped his fingers and bounced up in his chair—"you're up." His previous career had been at the other end, the safer end, of the architectural life cycle—as a carpenter with the city—and had allowed him to spend his nights with his wife and two young children; but it hadn't offered the same room for advancement as the fire department.

The radio called again, and McCrae did more than listen. "Truck Three transfer to Truck Nine," it said. "Truck Three transfer to Truck Nine." Truck 9, housed at another station, had responded to a mattress fire on Wyoming Avenue, and Truck 3 had to cover for them while they were gone. He rang a gong that resounded like ringside at a title fight, and he switched on the upstairs bunkroom lights. He also put on his helmet; Truck 3 was his piece. Several bleary men dropped through the ceiling, sudden and surreal, sliding down the brass poles. The truck pulled out onto Thirteenth Street, red lights flashing and McCrae riding its side.

It was the fifteenth run of the day, and a reminder that firefighters work on the line between order and chaos, always crouched in a sprinter's stance. Their jobs were among the most dangerous the peacetime world requires— furnace flames; collapsing floors underfoot; tumbling walls; silent, deadly smoke—and also among the most boring. Like firefighters in many cities, they worked twenty-four-hour shifts, followed by forty-eight hours off, and naturally settled into the domestic routines of any household, but what distinguished them was the speed and frequency with which these routines were often upended. They might be working out in the basement weight room—or playing a video game, or eating a meal prepared out of the separate refrigerators each platoon kept, or sleeping behind the blacked-out windows of the bunkhouse, where they were allowed to retire between 8 P.M. and 6:30 A.M. each night—but they knew they were just a frayed wire, an arsonist's match, away from a four-alarm inferno. The line was especially sharp at night, when the sirens echoed louder down the empty streets, the leap between sleep and action lengthened, and the flames blazed brighter against the dark sky, like a window into hell.

Truck 3 was back thirty-five minutes later, an uneventful trip, and McCrae went up to bed. Mark Wynn, at nineteen the city's youngest firefighter, took the watch, still wearing his rubber boots and waterproof, suspendered turnout pants; underneath were the doctors' pants he had been sleeping in. "Any fire looks way more terrible at night," he said. "They don't look so bad during the day, but at night you see that big orange glow, you see the rolling flames." He was sneezing from spring hayfever, his deep-set eyes watery, and he put on a blue D.C.F.D. baseball jacket over a blue D.C.F.D. T-shirt. "Complacency, that's a big word on this job. You never know when you're gonna get the big one. You sit here and sit here and do nothing, and then all of a sudden one night you're sleeping soundly and at three-fifteen there's a box alarm. It's thirteen degrees out and you've been sleeping under these warm blankets, you've done nothing for three months, and then you're in your gear and out in thirty seconds. Fire's rolling out the windows, children are trapped, there's all this whooping and hollering. You do that for twenty-five years and that's a whole lot of stress. That's why firefighters die ten years earlier."

The fire department had introduced Wynn to a side of the city he hadn't seen before. "I came up in a middle-class family," he said; his father had a small trucking business. "We were inspecting a building, an apartment building with one bathroom for seven different apartments. I didn't know they had stuff like that in D.C. Man, I was shocked." Firefighters were dispatched to medical emergency calls when ambulances were short, and in his first month on the job Wynn saw five drug overdoses. "It doesn't make it right, but if you're young, fourteen or fifteen, your parents are poor, you're poor, and you see a guy stand outside for fifteen minutes and he makes two or three thousand dollars, it's hard to say no. You have to say 'I ain't gonna do it, that's wrong,' but unless your parents tell you stuff, put your head on straight, that's hard. Congress says 'Say no, no,' but they haven't experienced poverty themselves."

Wynn shut the doors and went into the back room, where he sat in one of the hand-me-down chairs that gave it the look of a basement rec room. Flecks of orange dotted the walls—the flames in the photos of fires past. "I sit here sometimes, especially being my age, and I wonder what everybody else is doing now." He looked out toward the five brass slide poles, a kid's firehouse dream. "I found them exciting at first. Now they're just the way to get to work."

Kenny Mallory sat at a computer console in the fire department's communications center, facing a wall-sized map of the city's streets and wearing a radio headset that, all night long, told him of the troubles hatching out on those streets. At 4:15 Ambulance 12 was in Southeast Washington, responding to the call of someone complaining of abdominal pains, but they weren't quite sure where the street was. Mallory stepped on his foot pedal to speak to them. "Ambulance Twelve, come in. You're going to have to spell that for me. . . . Bass? Like the fish? B-A-S-S? Okay." He gave the directions—straight on East Capitol, then right, "You okay on that?"—and they were on their way.

The communications center, in a nondescript building behind a locked fence overlooking a reservoir near Howard University, was a clearinghouse for the city's woes. The room Mallory worked in had no window onto the reservoir, but it did offer a window onto an urban landscape of drug abuse, murder, assault, fire and a sickly health care system. It was the source of the voices that directed the city's firetrucks and ambulances, and it had been directing them to more places more often these last several years.

"It used to be that if somebody got shot, that was a big thing," said Mallory, who had watched their news value plummet. "We've had seven shootings tonight. I don't know how many are gone yet." He wore a denim jacket over his light-blue uniform shirt, and he smoked from a pack of Newports. "You think of Washington and you think the White House, the Lincoln Memorial—that's a hell of a place to take the kids on vacation. Then you see three hundred and seventy-two people killed last year. Well, goddamn, there's only three hundred and sixty-five days in the year. It makes you wonder what's going on."

He lived in Northeast Washington, but when he took his young daughter out to play, he went to a park in Chevy Chase, a Maryland suburb.

A Day in the Night of America

"Somebody came in here once with one of those stress cards, where you put your finger on it and it turns a color. I had my feet up, I was smoking a cigarette, I didn't feel like I was stressed. I put my finger on it and it fucking was black. I went out and played some pinball and came back and it was blue."

Another call came in from Southeast: a narcotics overdose in a vacant house. "You may not wanna go in right away," he told the ambulance.

"Are the police on the way?" they asked.

"Yes, they're on the way."

If you were to fly straight up from Earth, up through the gradually darkening skies, you would, at about 6,000 miles, cross the fuzzy border that separates the atmosphere from the void of interplanetary space, where the night, like the night in the Arctic in winter, is unrelieved. If you continued on up through the lasting night of space, you would, at 22,300 miles, reach a beltway something like the suburban highway that rings Washington. The traffic up here, though, is satellites. The 22,300-mile mark is the magic level at which the speed of a satellite's orbit around Earth's equator exactly matches the speed of Earth's rotation around its axis: A satellite lofted up here will appear to hover in a fixed spot in space, even though it is actually yoked in perpetual motion with Earth, much as a gondola is with the spinning hub of a Ferris wheel. A satellite is to the universe far less even than a grain of sand is to the ocean, but it is to Earth a vital perch from which to see, literally, the big picture. There are satellites that spy on Soviet airbases, that relay telephone calls and television images, that collect scientific data, and there are satellites that tell you whether you'll need an umbrella in the morning—the satellites that concerned the six men working the overnight shift in a government building just inside the Capital Beltway.

Line by line, like a computer printer sawing across the screen, a picture emerged on a black-and-white video monitor that was set in a bank of blinking electronics. John Hoffman sat and watched, making sure the lines continued straight and unbroken. With each successive band the portrait grew rounder and clearer—an astronaut's view of Earth, silhouetted against black space. Clouds swirled over the heart of the continent, but the skies over the East Coast were clear, confirming what you could see from the vast, empty plain of the parking lot outside. It was the image the TV weathermen would stand before tomorrow. "It's like time-lapse photography," Hoffman said. "I can see all the fronts and storms developing."

The pictures arrived at half-hour intervals all through the day and night, every day and night, comprising a mosaic record of Earth's ever-changing face. The government agency that snapped these pictures, the National Oceanic and Atmospheric Administration, had a public profile as anonymous as the building that housed it—a sprawling, three-story, yellow-brick, generic-federal office, the architectural equivalent of a giant file cabinet, on a suburban strip in Suitland, Maryland. But it was a deceptive anonymity. The windowless, computer-crammed room Hoffman worked in, on the second floor of Federal Building 4, was the nucleus of a satellite network that gathered data on rainfall, earth tremors, crop growth, ocean currents, tides, river levels, forest fires, volcanic eruptions and, most visibly, the approaching weather—from morning mists to the great hurricanes.

Despite the stream of beamed-from-space data, a call here would yield little in the way of a weather update. The job of the staff at the Satellite Operations Control Center, the formal name for this electronic enclave, was not to interpret the satellite data themselves but to ensure they got to the people who did. "I could maybe pick out a hurricane," John Carlucci, the shift supervisor, said. He served in the air force before coming here, working with the kind of satellites that took political temperatures. "If I want to know the weather, I'll pick up the phone and call the weather number."

About the only place you saw the word *satellite* here was on the door on the way in; *spacecraft* was preferred inside, a term that better reflected the job's complexity. Space is not a natural environment for Earth-made objects. It strains a satellite, and when the strain causes something to break—a bulb, a servomotor, a piece of circuitry—you can't climb a ladder up to fix it. Imagine trying to repair a TV set blindfolded, hands tied behind your back. "Once it's up there, you can't touch it or feel it or fix it," Carlucci said. "You can't do anything other than take its pulse and temperature and play doctor and nurse to it."

They had eight patients tonight, and several were ailing. Of the five satellites in geostationary orbit at 22,300 miles—the ones that resembled an alien grasshopper head attached to an upturned bass drum—only one was able to send pictures back to Earth. Two of these satellites normally looked down on the continent like a heavenly stereopticon, one over the East Coast and one over the West, but the West satellite had recently failed. To compensate, the East satellite was moved over the Midwest, like a one-eyed man cocking his head for a better view. The three polar satellites—the ones shaped more like a robotic marine mammal—were reliably circling in a much lower orbit around the poles, about 540 miles up, cutting vertical swaths along the spinning Earth like a combine cutting across a wheat field.

At 2:45 the good eye of the transplanted East satellite was patched, too, and John Hoffman kept close watch on it. The blindness was temporary and intentional, occasioned by the onset of eclipse season, the period around the equinoxes when Earth daily blocks the satellites from their power source, the Sun. To conserve its batteries, the satellite had been switched off for the duration of the eclipse, sixty-nine minutes tonight. Because GOES-7, the satellite's given name, was the only civilian camera in space now, it had to be treated with special care; if it stopped, the weather pictures stopped. By 2:55 the eclipse had passed, and the eye was opening back up. "The functions are turning back on," Hoffman said, watching the computer screen. "Tank Heater One is on. Once it starts, it's real fast."

Little here was as fast as what Hoffman had seen in his previous career: He was one of the striking air traffic controllers fired by Ronald Reagan in 1981. His view of the skies was longer, more placid now, but he still put up with rotating shifts. "It's mostly psychological," he said. "Everything you've ever learned is that you're supposed to sleep at night, so you sit at work here and think 'I'm not tired but I should be, because it's the middle of the night.' " He was forty-four, with graying hair and a gravelly bass voice. He wore an unzipped black sweatshirt over a white button-down shirt and blue jeans. "People say, 'You mean you have to go to work tonight?' But see, tomorrow morning I'm gonna get a lawn chair and a cooler of beer and watch all you people go to work."

By four it felt as if a cold front had migrated off the screen and into the room's atmosphere. The temperature inside hadn't changed; it stayed at a constant 55 to protect the computer equipment, which included disk drives the size of washing machines. But my body temperature had, dipping into the circadian valley of the latest hours. Al Bressi felt it, too. He kept his ski jacket on against the chill as he checked the telemetry from a polar satellite. "We kid sometimes that the rest of the world is sleeping while we're up protecting the skies, but it's not so far from the truth," he said. The VCR playing in the background had finished *It's Alive!* a thriller about a monstrous baby's murder spree, and now started *Top Secret,* a spy spoof.

"Definitely I would've bet money that we were the only six guys on the East Coast up working. There might be six other guys in Philly and that's it. It's like some old science fiction movie, where they're in a bunker in East Texas when the world blew up and they're the last of mankind. You do get the feeling you're alone in the world, that if there were a nuclear war, this is the only place that would survive, just us watching Z-rated movies."

The sky outside the breakroom window was still dark at 5:30, but the latest picture from GOES-7 previewed the dawn due soon—the first line of sunlight spilling over the east edge of the globe, advancing across the Atlantic like an invading navy bound for our shores. On TV a leotard squad of women contorted their way through a wake-up exercise show, *Morning Stretch with Joni.* As the night ended, so too did the equipment's trouble-free torpor. The satellites communicate with Earth through two ground stations—antenna clusters in Fairbanks, Alaska, and on Virginia's Eastern Shore—and now the Fairbanks computers couldn't talk to the computers here. It was the first glitch of the shift, but the problem turned out to be in Fairbanks. "The equipment's tired," an Alaskan operator said. "It's been up all night."

William Hart sat at his guard post in a glass booth in an office building in Northwest Washington, eight video monitors before him showing, with a filmy blue-gray glow, the building's distant, empty corners. He saw back doors, hallways, loading docks. Jazz played softly from his small radio. "Sometimes I'll see a big rat run right across there," he said, pointing toward one screen.

Hart's job, like that of the 1.2 million other security guards in America, was based on the ancient premise that bad things can happen after sunset. His duties did not require him to make anything or sell anything or even enforce the laws of the city, but simply to sit and watch his territory, his presence serving as a human deterrent to encroachment. The private-security business is—and this probably isn't an altogether healthy economic indicator—a boom industry in America, doubling in size over the last twenty years. What was once a limited profession (bank guards, department store detectives, warehouse watchmen) now reaches into every corner of the economy: Guards are posted to the smallest stores; affluent neighborhoods hire their own security patrols; and even some robots are on the beat, sensing intruders as they roll through empty halls. Employers pay 1.6

percent of the nation's work force—a figure that doesn't include public-safety officers—to protect us against our own sins. Fear is an accepted, and rising, cost of doing business.

Hart was a watcher who watched other watchers. The building he guarded, a modest concrete-and-glass structure reminiscent of a 1960s-vintage high school, was home to a TV station and a radio station. His booth straddled the space between the outside doors and the inner ones, and he presided there as gatekeeper for the incessant work force that kept the stations broadcasting. "Did he know you were coming?" he asked a woman who had come to see a deejay. Media figures are often prey to strange, unwanted attention—*Play Misty for Me* and all that—so he was careful about after-hours callers. Notices posted in the booth warned against admitting several nuisance visitors, including a woman who claimed to be a federally protected witness in the Iran-contra case: Her papers were worth millions, she said, and she was eager to sell her story. Hart called up to the deejay. "There's a young lady here to see you," he said, and gave her name, which was, it turned out, the name of an expected guest, not a radio groupie. "He's coming right out."

Great waves of energy issued from the building, firing insomniac TVs and radios all across the region, but little reached into the booth. Hart was sixty-eight, a retired government worker and the overnight guard here just two nights a week, Fridays and Saturdays. Saturday nights brought more traffic—preparations for *Meet the Press*, broadcast from here Sunday mornings—but this was Friday night, and Friday nights, apart from the occasional radio-contest winners come to collect their concert-ticket prizes, usually left Hart alone with himself. He was in good company then. He had lived long and well enough to acquire a fileful of good stories, and he quietly broadcast a few to an audience of one, me, in his crisp, proper voice: his Georgia upbringing; his wife, his five children and his grandchildren; his time at a navy training school at Hampton Institute, a black college in Virginia, during World War II; his civil career with the Defense Department, the Veterans Administration, the city parking enforcement division; his early years walking the embassy beat, one of the few blacks in the city's police department at the time. "I was colored then, I've outgrown that," he said. "I'm well aware of the fact, and I don't want this to sound racist, that I've got to be two times as good as other people. I don't kid myself. I probably would've stayed with the police, but I didn't know what the chances were of going to the top."

He got up from his desk sometimes to keep himself awake: a gulp of fresh air, a cup of coffee, a splash of cold water. He was not by nature a night person ("I'm just convinced that night is meant for sleeping"), and his body clock was further confused by his other job, as a weekday security guard at a hospital; but he still managed, as he always had, without an alarm clock. "Your job's supposed to wake you up," he said. "They talk about computers; your body's had computers since day one." He generally did without TV here, preferring instead the company of Dizzy Gillespie, Illinois Jacquet and Duke Ellington—a fellow Washingtonian who, by choice, also worked nights, composing in the dark and sleeping in the light. The phone rang only infrequently. "A lady called here one night because the weatherman mispronounced the name of a town, some little place in the Midwest. She was furious. I said to her, 'Miss, I can understand, but I'm security. You and I could talk all night, but it would just be useless. It's a waste of your time to hassle with me about it. Call on Monday and register a complaint then.' "

A stack of fresh *Washington Post*s arrived at 5:30 along with the first light. The satellite dishes outside emerged from the darkness, and the signal tower, and the flagpole circle out front from which Willard Scott sometimes broadcast the *Today* show weather, and the view from the booth widened to take in part of the pleasant green neighborhood that surrounded the station. Hart pressed a button to let a TV staffer in through the locked glass doors. "How are you doing this fine morning?" he asked, getting a cordial greeting in return. "I try to be nice to people. Sometimes people just won't let you, but I'll give it a shot anyway."

By midnight almost all the one-hundred-plus members of the Associated Press Washington bureau had long since dispersed, their dispatches from the White House and Congress and the Pentagon and the other federal outposts had already moved on the wire and into the printing presses of the thousands of newspapers that would publish them in the morning, and just three reporters and editors were left in the empty, brightly lit newsroom, where they waited for the president to die. They had nothing against George Bush, and no reason to expect his imminent demise. One of the reporters had watched him disembark a helicopter on the White House lawn not long ago, and it was fair to assume he was asleep, in fine health, upstairs there now. But if he were to die, somebody had to be ready to tell the world about it. They had to be ready here, too, in case the United States invaded Panama or Iraq, or the general on the ceaseless command plane gave the launch order, or any other story of great import broke in the middle of the night. "What I stop to think about sometimes is that I could bring down Western civilization all by myself, just by sending one well-placed bulletin," said Laurie Asseo, who stood watch alone after 3, and who resisted the temptation to test history. "There's nobody to stop me from sending a bulletin that the president's been killed or that missiles are coming in. Of course, it would be the end of my career. It's like the feeling you have when you stand at the edge of a cliff and look down. You know you could just jump off. You don't do it of course, but you could."

Civilization held fast most nights, and the late-late bulletins that crossed the General Desk—the two tangent semicircles at the center of the room that served as the news command post—were infrequent. News is an incessant, Pavlovian business, often a matter of chasing bells and whistles; "Forget literature," the columnist Bob Greene once wrote, "immortality lay in a front-page by-line about a four-car fatal on I-70." The local reporters who covered Washington were on duty elsewhere, eavesdropping on police scanners and cruising with minicams, coiled to pounce on three-alarm blazes and last-call bar stabbings, heirs to the hoary fedora tradition of leg men and get-me-rewrite and bulldog editions. But they were covering Washington, the city, for a local audience. The AP bureau was covering Washington, the government, for the world audience, and Washington the government, like the eagle that is its symbol, is mostly a diurnal creature.

The phone rang shortly after midnight, and Tom Seppy, the reporter who had earlier witnessed Bush's touchdown, answered. He listened briefly, then relayed the question to the room. "Why was the movie *Rain Man* called *Rain Man*?" he asked. The Oscars had just been awarded in Los Angeles, and a foreign correspondent posted to Washington, now composing his dispatch on this glittery American ritual, wanted to explain the title's origin to his nation's readers; so he turned to the AP, as many other reporters do, as a living almanac. He had turned to the wrong page tonight: Nobody here had seen the movie. "Sorry," Seppy said. It was a typical query for Seppy, who comprised at this hour the bureau's entire reporting staff, and it was among the last of his shift, for he would soon be spelled by Asseo. He had worked through many nights in his twenty-nine AP years, starting back in Baltimore, where the overnight shift meant "steak and eggs at four A.M. at the waterfront with the guys from the *Baltimore Sun*," and freed his days for law school. "Part of the routine was to call all the state troopers' barracks to find out if anybody had been killed, if any planes had crashed. Everybody became real good friends immediately, because they were isolated, too, and they wanted you to stay on the phone, just to have somebody to talk to."

Congress was in recess this week, news was light, and Wayne Davis, the PM supervisor, having left his mark on the way the world would see that news tomorrow, was getting ready to leave, too. Everybody who read a newspaper tomorrow, or heard the news from radio or TV, would learn then what Davis, and the rest of the bureau, did today. The larger news outlets would use the AP to fill the holes in their own coverage, and the smaller outlets, those with few bureaus beyond their own city halls, would use it to fill most of their front page. The wire services, the AP the largest of them, are among those institutions, like the electric company, that wield power out of all proportion to their visibility, and the night here, as at the electric company, highlights that power. "I end up making decisions that would be made by seven or eight people during the day, from simple editing to what stories should be highlighted around the world," he said. "It's a little scary sometimes in a job like mine. You don't think sometimes about how your work reverberates. . . . There was one day when the Tower nomination fight [John Tower was Bush's initial, and unsuccessful, choice as Defense Secretary] was heating up. I thought the story didn't really discuss how serious the problem was, so I edited it to heighten the point that the nomination was in serious trouble. I went home that night and looked at the news on CNN, and they were kicking back my lead as the top story verbatim. For a good half hour it made me really uncomfortable. Suddenly there was a megaphone on what I had written, suddenly it was going everywhere. But that's part of what's attractive in the job."

The evening shift's main responsibility was to edit and update the stories bound for the nation's afternoon newspapers, a package that sometimes swelled to fifty or more, but that stood tonight at twenty-four. Oliver North's trial continued. The White House commented on the Alaskan oil spill. Barbara Bush spoke about her thyroid in an interview with the *Washington Post*. The Agriculture Department revealed that an artificial scent had been developed to detour the libido of the male peach tree borer, an insect that bores into the trees in search of females. "I wanted to say 'Pining Away,' but it was too much of a pun," said Robert Greene, alone on the desk with Asseo now that Davis had gone. Tonight was calm for him, far

A Day in the Night of America

calmer than the night almost two years before, when he was new to the bureau, fresh from serving as correspondent-in-charge in Cleveland, new to what he called the "minimal, austere life-style" this shift imposed—and when the *Stark,* a navy ship patrolling the Persian Gulf, was attacked by Iraq and thirty-seven American sailors died. "I was on a conference call with the Pentagon. It was about three or so. I took the bulletin and got it out. There wasn't much more I could do."

When the phone rang at 3:10, Laurie Asseo was the only one left to answer it; apart from the man baby-sitting the computer room, she was the only one on the sixth floor, the whole of which the AP occupied, and since the sixth-floor lights were the only lights visible from down on the street, it was a fair assumption that between the two of them they now constituted the building's entire population. Headquarters was calling from New York. The *Los Angeles Times,* its first edition just off the press on the West Coast, had published a story reporting that the Bush administration was urging Israel to withdraw troops from the West Bank and the Gaza Strip, and New York wanted to know if the story was worth picking up and putting on the wire. "Yeah, I would say it's worth a pickup," Asseo suggested. "The part about urging Israel sounds new. The part about the PLO we've had before, that they're trying to get the PLO to lighten up. I'll tell dayside." And then, off the phone, "It's absolutely amazing the stuff we're supposed to know about, everything in the world practically."

The AP runs along a militarylike hierarchy—go where you're needed, work up through the ranks—and the overnight shift here is like the military's war college for senior officers, an initiation reserved for those with the most stripes. Asseo's coverage of the fall of Arizona governor Evan Meacham for the Phoenix bureau had helped earned her a Washington berth, and the consequent privilege of riding the carousel schedule assigned the newest arrivals here: two overnights each week, two evenings and a single teasing day shift. Her days off were Mondays and Thursdays. "AP hell," she called it. She drank Diet Coke to stay awake, took the occasional Unisom to get to sleep, got headaches and colds more frequently, and waited patiently—it had been six months already—for someone new to arrive to boost her up the ladder.

The computer printers, successors to the retired teletypes, kept churning out stories: Salman Rushdie sympathizer shot to death at Brussels mosque; seven indicted in Boston on drug-money-laundering charges; USDA says yams aren't sweet potatoes; Bush leaning against federal role in oil-spill cleanup. Asseo assembled a package of Washington-in-brief stories. "A trained monkey could do it," she said. She wore blue jeans, sneakers, a white sweatshirt and gold earrings; "I miss dressing up." A TV tuned to CNN, a repeat of Larry King talking with Steve Garvey, played a commercial for Zamfir, "master of the magical pan flute."

The phone rang again. "What now?" she wondered aloud before picking it up. Some overnight news here could be anticipated—as when official Washington traveled to a European summit meeting for instance and was at work there under the antipodal sun. But most news here was a lightning flash—an action in the world that required a Washington reaction. It was a shift especially sensitive to Middle East tremors, coinciding as it did with the region's often tumultuous days; hostage rumors were not uncommon, and they carried the terrible weight of involving a colleague, AP's own Terry Anderson, who was then still among those held in Lebanon. The call was New York again. An earlier AP story out of Washington had reported that the State Department was welcoming the Arab League's call for a cease-fire in Lebanon, and now the bureau in Nicosia, Cyprus, where it was late morning, wanted to know more of what was said at the briefing. "I'm probably gonna have to write a story here, but I don't know anything about it," she said. "But that's our job, to figure it out. On a moment's notice I may have to write a story about a bombing in Lebanon and I have to know what I'm doing."

The wire-service ethic is that breaking news requires reporters to think and write faster than language. An AP reporter who witnessed a spaceship landing would instantly file a story in bullet prose, communicating to the world news of the encounter more swiftly and efficiently than the telepathy the spaceship's alien pilots might use. Asseo found the transcript briefing and called New York back: She only needed to send notes, they told her, not a story. "This is gonna be easy, not nearly the trouble I thought it was," she said, far from disappointed. "I've never had a byline story on this shift, and I don't even want to. I'd just as soon it were nice and quiet. If all hell broke loose, there's no way to win. You just can't deal with a story that big all alone. I like excitement and everything, I like a big story, but not at this hour of the day."

She sent the notes off toward Nicosia. The phone was silent, but the infobits posted on the bulletin board over the General Desk testified to the encyclopedic range of stories she could be called upon to write before the sun rose: 1988 trade deficit, $137.34 billion; a printout of the Bush cabinet; the correct spelling of *Gadhafi* and *Mitterrand;* "new style—no quotes on *Star Wars.*" The phone number for Domino's Pizza was up there, too, but that wasn't much use now. It closed at 1.

Back at the apartment where I was staying, the TV was playing in the background, tuned to *Good Morning America,* as my friends got ready for work and I got ready for sleep. "The Bush administration," I heard the anchor read, "is reportedly urging Israel to withdraw most of its troops from the West Bank and the Gaza Strip."

4

At 1:30, in a FLORIDA *radio studio, a talk-show host put another caller on the air, letting him broadcast his story across the listening night.*

Down past Richmond on Interstate 95, coming up hard on the North Carolina border, I noticed the stars again. The sky was raven black here, and the stars stepped forward in it like actors for an encore—unmistakable signals that I had escaped the gravitational orbit of the Northeast Corridor and no longer traveled under the luminous smog that clouds its night. Almost a fifth of all Americans, me included, are squeezed into the region I was now leaving, the same fractional seaboard band taken by the first colonists, and the megalopolitan light that drifts up from our settlements there dulls our night, obscures our view of the heavenscape, exiles the stars. The sound of the city was still with me in Virginia—WABC-AM from New York, which followed deep into South Carolina—but its stray light had dissipated. The road was mostly empty, and it made me think of space travel. I was alone but for the radio, speeding in a straight, smooth line, and outside the tunnel carved by my headlights, the only lights around, Earth appeared as just an extension of the same space that contained Venus and Alpha Centauri and the rest of the Milky Way. I resisted the temptation to enhance the sensation by pressing into warp speed, because I knew I had to answer, as an astronaut didn't, to the Virginia State Police.

That the sky was dark now was, at first thought, a given (sunset had, of course, switched off the lights), but at second thought it became a mystery. There were 100 billion trillion stars in the universe beyond my car—a number derived from science, not, as you might suppose given its incomprehensibility, from theology—but even on a clear night like this I could see no more than 2,000 of them. Binoculars would have turned up 5,000, a two-inch telescope 300,000, but where were the rest? Why wasn't the sky white with their light? If I stopped the car and walked into a deep roadside forest, I would see, in every direction I looked, only trees, not the fields beyond; so why did I see black space overhead, not a blazing wall of stars, like the unbroken wall of tree trunks in the forest? Astronomers called it Olbers's paradox and offered a string of wrong answers before Edgar Allan Poe, a writer deeply acquainted with the night, offered the right one: "the distance of the invisible background [of the sky is] so immense," he wrote, "that no ray from it has yet been able to reach us at all." Stars did cover the sky tonight, I just couldn't see them—because their lives are finite, the speed of light is finite, and the age of the universe itself (born 15 billion years ago in the Big Bang) is finite. Their light, traveling at 186,000 miles per second, hadn't yet had time to get here. I was driving under a sky shaped by the kind of mind-stretching physics and math and history and cosmology that can push a person across the border from science into religion. The darkness above me was anything but a formless void. It was instead the nightly evidence of Creation.

The roadside billboards were evidence that I was still earthbound, and hadn't lifted off into space. I-95 runs from Maine to Florida, the Main Street of the East Coast, sustained by the democratic premise that any so-inclined drivers in the snowy North can point their cars south on it, drive until their eyelids fuse, and then land, a thousand-plus miles later, in the tropics; and I was in its midsection now, one of its prime business districts. Motels and restaurants clustered at every exit, beckoning to travelers eager to bisect their two-day drive. Winter was over, and the motel lots were filled with the cars of sleeping snowbirds, whose mass migration back to their northern homes had jammed the road all the previous day. I flew past them all, aimed for the landmark that scores of billboards had hawked for the last 150 miles: South of the Border. PEDRO NEVER SLEEPS, one had read—back at the ninety-three-miles-to-go mark—but I wanted to see if he napped.

South of the Border is a garish 130-acre complex of travel services—chili dogs, cherry bombs, gas, motel rooms, miniature golf, souvenir maracas—linked by a Tijuana East motif that would have you believe the border it is south of is the one between the United States and Mexico rather than the one between North Carolina and South Carolina, and best appreciated by people who have just spent ten hours in a station wagon with three kids who want to be at Disney World RIGHT NOW. It started as a beer stand in 1950, in the infancy of the interstate highway system, and has since been visited by "100 meelion Amigos," to borrow the sí-señor Spangleesh that is the native tongue here. I drove through the orange arch formed by the bowed legs of the 97-foot Pedro sign—the largest incarnation of the ubiquitous, mustachioed, hugely sombreroed South of the Border symbol—and found I had arrived, at 4 A.M., during siesta time. Pedro's Hideaway Bar was closed, as was Pedro's Mini-Mex Golf, Pedro's Martial Arts Stuff, Pedro's Leather Outlet, Pedro's Tee-Shirt Shop, Mexico Shop West, Café Olé, Pedro's Myrtle Beach Shop and Fort Pedro Fireworks. The 200-foot Sombrero Tower, which looked like an oil derrick in a carnival costume, was also closed, so I could not, as the brochure promised, "ride the glass elevator to the Sombrero observation deck and see almos' all ze way to Mexico," or even just out over the dark, piney flatlands of Dillon, South Carolina.

What was open catered to the most basic 4 A.M. needs—the gas station, the motel, Pedro's Diner, the Hot Tamale fast-food restaurant and Pedro's Pantry, an all-under-one-roof greatest-hits package of South of the Border wares. Inside Pedro's Pantry two small boys traded head blows with squeaking plastic music hammers. A couple dozen people browsed the brightly lit aisles that offered smoke grenades, Black Cat bottle rockets, Saturn missiles, the Johnny Reb Fireworks Assortment, Spam, milk, bread, Vienna sausages, peach wine, Pedro keychains, Pedro T-shirts, Pedro's Generic Toilet Tissue ("for cheap assholes"), .44 Magnum water pistols and long-billed caps that declared BET YOU MINE'S LONGER THAN YOURS. A man and his young son took turns trying to crack a bullwhip. A pair of friends, college kids, were buying armloads of fireworks, one at each of the two cash registers going. "How much you spend?" one asked, after paying $103.74, in traveler's checks, for his arsenal.

"About a hundred," his friend answered.

"Me too," he said, and put his thumb up.

Back by the car wash outside, someone who couldn't wait to try their new fireworks had launched a white Roman candle, sparkling, silent, against the night. I drove through Pedro's legs again, and returned to 95. Tonight was the spring-ahead night of daylight saving time, when time is cheated at 2 A.M., instantly fast-forwarded to 3 A.M., and nobody, it is thought, is around to notice the missing hour. The sliver of a yellow crescent moon hung low in the east. The talk on WABC was about gun control when it finally faded out. The sky above me illustrated a James Joyce line—"The heaventree of stars hung with humid nightblue fruit"—as the road beneath me brought me nearer the only star that really matters here on Earth: the Sun.

Facing a pair of cameras from behind the anchor desk in a darkened Atlanta TV studio, Steve Schatz ran his face through a series of contortions of the type you might use to entertain a cranky baby. He stretched his mouth open wide, then brought it back into a tight O. He fluttered his tongue. His eyebrows did push-ups. He scrunched his eyes closed, then burst them open as if in astonishment. Like a batter stretching in the on-deck circle, he was limbering up his most critical muscles. Above the waist he was smartly turned out in a blue blazer and a red pocket handkerchief that echoed the highlights in his tie. Below the desk he was backyard casual: white Reeboks and surgical green Bugle Boy casual pants he had found on sale for six dollars at K mart ("It would be silly to sit here in a thousand-dollar suit and alligator shoes at 4 A.M.," he said later). He sipped from a can of Tab. His face appeared, healthy and well-complected, on several monitors in the adjacent control room. But if you looked at him through the control room's glass wall, at his actual face and not the televised version, you could see it was made-up in a particularly unnatural shade of orange; to look real on-camera you must look fake off-camera.

At 1:30 his Tab was set aside and his game face was in place. The opening titles for the show he was anchoring, CNN's *Newsnight Update,* were on the screen now, accompanied by a dance-club beat and a jump-cut sequence of nocturnal scenes: the White House, the Capitol, Times Square and, finally, a self-portrait of this very building, CNN's Atlanta headquarters. Footage from several lead stories followed—Oliver North's trial, Foreign Minister Eduard Shevardnadze in Soviet Georgia, the Illinois Lottery—as Schatz read the headline voiceovers. Then his face appeared on TV screens in 200,000 American households. "Hi, and welcome to *Newsnight Update.* I'm Steve Schatz"—pronounced as in "four shots were fired"—"in Atlanta. Those reports and a weather update in the next hour, but first our top story." He turned to look at the second camera, and a graphic of the Capitol under the words "D.C. Crime" appeared in a little box over his left shoulder. "Federal drug-policy chief William Bennett says drug-related crime in Washington, D.C., is growing out of control, so he's devoting nearly eighty million dollars in taxpayer's money to crack down on crime in the nation's capital." His face was replaced by footage of a murder victim on a dark D.C. street, the body covered by a white sheet, the blood puddled on the sidewalk a garish, unreal red, like spilled paint. "The District of Columbia has a murder rate seven times the national average, a murder rate so high the city is known as the murder capital of America."

Ted Turner built his Cable News Network around the premise that the news never stops, so neither should the telling of it. Since it started broadcasting in 1980, CNN has come to illustrate, maybe better than any other American institution, the restless incessancy of modern life, and it has helped feed our endless appetite not only for information, but for pictures to render that information visible. It has altered our news-consumption habits, because it subverts the comfortable old illusion that the news unfolds in an orderly line each day, ready for scheduled delivery in the neat packages of the evening news shows and the morning papers. It functions as a sort of illustrated wire service for anybody. "In many cases it's the first communication we have," Marlin Fitzwater, the president's press secretary, has said of CNN. The sense of plugged-in omniscience CNN offers can be addictive, and it has hooked a wide following: Eighteen million American households, including the White Household, watch each week, plus an uncounted number more in the ninety other countries where CNN goes but Nielsen doesn't. Generals in the Pentagon war room monitor CNN, and CIA analysts gather to watch it in the library at their Virginia headquarters when a big story is breaking. During the Gulf War the whole world mainlined CNN. And at the Varsity, Atlanta's landmark drive-in restaurant, customers can choose among different TV dining rooms, each one devoted to a different channel: One room, naturally, is the CNN room.

"Texas Air Corporation says no deal yet on Peter Ueberroth's proposed purchase of Eastern Airlines," Schatz read before yielding to tape of a weary Ueberroth on the steps outside bankruptcy court in New York. "We're gonna all try and get some sleep," Ueberroth said, "and tomorrow come back and meet on these issues."

Pat Neal's post for the night was a desk at the center of the newsroom, raised slightly above the floor and positioned like the prow of a ship, and not long before *Newsnight Update* went on, she sat there deeply engrossed in an apparent conversation with herself. "The man with the famous daddy, Hank Williams, Jr., went home with his third consecutive . . ." she said, speaking into a microphone with her clear, modulated voice. She was at the command post because she was supervising producer, and she was talking about Hank Williams, Jr., because she was working on a story about the Academy of Country Music awards ceremony, hoping to finish in time for it to run as a kicker at the end of *Newsnight Update*. Assembling a piece for broadcast involves not just gathering the information but also getting the right video, file tape or fresh, writing a script that links it together, reading that script aloud, then editing it all into a size that will fit the allotted slot. "When I first worked an overnight, I was so worried I'd fall asleep that I kept myself busy," she said. "I wrote four packages."

The CNN newsroom rose in gentle steps like an amphitheater behind the anchor desk, separated from it by a glass curtain and visible on home screens as the backdrop over Schatz's shoulders—a blurry glimpse of TV monitors and computer-topped desks. It was largely empty now, the only real lull of the broadcast day. The soothing-tested color scheme of mauve and gray, decorative tones designed to calm the war-room deadline din, was a little too soothing at this hour, almost soporific. The news and production staff that was here was, on average, young enough to make it seem like an extraordinarily well-endowed college TV station. Because it was a nonunion shop, CNN was thick with young staffers not long out of school who, in the absence of union-defined job categories, might find themselves focusing a camera on Schatz, or capturing pictures off the satellite of Soviet tanks, or serving, as Frances Causey was, as an assignment editor on the national desk. "Yes, ma'am, I understand, I understand. . . . The best way I can help you is to give you the station there in Houston," Causey, twenty-six, was saying into the phone. Conspiracy theorists seem to see the outlines of their conspiracies more clearly at night and are more inclined then, unencumbered by the harsh logic of daylight, to share them with the world. This one came from Texas and had something to do with drug dealers, an apartment building, the FBI. It did not send Causey scrambling for a satellite feed. "Right. . . . Again, the only thing I can tell you, ma'am . . ." Three overnights a week were part of the deal when she was promoted into this job. "Around three the eyelids start getting real, real heavy," she said. "It's dark in here, you never see the sunlight, but I can always tell when things are about to start picking up in the morning, I can sense it. There's an electricity you can sense in the air."

"Can somebody ask how much LSD Jim Morrison did before a concert?" a producer, hand over the telephone mouthpiece, wanted to know. Every line in the control room was lit, and every caller had a question for the guest Schatz was interviewing: Danny Sugerman, who had as a teenager worked for the Doors, had written a book about them, and now had written a book about himself. The calls came from—and this was not a toll-free number—Baton Rouge; San Diego; New York; Albuquerque; St. Paul; Lancaster, Pa. The LSD question got the go-ahead.

The talk was of drugs, alcohol, rock 'n' roll and the Doors, a band whose music had made it seem a natural inhabitant of this postmidnight world; "Try to set the night on fire," Morrison had screamed, almost a command, at the end of "Light My Fire." Sugerman spoke by satellite from Los Angeles, the lights of the California night spilling down the valley behind him. His white shirt was open at the collar, his hair was long and wavy. During the commercial breaks, his face still up on the control room screens, he adjusted his round glasses and smoked a cigarette. A caller asked what Sugerman had learned from Morrison. "It took me a long time, you know," he answered, "it took me about twelve, thirteen years, to learn that if you live like that, you die." The LSD question didn't make it to the air. "I'm sorry, we ran out of time," the producer told the caller. "It's not gonna happen tonight. Thanks for calling, though."

After a commercial Schatz returned with the final segment. "The Academy of Country Music presented its twenty-fourth annual awards Monday night," he said. "CNN's Pat Neal takes a look at some of the winners." Her story had made it out in time from the warren of editing rooms along the newsroom's rear wall, where she had shaped it, amid the high-pitched squeal of fast-forwarded tape, into a neat 105-second package of clips of Alabama, George Strait, K. T. Oslin, the Judds, Buck Owens, and the other winners, including, of course, Hank Williams, Jr.

"The show wasn't over until two," Neal said later. "That was quick to turn a piece around."

"And the news continues," Schatz said, signing off, and it did.

Schatz had six more minutes of on-air work left—two-minute updates at 4:20 ("Prime Time Fiji, we call it"), 4:40 ("I'm the Bryant Gumbel of

A Day in the Night of America

Iceland") and 5:25 ("My father gets up to watch that one to see if I'm all right")—but it would be three more hours before his shift ended. "It's not the idea of doing nights that's repugnant to me, I don't think I'm above it, it's the abuse of the schedule," he said. He worked two overnights, three days, had Wednesday and Thursday as his weekend, and described it as "physically and mentally the most deleterious exercise I've ever participated in." He was forty-seven, and had anchored in Boston and Detroit before becoming one of the dozens of anchors at CNN. "If the circus were in town, and the elephants worked this schedule, there'd be pickets around the Omni arena."

The bright CNN cafeteria was heavy with the smell of morning bacon as Schatz, coffee in hand, awaited his next update. "There's some heavy symbolism if I'm putting the coffeepot on at home at night when everybody else is asleep. That's what gets me. 'The World Turned Upside Down,' the song the British played at Yorktown, that's our marching song."

Outside in the Atlanta night, a giant red Coca-Cola signature hovered over the skyline as if the city were an all-night diner. Down on Auburn Avenue, where Martin Luther King, Jr., lived as a boy and preached as a man, his tomb was bright white in a floodlight, seeming to float weightless in its reflecting pool, much like the reflecting pool at the Lincoln Memorial, the site of his "I Have a Dream" speech. A gentle rain fell, and his eternal flame whispered like a breeze as it burned.

The sun was shining nowhere in America now, and it was hard to believe that anyone anywhere was watching TV; but Schatz did. "That's like asking a baseball player if it's any different coming to bat at one A.M. in extra innings when there's only fifty people left in the stadium. It's still your at-bat, and if you have any pride, any sense of professional dignity, it's the same as batting cleanup on Fourth of July afternoon with the stadium full. When the red light goes on, it might as well be the Fourth of July in Yankee Stadium."

At 5:25 he did his final update. Little had changed since the last one: North's trial, Ueberroth and Eastern, a chemical-plant fire in California. He signed off, his workday done, ready to drive out home past the inbound cars of the people whose workdays were just starting. "I envy the shit out of them."

Kevin Coyne

The causeway lay across Tampa Bay, stretching miles through the night, like a necklace across a black velvet cocktail dress. At either end of the road were the lights of the two cities that anchor this magnet Sun Belt metropolis, Tampa on the east and St. Petersburg on the west, but out here on the water, whether looking ahead through the windshield to one or back through the mirror at the other, the sensation was of sailing offshore on a cruise ship, bound for a new port of call. The air had sagged with moisture all evening, and now had grown so heavy that I felt like I was driving through the bay, not over it. I was midway across when the sky finally opened, a razor to a water balloon. It was a quick, violent downpour, finished within five minutes, as if it knew its rain wasn't welcome here and so had waited to dump its payload furtively under the cover of midnight.

Unsettled weather had followed me down the coast, echoing the unsettled weather in my own body. I was losing sleep, losing weight, losing track of hours and dates, and sometimes while lying in bed, still conscious of the shadows of the trees playing over the ceiling, I had the eerie sensation of slipping into a dream while I was still awake. The five years of your life you spend dreaming, unlike the years you spend watching TV, are of more than just entertainment value: Dreams recharge the day-worn brain, and sleep-lab subjects who were deprived of dream sleep, awakened whenever their REMs revved up, started showing signs of mental instability after just fifteen days; dreams, it turns out, while they may seem crazy at times, actually help keep you from going crazy. My hypnagogic fantasies, as these pregame falling-asleep dreams are called, were my brain's way of telling me it craved more dream time. Heat lightning blinked over the eastern horizon, as if all the tourists at Disney World, ninety miles away, had flashed their cameras in unison, trying for a farewell shot of Cinderella Castle against the night sky.

I drove out to the end of the Pier in St. Petersburg, which reached solid as a city street out over the bay, and watched a dozen fishermen watch their lines. One line finally jerked taut, snapping its owner to attention. He played the line, the fish leading him down the pier as the other fishermen respectfully lifted their own lines to let him pass under, clear and untangled, like a boy under a fence. "Get the gaff, Jim, get the gaff," he yelled to his partner. He hauled up from the darkness a thrashing silver snook, a Porsche-shaped fish with dark racing stripes. He unhooked the landed snook, grabbed it by the eyesockets with his thumb and middle finger and tossed it, twenty pounds of suppers, into the bed of a pickup. "I'm eating," he told a fishless fisherman who was admiring the catch, "not selling."

A Day in the Night of America

I drove back across the bay to downtown Tampa, giving the traffic lights at least one reason for continuing their cycles. The night felt cleaner now, rinsed and emptied by the rain. I drove down along the waterfront, past the lights of the docked freighters. In the historic, Latin-tinged Ybor City neighborhood, I passed under the festive white lights strung across the deserted main street, and I heard, while stopped at an intersection, a blues guitar lead coming from a second-floor window. My radio was tuned, as it always was, to an AM talk station. I drove along silent streets lined with long, low bungalows, their roofs overhanging their wide porches like a hat pulled down over the eyes of an old man dozing in the afternoon shade. "If you wake up in the middle of the night and you feel lonesome," Liz Richards was saying over 970 WFLA, "we'll rub your tummy and make you feel better."

"Oh, brother, this is great," Tom from Bradenton said. "I've listened to you for so long and never got a chance to call you, because I've been admiring you from the seat of my van. . . . The dynamiteness is excellent."

"It's really wonderful," Liz Richards said. "It's like having an affair long-distance."

"Yeah, it kinda is. Even my girlfriend gets a little jealous once in a while."

Tom's girlfriend had little to be jealous of, because the affair consisted of no more than the sort of casual conversation you might have with a barstool companion. They talked about his old girlfriend (she left him when he said he was moving to Florida), his old job as a night-shift cop (he had loved the serene breezes of the hour before dawn), his songwriting (the songs he wrote at night came out better than the songs he wrote in the day) and fellow citizens of WFLA-world (the Vietnamese woman whose call had touched him last night) before Richards had to say good-bye and break for the news.

Radio waves travel farther at night, a function of nature and physics, and perhaps of psychology, too. The ionosphere is what makes radio possible, a dome in the upper atmosphere that reflects upward-bound radio waves back down to Earth, and at night, in the absence of ionizing sunlight, it lifts like a hat and absorbs fewer waves, allowing them freer and more distant passage. The principle is the same as bouncing a rubber ball: The more oblique the angle you bounce it at, the farther it travels from you, just as a night radio signal might bounce across a half-dozen new states. At night the radio dial also clears of the small, low-wattage stations that sign off at day's end, leaving more room and less interference for the stations that don't sleep. And at night the brains of radio listeners, cleared like the AM band of daytime static, seem to absorb, unlike the ionosphere, more waves.

The late Denver talk-show host Alan Berg once called talk radio "the last neighborhood in town," which is about the best explanation I've heard for its appeal. I listened to talk radio during the day on my trip because it was a fast way to take the pulse of a new place, but I listened at night because its live voices were a reassuring confirmation that I wasn't alone in the darkness. The sense of community it provides is an illusion, of course, sometimes sad and cheap and pathetic and even dangerous—Alan Berg is "the late" because his strident opinions made him the victim of a machine-gun assassination by a band of neo-Nazi white supremacists—but at 3 A.M. you take whatever community you can get.

"I specially stayed up tonight just to talk to you," Alan from Clearwater said.

"You did?" Liz said. "You don't know what that means to me. I would've preferred a diamond Rolex, but I'll accept this."

"I'm goin' out now," Tom from Tampa said with a Philadelphia accent. "We're gonna go out and barbecue steak tonight, how's 'at grab you?"

"Where are you doing that?" Liz asked.

"Over on the causeway, you know, over on the Clearwater side."

"Oh, yeah, and you're gonna sit out by the bridge and barbecue steak."

"And catch fish. Maybe I'll bring you a fish up."

"Liz, are you the same Liz Richards from Cleveland that used to be on *The Morning Exchange*?" Ken wanted to know.

"I am," said Liz, who had hosted a TV talk show in Cleveland before coming to Tampa.

"Oh, my god, I used to watch you on my way to school in the morning, and awwww, I got to tell you I had the biggest crush on you and I still do. You were always so cute."

"Well, I'm far from cute. Voluptuous maybe, but . . ."

"How 'bout gorgeous, then?"

"You're getting closer, you're getting real warm."

"Listen," Claude said, "I wasn't the one that called you a femi-Nazi, that wasn't me."

"Liz, that's a purty name, 'cause my daughter's named Liz," said Robby, who went on to give a crate-by-crate account of his years as an early-early-morning milk-truck driver in Wheeling, West Virginia. ". . . and a lot of the time you'd be goin' over those ridges goin' into the Ohio River when the sun was comin' up, and some of the most beautiful scenery you ever wanted to see, comin' in there. . . ."

"You dirty bitch . . ." Joe from Tampa growled, breathing heavily, but Liz, who started every phone call with her finger on the dump button, cut him off before he got any further, and the seven-second tape delay kept his voice off the air. "Got him," she said. "I just love to do that to some guys."

"I just hadda call you and let you know that I'm still swinging on the back burner, I'm still playing the piano," said Bud, an out-of-work musician from St. Petersburg. "It used to be very fruitful down here musically, but it's not too much happening down here now."

"Liz, I wanted to ask you, how'd your son's birthday party go?" Jan asked, not because she was a friend of the family but because she had heard Liz talk about the planned party the night before. She listened to the show in Sarasota, where she worked the overnight shift as a private aide to an ailing eighty-four-year-old woman. "I clean house and, you know, I go in and check on her to make sure she's still alive, she's still breathing, because she's up in her years."

"Tell your patient we say hello."

Richards spoke to the night through a suspended gray microphone, looking at it, making expressive faces at it, as if she were looking at the eyes of her callers. Her hands moved with the rhythm of a kitchen-table discussion. Her red nails matched her lipstick, and her dark hair had a henna tint to it. She wore a purple jumpsuit. She fielded the calls from an executive swivel chair, her black bomber jacket draped over its high back, in a small glass-walled studio in a low brick building with castle-slit windows in downtown Tampa. The overnight wasn't her regular time slot, or anybody's, here, because the national radio networks—led by Larry King, with his 3.5 million listeners on 355 stations—had all but killed local late-night talk radio: It was cheaper for stations to tap into a satellite feed and send their overnight hosts home. WFLA was in the process of switching networks, from Talknet to ABC (home of Sally Jessy Raphael and Tom Snyder), and Richards, a daytime host, was just helping bridge the gap. "I fully expected to get on the air and talk to nothing but mental patients and nuts and sexual perverts all night long," she said. "But I learned that not everyone who stays awake all night is a crazed maniac. I have gotten less rancor, less sexual perversion than I ever did in the day. People are reasonable, they're kind and they're very friendly, they're a lot less tense, a lot less competitive. They just don't seem to be out trying to prove something, they're just doing their job. They're less combative, they don't want to fight you all the time. They want to talk more about relationships, about gentler subjects."

"I think night is a time of great freedom," said David Fowler, who until recently had held court from 11 P.M. to 2 A.M. across town at the Sun Radio Network, whose talk shows were picked up by 150 mostly small stations "from Maine to Rancho Cucamonga," as he liked to say in his deep, rolling, born-for-radio voice. "The greatest ideas I've ever had, and how great they are I don't know, but they've always come late at night, always. It's as though you can just feel something move off the front of your mind that says 'Okay, let that out now,' and it absolutely can't happen during the day, when you're just bombarded constantly on all sensory levels."

At 1:30 the lights on WFLA's Telemix console were still blinking green with on-hold callers, a classroomful of raised hands clamoring for a chance to be heard. Richards punched one up, Jesse from Clearwater, and listened to his story through her yellow-foam headphones. "Listen, Liz, I've been gay for about three years and I don't know how to tell my parents," Jesse told Liz, and also the entire nocturnal audience of Tampa's top-rated AM talk station.

Richards kept her finger on the dump button, unsure if Jesse was a legitimate caller. His voice was a strained monotone, and his story was marked by long pauses and off-key notes ("Well, I dunno, it's fun, I've never been with a chick"), but she kept him on the air, drawing him out and offering commonsense advice about safe sex and support groups. "You've chosen a very difficult life-style, and this is your first trial," she said. "There is no convenient time and there is no good time to do this."

He was twenty-five, gone from home since eighteen, but he said he still feared his father. "I used to get punched all the time," he told Liz.

"I would just hate to see any physical violence come out of this," she said. "I suppose the best way to do it, then, would be to take somebody with you. How about a friend of the family? An aunt, an uncle?"

"Yeah, that's a good idea. Because if he punches me anymore, I'll call the cops on him."

"Well, and I think you should. You're a grown man, no one has the right to hit you."

"And then he'll go to jail and he'll find out what it's like."

Doug in Palm Harbor wasn't quite sure what ailed him, or even why he had called in the first place (aside from "Well, I just got done doing my taxes"), until he hit upon the subject of the vacuum cleaner. The previous afternoon, he told Liz, he had asked his wife if she wanted to go shopping for a new vacuum cleaner. "What are we gonna do with the kids?" was his wife's sharp reply, unaccompanied by a yes or a no. "I mean, I just throw up my arms and go 'What kind of answer is that to any sort of question?'" he said. It was the kind of answer from which Liz could extract a sixty-five-minute discussion, stretching across one news break at 2 and almost into the next one at 3, about "noncommunicative relationships" and "passive-aggressive behavior" that revealed, in successive layers of frustration and bitterness and anger, the marital troubles he couldn't discuss for even five minutes with his own wife.

"I wanna tell you, there is nothing lonelier than being married and being lonely," she told him. "She feels steamrolled, and that's her way of getting back at you. She was being aggressive with you in a very passive way, and that's dirty pool. She was putting you down, or putting your idea down, because she doesn't have the nerve to do it outright like I just did and tell you to shut up."

While Doug's marriage unraveled on the other side of the glass, Gary Fitzpatrick sat in the control room and stitched calmly at his needlepoint. He picked up the phone occasionally to check on the callers still stuck in traffic, bottlenecked by Doug's jacknifed marriage. "Doug's going for the record here," he said. The phone rang with another caller wanting to join the line. "Hey, Bob, whatchew wanna talk about? . . . So you're gonna help the dude out? Hold on." He typed the call into the computer keyboard and onto Liz's screen, where Bob waited with the others and hoped to crack Doug's monopoly.

Radio at night is like the great and powerful Oz, penetrating invisibly across the land, and Fitzpatrick, a linebacker-sized engineer with an expansive voice, was like the lone man behind the curtains in the Emerald City, pulling the levers that animated the wizard. It doesn't take many people to keep a radio station broadcasting, even one as big as WFLA. His only company, besides Liz and his needlepoint, was a news producer, across the hall preparing hourly news breaks, and a deejay, playing classic rock on the FM sister station, but that would have been a crowd at one station he'd worked at before. "It was out in this swamp, by a river, and I was all by myself all night long. You've really got to be nice to people then, say, 'Yes, sir, I'll play that song.' I was alone, I had to walk out of there, and they knew where I was, so I was nice to everybody." Fitzpatrick worked this shift even before he started in radio, on the night crew at a Buffalo supermarket, and he continued on it by choice, leaving his days free for his four kids and his soap operas. He was happy about the return of daylight saving time, with its dark mornings and light evenings. "If you can go home and go to sleep in the dark and then get up in the light, you feel better, it's like getting some of that night sleep. If you don't, it's like 'Hey, they started the day without me and I got things to do.' "

The phone rang again, Charles from Tampa. "Whatchew wanna talk about?" Fitzpatrick asked. "You want her to get Doug off the air?"

Doug's call was in its final act by now, as was his marriage. "Maybe you oughta consider the alternative?" Liz suggested.

"Which is?"

"Which is, the relationship ain't gonna work."

"I think that's pretty much what I feel." He and his wife had almost divorced two years before, he said, but decided against it for one reason: "I have two gorgeous little girls."

"But you and your wife are in an emotional war, and the kids are right in it, battling it right along with you."

"They need a mother and a father."

"They still have a mother and father, and they will have a mother and father. They just don't need to see their mother and father emotionally beating each other up."

"I am totally a prisoner," Doug said, and Liz soon released him.

"I really think a lot of it has to do with the visual," David Fowler said. "At night, let's state the obvious, you can't see outside. Outside is a mystery to you, so I think your mind, since it's not intruded upon by the visual, is more free to roam in any way it wants. I think at night you allow yourself to think things that during the day would never even occur to you. At night it starts to go, I think *cosmic* is a great word. You begin to wonder about your place, your size—you know, your meaning, all of that."

The second hand on the clock Richards faced clicked off the time incrementally, and the farther it got, the more it seemed to slow, like a fading racehorse. She still had two more hours before she would hand the mike off to the morning host at 5 A.M., but the callers were already thinning out, threatening to cut a dialogue down to a monologue. "I'm much better at eliciting emotions than I am on issues," Richards said. "But callers get tired, too, and it's easier for them to call on issues than on emotions. Every host has a few issues of their own they can pull out when things are slow that'll put calls up on the board. It's a cheap shot and you hate to do it, but sometimes you have to. I bash men. I take them down the rocky road and nail them as being lazy and slovenly and egotistical." But before she could even bait her hook, she reeled in Jacob, a semiregular caller with formal diction and an upright, Bible-quoting manner ("I'm almost sure he's a put-on").

"Does Irma know that you and I are meeting like this?" Liz asked, her voice bypassing flirtatious and moving straight into seductive. "She's worried, isn't she? She knows how I turn you on."

"I have met you, Miss Richards, and for all those people out there wondering, you are quite an attractive woman," Jacob said.

"Thank you. See, I knew I had you going, I knew you'd give up your religion for me."

"Well, you're not right there. No, the reason I called, I wanted to say that I think you have found your niche. I have never heard you exert—and I'm quite the critic of talk radio—I've never heard you exert such control and self-confidence."

"Really? It takes a lot of control when I talk to you." Fitzpatrick's laughter filled the control room, seeping through the thick glass into the studio; Liz strained to keep hers silent.

"In what way, Miss Richards?"

"I've just always had this thing for you. It's sort of like defrocking a priest." Jacob mumbled and sputtered. "Jacob, are you okay? I don't mean to rush you, because I know you have to be handled gently."

"Yes, I am. I cannot figure out your obvious, oh, how should I say . . ."

"Passes."

"Whorelike passes."

Her laughter finally escaped in a raucous burst, echoed by Fitzpatrick's. "Well, that certainly did it, that cooled me off. All right, what the hell do you want? You wanna play rough? I'll play rough. I can use four-letter words."

"Well, actually, *whore* is a five-letter word."

"Go on, Jacob, what do you want? You gonna bless my body for me?"

Jacob sputtered some more and seemed to swallow his own laughter. "Uh, there appears to be a problem on the line," he said, and with a click he was gone.

"Hello? Hello? Oh, Jacob, I can't believe it. We got him. We finally got Jacob. He'll never be the same."

Jacob's call pulled in some other calls from the small galaxy of radio addicts, the regular listeners who talked about the station's hosts the way most people talked about co-workers, and who asked Liz when she would be on next, as if they were asking for a date. Lee called from his job at the airport, setting aside his algebra homework for a moment ("You got Jacob all hot and bothered, now he's gotta go pray under a cold shower"). Wayne the trucker called ("After what you did to him, I think Jacob's in that little room that he doesn't allow Irma in") and caught Liz still in a double-entendre mood.

"My wife waits up for me, you know," he told her.

"Awww, she does? Isn't that sweet."

"And then after I get home and things are taken care of, she goes to bed."

"What things?"

"Well, I dunno . . ."

"You mean she unloads the truck?" Fitzpatrick's laughter penetrated the glass again. "I can't believe I said that. I just pulled a Jacob. It made my eyes water, it embarrassed me so much."

"If you can't hack the night, then you must be terribly insecure," David Fowler said. "It's not the people who are up all night who are insecure, it's the people who can't be up at night, it's the people who have to have this constant goddamn barrage of human contact to prove to them they exist. When you're up at night alone, you'd better have some hold on yourself, some little bit, because you can slip off into thinking you don't exist anymore."

The callers arrived in a slow, but almost unbroken, procession through the remaining night. None of them, it turned out, wanted to report an Elvis sighting at the Winn-Dixie, or a UFO touchdown in Plant City, or the imminence of the Second Coming; nor did they wish to discuss any of the hot-button issues—taxes, the death penalty, Social Security—that drive daytime talk radio; and only Joe from Tampa had outright obscenity on his mind. Their calls instead, when added together hour-by-hour, had the free-associative, drifting quality of a collective dream, and consequently the whole talk-show process, like the process of sharing an individual dream, had about it an odd, slightly shameful air of both exhibitionism (for the callers, their stories shielded by the anonymity of their first-name intimacies) and voyeurism (for the audience, sitting alone in the dark and listening in). "My daughter said to me today, 'Mommy, what do you talk about?' and I said, 'You know what, I don't know,' " Liz told Bob, who had called because his worries about a job transfer were keeping him awake. "Things, I mean, I don't know. Life."

The familiar chatter, unfortunately, didn't always sign off when Richards did. "It's the bane of my existence, when you're out somewhere and you meet people and they think they're good friends of yours," she said later. "Part of the talent, I guess, should be to make each individual listener feel as if you're only talking to them. If you achieve that, that's what you get. But when I'm out and I'm with my family, I'm not Liz Richards then. I'm 'Mommy' or 'Honey.' I'm not that person on the radio. I teach my children not to talk to strangers, and then people walk up to us and start talking. It's difficult for children to be able to assess that."

She stifled a yawn, her chair creaking softly, and punched up the lone blinking light. "Yeah, I've had this problem, it's been preying on my mind for about twenty-three years," Charlie from St. Petersburg said, his tone hinting at the arrival of the night's deepest hour, its low time of loss and regret. It is in the darkness—when your eyes, using their rods instead of their cones, are most sensitive to the color blue—that your soul is most sensitive to the mood of the same hue.

"I went out with this girl many years ago, about twenty-three years ago," he said, his words tumbling together in a pensive New York accent, "and she was a virgin when I met her, and we went out for about nine months, we dated consistently, but I never made love to her, but I had a chance to, and at the last moment I backed out. I gave the excuse that I had too much respect for her and I wanted to wait for marriage, and shortly after that we broke up." He was twenty-six at the time, and she was nineteen. "I just wanted your opinion on that, if I did the right thing or I should've made love to her."

"Don't tell me you've been saving yourself for twenty-three years, Charlie?"

"No, of course not. But after I broke up with her, I realized how much I loved her. I didn't realize it then."

"Well, that's usually the way it goes."

She didn't give him the counselor's hour she had given Doug, but she did hear out his melancholy tale. "There are people you can really do something for," Richards said later. "I know it's bad radio sometimes, but it seems cruel to have to make that judgment about them, because you hold yourself out to people, and some of them really need to talk to you."

"She was the perfect woman," Charlie lamented, "the kind of woman that you wanna bring home to mother, and possibly if I did make love to her, I probably would've been married today."

"I think you did the right thing."

"Why do you say that?" he asked plaintively, sounding disappointed by her conclusion.

"Because I think those were your initial feelings, and I think that if the relationship couldn't withstand a glitch like that, which was a glitch that was only done out of caring, out of feeling in love, if it couldn't survive that, which was minor, then it wouldn't have survived life's really tough problems."

He seemed to want a different answer than that—maybe a suggestion that he track her down and they try to reel back the years together, or maybe a nodding agreement that he had been wrong twenty-three years ago, so that he could then blame the absence of love in his life now (he later married someone else, he said, "but it didn't work out") on some ancient miscalculation and not on some flaw in his own character.

"I just can't believe you're still thinking about it after twenty-three years."

"Yeah, well, because I loved her so much. I think I still love her today."

When the second hand took its last step to 5 A.M., Richards yielded to the news and signed off for the last time in her short turn as an overnight host. Outside, the streets were still dark, and there was no sign of Tom or Ken or Joe or Jan or Jesse or Jacob or Charlie or any of the others who were out there somewhere, the calls had proved that, but who were hidden by the darkness. "Every night when I walk out of here I cross my fingers," Richards said. "They could be sitting in a car out there. They can chart my movements, they know when my voice is on the air. That's really scary. There's a lot of loneliness out there."

"I think that being up at night regularly, and wanting to be, is a form of anticipating death," David Fowler said. "I mean, is death a whole new freedom, or is it the final prison? See, I don't know, but when you're up at night alone, trust me, you think about these things a lot, and I think you're anticipating it, just by the very act of being up alone in the dark."

Becky Byers was forty miles from the Atlantic, sealed away from the night in a large windowless room in a low, gray, warehouse-style corrugated-metal building on a commercial strip in south Orlando, a steak house on one side and a muffler shop on the other, but at 1:30 she knew that a cruise ship had docked somewhere along the east coast of Florida. She heard through her headset the voice of a lonesome, far-from-home sailor. "What number are you calling in Korea?" she asked him through the tiny tab microphone on her headset, trying to get him home for a few minutes. "Say the telephone number in Korea, please. . . . In what city? Pusan? Are you calling the military or the city? . . . Your charges will be nine dollars and fifty-five cents for the first three minutes."

The call had already exceeded 32.4 seconds—the prescribed average time for an AT&T long-distance operator here to spend with each customer— and the sailor was just now dropping coins down the slot. He was Korean, like many cruise-ship crew members, and he had difficulty understanding Byers's patient instructions. He had deposited just a dollar when, hearing a Korean voice on the line, he started talking. "Hello, Korea, hello, sir, you can't speak yet. Hold the line, sir. You have to deposit another three dollars. Sir, put the money in, please." The pay phone could only accept coins in three-dollar lots, so she had to repeat her instructions after each lot. "Just a moment, Korea, please hold the line, just a moment, ma'am. Please deposit three dollars again. . . . Yes, you have to put another three dollars in, sir." International calls require enough jangling silver to stake a low-roller Vegas slots player, and the sailor was finally tapped out. "You only put in eight dollars, sir. . . . You do not have any more coins? . . . A collect call? Just a moment." She returned to him the two dollars the phone hadn't swallowed yet, and she asked the Korean operator to put through a collect call. "Operator, tell the customer to stay on the line when he's through for a refund by mail. He lost six dollars." And then, finally, to the sailor, "Yes, go ahead." When she checked back on him a few calls later, he was gone.

The voices that emerge through the telephone at night—voices that call talk shows and emergency numbers, that order Zamfir records and Japanese yen, that wake you with news of birth or death or simply unadorned loneliness—do not travel unimpeded through the atmosphere like radio waves. They must follow instead a more circumscribed route, along the seemingly infinite paths of the telecommunications network that webs the nation as capillaries web the body. Like the nation's other infrastructure capillaries (roads, for instance, electricity, water), the phone network is always on, and consequently requires incessant attention to ensure it stays on. Most of the network's guardians are as invisible as the network itself, traffic managers and repair crews and technicians, but the operators at the other end of the ring embody it in a reassuring, always-available human voice.

When Becky Byers started with the phone company in 1968, it was still The Phone Company, and an operator was a one-stop telecommunications general store, able to look up numbers, check out problem lines, place collect and credit-card calls, hook up long-distance calls, even summon the police. Automation streamlined some operator functions, replacing the plugs and cables of the old "cord boards" with the keyboards of computer consoles, and in the process allowed many women to pursue alternate careers: Without automation, an early-1960s Bell Labs study predicted, every American woman would eventually have been needed as an operator. The Bell split-up split up others: Local operators handle local calls now, information operators handle information calls, and long-distance operators like Byers, who chose to go with AT&T rather than Southern Bell after the breakup, handle long-distance calls. Her position was in an open, waist-high cubicle, sitting before a suspended video screen and a sloping console she played as deftly as an organist. Potted plants stood on the mauve carpet, and a wall sign reminded the operators to remind the customers that they were using AT&T, which was no longer the only long-distance carrier: BRANDING IS LIKE SEWING OUR LABEL ON OUR PRODUCT, it read, and the soft, constant chorus of "Thank you for using AT&T" was the sound of stitching.

Fifty operators generally worked in this room during the day; thirty-five were still here at 11; but by midnight, when Disney World's closing fireworks had faded and the tourists there had been replaced by the overnight cleaning troops, only eighteen were left. The emigration continued at planned fifteen-minute intervals throughout the night, reducing the operator force to four by 3 A.M. AT&T's staffing cycle, like its cheaper-when-later pricing structure, reflected the demographic biases of America's daily schedule: work at day, home at evening, sleep at night. Night calls were sparser, but their greater complexity, unpredictability and length made the late shift at least a rough approximation of the prebreakup operator's job.

"I'll try to connect you with an operator for Lebanon. . . . I'm sorry, there are no circuits to Lebanon."

"You'd like to make a collect call to Bahrain?"

"The lines to Syria are busy, would you try again later?"

"What city in Mexico are you calling? . . . Is that in the state of Chihuahua? *Momento, por favor.*"

International calls, spanning oceans and time-zone differences, accounted for more than half of the postmidnight traffic here. "You get around," Byers said. "You get to talk to a lot of different people. I like talking to Japan. Their voices are so lilting when they come on." Prisoners often made collect calls at night, and other lonely people called just to hear a live voice. Some late callers were anxious to speak to the governor or the White House. Nuisance callers were more active: "They'll give a weird name, like 'Bright Eyes,' and when the people they're calling don't know them, they'll keep calling back, and I'll have to tell them, 'I'm sorry, they don't know you.' " When spring-breaking college students descended on the Florida beaches, they could—since they were, like the alligators native to the swamps here, nocturnal creatures by nature—push the volume of calls on the 10-to-6 shift here from five thousand to twenty thousand. And many of the twelve million annual visitors to Orlando, those still up after their Disney World day, were fond of calling the folks back home to rave about Space Mountain.

"Your name, please? . . . Thank you, Celeste. Hi, this is A.T. and T., will you accept a collect call from Celeste?"

"I'll be glad to arrange credit for you. What number were you trying to call?"

"There's no answer, could you try again later, please?"

"Deposit eighty-five cents, please."

The room—which thrummed with a muted, steady conversation, although nobody here was talking to anybody else here—had an unusual sound to it for a night workplace: All the voices were female. The scene would have appalled Louis Brandeis, the former Supreme Court justice and, as coauthor of a tract titled "The Case Against Night Work for Women," one of the many leaders in the first part of the century, from both politics and labor, who wanted to prohibit women from working late shifts—to protect them, the logic went, from exploitative factory managers, and also to shield them from the danger and menace and immorality of the night, to conserve their health, to keep them near their home and family duties. The night-work bans have since been overturned, but the cultural traditions persist: Women commonly work the evening shift, but men still outnumber them two-to-one on overnight shifts. Telephone operators, traditionally an occupation where women predominate, explode that ratio.

The overnight shift had some advantages here—a calmer pace, a pay differential, more casual dress—and Byers, whose seniority gave her a wide choice of hours, chose it over days. Mary Siler, the 10-to-6 supervisor stationed at the head of the room like a dispatcher, was here by choice, too. "I could never have raised a family if I had to work days," Siler said. She also might not have had the chance to place person-to-person calls, as she once had, for Bob Hope, Victor Mature and Zsa Zsa Gabor. "We know everybody who's up."

No stars called tonight, and there were no tornadoes or accidents or airport flight delays or other calamities to cause a rush on the lines. Customers entered the network in a slow, even stream. But there was a mother worried about her daughter in Hawaii. "I'll be glad to try it for you, but I have no way to check it as long as it rings," Byers told her. The problem wasn't the lack of a ring, the mother said, but the lack of an answer. Byers rang a local operator in Hawaii. "Can you connect us with the repair service? She's been trying to get her daughter for about six days with no answer. Thank you." And to the mother, "Oh, you're welcome."

The small pool of light Thomas Hannah and Simri Dones worked in started fading just a few desks beyond their own, the darkness spreading out from them like pond ripples from a sinking stone, gradually shadowing the surrounding maze of chest-high gray cubicles, and finally obscuring the farther reaches of the fourth floor. From outside—from the empty parking lot, from the winding drive through this office-park campus in Maitland, just north of Orlando—their light was the building's only light, a dim glow that kept it from merging into the dark night sky. The elevator sat on the fourth floor with them, right where they had left it; there was nobody left in the building to call it elsewhere. Their attention was fixed on their computer screens. They punched up a series of separate displays like shuffled cards, checking the vital signs of the patient they were charged with monitoring: AT&T's internal computer network, one of the world's largest private computer networks. "I don't believe in ghosts, personally, but I do believe in gremlins," Dones said, and the gremlins that inevitably invaded the computers were why he and Hannah stood watch here through the night.

Although AT&T was no longer The Phone Company, it was still A Giant

Company, and its computer network—the one that handled internal functions, such as billing and payroll and orders and repairs, not the one that handled telecommunications—was consequently so immense that, as Hannah said, "it's hard to perceive the vastness of it." Almost a quarter-million work stations were tied into the network, and when they went down, and couldn't be brought back up locally, this was the hub their operators called. "We've got the A.T. and T. world in our hands," Hannah said. Some red on the screen and a beep were signals that some province in that world was restive. "People expect when a computer goes down there's rumbling and sparks and things falling down. It's not like that. When it goes down, it goes down. You don't hear anything."

Nothing was going down tonight, which made it harder for Hannah and Dones to stay up. "Between four and five, five-thirty, that's rough," Hannah said. "There are times when you literally black out. You look at the clock and it says four fifty-five, then you look again and it says five. You just pass out."

The valley didn't swallow him tonight. He picked up the phone at 5:10. "You see anything funny on your system?" he asked. He was talking to one of AT&T's data centers—sprawling storehouses filled with aisle after aisle of computers, humming with enough electronic brainpower that they might qualify as sentient beings, sifting the day's information like a dreaming brain. Sixteen data centers anchored the network, one of them down near the operators' building. The operators were in Orlando because operators were everywhere, but the Computer Network Management Center, Dones and Hannah's posting, was here because of the same factors that induced many other corporations to establish Sun Belt outposts: cheaper land and lower wages. "Not funny ha-ha, but funny." Nothing was funny, which was occasion for cheer.

By 7:30, the end of their shift, the elevator no longer waited for them, having been summoned to start carrying the day workers. Everybody was in corporate uniform, and the logic of Dones and Hannah's overnight attire—white shirts and ties—became apparent. They passed the network on intact. "A lot of people want exciting and challenging," Dones said, which in his job would mean a troublesome computer network. "I like boring and dull, the same thing every day."

Kevin Coyne

Land in Florida, where the continent makes its mad, swampy dash for the Caribbean, is a relative thing. The farther south you go here, the faster the land seems to be sprinting, spreading itself thinner as it rushes to the tropics, letting the water fill the gaps in its wake, until finally, at the end of the vast, riverlike Everglades, it gives out entirely and merges with the sea. This swath of central Florida is Sun Belt bedrock—from Tampa Bay, big enough to carry an NFL franchise, through Orlando, a factory town whose plants (Disney World, Epcot Center, Sea World and the rest) turn out a year-round assembly line of endless-summer vacation days, to Cape Canaveral, where the night sometimes blazes with the launch of a space shuttle on a secret military mission to deploy a spy satellite. But if you stray just a short way off the main corridor, past the raw strip malls and the instant-house farms that fill in the landscape, you can glimpse the other, older, often wetter Florida, where the night still belongs to a species not yet conquered by its only natural enemy: the alligator. "There's not too much that'll mess with them," Lieutenant Mike Wiwi of the Florida Game and Fresh Water Commission said of the gators—except a poacher with a rifle, whose only natural enemy was Wiwi.

Wiwi flicked off the headlights of his green Dodge four-wheel-drive and bumped slowly down a dark back road in Polk County, almost midway between Tampa and Orlando. His work hours were self-determined: whatever eight hours out of the twenty-four he thought would net the biggest catch. He worked a lot of nights. "At night the old boys are out doing their skullduggery," he said. He had personalized his truck with a picture of his two young children and a copy of the football schedule from his alma mater, Florida State University. "It's always fun to go out at night. You're still in the same environment, but it's so eerie that it doesn't feel like the same environment. You can't see all around you, it's an area of the unknown, and that little bit of the unknown adds to the excitement."

Florida has an exotic, cacophonous ecosystem—alligators, panthers, bobcats, wintering circus elephants, wintering tourists, five-foot-tall mice named Mickey, migrant farm workers, Cuban exiles, colonizing retirees, even some people, like Wiwi, who were actually born here—and his job was to try to keep it in some balance. It was a job made harder by the wild night. At night alligators—like thieves, card sharks, wolves and many other fang-and-claw, meat-eating predators—emerge to hunt; timid deer come out to forage; poachers sneak around after both quarries; and game officers try to prevent the furtive, bloody encounters between the two sides. Game officers, as you might deduce from the scenario, are assaulted at a higher rate than most other law enforcement officers. "You're out there on foot, at night, by yourself. Number one, he's gonna be startled. Number two, he's armed. Number three, it's usually you and him and his buddy. The element of surprise is about the only thing on your side."

Wiwi checked out a reservoir that poachers, trawl-seining for wholesale lots of bluegills, sometimes regard as an all-u-can-pick fish farm. The only wildlife apparent here tonight were mosquitoes. His rendezvous with a fellow game officer was cut short when the other officer was called away by the dispatcher: A woman had reported a casualty among her ducks, killed, she thought, by a panther. A panther was an unlikely backyard duck hunter up here—there were only about forty in the whole state, virtually all in the Everglades—but the culprit could have been a cougar or a tiger or some other large cat, escaped from either a wintering circus or one of the drug dealers who kept exotic animals as status pets. It turned out, Wiwi later learned over the radio, to be a bobcat. "That consoled her pretty much," the officer said.

An alligator would have been an even more likely suspect for backyard trespassing. Back in the late 1960s the gator population had dipped low enough to earn them protection under the Endangered Species Act, but they had since staged a dramatic comeback, almost a million of them lolling now wherever water gathered in Florida—roadside culverts, cypress swamps, even apartment-complex retention ponds—their menacing, armored, prehistoric visages a reminder that evolution got some species right a long time ago. The rising number of gators had coincided with a rising number of state residents, which had meant a corresponding rise in the number of meetings between natives and newcomers. "They don't go after people," Wiwi said. "It's hard to provoke a gator. A wild animal's first instinct is to get the heck away. When people get killed, most times it's by a gator that's been hand-fed. It's illegal to feed them, because that helps them get over their fear of human beings. If a gator expects to be fed and then he isn't, he's going after something to eat." It could be, since gators have poor eyesight, a poodle or a duck or an unlucky swimmer; they wrestle their prey underwater, drowning it before they eat it. "A gator doesn't know a dog from an otter or a raccoon. It's just a small, warm-blooded animal. The way a gator I.D.'s something is with its mouth, so if it takes a bite, you punch it or kick it, then the gator realizes it's not what he thought it was." He had no wish to test this tactic's effectiveness in his job, where he was sometimes called on to trap gators that presented a public danger; he once removed an eleven-foot gator from the porcelain-filled garage of a tile business, with no breakage and his extremities intact. "As a kid I'd catch baby gators to play with them, like you'd catch frogs. I thought it would impress the girls. But then I learned, number one, girls are not that easily impressed, and number two, you don't have a lot of room for error. You're looking at something that can kill you. I'd rather face a human being. You can react to a person based on your perception of his reasoning. But a gator's brain is about the size of a walnut. There's no reasoning there, just survival."

Despite their natural advantages—six feet is a common length for a Florida gator, but they can get close to fourteen feet and top six hundred pounds—they are an easy target for poachers at night. Evolution didn't anticipate high-powered flashlights that, when shined out over the water, reveal a pattern of glowing red-orange spots, reflective gator eyes, about the color of the lit end of a cigarette. Just point at the spots and shoot, and you have a gator, worth more than five dollars a pound for its meat ("It's a rich, white meat, a consistency like lobster," Wiwi said) and fifty dollars a foot for its belly skin. The poachers' market had been undercut in recent years by farm-raised gators and by the limited, legal September hunt that started in 1988, but the poachers still emerged, on late-spring nights, when the breeding gators were most active. The game officers would start their stakeouts within the next few weeks, long, mosquito-inhaling sessions on boats and airboats in the dark swamps. Tonight Wiwi kept his lookout from land, where he was, he knew, almost as likely to find drug skullduggery as he was poachers. "No area is immune to drugs," he said, least of all the vast, sheltering backwoods night. "A lot of these old boys never had more than a one-acre dirt farm and some guy says to them, 'Here, sit at the end of the road tonight and here's a thousand dollars.' "

He came upon three cars by the side of the road, not at the end of it, at the Hopewell pits, a reclaimed phosphate mine now filled with enough water to attract gators, and possibly, he had thought on the way here, poachers, too. He put the cars in his spotlight—primer-gray Camaro, yellow VW Beetle, black Olds—and took his hat from its holder over the rearview mirror. "These guys are probably swapping some dope," he said, getting out to find out. Lawbreakers sometimes had the mistaken impression that a valid fishing license granted them blanket immunity from a game officer. In fact Wiwi had as much authority as, say, a Florida highway patrolman to arrest these guys; and he did. He had apparently interrupted a wholesale marijuana transaction between the driver of the Camaro and the front-seat guest. He found $179, a tray flecked with seeds and stems, empty plastic bags and a paper bag filled with a felony quantity of marijuana. He took their wallets to the truck to check their ID's. None of the four, the two in the car and the two who had been standing outside, were over eighteen. They shuffled silently, nervously, in the spotlight, the boys smoking Marlboros, the girl drinking from a long bottle of Mountain Dew. "I have two ten-fifteens, possession of marijuana felony," Wiwi said into the radio, using the signal for a prisoner in custody. "I need assistance in transporting."

Two Hillsborough County deputy sheriffs arrived, and Wiwi released the two teens who had been wise, or lucky, enough to stay out of the car the marijuana was in. "Okay, Vicky, you're free to go," he told the girl, and she did, fast. A tow truck hooked up the now-impounded Camaro. The two 10-15s went with Wiwi and the deputies to the sheriff's office. "Man, I didn't know it was in there," the shotgun-rider protested. "Sure," a deputy said. "You were just sitting there bullshitting."

Wiwi had a polite, subdued arrest-side manner, a useful quality for a small, muscular man whose job it was to exert authority, alone, in the dark woods. "I find you get a lot further treating people like human beings than you do if you give them a hard time," he said. But when respect fails, some creative bluffing can help. On one of his first solo night patrols he had turned up three drunk men "monkey-fishing" in a canal at 3 A.M.—an illegal technique that uses a device resembling an organ-grinder's box, hence the name, to send an electrical charge through the water, making easy pickings of the stunned fish. "They start mouthing off, like, 'We know you're all alone here, we oughta just throw your ass in the canal and be done with you.' I made a mistake and used profane language. I said, 'You touch me and I'll have your ass,' and that got me on the defensive. They said, 'Hey, you're in trouble now, you ain't supposed to curse.' So then I start blinking my flashlight up the hill. They ask, 'What're you doin'?' and I say, 'None of your business,' and they say, 'You're signaling your buddy up there.' Next thing I had their IDs and I jogged back to my vehicle. I got on the radio and said, 'Get a deputy down here.' I go to church, and I was always taught not to lie, but sometimes you've got to stretch the truth."

At the sheriff's office Wiwi weighed the marijuana: 207.5 grams, which translated as 7.4 ounces. He called the home of the younger boy, the sixteen-year-old in the passenger seat. "That's Wiwi, ma'am, W-i-w-i," he told her ("It never fails that I have to spell it," he said later of his name, which was of French and Indian extraction). "Your son's been arrested. . . . It's a felony, ma'am, that's very serious." Reports were typed, and the deputies took custody of the Camaro's driver, eighteen and now charged as a dealer. A detective took him into an interview room, explaining that life would be easier if he pointed to a bigger fish. "Think real hard about what I said, Jimmy, real hard," the detective said when they came out, but Jimmy, silent, just shook his head.

Wiwi drove the sixteen-year-old to the county jail in downtown Tampa, just a few blocks from the WFLA studios, and accompanied him through booking. The boy gave fingerprints and stood for pictures, the camera's flash harsh as the noon sun. Wiwi uncuffed him when his parents finally arrived. "It's just for possession," he told them. "I didn't believe it was his marijuana. He'll have to go to a juvenile hearing, then maybe drug rehab or probation or community service."

The city streets were empty, but the lights still shone in the bail bondsmen's offices that orbited the jail. Wiwi's truck and his uniform—green pants, tan shirt, green epaulets—seemed far from their natural habitat. Tomorrow night he would start off on the back roads again, maybe stalking firehunters (an Indian term now applied to nocturnal poachers who cheated with Q-beam spotlights and 12-volt batteries) or chasing a pickup out cruising for wild hogs (pit bulls bred for the job were loaded in the bed of the truck, then set on a hog when one was spotted) or even running across, as he did deep in the woods one night, a weekend encampment of paramilitary survivalists. "It was eerie," he said of that encounter. "We were looking at machine guns, guys dressed in full camouflage, bayonets. It was like a mercenary camp. But they all had permits, they weren't breaking any laws, so there was nothing we could do. You don't know what you've got out there. It gives you a little rush." Tonight he stayed on the four-lane highway back to the Lakeland station, where paperwork on his arrest would consume the rest of his shift and beyond. He passed a billboard for WFLA: OUR NEWSROOM NEVER CLOSES, it announced.

At 2:00, a the MEMPHIS *airport, a Federal Express loading crew rolled just-filled cargo containers into the empty belly of an outbound DC-10.*

The Mississippi River looked as still and silent and black as an empty interstate. The night cloaked its nation-draining power with a deceptive calm. It was moving south, about as fast as a person walks, but in the darkness it seemed to offer a solid path from Memphis across to Arkansas. A lone light moved south with it, a towboat hauling a shadowy barge. The quiet rose up from the river to envelop the overlooking streets of downtown Memphis. The cotton warehouses along Front Street were all sewn up tight. The guest-room windows were dark at the venerable Peabody Hotel, and on Beale Street, dotted with nightclubs and famed as the home of the blues, it was past closing time on a weeknight, and the blues had apparently gone home elsewhere for some sleep; the police station was the only place still awake there. But not far from downtown the streets rumbled with an intermittent stream of trucks, all either going to or coming from the same large, windowless concrete building: the U.S. Postal Service's general mail facility for its Memphis division.

"You got all of Truck Twenty-one out?" Ed Garner, the South Dock supervisor, asked one of the mail handlers bustling around him on the loading dock. Sacks slid down chutes, and carts were rolled in and out of the yawning trucks—the mail arriving in and departing from, as it did around the clock, the city of Memphis. He wore a blue windbreaker against the chill night air. "People ask me, 'What do you all do at night?' They think they just drop the mail in the box and a carrier goes and delivers it."

More than 800,000 people work for the Postal Service, one of every 150 American workers, making it the largest employer outside the military, but the public sees fewer than half of them: the familiar cast of letter carriers delivering bills and window clerks selling stamps. Supporting the public Post Office is the hidden Post Office, a network of vast, factorylike buildings where workers sort and move the mail all through the night so that the letter carriers will have letters to carry the next morning. Memphis was an average-sized facility, about 120,000 square feet, and it generally handled between 2 and 2.5 million pieces of mail daily; the national total was 537 million pieces daily. The flow of mail was as relentless as the Mississippi, and similarly capable of flooding. "Once you get behind, it will just overpower you," Abraham Parker said. As an operations officer in the engineering technical unit, his job, much like that of the engineers assigned to control the Mississippi, was to help keep the flow straight and smooth. "A visitor will come in here when it's busiest and say, 'You'll never get that mail out,' and then they'll come back when everything's cleared and they wonder how it got done."

It got done much differently than it did back when clerks read each envelope and tossed it into its proper bin. The facility functioned like a city-block-sized computer, shuttling information to its assigned place, except here the pieces of information shuttled were actually pieces of mail— solid, unwieldy, heavy when gathered together, susceptible to tearing—not invisible electronic pulses. In the evenings, on the shift known as Tour 3, the job was to get the mail out of Memphis and into the world. Raw mail arrived in sacks from all over the city and other collection points within a hundred-mile radius of here, a territory that encompassed western Tennessee, eastern Arkansas and northern Mississippi; was canceled; was herded through a series of sorting machines that were updated, high-speed versions of those old quick-draw clerks; was resacked; and was loaded onto trucks bound for New York, Chicago and the rest of America. "Who else is gonna deliver a letter to Minot, North Dakota, for twenty-five cents?" Parker wondered.

At 11:40 the tide abruptly reversed. Throughout the remaining night, on the shift known as Tour 1, the job was to take the mail from the world and get it into Memphis. The same machines were used, but their flow was reversed: They sorted for the little picture now (sections of Memphis, "associated offices" such as Tupelo, Mississippi) rather than the big picture (Omaha, Los Angeles). "Everything looks clear here," Parker said, pleased at not finding any left-behind mystery trays, sacks or carts of unprocessed mail. Days were his usual shift, but he sometimes worked nights to check the flow at its highest crest. Running overhead through the whole fluorescent cavern was an enclosed blue catwalk that resembled a heating duct dotted with one-way mirrors, a low-tech version of the surveillance system casinos used to spot cheaters; inside were postal inspectors—nobody on the floor knew when or where or how many—watching for workers poaching in the river of mail.

The first sorting machine, the optical character reader, was the most efficient. Clerks (clerks "work the mail," mail handlers move it) loaded the device with stacks of mail like soldiers feeding a bullet belt into a machine gun; it read the addresses and ZIP codes at the rate of nine per second; then it rifled the envelopes down the long center runner, where they were deflected into the proper bins. About 64 percent of the envelopes were legible enough for it to sort. "This looks pretty good, it's possible it will read this," Parker said, plucking from an inbound tray a handwritten envelope headed for ZIP code 38101. He picked up a rejected letter: The bar code printed on it by the machine had smeared on its blue paper. "It could've been gone, and not been delayed. It may only be a couple of hours, but that means extra handling, extra costs, and it's just because of the paper."

The blue envelope, and the rest of the rejected mail, went into the Letter Sorting Machines, where the optical character readers were humans. The LSMs required their operators to become letter-sorting machines themselves, and they tested, like a big-league curveball, the outer limits of human hand-eye coordination. The operators sat at long consoles arranged in rows like a secretarial pool; a device that looked and moved like a pudgy little baby arm picked up a waiting letter and dropped it in front of them; and they then had seven-tenths of a second to read the address and three-tenths to type in the proper code before it was whisked away. It looked like a Charlie Chaplin technology-hell nightmare, but the LSM jobs did not go begging: The pay was higher, the breaks more frequent. "You'd be surprised how fast the eye and hand can move," said Parker, who spent eight years on the LSMs, working nights and going to college days. But even the fastest sometimes faltered in the face of the numbing repetition: Error rates rose after 3 A.M., when lunch break was over and circadian rhythms naturally slowed. "I used to keep a wet towel on my forehead and temple until I got over the rough period and woke up," said Levi Hibbler, the acting tour superintendent, who also spent eight years on the LSMs. The fraction the LSMs missed were sorted the nineteenth-century way, the least-efficient method of all: by a clerk standing at a pigeonhold board, sliding letters into labeled slots.

Some letters, of course, did get missorted, and at 4:40 John Register caught one—and thereby saved a young man on Greenbrier Cove in Memphis from the heartbreak of thinking his love might be unrequited. "There was something about it that caused me to scrutinize it," Register said, holding a card he had found misZIPed and mixed in with mail bound for the Internal Revenue Service. "At a glance I could tell it didn't belong there." The return address, in a giddy, loopy script, read simply, "Someone Who Loves You," a sentiment rarely expressed to the IRS. His twenty-five-year tenure had left him with a ZIP code map imprinted on his brain and an instinctive sense of what mail was going where, and had led to his present job, which offered a level of freedom unusual within the military-style hierarchy (the title Postmaster General was no accident) of the Postal Service. His title was review clerk, and he worked without a supervisor, specializing in general troubleshooting. He chose the night shift because his wife worked nights as a nurse, his six children were grown, and it afforded him time to work for his church. "I'm just opposite the rest of the world," he said, and he sent the love note on its way to Greenbrier.

"How many people you see laughing?" asked Larry Moore, who wasn't. His forehead beaded with sweat, and carts full of magazines—*Circus, Billboard, Architectural Digest, Shotgun News*—surrounded him. Wearing a green T-shirt and tan chinos, Moore pushed a mail-heavy cart out into the cool dawn air and onto one of the trucks that fed the substations through-out Memphis. "What you pay your twenty-five cents for, this is what it is, this is the main event here," he said. "Everybody does it, everybody moves it." He had worked twelve years of nights and was the incoming group leader. "It's like that song 'Nightshift' by the Commodores. We'd play it here and everybody'd clap and say, 'Yeah, that's our song.' " The 1985 hit was the Commodores tribute to the late singers Marvin Gaye and Jackie Wilson: "Gonna be some sweet sounds, comin' down, on the nightshift," the chorus went, "Gonna be a long night, it's gonna be all right, on the nightshift . . . I know you're not alone on the nightshift."

By 6:30 the letter carriers were in, breakfast-sharp in their uniforms, putting in route-order the mail that had wound through the building and toward their stations all night long. By 7 the trucks were launched, the machines downshifted to a hum, the 482 Tour 1 workers were leaving, and the 231 Tour 2 workers were arriving to replace them. The mail had moved out on schedule, and if the schedule held down the line, it would be in St. Louis's mailboxes tomorrow, Los Angeles' the day after. "There's a greater feeling of accomplishment on this tour," Levi Hibbler said. "You can see the results. There's not enough action for me on Tour Two."

Well past midnight, at an hour when the traffic in the skies over most cities had slowed to a twinkle, the sky over Memphis blinked brightly, busy with more traffic than Beale Street. Enough lights traversed the night here to leave the impression that the city stood under some congested astronomical confluence—a heavenly intersection thick with shooting stars, meteor showers, comets, maybe even UFOs. The actual explanation was less cosmic: Virtually all the lights belonged to Federal Express jets, departing the Memphis Superhub. Almost one hundred planes landed each night on the Federal Express runways at the Memphis airport, and almost one hundred planes took off again a few hours later. Memphis was no longer the company's sole hub—some sorting was handled now by regional hubs in Los Angeles, Oakland, Chicago, Indianapolis, Newark and Brussels, Belgium—but it was still the main channel: 800,000 of the 1.3 million items Federal Express delivered daily briefly visited this river city.

Federal Express created a new industry (and added a new verb, *to Fedex*, to the language) by exploiting a previously neglected resource: the empty hours of the night. By working through the night, the logic went, by flying all the items to a central location, quickly sorting them and then flying them back out to a squadron of waiting vans—the "hub and spokes" system first outlined by founder Fred Smith in an economics paper at Yale that, according to company lore, earned him a C—you could deliver letters and packages the day after they were sent, a service for which customers, the logic continued, would willingly pay many times the price of a first-class stamp. Because most customers slept while their packages flew, the process seemed even faster than it was. It was a breakthrough transportation idea, using the natural resource of the night, and it was enormously profitable: Federal Express grew into a $4.6-billion-a-year company in just sixteen years. Federal Express was a far-flung empire now, responsible for 45 percent of the overnight delivery market, employing 64,000 people (1,060 pilots among them), 258 planes (from DC-10s and 727s to Cessnas and Fokkers), 24,000 vans and trucks, its own weather bureau, its own flight simulators, even its own reservations counter for vacation-bound workers exercising their privilege to fly for free in the jump seats back with the packages.

Federal Express was the reason for a late rush hour down on the southern edge of Memphis. While Johnny Carson, broadcast at 10:30 here in the Central time zone, bantered with his *Tonight Show* guests, the roads leading to the airport filled with commuting cars and the crosswalks streamed with brigades of workers, almost 4,500 strong, in blue uniforms and steel-toed boots, marching out of the night and into the Federal Express complex, through the long, wide, sci-fi-white corridor and toward their stagemarks for the nightly one-act drama called The Sort—a three-hours-or-so sprint wherein the delivery cycle reached its busiest peak. More than three-quarters of them were college students, the moonlighting, part-time backbone of the sorting process. For a few hours, at an average wage of nine dollars an hour, they would work at a pace few could sustain over a full eight-hour shift, human cogs in the din of a vast Letter Sorting Machine, emptying and filling cargo containers, depositing and withdrawing packages from 127 miles of conveyor belts, leaving finally when the last loads were headed for the planes.

Jacqueline Mitchell's position in The Sort was amid a flurry of overnight letters. Days she studied at Christian Brothers College, aiming for a job as a hospital psychiatric technician; nights she aimed to drop the right letters in the right slots. "I feel like everybody should be up at this time," she said, an understandable bias for someone who had been up at this time for five and a half years here. She was twenty-four and just back from a trip to Switzerland; she had previously jump-seated to Florida, Los Angeles, New York and South Carolina. "When I was younger, I used to go out and I'd think, 'Two o'clock? It's late.' Now I go out and I think 'It's just two, it's only two.' " She was a checker-sorter in the primary sort, the person who met the letters as they were dumped from their big blue sacks and who then dropped them through slots onto the belts that sent them on their proper course. "I learned as a freshman not to take eight A.M. classes if you work nights. I only took two the entire time, and those were because I had to."

Boxes entered the system by a different route: cascading down a Niagara-wide slide, funneled onto belts by sorters whose keypunches determined where the boxes would be kicked off onto other belts. Letters, packages and boxes all met up again in the primary matrix, the hub of the Superhub, where they were sorted automatically by ZIP code; the effect was something like a dealer collecting the cards, shuffling them and dealing a new hand—except this dealer knew exactly which cards were going to which players. Next stop was the secondary sort, which directed everything to the correct outbound flights like a travel agent. The whole process—the flood of packages and letters, the tugs hauling snaking trains of containers and honking at each intersection, the rising crescendo of machinery echoing through one million square feet of roofed space—looked much more haphazard than it really was: Computers tracked each shipment, and a central control room orchestrated The Sort, monitoring the flow and rerouting traffic around snags the way the phone company reroutes long-distance calls around busy circuits.

For the pilots, grounded while their planes were emptied and refilled, The Sort was a slow time, more like The Wait. A ground-floor room in the Flight Administration Building was thick with blue-suited pilots, gathered like a war-movie squadron on the eve of a big bombing mission. Some filled thermoses at a diner-sized coffee urn. Jim Keeling sipped tea from a Styrofoam cup. He had arrived in Memphis at 11:45 from Dallas, where he lived and where he spent the day, and was due to take off for Los Angeles at 3:45. "Night flying is rough," he said. "People say you get used to it. You tolerate it, but you never entirely get used to it."

The world was a small place to a pilot, cruising 30,000 feet above the interstates at ten times the legal ground speed. Keeling was the number-two Federal Express pilot in seniority, his roots in the company's lean beginnings, so he mostly got the routes he bid on: He flew to Los Angeles, Oakland, Chicago, Atlanta, even Japan, as routinely as most people drove to the mall. He averaged three and a half trips a week. Yesterday he had arrived in Memphis from Los Angeles at 12:45 A.M., then flew home to Dallas. Tonight's flight would land him at 6 A.M. back in Los Angeles, where he planned to spend the day sleeping and exercising; at 7:30 tomorrow evening he would pilot a loaded plane back here to Memphis. "The worst case is when you fly every other night," he said. "The best is to fly six days, be off six days, then fly six days again. If I'm off for a week, I get back in sync with my family. If I'm home just for a couple of days, I don't even try to get back in sync." Staying fit was one defense against his schedule: His routine included riding a Lifecycle, pumping weights, walking a treadmill, taking a sauna. His sleep patterns were less predictable. "If I'm tired, I go to sleep."

When the night was clear, Keeling's pilot seat offered a transcendent view of the sleeping nation, as much as two hundred miles in a single wide-angle glance, the lights of its settlements spread out below like phosphorescent plankton floating in the dark sea. Sometimes the lights dropped from above, too. "Two weeks ago, coming in from L.A., I saw the prettiest Northern Lights I've ever seen. They went from Oklahoma City to Fort Smith, Arkansas, before they died out—fingers and rays of light. They were scarlet. I hadn't seen such a pretty scarlet color before." Not all the night lights were so benign. "You get in a thunderstorm and lightning's banging all around. You look down on those big clouds and you can see one hundred miles of thunderstorms, where on the ground you might only see two. You can see bolts all down the line, and it appears like they're firing in line, like a pianist dragging his fingers down the keys. It's a beautiful sight. It's also extremely detrimental." No lightning performances were in tonight's forecast, which he had already checked. The only weather trouble nationally was in Akron—a spring snowstorm there had reduced visibility to a quarter-mile—but Keeling had no business in Ohio. The conditions in Los Angeles were a welcoming 1,200-foot ceiling (the base of the lowest clouds the plane must swoop down through) and four miles' visibility.

By 2:15 the belts were clear, The Sort finished like the fading aftershock whisper of a cymbal crash. Crews were sliding containers—heavy with contracts, spare parts, even "human tissue for transplant," as one box was labeled—into the seatless, warehouse bellies of the planes. (They loaded trucks, too; some shorter distances were bridged by highway.) The jump-seaters had mostly departed the small waiting room by the reservations desk. The tour groups, here on the unadvertised late-night visits the company offered, were gone. Workers trooped back out into the night, where sodium-vapor lights glowed pale orange against the darkness like hazy setting suns. Although The Sort required a lot of bodies, Federal Express spent much less of its budget (about 51 percent) on labor than did the Post Office (85 percent): Short Sort shifts and a nonunion work force were why.

At 3:30 Jim Keeling started the engines on Federal Express Flight 217—a DC-10 painted the same company-logo purple-and-orange as the familiar vans, carrying a crew of three, four jump-seat passengers and 200,000 pounds of freight. At 3:45 he took off, just about the last flight out tonight. He flew west through the night, slower than a fax but faster than most first-class mail, over the Mississippi, the southern Plains, the tailbone of the Rockies, the southwest desert and finally into Los Angeles,

A Day in the Night of America

where the empty dawn runway, not yet clogged with passenger traffic, would grant him a clear and free landing. "You'd be surprised," he said, "how many lights there are out in the desert."

●

The big jet parked across the highway from Graceland—the *Lisa Marie,* Elvis Presley's customized 880 Convair, grounded now, a tourist attraction that looked as if it had undershot by a few miles the runway at nearby Memphis Airport—carried no packages, only memories. "I miss him an awful lot," Osie Nicholson said about the man who, in a bedroom interview in 1974, had hired him as a security guard. Tonight Nicholson sat in a darkened guard booth at the entrance to the adjacent parking lot. The postmidnight traffic on Elvis Presley Boulevard, a six-lane commercial strip, murmured softer and slower even than "Love Me Tender." The main house silently crowned a small rise, a white-columned manor soaked in green, orange and yellow lights that made its beige Mississippi fieldstone incandescent against the night. The long drive leading up to it was closed, the Music Gates swung shut across the entrance. "It was a lot of fun back in those days. You'd see these women climbing the trees out front to see if they could get a glimpse of him." Tree climbing was no longer necessary: Elvis's grave was in the Meditation Garden beside the house, the finale of a Graceland tour.

Like many creative souls (Joyce, Proust, Keith Richards), Elvis was a nocturnal creature, and when he was alive, the lights of Graceland often met the dawn. Sometimes he worked through the night in recording sessions, but more often he played, enjoying a degree of personal freedom then that his celebrity denied him in the day. "We went to make sure somebody didn't mess with their cars," Nicholson said of the regular trips by Elvis and his entourage to a local movie theater for private postmidnight screenings. The Graceland kitchen was staffed round-the-clock, always on call to pre-pare Elvis's favorite fried peanut butter sandwiches. A drunken Jerry Lee Lewis—waving a .38, demanding an audience with the King, threatening to commit regicide—tried to ram his Lincoln through the Music Gates late one night. "I was guarding the back gate," Nicholson said about that night, and by the time he was called to the front, "they had him handcuffed already, putting him in the squad car." And at 4 A.M. on the last night of his life, Elvis played racquetball in the indoor court behind the house, and when the game ended, he sat at the piano and played "Blue Eyes Crying in the Rain."

But Graceland was a museum now, and its 700,000 visitors this year all came during the day. "Night wasn't meant for a person to work," said Nicholson, who didn't share his late boss's habits. He left his booth for a short foot patrol, letting the cool night air revive him as he walked along the locked-up strip of gift shops and restaurants in Graceland Plaza. Somebody had stopped to take a picture of the house earlier, but he was alone now. He wore a white shirt, blue pants and a blue tie secured by a diamond clef-note tie tack. His shift ran from 5 P.M. to 5 A.M., which left his days free to pick up his young granddaughter, one of his fourteen grandchildren, at school. At various times four of his eight children had worked at Graceland; his wife had been a cook and maid here for twenty-five years. His busy season was nearing now—the summer tourist months, bringing upward of 3,500 paying customers daily and peaking on August 15, the anniversary of Elvis's death, when Graceland opened its gates, the city closed off Elvis Presley Boulevard, and 10,000 people spilled out from the gravesite, over the grounds and into the street for an all-night candlelight vigil. "He had something," said Nicholson, who had seen all of Elvis's movies and was partial to his gospel records. "I don't know what you'd call it, but I never saw anybody or anything draw people like Elvis did."

The people Elvis still drew, even in death, often left messages for him, scrawled on the fieldstone wall that Nicholson now watched from across the highway. His concern was with wall climbers, not wall writers: Graceland let the wall serve as a sort of bulletin board for fan tributes. Most of the messages were yearbooklike endearments—names, dates, hometown, variations on the themes of "I Love You" and "You're Still the King"—but somebody had inscribed a quote, slightly edited, from Shakespeare's *Romeo and Juliet*:

When he shall die,
Take him and cut him out in little stars,
And he will make the face of heaven so fine
That all the world will be in love with night,
And pay no worship to the garish sun.

6

At 2:30, in a CLEVELAND *steel mill, a steelworker sent a glowing steel bar through a wringer-like roller, squeezing it thinner than a train-flattened penny.*

The fire that fueled the Cleveland night—its streetlights and bedside lights, its refrigerators and televisions, its factories and convenience stores—towered ten stories high. It was a violent, whirling cyclone, a 2,800-degree inferno so immense that, if not purposely contained the way it was, would have required fire companies from both the East Side of the city, where it burned, and the West to extinguish it; yet it was as invisible to the world as the electricity it generated. It was hidden inside a building-tall boiler, under one of the smokestacks that emerged from the roof of the Lake Shore Power Plant like cigarettes from a package. Even inside the old brick plant, where the fire's heat and noise were steady, you could only see hints of it, glowing a bright orange that looked as fake as a plastic hearth light, through small portholes in the boiler's wall. Up in the ninth-floor control room, Dan Curtiss had a better angle: A black-and-white video monitor showed an over-the-brink view of the fire, ashes falling like sinners through the swirling flames. "You can see what hell looks like," he said.

Curtiss's job, as a Lake Shore shift engineer, was to help keep the night from swallowing Cleveland. The Lake Shore plant, one of five power plants operated by the Cleveland Electric Illuminating Company, could produce 517 megawatts of electricity, enough to supply half a million homes, but to do that, it needed 10 tons of coal an hour, 240 gallons of water a minute, a fire that burned twenty-four hours a day, every day, and a work crew that kept the same hours as the fire. The water was pumped from neighboring

Lake Erie, up into the miles of steel tubes in the boiler, where the coal-fed fire converted it into high-pressure steam, which then spun the blades of a giant turbine, which in turn spun the generator that made the electricity that illuminated the darkness. "The city doesn't know all the electricity it relies on us for right now," Curtiss said, setting out from the control room, a fluorescent cave of dials and gauges and switches, to continue his rounds through the dark plant, checking its continued reliability.

Lake Shore, for all its megawatts, lit itself only sparsely. Its interior—a shadowy, sooty, slightly ominous, undercarriage maze of pipes and ducts and narrow stairs and steel-grid floors—was faithful to the plant's role as the furnace in the city's basement. Curtiss, like a miner, wore a hard hat with a headlamp. He ducked under and stepped over and played his light across dark recesses. "We just had a real good run the last three months," he said. Walking along the top of the seven-story coal feeders, he watched the black surface sift slowly down like sand in an hourglass, evidence that the coal below was blowing steadily into the boiler. Because the coal was pulverized fine as baby powder, it also blew, unintentionally and invisibly, outside the boiler; when you set your hand down, it often came up dusted gray.

His inspection turned up few other people. Days brought 150 workers to the plant—fixing equipment, filling the coal bunkers—but nights got by with just a ten-person operations crew. Curtiss passed one of the four boilers that were cold tonight, shut down and opened for daytime maintenance, and inside it the tubes climbed dense and high as heaven's own pipe organ. On Unit 18, the fifth boiler and, at 250 megawatts, the largest of them by far, he checked a pinhole leak in an external pipe, steam hissing from it like a vengeful radiator. "It might go on hissing like this for another month," he said. "Most times it doesn't blow like a cannon, it just wears out. But I have seen two leaks really blow, the kind that scare you."

Just after midnight Bill Mockler called Richmond Heights to see if the darkness had lifted. "Yes, ma'am, this is CEI calling," he told a customer on Donna Drive, where power had failed earlier. "We wanted to make sure your lights were back on." Stretching behind him, covering the wide back wall of CEI's downtown dispatch center, was a hospital-green pegboard—a knotty, connect-the-dots schematic drawing of the intricate, branching network of substations, transformers and transmission lines through which electricity traveled from generating plants to the homes of greater Cleveland. A bad underground cable near Donna Drive had interrupted the flow, but a repair crew had now patched it. "Everything else is back on okay?" Mockler asked the woman, who didn't know how to resurrect her microwave oven. "I'll have someone stop by sometime after nine to see if they can give you a hand."

Because any piece of the network could falter at any time, dispatchers were always on duty here—on the fifth floor of an office building just behind CEI's headquarters and just off Public Square, the central hub from which all the city's main avenues radiated—and repair crews were always ready to roll. On stormy nights, when ice and lake-driven winds felled power lines, scores of crews were mobilized. On a night like tonight, when the spring breeze through the opened fire door cleansed the bottled office air, three bucket-truck crews and one underground-line crew were standing by between midnight and dawn. Their busy time was often determined by the level of civic inebriation. "Around three you start getting drunks banging into things," said Mockler, who was a lineman himself before a fall hurt his neck and back. "One night I remember seven poles being hit."

Dan Curtiss descended the steel labyrinth that surrounded the boiler the way a gantry surrounds a rocket, following the steam's path to the turbine room, a dim yellow-tile and glass-brick expanse that resembled a grimy high school gym. The turbines, stretched across the floor like giant drive shafts, spun invisibly inside their file-cabinet-green steel shells at 3,600 revolutions per minute. The only evidence that Cleveland's electricity was being generated here was the noise: The room was still, nothing moving, but the turbines' roar echoed through it like a ghostly crowd cheering a game-winning buzzer-beater. The view from outside the plant, from the cars passing on the eight-lane lakefront Shoreway, was even more concealing, just a dusky glow through the glass bricks hinting at the blaze inside.

Leaving the turbine room to inspect "the morgue"—the decommissioned original wing, a crumbling, vacant, shadowy relic—Curtiss left the plant's present and entered its past. Lake Shore was CEI's mother plant, built in 1911, just thirty years after the company's horse-and-wagon crews strung the first power lines across downtown Cleveland's rooftops to light eighty-eight streetlamps, and the morgue was where it was born. Tonight, with its rubble and scabrous paint and decapitated pipes, it looked more like an industrial archeology excavation site. "It'd be a beautiful place for a horror movie," he said. He crossed over a water channel that called to mind *Phantom of the Opera*. There was no power to check on, only intruders: Fox and opossum sometimes visited, and bats, rats and pheasants; shad swam in from the lake. Homeless people sometimes sought shelter in the gutted offices that hovered over the shell like a tanker's superstructure. He stood at the foot of a staircase to nowhere. "It looks like Boris Karloff should be coming down," he said, but tonight it was untrodden.

From his post in CEI's command module, its Systems Operations Center in the southern suburb of Brecksville, Ted Zenz watched northeastern Ohio nod off. He sat before a wall of gauges that monitored the utility's metabolism—the output of the five generating plants strung along the lake like a necklace (Lake Shore, the three other coal- and oil-fired plants, the nuclear plant in Perry) and the intake of the 720,000 customers (including 7,500 industries and 62,000 businesses) in a territory reaching from the western suburbs to the Pennsylvania state line. The dial showing Lake Shore's output had settled around 104 megawatts. The dial showing the gross load, the total amount of electricity being consumed, had been clicking like a backward odometer, from 2,124 to 2,115 to 2,085 to 2,056 and now at 2:40, after the bars had closed, down to 2,005, a decline that mirrored the dipping circadian rhythms of the sleeping populace. By 4 it would drop to 1,975. Zenz called the plants, telling Avon Lake to lower its output by 30 megawatts, Eastlake to drop by 25; Lake Shore was already at its minimum operating capacity.

The center of the Operations Center ("They're the conductors," Curtiss said, "we're the locomotive") was about the size of an amphitheater, dominated by an electronic version of the downtown dispatchers' map and occupied overnight by a three-person shift. No markings identified the building's exterior, a precaution against anyone bent on shutting down Cleveland. The view from the center tonight was of a system flush with electricity. Come summer, hungry air conditioners would boost the load beyond CEI's generating capacity of 2,978 megawatts—it had peaked the previous summer at 3,723—and force the company to buy power from other utilities; but now it was still spring, when open windows sufficed, and the load was low enough to permit the shutdown of the Perry nuclear plant for refueling. The giant circuit board illustrated an unbroken transmission network. When a string of green lights did start flashing up on the map, between the Ashtabula plant and the Zenith substation, it was expected: The line had been shut down so that a crew could work on the steel towers there tomorrow.

A Day in the Night of America

By three the load had crossed the 2,000 mark, and Zenz had called his counterpart at Toledo Edison to exchange price quotes. Power didn't always travel a straight path from CEI plants to CEI homes: it entered a grid, where it could be bought and sold among various utilities. Zenz was a seller tonight. He expected the load to stay low until 6, when alarm clocks rang as one and lights and coffeemakers followed, and then drop again at 7:15, when streetlamps switched off—the pattern that usually held, unless NASA called. NASA's Lewis Research Center in Cleveland was a $12-million-a-year CEI customer, using much of that power to drive its wind tunnels, and it sometimes ran late shifts at the tunnels to take advantage of bulk electricity prices that, like long-distance rates, dropped during off-peak hours; NASA alone could add 330 megawatts to the load. But tonight the wind tunnels were calm, and Zenz watched the night breathe slowly, deeply, toward dawn. "Somebody's gotta be out there," he said. "They're using 2,000 megawatts of power."

Curtiss, back from the morgue, traced the steam's route again, down to the condensers, where, its turbine duty done, it turned back into water. The network of steam pipes that webbed Lake Shore kept the plant far hotter in summer than the homes it air-conditioned, and also offered a lunch-break alternative to the bachelor-style kitchen up by the lockers. "Everybody has a favorite spot where they'll put a sandwich or some soup on a hot steam line," he said. "There was one guy who used to take other guys' lunches. He'd smell a meat-loaf sandwich as he was going by and he couldn't resist so he stole it. So we took three shad and some ketchup, made a sandwich, wrapped it up and put it on a steam line. Every now and then you'd see it pulsate." He moved his hand like a twitching fish. "Nobody saw him bite into it, but lunches didn't disappear as fast after that." The shad weren't hard to find: when the intake screens failed, and fish spilled from the cooling pipes, the plant operators shoveled like Gloucester deckhands.

The navy had taught Curtiss about turning fire and water into power. "For some reason the recruiter didn't like me and I ended up in boiler school. 'Put him in the hole and sweat him to death.'" CEI taught him about turning your life upside down with rotating shifts. "We always say among ourselves—we have to say it because we're on it—that shift work has its advantages. The reason we say it is so we're not depressed constantly. One disadvantage is that you miss a lot of things, like weddings. But sometimes that's an advantage, too. If you get an invitation you're not too thrilled about, you have a perfect crutch. You can say, 'Gee, I'd like to, but I can't. I have to work then.' " The plant itself taught him who was boss. "We have all the ingredients here for one heck of a disaster. I've been in two serious fires here, and after being through them I feel more humble. I respect the place. After you see things go wrong, you get that sense of respect for your surroundings."

Curtiss walked out into the night, out along the discharge channel, thick with fish drawn by the warmer water there. The breeze off Lake Erie was cool, the traffic on the Shoreway light. "By about four it seems like you've been here forever already."

The Flats sprawl along the banks of the Cuyahoga, the river that bisects Cleveland, like the aftermath of a flood—as if the receding waters had left behind not fertile cropland, as the Mississippi had, but an industrial bog instead. In the daylight the Flats are a sooty intestine, a tangle of factories and mills that testifies to the city's manufacturing base. At night, seen from the interstates that bend around them, they are the bubbling surface of another planet, fire and smoke rising from a darkness unbroken by the lights of houses and streets. Down in the middle of the Flats, spilling over fifty-seven acres on both banks of the Cuyahoga, was LTV Steel, where the alchemy of turning iron ore and limestone and coke and manganese into steel required temperatures so unnaturally hot that the fires burned straight through the nights.

Down in one of LTV's rolling mills, the eighty-four-inch hot-strip mill, the flames licked out of the ovens that cooked the steel. The stadium-scale building was tall enough to play football in; long enough, at five-eighths of a mile, to accommodate the process of squeezing thick steel bars out into thin sheets suitable for subsequent shaping into, as foreman Chris Bewley said, "anything from sinks to submarines"; and dusky and forbidding enough to make you feel, as you walked its length, like a shrunken visitor inside a railroad locomotive. "In a place like this, with everything so big, if you get hurt it's bad," Bewley said, as a steel bar emerged from an oven and started down the rolling table. It glowed a molten orange, like a sliding door into the underworld, and you could feel its heat as it passed.

The steel was moved by distant hands. The mill floor was empty, the steelworkers perched in glassed-in pulpits, sealed away from the steel they worked. The cold bars—forged earlier in LTV's furnaces and cast into obelisk slabs—were slowly pushed, one by one, into the ovens; roasted for three hours, at almost 2,500 degrees; fed through the first set of rollers, the five roughing rollers, like a wet shirt through a washtub wringer; flattened by the two thousand tons of pressure like a penny on a train track; fed through the second set of rollers, the seven finishing rollers; and coiled up like a roll of newsprint. Workers were posted all down the line, but their sweat and instincts had largely been supplanted by blinking computer controls. "What you see here tonight is the last of the steel industry," Skip Young said at his post in the finishing pulpit. More than one hundred people had worked each shift in this mill once; thirty-five were here tonight, and Young could foresee a time when automation would reduce that number even further, maybe to as few as three. A hoax ad in the *Cleveland Plain Dealer* had people camped outside LTV a few nights earlier, looking for jobs that didn't exist. "If you come back in ten years, it won't be here like this."

A bar approached the finishing rollers, as one did every couple of minutes, and Young took its temperature with his eyes. "That's about 1,970," he said, degrees that is, extrapolating from the intensity of its glow. A digital display measured it at 1,967. "If it's 1,920, I'm in trouble." A single bar could be worth as much as $60,000, a sum that could be lost at several turns—by rolling a bar too cold, by overheating it in the oven, by squeezing it to the wrong thickness. A bright computer room, just behind the finishing pulpit, had removed most human decisions from the process, controlling the machines and sending signals to the operators in the other pulpits; but it was Young who, like a conductor, set the mill's pace. "Let's go back to 1,500 on the push," he said into the phone, telling the heater, the man who ran the ovens, to increase the speed at which the steel moved through the ovens and onto the rolling table. "We ran two hours halfway decent at that, let's try it and see what happens."

Geography made Cleveland a steel town: It was near coal (western Pennsylvania and southern Ohio), limestone (western Ohio) and, by way of the Great Lakes, iron ore (northern Minnesota). The Cuyahoga provided water to cool furnaces hot with production. Steel-company profits were as sturdy as their I-beams. Skip Young, the son and grandson of steelworkers, graduated from Findlay College in 1968 with a degree in economics, and it was economics that told him the best money around at the time, $640 a month, was at Republic Steel. He then watched as economics turned the steel industry, once the symbol of American industrial might, into a symbol of American industrial decline. Steel's troubles are attributable to a complex mixture of factors, each weighted differently depending on your angle: companies that considered themselves inviolable fortresses, slow to invest in new technology, stingy in research-and-development spending; unions that demanded too-high wages, too-rigid work rules and overstaffing; too much production capacity chasing too little demand; increased competition from cheaper foreign imports. By 1984 Young was working for LTV, which had taken over Republic, and by 1986 his new employer was bankrupt, filing for Chapter-11 protection and claiming it could no longer afford to pay its retirees' pensions. LTV continued making steel, even profits—8.4 million tons of raw steel this year, $4.1 billion in revenues, the third-largest American steelmaker—but the cost was fewer jobs: the company had 43,000 retirees and 75,000 workers in 1977, a ratio of .58 retirees per worker; by 1989 that ratio had ballooned to an alarming 4.8, with 87,000 retirees and only 18,000 workers. Earlier in the shift tonight the overhead crane had changed a roller, revealing a large, scrawled message: FUCK THE MILL.

Young sent another bar through the rollers, pressing it to just .155-thousandth of an inch and watching it slide out the far end like a red river. "For us the hardest time is about four A.M. That's when I have to be awake and when I have to keep these guys awake. We'll start talking, just to pass the time, and we might talk about anything from raising corn in Alabama to fishing." Conversation was unnecessary tonight; they had a fire to rouse them instead. Farther down the rolling table flames suddenly shot up thirty feet high—grease ignited by an electrical short in a table motor—and Young shot down from the pulpit to douse them. Within four minutes the fire was out, Young was back in the pulpit, the damaged table rollers were disengaged from the motors and left to freewheel, and the steel rolled over them again, beacons through the hovering smoke.

The night's tally, when Young's shift was done at 7:45, was 233 pieces of stainless steel rolled, 3,000 tons worth (stainless took longer than plain), and no costly shutdowns (overhead here was $14,000 an hour). "That's a pretty decent turn on stainless," he said. As a roller he was part of management, not the union, but he worked the same rotating schedule. "If I had to do it all over again, I wouldn't do it. The shifts'll kill you." The morning light outside opened a clear view downtown to Terminal Tower, the 1930s-vintage skyscraper that was once the tallest building between New York and Chicago. The flames on the Cuyahoga had long since been extinguished: Its surface had caught fire once, a symbol of pollution so bad it could seemingly make even water burn, and a modern incarnation of Phlegethon, the river of fire in Greek mythology, one of the five rivers separating the underworld from the world above. Downstream on the river now, up near downtown, the banks were freshly lined with bars and restaurants, busy at night with people who spent the dark hours playing, not working.

Deep in the heart of Ford's Walton Hills Stamping Plant, just south of Cleveland, the highlight room gleamed, just after midnight, sunglass-bright. The room resembled a photographer's studio in a loft—floods of squinty light, white walls rising partition-high and then yielding to the dim factory above and beyond them—except that its cast of models was limited to fenders, doors, roofs, quarter panels, deck lids and assorted other unassembled auto body parts. The lights, bright enough for biological-clock-resetting and photography alike, were instead, like the lights in old detective movies, interrogational. Quality-control samples were brought here off the production lines and, under the harsh, revealing glare, inspected for imperfections. But the grilling was ending now, the lines shutting down, the manufacturing day done. Some evening-shift workers clustered around coffee and cake just outside the highlight room, toasting the retirement of a colleague whose thirty-eight Ford years had ended tonight. The night shift—known here as the first shift, in recognition of midnight's delivery of a new date—was taking over, ready to, as shift manager Bruce Toburen said, "tear the guts out of the plant and put it back together again" before morning.

Toburen sat at the head of a horseshoe-shaped array of long tables in a neighboring conference room, presiding over the changing of the guard. Sitting on his left were the departing third-shift managers, facing, on his right, their arriving first-shift counterparts, twenty men in all, a gathering that, except for the hour, might have been a Rotary luncheon. Toburen, tall and thin with a rolling bass voice, sipped from a green Ford coffee cup. Windowless walls and a drop ceiling sealed the room off from the rest of the plant, but a low rumble slipped in whenever somebody opened the door.

"Ten Assembly was down for half the shift. The seal on the manifold was sorta burned up."

"Twelve Line was down the first two hours on the shift, but after that it started running and it ran pretty good."

"Seven Line is okay, but I'd like automation to take a look at the bottom sprocket on the exit line."

"The feed units gotta be moved north about two feet."

The start-up meeting proceeded with little small talk. The third shift reported on their designated areas, each man leaving after his hand-off, as the first shift asked terse questions and took notes on what needed doing. The American automakers do not, for the most part, make vehicles through the night: Days and evenings are for production, nights for maintenance. Companies have pushed for round-the-clock production—General Motors boosted production by as much as 50 percent at several European plants by using three shifts—but the United Auto Workers union has generally opposed such plans, fearing cuts in overtime pay and the possibility of job losses due to plant consolidation. Days and evenings Walton Hills turned raw steel into pieces of Thunderbirds, Escorts, Cougars, LTDs, Tauruses, Topazes, Sables, Lincolns and other models; nights, it took a look at 7 Line, 12 Line, 10 Line and all the other lines, preparing them for the next day's orders. Toburen lit a cigarette.

"Seventeen Line ran very well tonight. I want to thank you guys for correcting the oil leak. You did a good job. The operators are tickled to death."

"Twenty-three Line is okay for morning."

"Twenty-four is okay for A.M. production."

If, by the A.M., all the lines were okay for production, then Walton Hills' first shift had done its part toward helping Ford—the world's second-largest automaker, after GM—keep up with the Japanese. The parts produced at Walton Hills today were bound for the 6.4 million vehicles Ford would build this year, when its share of the domestic market was higher, at 24.5 percent, than it had been in a decade, but lower than the collective Japanese share, 26 percent, their highest yet.

The meeting over, Toburen walked the plant, the black wood blocks that paved its floor cushioning his steps and deadening what was left of the factory din. On one side of the two million square feet, at the start of the lines, were coils of steel, the end of the LTV line; on the other side were racks of finished parts, waiting to be loaded into the empty boxcars that rolled right inside the plant and that would deliver them to Ford's assembly plants; and in the middle were the now-silent machines, simple as cookie cutters in concept but tectonic in force, that transformed the one into the other. "I don't mind it, but I don't prefer it," Toburen, thirty-five and a second-generation Ford employee, said of the shift. "I like being my own boss. I call all the shots on the shift. I take full responsibility for the whole operation, and that means I also take full responsibility when something goes wrong. Between three and five, when things start gearing up, that's when the tension and stress start to get to you."

An overhead crane, cruising above Line 23 faster than a person walks, carried one of the dies that needed changing tonight. Most dies—the jagged metal blocks, the size and weight of glacial boulders, that stamped the steel into shape—traveled by night here: A pressing line that today made left-inner-quarter panels for Topazes might tomorrow be needed to make right-inner-quarter panels, so it was the first shift's job to remove the old dies and install the new. The crane stopped over Milford Douthett, who stood by the line's first press. Following his signals, it lowered the die toward his guiding touch. He brushed off its bottom with his hand, then nudged it into position, pushing from the side, as its descent continued, not letting go until it had finally settled into place. "Okay, that's it," he said, and he unwrapped the chains.

Of Ford's 170,000 American employees, 18,000 were in the Cleveland area, which the company referred to as its "second city," 2,400 of them at Walton Hills, and 300 of those on the first shift—half because they didn't have enough seniority to get off it, and half, like Douthett, because they had enough seniority to stay. He started with Ford in 1954, became a die-setter the next year, and went on the night shift to stay in 1961. "One thing about it is the quietness. You can go in, do your job, and there aren't too many people around to bother you." It also gave him time with his five children. "I was free during the day to take the kids different places. I'd sleep while they were in school, then pick them up after school. They were all involved in sports and things like that." He turned a key on the press, tall as a two-story house, that dropped the ram onto the die, then bolted the two together, turning the nuts with a forearm-long wrench. "When you're pulling on the wrench and handling the chains, your upper torso really takes a beating. It gets you in your shoulders and back."

A stripped thread on one bolt was giving his partner some trouble. "How you making out?" Douthett asked. He took the bolt to the grinding wheel, walking the line at almost crane-speed ("I don't smoke or drink, I do a lot of walking, and I pull on the wrench"), and ground it down to good thread. He wore gray-green coveralls and a black Walton Hills baseball cap. "That took care of it," he said, twisting a nut on it. He secured the bolt, both hands on the wrench, the die now set. "When you're torqueing these bolts on, you can't get it too tight." He knocked the nut lightly with his wrench. "It's a little thing. I just give them a tap, but if they don't move, then you know they're tight."

After the dies were set, the automation crew took over, resetting the electronic machinery that moved the steel through the pressing lines. Line 10, yesterday the birthplace of Cougar deck lids, would tomorrow be making Sable deck lids, so tonight Jim Burke took out a wrench, much smaller than Douthett's, to adjust its automated equipment accordingly. "The new die is lower than the die coming out, so we have to change the dip balance," he said. He was working on the loader—an armlike device that slid the steel blanks under the die like a waitress sliding a breakfast plate onto your table—trying to figure out why its aim was off. He used hand signals to communicate with his partner, who stood at the control panel, until they got the plates onto the table smoothly: "One of the limits was set the wrong way on the carriage." They watched the outline of a Sable deck lid appear as the die rammed down on a steel blank the loader had properly loaded, then moved on down the line to the next piece of automation. Burke had, by choice like Douthett, worked nights twenty of his twenty-four Ford years. "When you get tired enough, you can sleep anytime."

By morning the first shift, each worker earning a 10 percent differential over the average fifteen-dollar-an-hour wage had changed forty-four dies, adjusted the automated equipment and gotten it out of the aisles and back in the lines, and handed over a factory ready to start stamping the parts that would collect again tomorrow by the boxcars. The next night they would be back to do it all again: There were 24 major pressing lines, some of which needed changing every other night, and 800 dies to choose from. "The night goes by like that," Bruce Toburen said, and he snapped his fingers.

As the evening faded toward night in Newark, Ohio, the lights in the houses along Hudson Avenue—rooted brick and wood-frame homes, the century's biography written in their familiar architecture—ascended toward heaven. The windows darkened first on the first floors, the TV and company floors. The lights then reappeared in the windows on the second floors, the bedroom floors up the stairs, where they oversaw the good-night routines that ended the day before they, too, retired, leaving the eye outside to follow the light up through the streetlamps, up past the tree canopy of green spring buds that overarched the silent street, up toward the stars. In downtown Newark, Main Street was doubly wide, the generous space allotted for angle parking now unparked-in, as it led toward, and then respectfully detoured around, the green civic square where the county courthouse presided among stately trees, tulips, a fountain and a gazebo. The courthouse's tall, narrow windows were dark, but the lights had risen to showcase its clock tower. Back by Hudson Avenue, a few streets behind and across the railroad tracks, lights traced the tangled outline of a tan factory, a signal, along with the slightly sweet toasting smell, that Owens-Corning was, as it did round-every-clock, making Fiberglas.

Owens-Corning, Newark's signature industry, kept the city's metabolism, as well as its economy, running straight through the night. Although it was small, its population just over forty thousand, Newark was proportionately more nocturnal than many cities many times its size. Night workers here were neighbors to sleepers, not exiles isolated in an industrial pocket like Cleveland's Flats. The shift-work lifestyle was a common burden, a tradition even, shared by thousands of families, not a suspect aberration. But if the night fell lighter within the town limits, it pressed heavier just outside: Newark, thirty miles east of Columbus, was surrounded by farmland, not a tiara of suburbs, and the unlit fields merged at night with the shrouding sky.

The night shift descended the stairs to the shop floor at Owens-Corning like sailors disembarking a ship. Blue jeans and flannel shirts were the predominant uniform. Tom Fisher, the shift supervisor, stood at the foot of the stairs, checking them in on his clipboard—125 people worked here in the wool plant, the factory's heart, where the Fiberglas was actually made, and 125 more were scattered elsewhere—and dispatching those without fixed assignments to their posts for the night. "I've got everybody but one in," he said at 10:30, the shift's start, and then the one showed up.

"I gotta work, Tom," the last straggler slurred loudly. He staggered unsteadily, a burly bearded man who had apparently forgotten that he was not free to celebrate this Saturday night, just another worknight for him, in a traditional Saturday-night fashion. "I gotta work," he said again, though he could barely walk. Fisher sent someone to take him home. "If it happens again, I'll suspend him."

Ohio, maybe better than any other state, depicts the nation in miniature—both rural and urban, agricultural and industrial, black and white, between east and west and bordering the south—and Newark was a microcosm of Ohio. Named for the hometown of its first settlers, the larger and more familiar Newark in New Jersey, it was the starting point in 1825 for construction of the Ohio-Erie Canal, which led north to Lake Erie via the Cuyahoga and Cleveland, south to the Ohio River, and which opened the state's interior to industry and trade. It was now the county seat, was still a farm trade center, and it had retained the manufacturing base that kept it from becoming a ghost town when the railroads killed the canals. Owens-Corning originally made glass bottles in Newark, later switching to Fiberglas, a product it invented, trademarked and capitalized, and despite some recent troubles it remained a shaping force in the region's economy. Many local homes were insulated with scrap Fiberglas the company had sold to its employees.

Glass, whether it ends up as Coke bottles or as the tiny fibers that comprise Fiberglas, starts out as molten, primordial soup, and the ovens that cook this soup, too hot to turn off at day's end, are what keep glass plants up through the night. About half of all glass workers work late shifts, one of the highest industry-wide percentages, slightly higher even than steel. Four ovens were cooking tonight, brick hearths at the starts of the production lines, and to walk nearby was to walk into a July desert. Sand, lime, soda and cullet (scrap glass added to the recipe) were mixed back at the batch house, then cooked here at 2,500 degrees until they became a fiery, bubbling liquid: Peering into a hot oven, preferably through sunglasses, was like peering down the lava throat of a volcano.

The cooks who tended the ovens here were spared the intense heat, watching from a small, dim, cool control room, sealed away from the factory innards like a space capsule; banks of computers translated oven activity into red and green and yellow blinking lights. "When it's a hundred forty degrees there," furnace operator Mike Idleman said, "and it feels like it could burn the hair out of your nose, it's seventy in here." The control room's relative comfort didn't make the night any more inviting to Idleman, who visited these hours, on a rotating shift, more often than he would have liked. "I hate them with a passion, even if I get a ton of sleep," he said of midnights. "I get grouchy and grumpy on the day before midnights. I start getting depressed, my whole mood changes. We have four days off before midnights, and if the first night is Wednesday, by Tuesday night I'm an S.O.B." The glass cooked steadily, as had his dinner. He spooned from an open can of Campbell's Chunky Beef soup, heated by setting it near a furnace—"a West Virginia microwave," he called it, a playful reference in which the neighboring state figured the way Poland does in a Polish joke. "You have to find a spot that's just hot enough, but not hot enough to blow it up."

On the other side of the furnace Pete Peterson's post was more like the narrow, gray bridge of a battleship. He watched through his window the enginelike room, the forehearth, where the molten glass, pouring down from the furnace through a single row of holes, was fiberized—pouring, thick and syrupy and shaped like glowing wineglass stems, into small buckets that swung back and forth like a line of clock pendulums; spun out from the buckets as tiny glass fibers; sprayed, as they fell, with a blizzard of foamy white binder squirted from hoses set along the rim of a rectangular pit; dropping into the pit, Fiberglas now, held down by sucking fans, the headwaters of a snowy Fiberglas river. A snowball had accumulated on one of the binder hoses. Peterson inserted his earplugs and went out into the thunder—so loud that, he said, he had lost 50 percent of the hearing in his right ear—to blow it off with a steam gun. "Right now the buckets are going just about right," he said. Earlier they had been swinging too far north, making the Fiberglas minutely lopsided, but his most recent fiber check, one of four he did each shift, confirmed that his adjustments had evened it back out. Peterson—tall and thin, with a graying goatee, a union cap and twenty-seven years' service—disliked midnights as much as Idleman did. "All day long you know you gotta come in." The light glared against the inside window, so he sat and watched in the dark, focusing on the blinding stream of liquid glass less than he would have had he not left his sunglasses in his car tonight. His radio was quiet. "The guy I work with," he said, referring to the operator at the other end of the room, "doesn't like country and western. He likes rock 'n' roll."

The river changed color after it left Peterson, baked at 550 degrees in a curing oven that made it look like a scratchy, tawny wool blanket of the sort found in cheap motels. The Fiberglass, like steel, was shaped according to customer demand. As it flowed down the conveyor belt, it was trimmed to its desired width and chopped to its desired length, a guillotine blade dropping at variable intervals, controlled by computer-programmed orders; binder formulas were changed back at the forehearth, too, depending on the desired consistency. The river, the D-5 line, ran smooth and swift tonight—making headliners for car roofs for a time, then switching, without breaking the flow, to insulation for cooking ranges. A neighboring line that made a more visible product, rolls of fluffy pink home insulation, ran less evenly, dammed up occasionally by a balky new bagging machine: Operators rushed to toss aside the backed-up pink slabs, building cotton-candy hills around themselves, until the bagger could be unjammed.

At the end of D-5, the river's delta, Steve Crumrine widened the guide rails by an inch and a half to accommodate the wider Fiberglas sheets of a new job. The last job had produced 57 rolls in 24 minutes; the next would take, according to the night's job sheet, 1.1 hours for 156 rolls. "At first I slept a lot, it seemed like all I ever did was sleep," Crumrine said. "Anymore I don't sleep as much, and I feel better. I have a pretty understanding wife." Larry King and four cups of coffee helped get him through the night—two cups when he first came in, one at his dinner break, and one now, in the 4-to-5 trough. "I try to take it easy for a few minutes, and just close my eyes." He watched the long sheets of Fiberglas wool, traveling at 95 feet per minute, feed into a machine that rolled them up, soft cousins to the coiled steel, and then kicked them out, finished, like hay from a bailer.

Back at the furnace Mike Idleman was heating back up as the night neared its end. "I die between three and five," he said. "I had my Snickers bar and my coffee and it didn't do a damn bit of good. But now I'm metamorphosing back into a human being." Pete Peterson blew off the binder snowballs one last time. Up in an office, a supervisor called off-duty workers at home, trying to fill four empty slots on the next shift. The five lines running tonight—a sixth was silent—had produced 350,000 pounds of Fiberglas. "I would've liked 400,000, that would've been a good night," Tom Fisher said, but the bagger problems had slowed them down. The D-5 line, handed over now in midstream to the next shift, had run well: 60,000 pounds. Outside, a front-end loader shoveled sand that would later leave the plant as glass. Downtown, the clock tower announced a time, dawn on Sunday, that nobody was out to see. Its lights were still on, a remnant of night, waiting for the sun to rise high enough to take over.

At 3:00, in a CHICAGO *shelter, 262 homeless*
guests slept in tight rows of narrow beds, granted
the welcome peace of an undisturbed night.

The evening prayer, shared by fourteen people gathered in a windowless room in a poor and broken part of the city, opened with a song. "The hymn is on page 604, 'Morning Has Broken,' " the young man with the guitar offered. "You can say evening has fallen if you want." They sat, thirteen volunteers and a Franciscan priest, on rec-room couches around a coffee table where a single candle burned, and at 7:15 P.M., the Chicago night nearing, they sang about dawn. "Morning has broken, like the first morning," they sang, "Blackbird has spoken, like the first day." Outside the building, a low brick and cinder-block former mop factory, fifty homeless people were already in line, waiting for the shelter doors to open and offer them refuge from the long passage of night. You could see from here the crown of the Sears Tower, the world's tallest building, rising beyond and above the battered dusk streets of the Near West Side, three miles due east, and a world away, in the downtown Loop. The prayers inside continued.

"Let us pray that the Lord may open the hearts of people to the plight of the homeless," someone said. "Let us remember all of the homeless, especially those who will not find shelter tonight, that they may find a safe place on the streets."

Night is when, if you have a home, you go there, and if you don't, you feel its loss most sharply. All over Chicago, in South Side housing projects and in North Side lakefront apartments, lights were coming up, comforting to those inside, lonesome rebukes to those left outside, alone, with no lights of their own. Chicago had a large homeless population—city officials put it between 25,000 and 35,000, homeless advocates said it topped 40,000—but there was only a small shelter network, about 3,000 beds, the largest collection of them here at the Franciscan House of Mary and Joseph. The respect this shelter had earned since it opened in 1983, amid the rubble lots and boarded-up houses on West Harrison Street, was evident in its façade—a rare unmarked gap in the street's graffiti canvas. Vacancies were rare, especially in winter, when the wind slashed in off Lake Michigan, and as many as 50 people were turned away nightly.

Their prayers dispatched, the volunteers were mustered out with a caution by the shelter's director, the Reverend Jim Hoffman, who had earlier surveyed the line outside. "There's at least five people out there drinking openly," he said, an offense that, according to shelter policy, would bar them from entry. There was more money than usual around—it was shortly after the first of the month, when some pockets still carried the windfall of just-issued government checks—and money often translated into trouble. "They're working on a fifth of Night Train. Be careful. I don't see any of the troublemakers tonight, but it could be a bad one."

Hoffman and three others, armed only with patience and clipboards, went out to let the homeless in. The nightly admissions ritual was an act of faith, and the shelter's tensest hour: four shelter workers trying to control scores of homeless people, many gentle and retiring, but others erratic, potentially violent, with alcohol, drugs and mental illness. There were no guards, no metal detectors, as there were at some shelters, just the judgment of the workers, and the knowledge among the homeless that those who broke the rules—by showing up drunk, for instance—would be denied a bed. The women went first, ushered into their separate dorm chamber inside. The men followed through another door, where they were assigned bed numbers and admitted in groups of fifteen. The regulars, those who got their mail here and whose reserved beds were held open for them until 9:30, arrived sporadically, passing the head of the line like season-ticket holders. Meanwhile, the disorderly were removed from the line.

"Sam, I'm gonna have to ask you to stay away tonight," Hoffman told a heavy man in a black beret who had earlier been working on the Night Train.

"I was telling you, I was just passing it," Sam protested.

"Sam, Sam, Sam." Hoffman shook his head wearily. "Don't argue with me."

"I have to go to work in the morning, I have to."

"You have to go to detox or somewhere else. You cannot come in tonight, nor can you come in the rest of the week." He moved down the line. "Jerome's not coming in here tonight, Jerome's going to detox," he told another man. "Please step out of line so the other men can come in."

"No, no, no," Jerome said.

"Yes, yes, yes. If you don't want to go to detox, you might as well start walking now."

"I'll go to detox," he assented, not too drunk to think he could win this debate, and he joined the six other men waiting for the city detox van. One man practiced karate chops on the air; another addressed himself, speaking a private grammar. A young boy sped down the twilight street on a bicycle; earlier some neighborhood kids had punched a homeless man who had left the line to buy cigarettes at a nearby store. The man in Bed 36 was added to the detox list: He had slipped through undetected and thrown up.

Hoffman met a spirited, apparently sincere denial when he barred a man he thought he had seen drinking from a paper cup of beer earlier. "Father, me no beer," the man insisted in English, his faltering second language. "Me no drink, no, Father. No smoke, no nothing." He continued his defense through a Spanish interpreter, claiming a case of mistaken identity, until Hoffman relented and he was admitted, grateful and sober. A young couple arrived, holding hands, and parted at the door with a good-night kiss, she into the women's dorm, he into the men's. A small radio softly broadcast the NBA play-off game being played just two miles from here in Chicago Stadium: It was late in the fourth quarter, the Chicago Bulls leading the Cleveland Cavaliers by six. "Jordan just missed two in a row," the man holding the radio said. Hoffman benched another man who had been drinking, a small, wiry Mexican in a heavy coat.

"I ain't goin' to no fuckin' detox," he said.

"We don't make you do anything," a volunteer said.

"Kiss my ass, motherfucker. That motherfucker's been drinkin'." He flailed manically, gesturing toward a linemate. "I'll kill you, motherfucker." He pulled a cheap pair of orange-handled scissors from his bag and lunged several times, blades open, threatening and defensive at once, aiming more, it seemed, at the world in general than at anyone here on the street. The shelter staff calmly retreated inside, emerging a few minutes later when the police arrived. The man had simply resheathed his scissors and walked off.

The man with the radio lingered before going in to bed. "He's a middle-class guy, he's not a ghetto guy," he said, arguing with a friend about Michael Jordan's background. He was intent on this point, refusing to concede, because he knew it made all the difference. Jordan hit four clutch free throws in the closing seconds. Chicago won.

By the time the lights went off at 9:35, some of the men were already fast asleep—stretched across their beds, safe at last from the public domain, exercising property rights over their one piece of real estate, however temporary and small. Several had withdrawn from the world entirely, pulling the sheets over their heads like shrouds. The beds were planted in tight, straight rows along the concrete floors of three separate rooms. The women slept on thirty-five beds and a couch in the back corner room. The regulars occupied the other rear dorm, stowing their goods in lockers along the walls and boxes under their assigned beds. The remaining men filled the main hall, sleeping under the high-arched ceiling and the heavy wood beams, reminiscent of railroad bridges, that supported it. The barracks effect of the cavernous, bed-carpeted dorm was relieved by the yard-sale patchwork of the donated sheets and blankets: "Happiness is being one of the gang," the "Peanuts" characters declared on one pillowcase. A banner on the far wall carried a verse from Isiah 49: I WILL NEVER FORGET YOU. UPON THE PALMS OF MY HANDS I HAVE WRITTEN YOUR NAME. At the head of the room, as at the head of a classroom, sat a battered wood desk of the type found in chalky old schools, illuminated by a single naked light bulb, the only light in the room.

Guests approached the shelter worker at the desk with occasional requests—a toothbrush, aspirin, soap, a towel, a wake-up call. (Homeless didn't always mean jobless: Many of the men worked, often at jobs—day-labor agencies, hawking newspapers, for example—that paid less and started earlier than the jobs of people with homes.)

"Put One-fourteen down for a four A.M. wakeup."

"Four-thirty for me."

"I got laid off my regular job and I been working for a roofing company. I gotta meet them at five A.M., so I gotta get waked up."

"I gotta get up at four A.M. and go to work. I'd like to snooze awhile."

"Three A.M. for Bed One-twenty-four."

The sleeping guests rested Hoffman's mind. He was fifty, with thin, graying hair—Father Jim to everyone here—and he had spent eight years as a missionary in Zaire and Uganda before coming, in 1987, to the shelter, where he often shed his clerical collar: Tonight he wore a gold shirt, black pants, sneakers. "There is an element of futility. I personally don't feel that, because I've reached a stage in life where I realized I ain't gonna save anybody. I don't attempt it. I talk from the angle that we have to know what we can do and what we can't do, and what we can do is provide a place for secure sleep, a facility for bathing, a bite to eat in the morning and the evening, and a little space for dignity for each person. If we stick to that, I think we're doing a great thing."

Most of the shelter's resident staff was asleep now, too—under the same roof as the homeless they served, in the small communal apartment they shared in the front corner. Private donations funded the shelter, and volunteer labor ran it. "After spending a week here," Bert Schroeder said, referring to the vacation when he and his wife, Nancy, traded their suburban home for a room at the shelter, "we felt we could not stay in Libertyville with three cars, one for each of us, and an eight-room house. It just wasn't right, after we'd seen what the other half of the people had." They started as weekend volunteers, but "that seemed kind of small," he said, so after their daughter graduated from college and married, they vacated their old life—the house, the cars, the things, the six-figure income, his job as a traffic manager in a factory, her custom-drapery business—and, on Ash Wednesday, moved into the shelter. Their home was now two small, dark rooms, their income dropped to ten dollars a week each, plus board. They planned to stay between three and five years, or until their daughter, who now lived in Seattle, had children, at which time they wanted to move nearer her. "There's something here, there's a spirit and love and commitment that's really hard to put into words," Schroeder said.

Two volunteers were still awake now, one in the women's dorm and another, Ron Otting, at the desk in the main men's dorm, watching over the sleeping crowd. Light spilled from the doorless bathroom on the side, trailed by the echo of the still-running showers; a steady trickle of men passed the desk on their way there, making full and frequent use of a facility that was often to them a luxury. Draped along the frames and over the footboards of many beds were damp socks and underwear, washed in the sinks. The air was close with the locker-room blend of body odor and soap. Rising occasionally from the beds, with shifting volume and tempo, was a chorus of mumbles, sighs, half-formed words, coughs, moans, sneezes, honks, and cartoon, wood-sawing snores; sleep is not silent when multiplied more than a hundred times. Otting left the desk at 11:30 to let in a late arrival, an elderly one-legged man dropped off by the police, and settle him into Bed 52. The man detached his ancient, oarlike prosthesis from his stump and, wordlessly, dropped into sleep. "I've never lived on the streets, and I hope never to live on the streets," Otting said. A Christmas celebration back home with his family in Ohio, heavy with presents and food and happiness, had convinced him that the scales were unbalanced and that he should leave his job as an occupational therapist in Colorado Springs, put his TV and VCR and microwave oven in storage, and at least try to set them right. "I love the work. I love the idea that I'm making a difference in some of these people's lives. But the poverty, the extremely high crime, the exposure to violence, got to me after a while. It's a pain in the ass to get up in the morning and find your car battery stolen and your windows broken. I'm used to being outside. You can't go to the park and relax in the grass and read a book. Sometimes I say to myself, 'I don't need this junk.' I could set myself up in another nice apartment and help only myself. Part of me wishes I could. Part of me is screaming, 'Don't be a fool. Take what you can get and enjoy your own life.' But the more spiritual part of me is arguing that I can't just do for myself, that I have to reach out. In one night here I help make a difference in two hundred lives. It might be just a small difference, but it is a difference."

The desk phone rang at 12:15. "Clarence, where're you at?" Otting asked. "What do you need? . . . Are you coming over? . . . When you gonna be here?"

Clarence arrived soon after with a knock on the heavy door, claiming one of the last empty beds, capping the night's guest list at 262, and closing his daily labors: He worked days as messenger downtown, nights distributing newspapers. "I had a place before Christmas and I had a job," he said, "but the job fell through and I had to give the place up." He had been coming to the shelter for three years because "they let me wash my clothes and look presentable" and few other doors were open to a forty-four-year-old who said he'd spent ten years in prison. "I'd like to be stabilized, but the economy won't let me. They say 'another day, another dollar.' Well, now it's fifty cents." He carried a small, worn green Bible. "Sometimes I sit up at County Hospital and witness there. I don't know how healthy the body is, but the spirit is." He took a towel and soap from Otting and headed for the bathroom. "I take a good-night shower. I gotta wash yesterday off."

The shower stream, after flowing undammed most of the evening, finally dried up when Clarence was clean, and the shelter settled into a brief limbo, just two or three hours long, that was neither yesterday still nor tomorrow yet.

A Day in the Night of America

Jay Griffin, eighteen and fresh to the city from North Dakota, sat at the volunteer desk now, a small high-intensity lamp shining on the book he was reading, *The Hobbit*. He had driven sixteen hours in a van with seven other people from the University of Mary, a small Catholic school in Bismarck where he was a freshman majoring in business and Christian ministry, to spend a week living and working in the shelter.

At 2 he turned on the coffee machine in the kitchen. As 3 approached he scanned the sheet of wake-up requests like a hotel desk clerk. A small statue of Jesus stood atop the fusebox on the wall behind him. "I'm a little nervous about the wake-ups," he said. The six resident volunteers—because they were needed for daytime duties like washing towels and picking up donated food, they were usually absolved of the 1-to-4 desk shift, which was taken instead by outside volunteers—were familiar with all but a few of the guests, and knew where trouble might rise, and who might come flailing up from sleep when awakened, startled and poised to fight; but Griffin, on his first night watch, did not.

He crept with a flashlight through the narrow aisles toward the earliest riser. He tapped the side of the mattress lightly and whispered, "It's three o'clock." The man woke gently, silently, then lay there briefly, eyes open, still, taking in the dark world he had returned to before getting up to prepare himself for it. His shower opened the morning bathroom stream that would run almost unbroken from now through dawn. Every half hour, then every quarter hour, a new round of guests was awakened, first by Griffin and then by Larry O'Toole, the resident volunteer who relieved him at 4. Each man had a reason, generally minimum-wage-or-less, for leaving while night was yet in the city.

"I do papers on Ohio."

"I'm goin' to work folding clothes at the Laundromat."

"I push boxes from one side to the other at McCormick Place, setting up a trade show. By noon your tongue's hangin' out."

"The papers'll go good today. It's Thursday, the food coupons are in 'em." A good day selling newspapers might bring twenty-five dollars; an average day, fifteen dollars.

"I'm getting five dollars an hour to picket in Hofmann Estates. They can't afford to picket themselves, so we wear their signs."

O'Toole's desk reading was *Utopia*, Thomas More's sixteenth-century vision of an ideal state where reason reigned and where poverty and its companion evils were strangers. "It's a common struggle: We provide a bed and a meal, but really, what more are we doing? Sometimes I wonder if

Kevin Coyne

we're being irresponsible by not pushing more, by not saying, 'You have to find a job, you have to find a place of your own,' that sort of thing. I struggle with that, and I wonder what I'm doing here.'' The problems here, he found, did not yield to easy answers—alcohol and drug addictions beyond the reach of the most sympathetic ear; mental instability magnified by the stress of life on the streets; an economy with little room for unskilled workers and ex-convicts. "It's not something anybody would choose if they had a choice," he said of the homeless life. "My sense is we're living off a lot of past sins of society that are not solved easily." He was just a few years out of Notre Dame, and he often took this early shift because his other job, teaching English to seventh- and eighth-graders at a parochial school in a Mexican parish, got him up early anyway. He set *Utopia* aside and went to wake the next group of men. "Look at these peaceful faces. They were a mother's son."

The morning light eased through the small, high windows after 6, a natural reveille rousing the remaining sleepers. O'Toole was its human counterpart. "Five minutes," he announced as he patrolled the aisles. "It's six twenty-five now." A man asked him if there might be an extra belt among the donated clothes. "I don't want to get up and shake hands and my pants don't get up with me," the man offered. He was grateful for the bit-too-long belt O'Toole found. "Perfect fit. I can always punch another hole in it."

West Harrison Street ran due east from the shelter toward the Loop— the downtown herd of skyscrapers, roped in by a circuit of elevated tracks, that looms over Chicago the way Chicago looms over the Midwest—but first it had to cross through a wide thicket where the city's biggest hospitals were silently gathered. It passed directly under the tall Corinthian columns that marked the entrance of Cook County Hospital and that recalled an age when architecture embodied the grand goals, both medical and social, of a public hospital. The columns were dark with city soot now, and many of the beds in the blocky, gray-white brick piles had been emptied, but Cook County, open nearly as long as the century, still served 34,000 patients a year, many of them among the city's poorest and sickest. Just a few blocks away, also on West Harrison, was the Cook County morgue—not the old morgue, which once held the bodies of John Dillinger and the victims of the St. Valentine's Day Massacre, but the sleek new one that was the destination of those who had traveled beyond the reach of the neighboring hospitals.

Just after 11 P.M., in a nursing administration office on the second floor of Cook County Hospital, Barbara Capdeville sat alone and worked the phone, sometimes three lines at a time, marshaling the night nurses for the campaign to keep the sickest patients alive until morning. "His condition is very critical? What's his diagnosis? . . . She's very critical, too? A diagnosis of dual hematoma? . . . Why'd they bring the patient to trauma? I thought he was coming directly to you. Is he on a ventilator? . . . Okay, what's her diagnosis? Is she having chest pains or what? . . . The monitor you want is in SICU. . . . What's your census up there? . . . I have no help to give you. If I can find another nurse, I'll send her to you, but I'm not promising." Her conversations reached across three buildings into the scattered units she watched over as night supervisor of critical care nursing: trauma, burns, medical intensive care, surgical intensive care, neurosurgery intensive care—a total tonight of forty-one nurses and sixty-four patients. Shift changes are a vulnerable time for a hospital—mistakes in patient care (missed medications, unnoticed equipment failures, unattended patients, accidental falls and other, sometimes life-threatening, lapses) peak between midnight and one—and her calls were meant to ensure a smooth transfer of power. "They have any DNRs up there?" she asked, referring to the "Do Not Resuscitate" order assigned, with consent, to those patients for whom medicine has no more answers. "You have a suicide in front? How bad is he? Has psychiatry seen him yet? . . . You said six units of platelets? No blood? . . . Wow, I thought my name was bad. What's his first name? Spell that, too. Does he speak English? . . . I'm sorry to do this to you, but I need her to go to Three Unit East. They have real problems there. . . . Who died? Oh, she died? What time? Okay, just do the best you can. You have to take care of the living people first."

Though hospital days are heavy with tests and meals and visitors and X rays and doctors' rounds and elective surgery and meetings on health-care policy and other scheduled medical business, hospital nights are left to a more elemental battle against death. The night nurses' mission was split roughly between watching and waiting. The watching staff, dispersed through the darkened and mercifully sleeping floors, maintained order, watching those patients whose faltering bodies couldn't be completely trusted to carry their occupants' souls safe into the next morning. The waiting staff, armed with blood and oxygen and machines that can wrestle lives back over the line, attacked chaos, waiting for, and hoping not to see, the victims of a gang skirmish, or a plane's collision with the Sears Tower, or a three-car crunch on the Dan Ryan Expressway, or a domestic argument that ended with a knife pulled from a kitchen drawer.

Cook County Hospital sat just south of the central border that, in the crude shorthand of Chicago's racial geography, divided the largely white North Side from the largely black South Side, the largest black neighborhood in America. It ministered to a mostly poor clientele—the 1.5 million people (from a total population of 5.2 million in Cook County, which encompasses the city and its inner suburbs) whose health insurance was either Medicaid or pure faith, and were thereby shunned by the brighter, newer hospitals. "They send us the patients they don't want," a nurse here told *Look* magazine twenty years ago, and the ensuing decades only magnified her complaint. The burden on Cook County, the worn flagship of a public health-care system in Chicago that spent more than one billion dollars a year, had since been swelled by AIDS, crack, the battlefield wounds from the streets, the closing of several trauma units in the city and the shutdown of several other entire hospitals; keeping its accreditation had cost $115 million in renovations over the last ten years. Local leaders were studying ways to overhaul the system, but in the interim the hallways were still clotted with waiting patients stretched out on their gurneys.

Capdeville finished her phone rounds and then set out to cover the same territory by foot. She wore a white hospital jacket over a pink sweater and black skirt, a more stylish uniform than the green scrubs she'd donned for fifteen years as a nurse in the trauma unit. "You can't imagine," she said of the things she saw there. "Somebody whose whole blood volume is on the floor. You open their chest and all their blood pours out from one great big clot, just pouring out. People with their faces blown off by shotguns. Somebody with one eye hanging out and the other blown away. Somebody whose face was smashed by an elevator coming up in a housing project. People say, 'Oooh, how do you work with all that blood?' My own philosophy is that God put me on earth for a reason. My reason is helping people, and my best way is as an emergency-room nurse. I missed it at first"—she had left trauma for the supervisor's job more than a year before—"but I was long overdue when I got out. Any time I want hands-on experience again, I can go up there, put scrubs on and work with the staff." She was a single mother with three children at home, a part-time job as a private-duty nurse and a talent for getting by with just four and a half hours of sleep daily. "When I'm up and walking around, it's okay. When I sit down to do paperwork at four, it's hard. That's why I do the paperwork first."

She passed through the emergency room, where the waiting crowd—sitting silently, slipped down asleep in the bright plastic seats, gathered before a lone TV—suggested a bus station. The most serious emergencies were directed to trauma, often leaving the emergency room to function as a family doctor for those poor families without one. "I can't run anywhere, officer," a young prisoner told the cop who was guarding him. "There's something wrong with my ankle." Up in the medical intensive care unit, the night's first casualty, a woman in her sixties with respiratory disease, lay covered by a sheet in the bed where she had died just an hour before.

Capdeville had no reason to expect that her shift would see any more deaths than the day shift. Death and night, it is often thought, are old companions—murderers, demons, car wrecks, "he died in his sleep"—but explicit evidence of their relationship is elusive. The National Center for Health Statistics didn't have any statistics on deaths by time of day. The Cook County morgue down the block did seem to notice more bodies arriving at night, but that could have more to do with the kind of cases it handled—violent and accidental deaths of all varieties, and unexplained natural deaths—than with death's daily schedule. Heart attacks peak not at night but in the morning, between 6 A.M. and 9 A.M., seemingly corroborating the ancient belief that sleepers will die if not wakened slowly, their night-wandering souls stranded, unable to return to their bodies in time. And the origin of a term often applied to these hours, "the graveyard shift," is less ghoulish than you might think: It was originally used to describe the graveyard silence of the midnight-to-4 watch on a ship.

"Her vital signs are fluctuating," a nurse told Capdeville about a young woman with Hodgkin's lymphoma. "We've gotta watch her close. It's not good." The monitors hooked to the living patients illustrated the effects of, among other ills, AIDS, strokes, cardiovascular disease and pneumonia. The neck of a man in surgical intensive care bulged with a tumor like a stopped garden hose. A tube emerged from the top of the head of a man in neurosurgery intensive care, the hematoma in his brain the result of an unnatural encounter with a lead pipe. A nearby bed was home to a man delivered into a coma, two months old now and running, by a gunshot wound to the head. A nurse answered the phone. "How are you related?"

she asked. "He just came from surgery. He just started to wake up. He's breathing with the machine. You'll have to get in touch with the doctor, but the doctor's doing another surgery now."

Crossing between buildings took Capdeville down through a subterranean tunnel in the hospital's bowels, as empty as a 4 A.M. subway platform and as threatening. "I don't like going through here. There are a lot of places somebody could grab you." Warm steam pipes followed her, hissing malevolently. A rumbling around the corner turned into a convoy of linen carts. She came up into the burn unit, donning mask, cap and gown before going in among patients whose skin was a tenuous barrier against infection. A seventeen-month-old girl sat up in a crib, her eyes spookily wide and silent, her head swaddled in white bandages that doubled its size. Bandages also covered her chest and stomach. "She wakes up every ten minutes and screams," the nurse, Maureen Moriarty, said. The girl had been scalded by hot water. Moriarty stroked her arm lightly and made comforting sounds in the universal language of toddlers. "My Spanish isn't baby Spanish, but she likes people touching her." Across the hall, where pediatric burn patients convalesced, another nurse watched over six sleeping children, ghostly in the still shadows in their white bandages. Night here was a gift, bringing unconsciousness that interrupted the long, slow pain.

Back through the tunnel and up in trauma, Capdeville found evidence of an apparent truce in the city. The floor was clear, the equipment waited along the sidelines, the IVs dangled from the ceiling like assembly-line tools. A doctor slumped asleep in a chair, resting her head against a suction machine. Two other residents curled up asleep on gurneys behind a curtain and found what rest they could on their marathon shift, a traditional rite of passage that has come under mounting criticism in recent years because of concerns about the logic, and safety, of requiring weary young doctors to make life-and-death judgments. The only people awake were two nurses, Natalie Wry and Marge Purdy, who knew that truces here lasted about as long as they did in Lebanon. "The night shift is where all the action is," Wray said. "If you want to learn trauma, this is the time to be here. We've seen things here that people just read about in books. We're up to our ankles in blood sometimes. We get blood in our ears, in our hair. People throw up in our faces. Somebody's artery is cut and it squirts like a hose all over. We've gone home saturated with blood, in our mouths, our noses."

Trauma is what happens when a hostile world collides with the body,

jarring, tearing, breaking and otherwise disrupting its fragile package, sometimes even exposing it the way an earthquake exposes the framework and
plumbing and electricity of a jolted house. Trauma—car accidents, murders, burns, falls, and so forth—kills 140,000 Americans a year and is the
leading cause of death for people under forty-four. Gunshot wounds were
the most common injury here; it was to a similar inner-city hospital, Martin
Luther King, Jr./Drew Medical Center in Los Angeles, that the army sent
its surgeons for combat training. Stabbings were next, followed by blunt
trauma (e.g., somebody beaten to a pulp with a baseball bat). In the
attached twelve-bed intensive care unit four other nurses tended a glossary
of trauma patients: a man left paraplegic by a bullet that bisected his spinal
cord; a woman whose seatbelt broke in a car accident; a severely beaten
woman; a man with a long psychiatric history who had jumped from a
second-story window and who was now under a suicide watch, sedated and
secured in full-length restraints; a woman stabbed under the sternum by her
boyfriend; a man, shot and stabbed previously, on his third visit, this time
with another gunshot wound. "Trauma is often a recurring disease," Wray
said. "These people need to change their life-style. They need to change
their friends. We see them and we see them and then we finally see them
and they're dead."

Another gunshot victim arrived at 4:25, a young man with blood leaking
from a gauze bandage on his upper left chest. A private hospital had
summarily patched him and then, because he was uninsured, shipped him
here: The average trauma-patient bill nationally this year was $13,000, and
hospitals lost an average of $5,000 on each, a sum private hospitals weren't
eager to swallow. He was twenty-one, unemployed, and his wound was
somehow related to—he was vague about the details—his membership in
the Vice Lords, one of Chicago's major gangs. Wray hooked him to a heart
monitor and an IV. "Are you allergic?" she asked him, one of a series of
diagnostic questions.

"I'm allergic to needles," he said. His face alternated between the
badge-of-honor grin, cocky and relieved at once, of somebody who has
survived a glimpse of death—a few inches south and the bullet would have
pierced his heart—and the pained grimace of somebody who, though
reprieved, still hurt when he moved.

"Use any drugs?"

"I smoke marijuana, drink beer," he said. "I'm not gay either. You don't
have to test me for that shit."

Wray asked his height (6 feet), weight (150 pounds) and the phone number of his nearest relative, which he had trouble remembering. "Do you know what place this is?" she asked.

"Cook County Hospital."

"What time is it?"

He glanced up at the wall. "Four thirty-one."

"You're smart enough to look at the clock."

At the neighboring gurney Marge Purdy kept company an old man waiting to be taken up for surgery on his spinal-cord compression fracture. He also had leukemia. "Any family?" she asked.

"No, my family all passed away. That's the reason I live at the nursing home." He looked up at the ceiling as he talked.

"Any children?"

"No, I never got married. I got drafted in the U.S. Army when I was twenty."

"And the ladies never got you."

"I bummed around my whole life."

As the old man talked, the young man, on Wray's orders, removed his high-top Nikes and modestly peeled off his black jeans. "Take it all off, shorts, too," she told him.

"Oh, man," he said, giggling boyishly. Using the sheet as a shield, he dropped his blue shorts to the floor at the foot of the gurney. The doctor who had dozed against the suction machine worked on him. The small-caliber bullet had passed cleanly through his chest, just above his clavicle—come and gone and presumably lying on the street somewhere now—but there was some concern about the potential for hemorrhaging: It might have damaged the main blood vessels off the heart. Wray explained to him about the angiogram that would test for vascular damage, a procedure that involved inserting a catheter into the femoral artery in the groin—and that seemed to venture uncomfortably close to vital turf. "You're gonna put a what in my where?" he asked.

The two nurses took a lunch break at 5:30 in a dim room behind intensive care—avocado salad for Wray, chicken noodle soup for Purdy. "It's easy to detach yourself and be businesslike with adults," Wray said. "The children are the hardest. It's difficult to get IVs in them, their veins are so small, and when they die, people get real upset. I think you feel bad because it makes you think about your own kids. It's real hard to put that aside." Two young teens shot on a street corner had been brought in the night before: One died there, the other was brain dead, though his heart was still beating. "They were so young and healthy, and it's all over before it's begun. They never had a chance."

"You really gain an appreciation for what you have," Purdy said, "when you look into a mother's eyes who has just seen her fourteen-year-old son dead."

The two patients waited side-by-side now on their gurneys—the young man for the vascular doctor and the dreaded angiogram, the old man for a vacancy in one of the three operating rooms that had been occupied all night. The old man waited alone. The young man joked with his friend and his girlfriend, who wore a Pirates cap and who was so hugely pregnant that it seemed she should be a patient, too. "He's gonna do all right," Wray said in an aside. "Then he'll go out and sin again."

Back up in the administration office Capdeville reviewed the night's toll: A second patient had died, but three babies had been born, leaving the hospital with a net gain of one. "They sleep good at night," another supervisor, Lucinda Glover, said of the daytime administrators, "so we must be doing a good job." Out on the car radio, 1450 on the AM dial still belonged, as it had since 10 the previous evening, to WVON, a popular black talk station; WCEV, a Polish-language station with a heavy polka playlist, would reclaim the spot for nine hours at 1 P.M.. The talk this morning was about gang violence, the source of last night's wound to the young man in Trauma. By the end of the year twenty-eight people on the West Side would be less lucky than he was—dead, victims of gangs. By the end of the year the Chicago Housing Authority had set up the Midnight Basketball League for young men, eighteen to twenty-five, in two West Side public housing projects, among the city's toughest—a program aimed at converting their energy into athletics in a gym during the hours 10 P.M. to 2 A.M., when it might otherwise be spent in crime on the streets. By the end of the year a bullet-wounded chest could have healed enough that it would no longer hinder a jumpshot.

The call arrived before midnight and stayed well into the next day—from a depressed college freshman in Idaho to a young hot-line volunteer in an unmarked storefront office near Wrigley Field on Chicago's North Side.

"I can tell you right now, things aren't gonna get better with your attitude," the volunteer, a college student herself, told the freshman. She sat at a folding lunchroom table, one of four arranged in a loose square. "The feeling that life is not worth living has taken over your life."

Several other volunteers, talking to several other callers, sat around her, all facing the empty center of the square, where neither their separate conversations nor their distant eyes converged.

"You ran away three months ago? Where have you been living? . . . Your parents don't know where you are? . . . You don't have parents? Who were you living with before?"

"You're saying that killing yourself is not a way of dealing with your problems."

"I can really hear the real desperation in your voice. How come you think she doesn't trust you? . . . How come she thinks you're wild? . . . Are your friends wild?"

An ambulance rushed by out on North Lincoln Avenue, its red lights flashing through the blinds. New phone lines had just been installed here, leaving sawdust and paint flakes and trailing cords on the floor and giving the office the transient look of a campaign headquarters. An antiques shop had occupied this space before Metro-Help, the nonprofit youth services agency that ran the hot line; the only things old here now were the troubles of the callers.

"You hate your dad?"

"You've been living with friends how long? . . . A year?"

"Do I sound like I want to get rid of you?"

Metro-Help started in 1971 as a twenty-four-hour phone-counseling center for Chicago's youth and had since evolved into the National Runaway Switchboard, a hot line open to all children and adolescents, not all of them runaways, who felt desperate and alone in America. Beside each phone was a Yellow Pages–thick computer printout directory, organized geographically, of seven thousand shelters, food banks, counseling centers, medical facilities, local hot lines and other agencies that could help. Before each volunteer were log sheets on which to chart each call—runaway, prerunaway, homeless youth, throwaway (kids who left home by their families' choice, not their own), suicidal, child abuse, sexual assault, alcohol/drug abuse. The phone number was posted in bus stations, shelters and other runaway crossroads, and tonight it had been broadcast nationally on the Fox television network, in a public-service announcement after an episode of *21 Jump Street*. The phones had started ringing right after the show, and the seven lines stayed occupied all evening; when one call finished, it was only a matter of seconds before another one started. (Names and certain identifying details have been changed here to protect the callers' privacy.)

"Basically what you really want to do is find your family. What if they won't take you back?"

"How about calling a shelter to see if we can find out how they might be able to help you? I don't want you to feel like you're alone. It's tough being out on the street."

"You talked about some dreams you had for yourself. Can you share some with me?"

"I'll tell you what I think you did tonight. You knocked on someone's door and started talking. . . . It's hard to reach out, but you really took the first step tonight. You reached out and started talking to somebody. You can reach out further now. You have a plan of action now, and you'll be able to get help face-to-face."

The calls moved westward across the nation with the night—from New York and Baltimore, through Akron and Houston, to Colorado and Oregon. Some volunteers—liners, they were called—held a phone to each ear; two phones let them hear better amid the steady surf. One liner broke between calls to tell a staff supervisor about his last caller. "He's eighteen, he's lived on the street for a year," he said. "Five of them live together, three are working. He works as a messenger. They pool their money. 'We're taking care of the two little guys,' he said. 'We keep them out of prostitution and drugs.' They decided they won't get off the street unless the little guys get off, too. They're not gonna leave them. Some of these kids are so good."

By 12:45 the ninety-minute session with the freshman was winding down. "I'm a night person, too. I hate to get up in the mornings," the liner told her. "But sometimes when you wake up in the morning, it feels better."

All around the clock all around America—a nation with a talk-show compulsion to air its griefs, a fierce loquaciousness unleashed by toll-free numbers, and an addiction to instant attention—hot lines rang with questions about alcohol, AIDS, cocaine, pregnancy, cancer, homosexuality, Alzheimer's disease, sexual abuse, suicide, anorexia, the proper way to baste a turkey, how to get the washing machine out of spin cycle, and other matters great and small, collectively forming a telecommunications safety net, a private and shadow talk-radio network, that ensured everyone within reach of a phone a listening ear against their fears. The Runaway Switchboard answered calls from a population that refuted conventional, hopeful notions about the innocent shelter of youth, hearing stories nightly that would be disturbing enough coming from adults but that were doubly so coming from children. "They're always running from something. They don't know what they're running to, they just hope it's something better," said Bob Taylor, the phone room coordinator and one of thirteen paid staffers; at least one staffer was always here, often silently listening on an extension, guiding and encouraging the volunteers. "It's not an adventure. A couple of nights on the street will confirm that very quickly. When you think that's better than home, that's a grim situation." Between 500,000 and one million young people, depending on whose estimates you accept, leave home each year, whether by choice (as runaways) or by force (as throwaways), and what they find out there is not some Tom Sawyer river dream but a dark, unwelcoming world. Between 68,000 and 250,000 of them were homeless on any given night. Between 100 and 150 youths—a number that excluded hang-ups and cranks and heavy breathers—called here each day, the volume regulated in part by time of day (it peaked in the evening, when runaways realized they were without a place to sleep that night), season (winter was busiest), and the geography of rainfall (wet nights meant more calls). "You can almost track the weather patterns by the calls," Taylor said. "It's not raining in Chicago, but it may be raining in the East."

By 1:30 the pizzas had been eaten, the volunteers had gone—most of the 150 were, understandably, unenthusiastic about the late-late shift—and the night was entering its darkest phase. "You get kids who have been up for a while, who really are serious about doing some harm to themselves," executive director Laura Thomas said. Suicide calls, complex and intense, can run for hours, far longer than the hot-line average of twenty minutes. "People here have never heard a gunshot. But callers have hung up abruptly, so you really never know." Two staffers handled the phones now.

"You're seeing a light?" Simcha Willick asked a young girl calling from a California hospital bed. He wore a gray pinstripe suit and looked a little like Richard Dreyfuss. He worked days here as program director, but occasionally took a late turn on the lines to hear the voices the program served. "This is not like a light in the ceiling? This light you're seeing is sort of like a passageway into the next world? . . . How's it make you feel, this bright light? . . . You feel like you want to go toward it but it makes you feel sad? . . . You're scared to make people sad?''

"You're at a friend's house?" Liz Kucera asked a runaway boy in Oregon. She was twenty-eight, the mother of three girls, and she had started here as a volunteer, taking the forty-hour training course, after her brother had committed suicide. "I wanted to help someone else," she said. Instead of burning out after a few months, as many volunteers did, she had become a part-time supervisor. "You're safe until morning? . . . Okay, I'll give you the address of a shelter in Portland."

At 2:30 Willick got exactly the kind of middle-of-the-night-and-nowhere-else-to-turn call the whole hot-line apparatus was set up for—a boy, seventeen, two days off a plane from Cleveland, running from an abusive father, reluctant to spend another night sleeping near a White Castle on Chicago's South Side. "Your father's been hitting you around a lot?" Willick asked. "What about your mom? You don't know her? . . . We'll keep calling around till we find you a safe place to stay tonight."

While Willick called around to youth shelters ("Thomas, it's gonna take a little more time to work it out," he told the boy) Kucera listened to the high-wire chatter of a teenage California girl who had vague thoughts of suicide. "I'm on crank," the girl said, her words racing ahead in fifth gear, lapping her ideas. "I'm a drug addict, I need fucking help. . . . I got a gun under my bed, I'm afraid if I go in my room, I'll blow myself away. . . . Hey, I love being a fucking white supremacist. . . . I'm watching TV, they got a commercial for this British invasion album, twenty-four ninety-five. Wow, you like Cream?"—she sang, tunelessly, the chorus of "Sunshine of Your Love"—"I wrote a song, I'm gonna send it to the Dead Kennedys."

Willick had by now found a bed for the runaway, but the problem of transportation remained. The boy refused to call the police for a ride. "I'm gonna sleep in the park," he said. "I ain't gonna talk to no cop. I don't wanna go back to Cleveland."

"I'd like to get you out of the park tonight," Willick said. "I'd like to get you a warm place to stay and something to eat."

"They throw out doughnuts at the bakery, I can eat some of them," the boy said. Willick offered to set up a conference call with the police. (The Runaway Switchboard could also, acting as a neutral third party, set up conference calls between runaways and their families.)

"I guess this is a bad time to call, three A.M.," the boy said; he had gotten the number at the airport. "But I just got up the nerve now. I got so many doubts in my head. This ain't no life for me."

"Believe it or not," Willick told him, "being out in the cold in a park at three A.M. is an emergency. I don't feel bad calling 911 for you. I'm not gonna tell them where you are, that's my promise." He brought onto the line a patient cop, who assured the boy it was no crime to be alone and far from home.

"You don't go to jail for being a runaway," the cop said.

"Let him know what the procedure will be," Willick said.

"It's up to him, whatever he wants to do. We'll send out a car, drive you to a bed, to food, to counseling. Where're you at?"

The boy, his fears apparently eased, gave the intersection. "I'm behind the gas station, the Amoco."

"Don't worry, nothing's gonna happen to you," the cop said, signing off to dispatch a car.

"I gather you liked what you heard," Willick said, and the boy said he had. "I don't have the answers for your problems. You're at the beginning of a journey. You know what? No one should be abused. No one deserves it. It's your choice how you wanna deal with your dad. . . . But let me ask you something, why Chicago?"

"It's like the melting pot of America. Here comes the cop. Thanks a lot," he said, hanging up and gratefully leaving the street.

"That's magic," Willick said, hanging up, elated, at 3:20. "Any liner will tell you, that kind of call makes their month."

Kucera finished her call soon after—having eased the girl back down to calmer realms of logic, challenged her racist rants against blacks and Jews, excised suicide from the conversation, and extracted a promise that she would, her song for the Dead Kennedys in hand, keep a previously scheduled appointment with a counselor tomorrow. Willick, due back in the morning for his regular hours, went home. Kucera set to tallying the log sheets from the previous day's calls. Two people usually worked this predawn slot, one to answer the trickle of remaining calls and one to do the paperwork, but since Kucera was alone, she shut off the phone. Anybody calling now got a busy signal. She listened to a Sting tape ("I can't do this without Sting") as she sorted the sheets by "type of caller"; one type was number 14, "repeat/problem caller," which included those men who, as they did at every toll-free number, treated the line as a phone sex service. "This one guy kept calling, and I finally said to him, 'You have a Visa card, use it.' " Number 4, "throwaway," was the type that troubled her most. "When I look at a little baby, a little kid, I think, 'How could a mother do that? Doesn't she remember what it was like when they were first born?' Once a kid's been treated like garbage thrown out in an alley, that's how they'll live their lives." Clouds hung low in the sky outside, a condition that in the daytime darkens the world but that at night, paradoxically, subtly brightens it instead, as the lights rise up from the city and reflect off the cloud ceiling like a pale haze. Kucera worked alone until 6, when another staffer arrived to open the phones back up and listen to the kids who, having made it through the night intact, were now having trouble facing the new day.

All through the night in the small mammal house at the Brookfield Zoo outside Chicago, 375 bats—the archetypal nocturnal animal, tagged by superstition as Satan in disguise, transfigured vampires, the ghosts of criminals and the unburied dead—slept undisturbed, hanging like rotten fruit from the ceiling of their brightly lit glass room. The kinkajous were asleep, too, and the owl monkeys, the black-tailed porcupines, the brush-tailed kangaroo rats, the two-toed sloths, the tree shrews, the dwarf lemurs, the spotted cuscus, the armadillos, the sugar gliders, the fennec foxes and the northern grasshopper mice. The display cages were illuminated along the dark hall like department-store show windows on an early winter evening, their false daylight a soporific to the animals inside.

Uncaged, all these creatures would have joined the vast night shift of the wild, shielded from predators by darkness as they searched for food, taking their place beside foraging deer and rabbits, dam-building beavers, migrating birds, swooping owls, spiders weaving webs, fireflies advertising for mates, and whippoorwills calling a song that some people hear as "night-is-here." The outsized, pivoting ears on the fennec foxes would have amplified the sounds that travel farther in the stiller, damper night air. The bats would have patrolled the skies unchallenged—as they have for the fifty million years since they emerged to feed on the banquet of nocturnal insects that had multiplied, unhunted, in the Mesozoic era—locking their Cold War–sharp sonar on their targets. (Humans—though we have no predators to hide from in the dark, except ourselves—are fairly well fitted for the night, too: Our eyes don't have mirrors to magnify the faint available light, as deer's and alligators' do, but once our pupils widen [after about fifteen minutes] and pigment concentrates in our retinas [forty-five minutes] we can see as well in the dark as an owl or a lynx, and better than a rabbit or a whippoorwill.)

But here in the zoo all the night animals were victims of a simple trick: Artificial light flipped their natural schedules to coincide with the diurnal schedules of their human visitors. The humans were mostly unimpressed. The building, one side of which was home to the nocturnal collection, stood just inside the zoo's south gate, but it was among the least popular attractions, far less visited than the bear grottos next door or, just across the wide flowering mall, Tropic World, where gorillas, monkeys, uncaged birds and other tropical species lived in simulated rain forests that produced thunderstorms thrice daily. Bats were a weak box-office draw after that. During the day the shadowy interior, as disorienting a departure from the sun outside as a movie matinee, was so little trafficked that you might easily think you had wandered into a closed area and that a guard would soon whistle you away.

"A lot of people don't give their eyes time to adjust—they think we have bats or something flying around in here," said Rodger Philips, Brookfield's night keeper. Specialized curators worked with the animals during the day, but at night Philips was the zoo's Noah, making rounds among all 425 species, from lions and elephants to snakes and penguins. "It's odd when I come here during the day, and everything's running around. I'm used to them sleeping." He was also used to attending at births, which were more common at night, helping raise babies and aiding the sick. "The best time is at dawn, when everything starts waking up. The elephants trumpet. The lions roar back. If there's a siren in the distance, the wolves start howling. It's kind of a primal thing."

Night fell in the cages just before the zoo opened at 10 A.M. The lights went out just the way they had come on the previous evening at closing time—instantly, with no slow, rising twilight, far faster even than dawn on the equator. The animals also rose as if by switch. Owl monkeys swung from branch to branch. Sugar gliders and kinkajous climbed. Spotted cuscus meandered. Crickets, breakfast here, chirped, making it sound like dusk; a northern grasshopper mouse, after running through its tunnels like a morning jogger, caught one in midair. A flying squirrel leaped across the upper reaches of its cage. A brush-tailed kangaroo rat hopped back and forth, demonstrating the origin of its name. A porcupine rubbed its face, reconnoitered its cage, bristles up, then humped a branch. The bats stretched open their prehistoric wings and soared down in a dense frenzy of flight that resembled a rush-hour highway. Outside, a sharp and sunny morning, visitors streamed past toward the elephants and the bears. The sloths still looked dead. "I don't think the sloths ever wake up," Philips said before going home to do what nocturnal creatures were meant to do in the daylight: sleep.

8

At 3:30, at a remote NEBRASKA *railroad crossing, the engineer on a mile-plus-long freight train blew a whistle that echoed across the deaf and vacant plains.*

The midnight sky over Iowa County, two hundred miles beyond Chicago in the dairying country of southwestern Wisconsin, was busy with thrown stars, astronomical evidence that the farther west you go in America, the farther behind you leave the artificial groundglow of human settlements, the more you see of the heavenly night. Under the sun the landscape here is a mural of children's pastoral drawings—rolling green hills swelling around silos, barns and farmhouses. Under the night, seen from the empty road, it is dark and horizonless as mid-ocean. The earthy, methane aroma of dairy cows surrendered the location of night-cloaked farmsteads. The cows must be milked twice a day every day, no excuses, and the farms would start waking in a few hours, at about 4, to accommodate their tyrannical routine.

The road came in from the fields at Dodgeville, the county seat, where the lights briefly challenged the heavy night. Downtown somebody was buying gas at one of the two open convenience stores, but everywhere else seemed under the spell of the deep collective sleep of a small town. The marquee at the Dodge Theater on Iowa Street, the main drag, was dark, as was the Heartland-Classical façade—yellow limestone, whitewashed wooden Doric columns—of the county courthouse, the state's oldest, across the street. The street signs in front of the courthouse prohibited parking between 1:30 A.M. and 5:30 A.M.; the curbs there were, respectfully, clear. Out on the north edge of town, next to the silos of the feed mill (FARMING IS YOUR BUSINESS, SERVING YOU IS OURS), several dark and immense warehouse-style buildings, out of all scale with the surroundings, rose out of a cornfield, almost invisible against the backdrop of night, and when you turned into the road that led among them, you exited one ZIP code (53533), the one used by Dodgeville's 3,458 citizens, and entered another (53595), the one used by the biggest local business: Lands' End, the catalog retailer.

Unlike the stores along Iowa Street, Lands' End was, as it always is, open for business. "Good evening, Lands' End. This is Rosemary, may I help you?" Rosemary Schaaf—one of seventeen operators on duty soon after midnight in the maze of gray cubicles deep in the main building—asked into the mouthpiece of her headset. Three operators awaited a ring; the rest, like Schaaf, handled customer calls. "What is the item number you'd like to order? . . . The five-pocket jeans for ladies? What size? . . . Fourteen?" Her computer screen said the five-pocket jeans, size 14, were available in the adjacent warehouse, the size of ten football fields, so she completed the order ("Your credit card number, please") and segued ("This is Rosemary . . .") into the next in an all-night string of calls from sleepless shoppers augmenting their wardrobes with pinpoint Oxford shirts, tropical worsted slacks, cotton crew sweaters, mesh-knit shirts, striped X-back swimsuits, stretch cargo shorts, squall jackets, rugby shirts, twill skirts, reversible jackets, Interlochen knit tops, canvas attachés and pages more of other items from the catalog that Lands' End mailed to ten million households, one of every nine in America. Until two years before, when she visited a daughter in Phoenix, Schaaf had never been farther than Rochester, Minnesota; but every night now she traveled by telephone around the nation and beyond. "When I get somebody on the phone, as soon as they start talking, I like to think to myself, 'Ah, they're from where?' "

Lands' End, started as a sailing-supply store in Chicago in 1963, had since evolved into a sort of Corn Belt L.L. Bean. Its move to rural Wisconsin gave it an anticorporate corporate address that embodied its plain-folks merchandising style. Dodgeville was not so remote as the company's name implied—Taliesin, the architect Frank Lloyd Wright's home and studio, was just up the road, and Madison, the state capital and one of America's loveliest university towns, was forty-five miles to the east—but it had helped Lands' End build an image as a national version of a small-town merchant, the kind who knows your first name and who gives you better, more personal service than your local mall. The company's ads often featured employees who rose early to milk their cows before driving to work, and its catalogs, thick with neighborly copy, offered "classic casual clothing" and little else. All through the 1980s the Lands' End formula was retailing gold, racking up annual sales and profit gains as high as 40 percent and landing founder Gary Comer on the covers of national business magazines. The five-pocket jeans Rosemary Schaaf sold contributed to a record sales year in 1989, $545 million, that put Lands' End within striking distance of Bean.

Lands' End—a catalog its show window, a toll-free number its sales counter—was among the hundreds of invisible merchants open all night to anyone with a phone and a credit card. All of these sales operations, from JCPenney to the Home Shopping Network, were awake now for the same reasons—twenty-four-hour service was convenient and reassuring to consumers; their equipment, like a factory's machinery, would otherwise sit idle, earning nothing; that pool of ten million awake-at-3-A.M. Americans was a tempting market; and the irrational power of the Slim Whitman factor was at work, the phenomenon whereby normal people, their defenses wearied by the late hour, start to believe, after seeing yet another TV ad for the Slim Whitman greatest-hits collection, that they can no longer live without it. Operators trickled out toward home as the night lengthened and the calls dwindled—eighty-five had started the evening—until, by 3 A.M., Schaaf and three others waited alone to hear from anybody who might have been browsing through one of the tens of millions catalogs scattered, beckoning, out there in the darkness. "The fishermen's sweater for ladies?" she asked a caller from Fremont, California. The skylight was black above the central atrium the all-but-empty operators' floor overlooked. "Large, in lapis. That would be it? . . . And you want that sent to your law office in Oakland?"

Schaaf had found at Lands' End one of the rare jobs in an early-to-bed county that could accommodate her natural late-to-bed inclinations. "People look at me sometimes and screw up their noses and say, 'Why do you want that shift?' But it couldn't be more perfect. It's like it was made for me. I'd probably have to get kicked off it. I always felt out-of-sync. I'd do housework at midnight, cleaning at one A.M." When her shift ended in the mornings now, she drove home and got her four younger children off to school—four others were in their twenties, grown and moved out—her husband went to his job as a tractor mechanic, she cleaned up the house some and then, "when my head hits the pillow, it knows enough to fall asleep." On the night shift she had learned that Monday nights were the busiest, Fridays the slowest; that nocturnal customers, relaxed, paging through the catalog, often bought more; that not all callers wanted just to talk business ("All she needed was somebody to pour her heart out to," she said of a woman whose son had committed suicide and who spent a grateful half hour on the line); that her sleeping mind was blanker ("I know I did more dreaming when I was on a real schedule, but I haven't dreamed for a long time now"); that driving the dark and lonely road to work could be hazardous ("I just about hit five deer tonight—there was a dip in the road and I saw some movement, it was a good thing I stopped"); and that she had plenty of wakeful company in the midnight world beyond Dodgeville ("For years I stayed at home," she said, "and I'm so happy to be out among people again"). Among the people out tonight was a son in Los Angeles sending a Mother's Day gift back home to Mansfield, Ohio, by way of Dodgeville, Wisconsin.

"I'd like to order a pair of shorts, the striped broadcloth coolers on page sixty-nine, in lemon," he told Schaaf.

"Anything else going to your mom?" she asked.

"Yes, one more thing, on page eighty, the sleeveless polo, in white. That should do it."

"You want that to say 'Happy Mother's Day'?"

"Yeah, 'Love, Tom.' "

The remaining night brought several other Mother's Day orders—to Milwaukee, to Virginia—before settling into near-silence, its usual pattern, between 3 and 4:30. The heavy breathers had taken the night off. "I didn't know there were so many perverts out there," Schaaf said. "The same guy once called fifteen nights in a row. Finally I told him to go soak his head in a bucket. He stopped after that. I don't know if he just needed somebody to tell him to behave himself." At 4:30, "like clockwork," the red light indicating a call started blinking on again occasionally, and at 5 the first of the morning operators started arriving. Schaaf was home by about 7, sixty orders after starting ("They say if you take a dozen calls, you more than pay your way, so I guess I paid my way"), but she was due back here later this morning, when she would usually be sleeping, for a training session on new products. The cubicles would be buzzing then, the atrium would open into a blue sky, the parking lots would look as if every car in Iowa County had convened here. "I'm wide awake now, but when I get in a warm room and I have to sit there, I don't know how I'll do."

Kevin Coyne

The road signs said I was in Iowa, coming up on Nebraska, but the radio said I could be anywhere. Denver, said one station; Louisiana, said another; Dallas, said a third, their signals sailing free across the flat and dark heart-land. I was halfway through the night, in the hour that was too late for yesterday and too soon for tomorrow, and halfway through the nation, in the vast abdomen of the great ungainly beast that America (New England its head, Florida and Texas its forelegs, the Rockies its spine, the West its massive hindquarters) resembles on a map. The long horizon, endlessly retreating in daylight, was hidden by the darkness, and the scattered lights of lone farms blinked like adjunct stars, annexing the land to the sky.

America is built around a sparsely settled, spottily marked, largely unfin-ished middle, much the way the night is, too, and the farther you travel into the heart of both lands—from Wisconsin to to Iowa to Nebraska in Amer-ica, from 2 A.M. to 3 A.M. to 4 A.M. in the night—the plainer view you get of their respective pasts. The nation's history is apparent here in a landscape little changed from the last century: Fields stretch unbroken from horizon to horizon, farmhouses fleck the wide spaces between the small towns, grain elevators rise like timeless classical monuments. The night's history is evi-dent in a heavenscape little changed from the last century: Stars stretch unbroken from horizon to horizon, a remnant of the pre-Edison age when they were familiar companions to earthbound humans who knew them by name and tracked their migrations through the year. The history of the universe is up there, too, because each point of light in the night sky is only a memory: The star it comes from might have died long since. Alpha Centauri, the nearest star to Earth besides the Sun, is 4.3 light-years away; its present light started toward us when Ronald Reagan was president. The light from other stars has been traveling since the Civil War, the Italian Renaissance, the Dark Ages. The Andromeda Nebula, a faint patch that looks to the naked eye like just another star, is actually the ancient light of a neighboring galaxy, two million light-years away, filled with 200 billion stars, twice as many as in our own Milky Way galaxy; when the light we now see from it left for Earth, our human ancestors had not yet learned how to make fire. To look up into the night here is to be an archeologist of astronomy: You can uncover the skeleton of time.

I crossed into Nebraska, the same flat black as Iowa. The land out here was huge and clear, as if an artist, drawing hand cramped from the tight detail work of the eastern foreground, impatient to reach the broad flourishes of the western background, had raced across this middle distance, leaving the canvas covered only with primer. The boxy state borders seemed as arbitrary and superfluous as the hours marked by a clock after midnight, small attempts at measuring a wide and vacant place. Accompanying me across the distance, rumbling along the roadside tracks, was a freight train. It was, when I first caught up with it, just a long shadow tail of cars, and a whistle a mile up ahead. I gained on it slowly, dark car by dark car, until I was abreast of the lead engine. Its headlight far outran mine as we rolled west into the night.

The Hobson Yard, Burlington Northern Railroad's sprawling rail yard on the outskirts of Lincoln, was a dusty web of tracks that all pointed toward the same tall spire on the eastern horizon—the Nebraska state capitol, the "Tower of the Plains," four hundred skyscraper-feet of limestone echoing the shape of the ultimate grain elevator. Locomotives painted Burlington Northern green shuttled among strings of boxcars, coal cars, grain cars, tank cars and flatcars. One engine, Jim Paap at the throttle, rolled slowly toward the west end of the yard, trailing behind it a second engine—*power* or *motor* was actually the preferred term here—and seventeen cars, most of them empty. Paap stopped just before an empty gravel road and put in his earplugs. The train's fireman rode with him in the first cab, a tight cell the pale green color of an old hospital ward; the conductor and the two brakemen were back in the second engine. He blew the whistle—two long blasts, one short, one long—eased the throttle up, crossed the road with a rising diesel rumble and drove southwest out of Lincoln on the fork that led to Denver, rolling toward the sunset and through the first mile of the night's journey. "My six-year-old just loves trains," he said. "We live five miles from the tracks and you can hear the whistle at our house. He always tells me, 'Whistle loud so I can hear you.'"

The train whistle, like a radio signal, drifted far across the open land, where little rose high enough to block it. The trackside wall of greenery grew squatter, eventually falling away entirely, the farther the train got from Lincoln. The capital is a pleasant, shady city, but trees are so few and precious in the rest of the state that Nebraska, alone among all the states, formally celebrates Arbor Day, the tree-planting spring holiday that started here. Paap gave the controls to the fireman and looked ahead through

Kevin Coyne

binoculars toward the signal in the distance. "I can't see it on the curve yet," he said. The signals were easier to read at night, when the red and green lights glowed against a black backdrop.

Railroads are the rivers of the West—carrying floods of goods, coursing unbroken through the dry land and branching off into tributaries, determining settlement patterns—and these cars were the headwaters of a stream that would widen as it flowed west tonight. None of the seventeen cars would be leaving Nebraska: Thirteen were addressed to Fairmont, three to Grafton, and one was going as far as Sutton. The crew's real mission was to assemble a grain train, picking up fifty-four cars of corn in Fairmont and fifty-four more in Halloran, and start it on its way toward the port of Tacoma, and ultimately Russia.

The train slowed to thirty miles per hour when it reached Crete, one of the alphabet towns—Dorchester, Exeter, Fairmont, Grafton, Harvard, Inland, Juanita, Kenesaw and Lowell were others, each letter farther west than the last—organized by Burlington Northern's corporate ancestor, the Burlington and Missouri River Railroad, when it first laid this line in the 1870s. Past the town, back, as they said, "out in the country," Paap throttled up to eight again, the top position, pushing the train back to the speed limit, fifty miles per hour, through fields hardly green with new shoots of corn. Without the railroads all this middle country might yet be wild grassland, the domain of Indians and buffaloes. The first westbound pioneers bypassed the Plains, the "Great American Desert" to them, but the railroads—so powerful and so desired that they were eventually given one-sixth of Nebraska's land—opened paths to new settlers, often just-arrived immigrants, who dispersed along the banks of the tracks like bottomland after a flood. The Union Pacific, still Burlington's chief rival, was first across Nebraska, racing west from Omaha to meet the eastward-racing Central Pacific Railroad in Utah and complete the nation's first transcontinental rail link; Burlington was first into Lincoln. The Burlington towns along this line were set about ten miles apart, an interval determined by the distance a farmer could reasonably travel to deliver his crop to a depot and get back home in a single day. Tall white grain elevators are the defining features of the towns, and late in the day they are, like mountains, the last places touched by the chiaroscuro light of the setting sun, luminous visions that call to mind the Emerald City rising over the MGM poppy fields. It is no surprise that L. Frank Baum lived on the prairie, in South Dakota, before writing *The Wizard of Oz*.

A Day in the Night of America

The rail corridor widened at Fairmont, population 767, much the way a rural highway widens into a Main Street when it hits a small town. The train slowed to a crawl, and the brakemen and conductor dropped off into the yard. The crew's orders here were to deliver seven of their empty cars to the grain elevator, several tracks over, an inertia-defying parallel-parking exercise that made a tractor-trailer seem by comparison as responsive and maneuverable as a Ferrari. As the daylight faded, the brakemen threw switches, gave hand signals, talked through hand radios. Paap pulled the train out almost to the edge of town, then backed through the switches onto the elevator track. The ground crew uncoupled a string of six cars, each car sixty feet long and thirty tons empty. "We've gotta spot one here," Paap said, depositing a car directly under the elevator loading spout that would fill it with one hundred tons of grain. They left six loaded cars on another siding—four for Shickley with molasses for cattle feed, two for Geneva with steel for irrigation pipe—and drove out on a branch line to pick up the first installment, twenty-seven cars, of the night's grain. Paap inched back, back, back until the grain softly jolted into place. The brakemen "walked the air," strolling the train's length to ensure the pressured air was cut in to the brakes on every wheel, then they all settled into the activity that, even on this busy artery, accounted for much of the job: waiting.

"We're gonna go on up to Main Street," Ben Hitch, the conductor, said.

"Do they have a Dairy Queen here?" somebody asked.

"I don't think anything's open," Paap said.

"There used to be a restaurant up there," Hitch said.

"I think that's closed, too," Paap said.

The wait now was for a rendezvous with the train that was bringing the second installment of twenty-seven grain cars. Other times they might have to wait for daytime maintenance work that blocked the track; or wait their turn through a busy intersection; or wait on a siding along a single-track stretch, yielding as a faster, higher-priority train passed. "Hot trains" went first: Amtrak passenger trains at seventy-nine miles per hour, piggyback trains carrying truck trailers, trains carrying goods worth more by the ton than corn. Grain trains were cold as morning cereal. "If you want to really rock 'n' roll, ride an Amtrak head end," said Paap, who had. At thirty-five he was young for an engineer, and without his mustache he would have looked even younger. "You get off and your stomach's like a milk shake."

A man and a boy, a father and his young son, admired the idle train from the grass of a trackside clearing. A crew member went out to be their tour guide, and among the features he highlighted was the small box on the last car that electronically monitored the train's tail: the rear-end device, better known as FRED. The *F* in its name stood for *fucking*, a measure of the railroaders' resentment toward the devices that had supplanted cabooses, the traditional punctuation mark of a train, and erased jobs. Working on the railroad now, as the FREDs illustrated, was like working in a steel mill: If you already had a job there, congratulations, and good luck holding on to it; if you didn't, maybe you should try a field that expected to need more workers in the future, not fewer. The railroad industry had stabilized since the 1970s, a crashing decade of bankruptcies, mergers, deregulation and shakeouts; more than a third of all freight in America still traveled by rail. The number of major carriers dropped (from sixty-five in 1977 to sixteen in 1988), as did operating costs (from 2.4 cents per ton per mile to 1.4 cents), as did jobs (by more than half, to 230,000); while sales rose ($28 billion in 1988, up 39 percent from 1977), spurred in part by a boom in grain exports, a market where truckers, their mortal enemy, just couldn't compete. (Burlington Northern, the nation's largest railroad, was also the largest rail grain mover.) Even more jobs will likely vanish, 50,000 more in the next decade according to the federal Bureau of Labor Statistics, as companies introduce more automation and fight the unions for smaller crews. But a FRED can't drive an engine from Lincoln to Fairmont, and when the twenty-seven new cars finally arrived, after 8, it required a synchronized choreography of signals, switches and radios between two crews, not two FREDs, to unhook the one train, then pull well into the fields beyond town to gain maneuvering room and then back, back, back to hook up the new train, fifty-four grain cars now, half a standard load.

"We got a green went red on us here, we don't know why."

"How many cars we need to clear?"

"We got fifteen, twenty cars."

"You just need to shove back five."

"Whenever you're ready, we can shove back."

"They wanna go back beyond the middle crossover."

"Right here is good enough."

"All we have to do now is the FRED test."

Spread wide in the sky ahead as they left Fairmont was a John Ford sunset, red like a city aflame over the horizon, graced with lavender clouds. The cab windows were open to the evening breeze. The clang of warning signals rushed up to meet the train as it approached each grade crossing, then retreated quickly as it passed. The short telephone poles running beside the track made the engine seem even taller than it was over the silhouetted land. They were coming through the country toward Grafton, the crescent moon sharpening in the faded sky, when the dispatcher lightened their load: A waiting train, he said, would take their remaining short cars, the three empty grain hoppers for Grafton and the lumber delivery for Sutton. "We're gonna swap power with them," Paap said. "They're gonna be sitting behind us anyway, so they might as well do the work. We'll both get over the road faster, and the quicker we get over the road, the better it is for everybody." The crew unhooked their grain cars, boarded the new engines—railroaders aren't wedded to their cabs the way truckers are—hooked back up and rolled through Grafton as an express. "We're hot now," Paap said.

The signals ahead were green, clear to an unaided eye. The engine's headlight, shining all day as a defensive light, now went on the offensive, boring a tunnel more than a quarter mile long through the darkness. The railtops were black lines under the headlight, their point of convergence now hidden somewhere beyond its reach. The low brush and the occasional short tree turned ghostly white, marking the light-tunnel's borders. Small signs imprinted only with the letter *W* were set at intervals along the track like notes along a staff: Whistle here, they said, grade crossing ahead. It was somewhere along in here—somewhere after they passed 10 P.M. and after they crossed the 98th meridian, the mapline beyond which rainfall is sparser and grain farms start giving way to cattle ranches, and the entryway, some people claim, to the American West—that the train, to the audience watching or hearing or imagining it from the outside, evolved from a means of conveyance into a symbolic creature. A night train is, in America, a picture of the national urge for freedom and possibility. It travels unseen paths, moving fast and straight and steady; its whistle, especially out here where it isn't lost amid the accumulated mutterings of civilization, sounds at the time when the mind, lying abed, is most vulnerable to the lure of journey and flight.

The view from inside the train was less romantic. "You get real tired of listening to that whistle," conductor Ben Hitch said. "You get out of the cab and you go, 'Huh? Huh?'" Heard from below, the whistle was not a lonesome call but the anguished "aughhhhhhh" of someone writhing in pain; seen from inside, the journey was not to some distant silk port but only to Ravenna, Nebraska—a town of 1,300 people, three bars, four restaurants (one of which the railroad paid to stay open all night), one pool hall and the "turkey sheds," the eight-by-twelve rooms in the modular housing units that were the railroaders' homes away from home. Each crew member averaged four trips a week, four thousand miles a month, back and forth, back and forth: A crew shepherded a train only from point A to point B, handing it off to the next crew like a baton in a relay race; nobody traveled as far as the grain did.

Freight trains, with no paying passengers, keep schedules that would incite much grumbling on station waiting platforms. Railroads are a capital-heavy industry—one million dollars for a mile of new track, one million dollars for a new engine—in which the capital investments never sleep. Trains run incessantly, day and night, not pausing to rest the way trucks do, forcing their crews to work erratic, carousel shifts. A telephone's ring, not a whistle blast, is the sound a railroader listens closest for. "Today I wasn't expecting the call when it came," Paap said. "I was out in the yard working. I figured it wouldn't be until later this evening." The crew came on duty tonight at 4:30 P.M. and would have to be off-duty by 4:30 A.M., the federal shift limit, but exactly how much of that twelve-hour allotment their jobs would consume would depend on how much waiting stood between them and Ravenna. If they were still on the train when 4:30 came, they would be spelled by a fresh replacement crew, ferried in by van, and would then finish their trip by road.

The trackside edge of the country unreeled in the headlight with a hypnotic rhythm. A light moved through a field off to the right, the only sign of extra-train life—a farmer on a tractor, readying it for planting tomorrow. "When we get on the other side of Grand Island, you'll really see dark," Hitch said. "You may see a farmer's yard light five miles away. It's so wide open it scares you. You go miles and miles and you don't see anything." The darkness lay thick inside the cab, too. "You sit here in a soft seat, looking ahead, seeing the light flashing, and see if your eyes don't get heavy." Sleep wasn't the only nocturnal hazard: A wrong step could break a leg, or worse; car markings were harder to read when hooking and unhooking; and fate-tempting drivers were more likely to challenge a train to a nerve-jangling race over a crossing.

Back in the second cab, Gene Noonan peeled an orange. "I work nights to feed my sons," he said. He had worked many nights lately—it was the height of trackwork season, which meant more trains were traveling by night—and his sons had eaten well: The older son, Danny, was a nose tackle with the Dallas Cowboys; the younger son, a high school star, was about to start his first year at the University of Nebraska. Their father, the brakeman, had the same John Henry build as his sons. He wore a mustache, a denim Oshkosh railroad jacket with a small American-flag patch over the right breast pocket, and he looked as if he could reroute the rails bare-handed. He was a tight fit under the low Ravenna shower heads. His father was a switchman, his brother a conductor, and in his twenty-three years on the railroad he had, like the rest of the crew, just about memorized every mile of track. "Lincoln's the only favorite spot I have."

When the train stopped, a little past 11, it was neither Lincoln nor Ravenna, but Halloran, the stop on the eastern edge of Hastings where fifty-four more loaded grain cars awaited them. Noonan and Randy Young, the other brakeman, dropped down to the dark tracks, lanterns in hand. Noonan cut loose the first fifty-four cars, Young threw the switches, the engines picked up the new fifty-four, then came back to retrieve the rest and complete the load. "Bring her back, Jim," Young said to Paap through the radio. "Ten cars to get over the switch . . . Five cars . . . Three more cars . . . Two cars now . . . One car." The gap closed with a bump half a train away. Noonan and Young walked the air one last time, clearing the grain for takeoff for Ravenna.

The train, grown to its full mile and a quarter length now, took a right at Hastings. Ravenna was 130 rail miles from Lincoln by the most direct route, but it was 169 miles by tonight's zigzag—west on one main line, then north on this connecting spur, then west again on another main line. Towns sprang abruptly out of the darkness now, so small that they emitted no warning glow to signal their approach. "You'd better look quick, we won't be here long," Hitch said in Giltner. North of Giltner they met the competition, Interstate 80—the highway that roughly follows the route of the Oregon Trail. As the train passed under, the running lights of a tractor-trailer passed above.

Red lights stopped the train in Aurora, where they waited forty minutes for traffic to thin enough to permit a left turn onto the main line. Two eastbound coal trains stopped them again before they forded the Platte River. Paap flicked off the headlight to cut the glare as each head engine passed. The coal hoppers were mostly shadows, rolling like fleet ground fog, their presence confirmed more by noise than by sight. A brakeman marked the end of the second train, swinging his lantern from the caboose platform. By 2:15 they were in Grand Island—the prairie was the open sea lapping this small island of a city—passing a meatpacking plant where cattle stood in outdoor pens, nudging houses set so close to the tracks that, as Randy Young said, "if we ever derailed we'd be right in their bedrooms," and slowly coasting through the busy diamond where the Burlington Northern track intersected with the Union Pacific. "Once we get the tail end over 281," Paap said, referring to the main north-south highway, "we'll be able to take off again."

Paap eased the throttle toward eight, the engines climbed to a higher pitch, the train gained speed almost imperceptibly, stretching back out slowly like a thick rubber band. "If you just throttle up, then somewhere we'll break in two." Railroad engineers, like other engineers, need a practical understanding of momentum, inertia and other physical forces. How they handle the controls determines how a train rides—whether it flows smoothly or is instead jarred by run-ins (the cars pushing forward faster than the engine) and run-outs (the cars snapping back slower than the engine). "You have to keep a hundred and eight cars in your mind at one time. You've got some short hills where the train's all stretched out"—there's an engine's length worth of slack in a mile-long train—"and when you get to the top of the hill and start going down, half the train is still coming up. At some point you have to stop pulling. You're thinking like that all the time, especially when there's a caboose and you've got guys riding back there."

A green signal opened the way, like a light on a rocket gantry, into the dark and starry territory ahead. The train, level as it seemed, moved nearer the sky now as it moved west. The Plains were starting their long, slow upsweep toward the Rockies, a rise that causes an empty, westbound, upbound train to burn more fuel than a loaded, eastbound, downbound train. The land was fenced and settled now, no longer as infinite as it once appeared to nineteenth-century pioneers, but the night here was still much bigger than the species that had risen to challenge it. "We see meteor showers, eclipses, things most people wouldn't stay up for," said John Mumgaard, the fireman, who had been swapping turns at the throttle with Paap. "A couple of years ago I saw the Northern Lights. I kept wondering what the spotlights were, what was going on this time of night." Tonight the Big Dipper looked close enough to ladle up some fresh water. "You go by houses at three or four A.M. and you see a light on and you wonder why they'd be up, why any person in their right mind would be up. When I worked days, I thought everything folded up at eleven." The only sign now of anybody else awake was the oncoming headlight of another train, a coal train rolling down east.

Mumgaard leaned forward when a rising alarm, like a manic bird chirping, made the dark cab sound like dawn. He silenced it with a punch to the yellow button of the alerter, a safety device triggered if an engineer goes too long without touching any of the controls. The alerter had supplemented older tricks for staying awake, like holding a heavy fuse down between your legs so that it would drop and wake you if you started drifting off, your grip relaxing. Mumgaard's habit was to sit on one leg. He often hit the button with preemptive strikes, stopping the alarm before it could start. An eerie, disembodied voice occasionally spoke into the cab. "No defects," it said, reporting from the failed-equipment detectors that electronically inspected the passing train. "Repeat, no defects." Trackside milepost signs imposed some external order on the void—Milepost 114, for instance, meant they were coming into the Sand Hills, pasture land now, nearing Ravenna—but the crew had long since imposed its own internal order. "You have to know every inch of rail," Mumgaard said, and not just on this line, but on all the lines out of Lincoln. "You have to know if it's uphill or downhill, what's up the hill and around the bend, whether you've got to slow down or what." The weather held clear tonight, setting no obstacles to test their knowledge, no fog ("The other night the fog was so bad, you couldn't see fifty feet. You wouldn't see the signal till it went by you. That's when you find out how well you know the track"), no snow ("Sometimes there's five, six-foot snow drifts as far as you can see. You just plow through, you just hold on and hope you come out the other end").

Ravenna received them at 4 A.M. with no fanfare. The train stopped long enough only to let off the crew that had assembled it, their twelve-hour shift clock now running down, and to let on the replacement crew, who had emerged from the shadows as it crept into town. The Lincoln crew walked south across the wide tracks, bags in hand, as the train rumbled out of Ravenna, a river of corn flowing northwest to Alliance, Nebraska, where yet another crew would take over, through Dutch, Wyoming; Billings, Montana; Sandpoint, Idaho; Spokane, Washington; and finally, probably less than two days from now, Tacoma. They were assigned rooms in the long, low white buildings that looked like a motel without cars. "They should let us vote in Ravenna, all the time we spend here," Ben Hitch said.

*   *   *

Kevin Coyne

Rolling back home into Lincoln the next night, on a train hauling power-plant-bound coal from Wyoming's Powder River Basin, the illuminated state capitol tower rose straight ahead in the distance, a red light flashing on top like a final stop signal anxious not to be missed.

The elevator inside the grain elevator was a cage barely bigger than a phone booth, piloted by Billy Allen and rattling up through a concrete tower that rose over the Iowa banks of the Missouri River. At the top Allen walked onto the roof and saw the night covering three states at once. Across the river, revealed only where it reflected a few riverside lights, was Nebraska. To the northwest, above a bend in the river, was the tail of South Dakota. He was in Iowa, just south of Sioux City in Sergeant Bluff—not far from the bluff where Sergeant Charles Floyd was buried in 1804, the lone casualty on Lewis and Clark's epic two-year, forty-man exploration of the Louisiana Purchase and beyond—standing atop one of the twenty-seven elevators that had bred here with a series of refinerylike structures to form the AGP soybean processing plant. A toasting, nutty smell hung in the air like dust. About 2,500 bushels of soybeans were traveling through the plant's innards each hour on this shift, being screened and cracked and flaked and extracted and ground by machinery tended by just seven men. "You come out here when you've got a full moon, you can see it shining on the river there," Allen said. "It's pretty nice."

The soybeans at the plant, millions and millions of bushels worth, were still in their most unfamiliar form, raw, just off the bush. You use soybeans constantly, often unknowingly—in pencils, paints, diesel fuel, soaps, linoleum, cement, face cream, wallboard, disinfectants, printing ink, rubber substitutes, plastics and, of course, food products, from cooking oil to chocolate bars—but unless you grew up on a soybean farm, as Billy Allen did, you might not recognize these hard, khaki-colored peas. Cultivated in China for five thousand years, where it was known as the miracle bean, soybeans were late coming to America. Henry Ford was an early enthusiast: In the early 1930s two pounds of soybeans were in each Ford, in gearshift knobs, horn buttons, window frames, accelerator pedals and other parts; Ford himself had two suits made from soy-based textile. It wasn't until after World War II, in the prosperous, carnivorous 1950s, that soybeans finally took root as a major crop—not because they were a remarkable source of protein for humans but because they were a remarkable source of protein for animals. America's 500,000 soybean growers produced 1.9 billion bushels in 1989, at sixty pounds per bushel, making it, with corn, wheat and alfalfa, one of the nation's top four crops. Most of the beans went to animal feed and to exports; less than one percent went to direct human consumption. Soybeans are more a raw material, like coal, than a food, arriving here by truck and rail car ($7.50 per bushel today) and leaving, after the plant has transformed them, as meal ($220 a ton) and oil (22 cents a pound).

The workers were spaced widely throughout the plant like watchmen. They had come on at 11, but the beans hadn't stopped to meet them even as long as the train in Ravenna. The plant ran without break, except for an annual one-week shutdown, and the shifts rotated to accommodate the constant stream of beans. "If you want to divorce yourself from all civilization, this is a good way to do it," said Jack Valentine, the production supervisor on the previous shift. "Fifteen years ago I leaned toward being an extrovert. Now I go off by myself, thumb my nose at the world and say the hell with it. I attribute that to nights."

Larry Heatherington—the plant's safety supervisor, a daytime job, but he was filling in tonight as Valentine's successor—toured the beans' progress, starting where they started, back at the elevator. His khaki pants were like camouflage. Six percent of the raw beans in the last sample were split, he found, an acceptable ratio. Billy Allen bisected a whole bean with a scalpel. "As long as it's yellow inside," Allen said, and it was. The bean flow started as a sandy, pebbly stream bed, then was shaken on screens like mechanical gold panners. The nuggets were cracked into eight equal pieces by sharp-toothed rollers; the hulls were sucked off; the cracked pieces were heated in long, revolving tanks, then flattened into flakes by wringerlike rollers, scale models of the rollers that flattened heated bars at the steel mill. A factory roar—disproportionately large, it seemed, to the small beans— filled the lonely stretches.

Heatherington stepped out into the stiller night, picking his way carefully over the roof of the main prep building. "I don't think a one of us here hasn't missed death by this close," he said, his thumb nearly touching his forefinger. The far view showed the neighbors were still up in this isolated riverfront industrial area: the gelatin plant, the fertilizer plant, the power plant, eight megawatts of its electricity making the short trip here to the soybean plant. A few stories below, an operator tested a sample of cracked beans: 9.14 percent moisture, he found, and a temperature of 163 degrees, perfect for flaking.

The flakes traveled to an adjacent building to have their oil extracted, a process more complex, and more hazardous, than squeezing juice from oranges. Ron Rathman stood alone at the extractor, checking through a washing-machine porthole for the level of miscella, the mixture of hexane and soybean flakes. The hexane, a clear, flammable liquid, extracted the oil (soybeans are, despite their stony look, 18 percent oil) and was then steamed off, leaving the oil behind. Rathman had no radio for company: The lighter-fluid quality of the hexane precluded any such potential electrical hazards. "As I get older, I become more tired," he said of the rotating shifts. "Several times on my way home I've been driving and I don't remember passing some of the landmarks on the highway. It's not a job for a young man who wants to get his personal life going. You're not gonna meet the girl of your dreams working nights."

Lean as marathoners now, the flakes went back to be ground into meal. Bob Shupe brought a sample of finished meal, about the consistency of flour, into the prep control room for its four-times-a-shift checkup. The lights and gauges on the room-length electronic panels charted the plant's performance. He took the meal's temperature (107 degrees) and inserted a moisture meter (10.44 percent). "If it's too wet, I call the extractor to add more steam." It wasn't, so it continued on to be loaded out.

Tim Girard and Dave Beechy, masked against the dust cloud, directed a stream of meal from a thick, dangling hose—an elephant prick, they called it—into a railroad hopper. During the day truckers waited their turns for their shares of the two hundred tons of meal loaded out of here each hour. At night only silent hoppers waited. This one had forty-five tons in it already; ninety-five tons would fill it. They would fill five tonight. "You see a few planes fly over every once in a while, so you know you're not the only one awake," Girard said.

●

The sugar was white, the flour in the washtub-sized mixer was white, the cake icing was white, the animated hill of raw dough crowding the wooden table was white, the doughnuts rising in the steam box were white, the doughnuts heading for the deep fryer were white, the pie shells and the bags of pizza dough in the cooler were white, the clumps of unbaked rolls were white and the aprons and T-shirts and pants and caps and flour-dusted hands of the bakers were all white. The streets outside the Sunkist Bakery, in the Morningside section of Sioux City, were black. "You've got to give up a lot, but it's something you're kinda proud of," said Bob Kolar, the owner, who had been working with his crew all night so that Sioux City could eat fresh baked goods in the morning. "You know you've put out a good product." The rolls coming out of the oven were golden brown.

For fifty-six years, Sunkist had survived as one of the dwindling few independent bakeries in an industry increasingly dominated by chains and grocery-store bakeries. Like dairy farms and wholesale produce markets, bakeries rise at night preparatory to the coming day, and because of the tyranny of stale passing time, eroding their wares and prohibiting any stockpiling of inventory, they must rise again each successive night for an encore performance. A driver had been out since 3 making deliveries to the forty-six wholesale customers Sunkist supplied. Nine people were busy in the kitchen at 4:30, working on some of the four thousand pounds of flour and four hundred pounds of sugar that passed through here each week.

Ken Vanderlinden slid another pan of rolls out of the oven. Burn scars up and down his forearm chronicled his thirty years as a baker, many of them as Sunkist's co-owner. He had sold the business to Kolar two years before. "I got tired of it," he said. His partner, his brother-in-law, became a salesman; he continued baking, but no longer worried about managing. "Volume is the only way to make it, not profits. The only way to make a good living is to work twelve-hour days, seven and a half days a week. That way you don't spend any money." He had started work at 2:30, setting up the first batch of bread and calculating what the morning appetite would be, a formula easily upended by bad weather and unaccountable shifts in tastes and buying habits. He commanded the two twelve-pan ovens, 400 degrees each, turning pans and watching for the color of doneness. He counted out five dozen special-order turnovers, apple and raspberry. His glasses fogged as he checked the yeast dough rising in the steam box. A timer buzzed and he took two more pans of sub rolls out of the oven. Later he would make three or four batches of cookies. He was fond of glazed doughnuts, but so thin that he looked as if he never ate any. "You don't gain weight, because you're busy working."

Ken Vanderlinden, Jr., readied a batch of dinner rolls for his father's oven, setting islands of raw dough in formation on a pan. He had worked other jobs, meat cutting among them, but he kept coming back to baking. "When I was on days, I thought I'd be satisfied and happy, a normal person again. I wasn't. It didn't seem like normal work." He dipped rounds of dough in cinnamon. He cut clumps off a breathing pillow of raised doughnut dough. "Sometimes when it's really warm in here, it crawls across the table."

Trays of doughnuts, muffins, buns, rolls, cakes, cookies, turnovers, Danishes, croissants, éclairs and other newborn treats filed out of the kitchen, taking center stage in the glass display cases out front, accumulating into a seductive, ephemeral banquet. "Nothing smells better," Bob Kolar said.

A customer came in at 6:30. "I'll take half a dozen glazed doughnuts," he said. The meadow-sweet smell of baking sugar followed me as I drove off, lingering in my nose and memory long after I had left fragrant Morningside, finally and rudely replaced downtown by the stench of the packinghouses, so foul as to make you wonder why you should ever eat anything but glazed doughnuts ever again.

Somewhere out here, somewhere among these scores of parked trailers waiting tiptoed on their front legs in the packinghouse lot, was the trailer Emery Weinfurtner was looking for. He cruised slowly, reading numbers. "There it is," he said: Number 324, a refrigerated trailer loaded with 44,000 pounds of beef. He backed his empty trailer into an empty space, leaving it to be filled later with its own load of beef, then backed up under 324, coupling with it like a rail car. The packinghouse, out in a field outside Schuyler, Nebraska, was closed this Saturday afternoon, but its smell was open, a rank blend of blood, offal, cattle gas and death. Weinfurtner pulled out of the lot, out of Schuyler, east on Route 30, east toward Philadelphia, where the beef was due on Monday morning, bouncing in the air-suspension driver's seat in the cab that would be his home, night and day, for the next week—a squat bed behind him, a tiny TV, a CB radio, an FM radio and cassette player, ten fresh shirts on hangers, a winter jacket (the week could take him to any climate), an atlas he wouldn't likely need, a case of Dr Pepper, a loaf of Wonder bread, Chips Ahoy, little cereal boxes, a can of beans, iced-tea mix, and a cooler stocked with lunch meat, cheese, tuna, mayonnaise, oranges, apples and three quarts of milk. He drank from a can of Dr Pepper. "They'd starve to death," he said, considering what would happen to the East Coast without his link in the food chain.

Weinfurtner, herding dead meat to market, was a cattle driver in the modern meat industry. Live cattle no longer traveled directly to local butchers, or even to the great stockyard cities like Chicago, but instead to the packinghouses dispersed widely through the Heartland. The beef riding in the back now was all packed in boxes, stacked only about a third of the way up, as high as it could go without putting the truck over the 80,000-pound federal limit. Even at 29 degrees, the temperature the reefer was chilled to, the beef was far more perishable than grain, and the faster it got over the road, the better.

In Fremont, still in Nebraska, a long train blocked the road. "This train gonna move or what?" Weinfurtner asked. Construction had also delayed him here, forcing a tight-turn, corner-squeezing detour. He pulled into a truck stop to refuel. His truck hadn't been fed since Dalton, Georgia, on the previous week's trip, and it took 170 gallons of diesel, $192 worth, two pumps filling it from either side and the numbers spinning forever like a four-wheeler's nightmare. He hadn't eaten since before leaving Omaha at lunchtime, and he took a hot turkey dinner and a glass of milk. He called home and asked his wife to meet him at an interstate intersection in Omaha with the ulcer pills he had forgotten. "The more coffee I drink, the more I need 'em."

Across the Missouri River into Iowa, Weinfurtner rolled east on Interstate 80, laid as straight across the state as a ruler across a map, the first segment of a trip he had long since memorized: 306 miles across Iowa, 156 across Illinois, 145 more to Fort Wayne, Indiana. "Before I go to sleep, I like to be halfway," he said, and halfway was Fort Wayne, 5 A.M. the estimated arrival time tonight. The dusk landscape passed like the repeating backdrop of a cartoon chase, farmhouse barn silo fields farmhouse barn silo fields. A rising hill wrinkled the land and slowed the truck to thirty-four miles per hour. "There ain't hardly any hills after Grinnell"—a town past Des Moines, halfway across Iowa—"at least until you get over to Pennsylvania." On the flat, clear stretches, the cruise control holding at a steady sixty-two miles per hour (a governor on the engine prevented it from exceeding sixty-four), driving almost became a desk job. Each new mile earned him twenty-four cents from American Transport Inc., of Omaha; for each mile over 10,000 miles he drove this month he would earn an additional eight cents. He had made $31,000 the year before; he expected to make $32,000 this year.

"I see more of the U.S. in a week than most people do in a lifetime," Weinfurtner said, but it was usually, like the railroad, the same narrow strip of the United States he had seen last week and would see again next week.

He had collected every contiguous state save Maine; he knew which truck stop showers were hot and clean and which were cold and dirty; where the diesel was cheapest; where to feed his two-pack-a-day habit with cheap cigarettes in Kentucky, North Carolina and Virginia; where the gear-strain-ingest hills were (West Virginia); where to get a fine $4.95 steak (Williams-burg, Iowa: "It's every bit of sixteen ounces, and you get a roll, a potato, vegetables, everything"); which states' roads were smoothest (Georgia and Tennessee); which states liked to slow speeders (New Jersey and Ohio) and weigh trucks (Illinois, Kentucky, Tennessee); and, by logging 120,000 miles or more a year, he knew the interstate system better than most people know their hometown street grid; but, reined by deadlines and route maps, he had missed some of the sights that wait off the main drag. "I've been real close to Niagara Falls, but I ain't made it there yet. Man, I'd like to go there, but I don't wanna run thirty, forty miles out of the way. The other thing I'd like to see is Atlantic City."

Weinfurtner held the big white steering wheel like a serving platter. The green dashboard light signaled the cruise control was on. Every six miles, mile after treadmill mile, another gallon of fuel was gone. A half-moon dropped pale light into his lap as if he were parked under a streetlamp. Another truck drifted slightly, drowsily. "You better wake up," Weinfurt-ner said. The green milepost markers apportioned the dark sameness, telling how far he'd come and, more importantly, how far he had yet to go: 251, 262, 273. The concrete road joints bumped under-wheel as steady as a metronome. A deer, drawn and startled by the swift lights and then killed by one of the heavy shadows behind them, lay dead on the shoulder near milepost 274. He passed the last of the three Iowa weigh stations and, gratefully, found it closed like the others. He got on the CB to reconnoiter the weigh-station situation up ahead in Illinois. "Are all the coops locked up?" he asked.

"The Land of Lincoln's all locked up," a westbound trucker answered. "It's been awful quiet. I dunno what the hell's been goin' on."

"I should be clear sailing now."

The dashboard glowed in the dark cab like a golden hearth, and the CB gave voice to the silent neighboring trucks. Weinfurtner mostly just lis-tened. "A lot of guys talk on the radio at night to keep themselves awake. You'll hear 'em go off and say, 'If it wasn't for you talking to me, I woulda been asleep back there.' " When he did talk, he used no handle other than his first name ("It just don't sound right to me"), and he was more interested in information than conversation, either dispensing some ("Hey, Carolina, you got your ears on?" he asked a truck with North Carolina plates. "One of your lights is flickering in the back") or seeking some, about scales, traffic, detours and cops. "It don't really matter about the cops, since we can't run that fast anyway. It's just a habit, I guess." He was more interested in the other radio—not the farm reports (he only drove beef, he didn't raise it), not the all-night trucking shows blasted by 50,000-watt clear-channel AM stations (Dave Nemo's Road Gang from WWL-AM in New Orleans, Bill Mack's "U.S. 1 Truckin' Show" from WBAP-AM in Fort Worth, Dale "the Truckin' Bozo" Sommers from WLW-AM in Cincinnati), but Saturday Night Gold, a syndicated oldies show. "As long as I can listen to oldies, I can keep going." He kept a list of FM oldies stations on the visor—from 99.9 KGOR in Omaha to 101.1 WCBS in New York—and switched from one to the next as he crossed signal boundaries, spinning a seamless loop of music like a deejay at a 1966 junior prom.

The highway bent south around the Quad Cities—Davenport and Bettendorf, Iowa; Moline and Rock Island, Illinois—crossed the Mississippi River, the same deep blue as the sky, and took Weinfurtner, just before midnight, into a new state that looked much like the last one, except that it was one state farther from home. "It always feels nice to go into the next state, because you know you've made some miles at least." The chill air through the open window ruffed his hair, straight and combed back off his forehead. Small and wiry, he wore silver-rimmed glasses, black boots, jeans, a red-white-and-blue plaid short-sleeved shirt and a tattoo on his left forearm: a flower with his wife's name in it—DELORES. "When you're out here, you think more about your family than you do when you're at home. You talk to drivers who've been gone from home six months. That's bullshit. In my book two weeks is long enough, that's the way I look at it." He had three daughters, had been married twenty-three years, and he rang up a two-hundred-dollar phone bill calling home each month, a sum that exceeded his mortgage and usually consumed his bonus check. His wife drove with him for a couple of years, and his youngest daughter would ride with him this summer, much as he had once ridden with his father, who was also a long-haul trucker and who still, at sixty, drove mail from Omaha to Denver. When he got home, weekly mostly, he watched *Dallas,* taped by his wife while he was gone. He had returned from an eight-day trip Tuesday at midnight. Last night he had stayed up late watching a movie with his wife.

A truck cruised by in the left lane, its trailer slipping long and slow from the shadows as it passed. Weinfurtner flashed his lights when it was far enough ahead to return to the right lane, a gesture acknowledged with a thank-you flash. The road was a clean, vacant corridor now, a trucker's dream, dominated by yellow running lights that outlined its ceiling and second-story drivers perched high in their cabs. The amateurs who clogged the road by day, reckless salesmen and poky Winnebago vacationers alike, had by now largely ceded it to the professionals. He looked down on only a few cars, and one of them was hooked to a tow truck on the shoulder, strobe-lit by police flashers, a drunken-driving arrest most likely. "You're better off if you can stay awake because there's less traffic," he said. He leaned forward over the wheel, a position that was easier on his back. "Four-wheelers are bad all over. In my opinion most people are just smartasses to trucks. In my opinion back East they're even more smartass to trucks." But tonight his weariness cut into this grace period, and the goal of Fort Wayne by dawn was fading. He yawned again, the latest in a sporadic series that had started back around Iowa City. He passed Exit 45 and its sign pointing the way toward the birthplace of Ronald Reagan, the president who allowed trucks to grow longer and heavier, and he started flipping through his mental atlas of rest areas and truck stops for a place to sleep.

The roadside here, though, offered no place to pull over. "Goddamn rest area's closed," Weinfurtner said as he passed a barred ramp. The rest areas he had passed that weren't closed were already booked up with sleeping drivers, their trucks parked wall-to-wall in the small lots and lined up and down the access ramps. "I just hope a guy can get in one." Most truckers like to shut down by 3 or 4 A.M. if they can find a safe place to park and sleep; the rate of fatigue-related accidents for single trucks is ten times higher between 4 A.M. and 6 A.M. than it is during the day. "They don't make these rest areas big enough, and they're too far apart." The shoulder is illegal, some truck stops charge to park, and many private lots will run you off if you stop even long enough to eat, let alone sleep. "I went to go in a Bonanza once and there was a big sign, 'No trucks.' I don't think it's right. How do they think the steaks get to where they're at? That makes me mad as hell."

A truck stop west of Joliet had a space in the last row of its lot. As Weinfurtner backed in, his eighteen-wheel, 80,000-pound, diesel-gulping, nation-bridging rig turned into a tiny studio apartment. The truck belonged to the company—ATI number 553, a midnight-blue Kenworth anteater with 333,000 miles on it—but he was its only driver. He had just installed a new TV antenna, and he hoped to add a VCR soon. "Hell, I got a TV and everything else, there ain't no other reason to get a motel." He worked on his log book, the federally mandated record of all his trips, using the cab light to power his solar calculator. The truck stop was as open as if it were 2 P.M., not 2 A.M.—fuel pumps, restaurant, video games, a store stocked like a mini–K mart with truck accessories and CB equipment, a washroom marked PROFESSIONAL DRIVERS ONLY—but most of the truckers were outside, asleep. The trucks snorted and chuffed in the dark lot like horses; the hard-to-start diesel engines were rarely turned off. Weinfurtner crawled into his small, neat bed, leaving open the curtain that separated it from the front seats. "With that curtain open you never sleep straight through. I never use an alarm clock. I wake up with the daylight." He was out instantly. The truck idled at 900 rpm while he slept.

The dawn was pale, misty and sluggish, but it woke him like a bell soon after six. Sunday breakfast was a cigarette. He climbed slowly through thirteen gears back onto Interstate 80. "This is a pretty time to drive." America's congested eastern third had hold of him now as he finished with Illinois and started with Indiana. The gaps between settlements shortened. Traffic joined the road like tributary streams to a swelling river. Potholes and patches roughened the ride. The truck, still about the size of a railroad locomotive, seemed to be expanding in a shrinking universe.

"I'm gonna get off here," Weinfurtner told the two truckers, one just ahead and one just behind, he had been conversing with on the CB. "You guys have a good one." He exited 80 in Gary before it became a toll road, then took 65 south to Route 30, a four-lane divided highway smaller than the interstate but still bigger than the two-lane roads his father once drove from Omaha clear to the East Coast. Trees broke the monotony of the fields. Plymouth still celebrated with a sign the state championship its high school basketball team won in 1982. In Warsaw the road was "just like a washboard" and the speed limit was forty-five, "and they enforce it." The John Birch Society had a roadside message: WHEN THE GOVERNMENT TAKES OUR GUNS, FREEDOM IS GONE. "We're just going over not even half the country, so it doesn't seem too big. But when you go from the North all the way to the South, then it feels big."

In Fort Wayne Weinfurtner stopped for a real, nonnicotine truckstop breakfast and added up on a napkin how far he had left to go—280 miles to Hubbard, Ohio, where he planned to shower, nap and refuel; 160 to the exit for Route 322 in Pennsylvania; 80 to Harrisburg; 68 to Lancaster ("That's only forty miles from where I've gotta go"). He hoped to cover all 588 miles today so that he could spend tonight in Lancaster and be at the loading dock first thing in the morning; miss a delivery appointment by thirty minutes and you might sit all day waiting to unload. The rest of the meat was going to the Hunts Point Market, the vast wholesale food market in the Bronx. "I'll hurry up to get over into the Bronx before nightfall, because if you get there at night, that's when they try to rob you. Once you get inside the market, you're safe. When you go to Hunts Point at night, you might come out, you might not. You come around a corner and there they are trying to stop you. You don't dare stop because if you do, you're dead. You just keep right on a-goin'. The cops tell you the same thing. If you stop, that might be the last stop you make. You hit a red light, you keep goin'. In winter they stand with bonfires to keep warm and they wait for the trucks. Before I get there, I'll hide all my money and leave twenty dollars in my billfold, that's it." He had learned his lesson about the billfold at an Atlanta truckstop: His truck was broken into while he slept late one night, and his billfold, with $145 in it, was stolen. When his trailer was empty, he would await orders from the company dispatcher about where to go next, what to pick up there, where to deliver it, and when to come on back home. A waitress brought him his plate of ham and eggs. The place was full—a few people in churchgoing clothes, but mostly bleary truckers, sitting alone. "It always feels good to come into Omaha again," he said. "I try to stay out of cars when I'm off. I figure I drive enough when I'm gone, I don't want to drive when I'm home, too."

South out of Omaha on Route 75, on a suburban strip like any other, just before the gate to Offutt Air Force Base, a sign warned drivers, DO NOT BE ALARMED AT SUDDEN LOUD JET ENGINE NOISE. It said nothing, though, about the suddenest and loudest potential noise of all: a nuclear war in which Offut would likely be ground zero. The Strategic Air Command was headquartered here, keeper of most of America's nuclear missiles and bombs, and its Underground Command Post was buried three stories down, sheltered behind reinforced concrete and immense blast doors and staffed, in an eternal string of eight-hour shifts, by the surrogates entrusted by the president and the Pentagon with the terrible, majestic power to end the world. Tonight the road was empty, the jet engines silent, the Cold War all but over. Entering the SAC headquarters gate, I fully expected to exit it again later, after the dawn had returned, yet a tiny part of me couldn't help wondering, as John Donne wrote, "What if this present were the world's last night?"

The agricultural heartland of America is also its nuclear heartland, because coiled beneath the fields that feed the world are the weapons that could kill it. Missiles and bombers were planted in a wide swath from North Dakota to Texas, deep inland from the vulnerable coasts, a military archipelago that would comprise the front lines of a nuclear war. The trigger was always cocked here. The bombers, loaded and waiting, crouched on tarmacs, their crews on round-the-clock alert in adjacent buildings. The missiles stood at attention in silos, their two-person crews buried, too, down in cramped launch capsules with the red box that held two launch keys, one for each of them, to be turned simultaneously. A billboard for Wall Drug in South Dakota, the South of the Border of the Plains, offered free coffee and doughnuts to any visiting missile crews, stimulants they needed more when they were on duty, twenty-four hours at a stretch, than when they were off.

The three aboveground floors of SAC headquarters were a benign façade of yellow brick and smoked glass that could pass for a big suburban high school or a software company in an office park. By day it bustled with the bureaucratic routines of thousands, from airmen to four-star generals, a self-contained village with its own barber shop, credit union, cafeteria and PX. By night it was deceptively calm, stripped of all but a watchful skeleton staff a couple hundred strong. The off-white halls, a muster of locked door after locked door, were carpeted in sedate mauve and burgundy. Elevator music played softly. The corporate somnolence was broken by the Security Response Team, armed men patrolling in battle-dress uniforms like a martial-law force imposed on a chaotic, war-emptied city.

In a corridor one floor down, where the fluorescent glare was harsher, Senior Airman Wallace McCullough stood at the entry to the restricted underground area and scrutinized the ID badge of a blue-uniformed officer. "Subconsciously it's always in your mind," he said about what lay beyond his post. He wore a 9mm Beretta at his hip, and a black beret. "If somebody's really serious about it, from here back is the most important part of the building. You make sure you check the badges real thoroughly." He let the officer past.

The sanctum sanctorum itself—past more windowless corridors, past where the lulling music stopped, past the weather squadron that forecasted clear skies at most bases but more rain and three miles' visibility for Pease Air Force Base in New Hampshire, past the big double doors meant to protect against a crippling electromagnetic pulse from a nuclear explosion— was, like most things that loom large in the imagination, much smaller in reality than you'd think. I half thought I'd be dwarfed by a shadowy, edgy cavern like the United Nations General Assembly and watch beribboned generals push division markers around a giant Risk board with croupier sticks. It looked instead like a Hollywood producer's plush private screening room. The new command center—it had just opened, replacing the adjacent 1950s-vintage original—rose in three gentle steps like an amphitheater, carpeted in blue and lined with desk consoles where the battle staff would sit to wage war. Each station was equipped with a burgundy executive chair, a computer screen, a multiline phone and a microphone that stood up like a cobra. Everything faced the eight big video screens that covered the front wall. CNN filled Screen 2, reporting on, among other stories, the latest Midgetman missile test; a Daffy Duck cartoon appeared briefly on Screen 8; the other screens were blank. Digital clocks above the screens showed four versions of the time: local, Zulu (the military's name for Greenwich Mean Time), Moscow (nine hours ahead, day there when it was night here), and Guam. During an exercise, when screens are displaying maps and graphics and mock orders are going out to bombers and missile crews, thirty officers might be busy here trying to manage a theoretical skirmish in Eastern Europe that has escalated into a nuclear standoff. But tonight, like most nights, the seats were empty, the world was mostly at peace, and the Heart of the Bomb was still. The custodians of power were up behind the glass wall in the balcony overlooking the theater: a support battle staff of eleven, sealed in with their own kitchen and bathroom for an eight-hour shift.

"I watch some things," Captain Don Wardle said. "Let's leave it at that." The things he watched, as a warning-systems controller, he watched on the two big monitors he sat before in the balcony from 10:30 P.M. to 6:30 A.M. His method for staying awake through the night-shift weeks of his rotating schedule was better than caffeine. "It's no problem. You don't sleep in front of a full colonel." The father of four and the son of a career army man, he worked in missiles before coming to headquarters. "The nuclear responsibility never really bothered me. I've always been at the edge. I like being at the heart now."

A Day in the Night of America

The heart had many chambers, far-flung and, like the body's own heart, on constant duty, determined not to repeat the mistake the American military made in 1941. Japanese messages intercepted in the dark, early hours of December 7 indicated an imminent surprise attack somewhere in the Pacific, but intelligence aides couldn't reach anyone with decision-making authority until Army Chief of Staff General George C. Marshall got to his office. By then, of course, it was too late. An elaborate chain of command facilities now bridged the gap left by the natural, nightly human power outage: the Underground Command Post here; the NORAD Cheyenne Mountain Complex in Colorado; the National Military Command Center at the Pentagon and its underground backup, the Alternate National Military Command Center at Fort Ritchie, Maryland; the National Emergency Airborne Command Post (say "kneecap" for its acronym), the plane on constant runway alert that would carry aloft the president and top military leaders if Washington were bombed. And because this underground post wouldn't survive a direct nuclear hit, SAC kept a fleet of airborne surrogates that mirrored its command functions—the "Looking Glass" planes, nine modified Boeing 707s that carried a crew of twenty, including a general who would assume command of the nation's nuclear forces if everybody on the ground were wiped out. The initial Looking Glass plane took off from Offutt on February 3, 1961, the first in an unbroken line, one plane relieving the other at eight-hour intervals, that flew continuously over mid-America until 2:28 P.M. on July 25, 1990— when the superpower thaw finally made it a costly anachronism. (SAC itself would eventually be grounded, too, replaced by a smaller, reorganized unit composed of air force, navy and army personnel.)

"There's been no really serious situation between the two countries in the time I've been doing it," Colonel Terry White said. "A bolt out of the blue is unlikely. I think there'd be plenty of indicators available to us about what was going on." White, the senior controller, was the officer in charge tonight, the colonel Captain Wardle couldn't sleep in front of, the pivotman at the consolelike switchboard at the center of the room, the shift commander at the world's most important police precinct, where the work was, like much police work, routine and boring. "This is pretty serious business. I take it as serious. I think all the people here do." Nights were slower and quieter than days here, the 1:30-to-5 stretch the slowest and quietest of all, and the last hour or two was the hardest time of all to keep alert: They had an electronic window on the world, but they had no glass window to let in the jump-starting light of the Omaha dawns. "We're far enough underground that we can't tell if it's day or night anyway." His previous assign-ments were mostly ground-level and above: flying tankers and B-52s, a tour in the Pentagon. "I try not to do any heavy reading. It puts you to sleep." He kept an eye instead on CNN, but neither that nor the more classified network screens showed any significant movement by the subjects of the SAC stakeout.

"There's nothing interesting on TV," Captain Roland Robitaille said. They got ten channels down here in the military underground—eight more than at his previous job tending missiles in Montana—but once the late sports scores were in, the viewing options were as dim as they were up on the civilian topside. "What makes the night drag on is that there's not a helluva lot happening." An emergency-actions officer, his phone had more than one hundred lines, and when he answered it, he might find the Joint Chiefs of Staff with a message for the SAC forces. (Omaha's state-of-the-art phone system, first installed to meet SAC's telecommunications needs, had made it America's toll-free capital: Ten thousand people at twenty-five companies answered 800-numbers round-the-clock, authorizing credit-card transactions, placing hotel reservations and taking orders for anything imag-inable.) "Like any other job, you get so wrapped up in the humdrum routine of it that you really don't think about the implications. We could go to war in the next ten minutes, but it hasn't happened in the last ten years, so it's probably not gonna happen tonight. I haven't seen anything on CNN." He often read through the humdrum hours; Tom Clancy was his favorite author. "We talk about it," he said about the brink-of-war plots and the familiar military hardware in Clancy's politico-technothrillers. "It doesn't really connect to here for me." When he came back up at shift's end, the night was gone, the sun had risen again, and Clancy's world was safely bound in novels.

9

At 4:00, along a blank South TEXAS *highway, a Border Patrol officer staked out a car he suspected of ferrying Mexicans north into America.*

The storm started gathering over Kansas after suppertime. The west side of the sky was clear blue as I drove south through the wheatfields, while the east, in as sharp a division as a scrimmage line, was black with clouds that looked angry enough to spit out a tornado. They held their peace all the way down the interstate to Oklahoma City, where their attack was finally launched with a prefatory, testing skirmish of scattered lightning. The full artillery barrage—an It's-Alive-Frankenstein-night epic that generated enough electricity to raise the dead, a Big Bang reprise of the birth of the universe—started around Pauls Valley. I kept driving through it, thinking it would soon burn itself out, but it raged through forty miles, fifty miles, sixty miles, no more than a second between lightning flashes at its peak. There was little rain and no thunder, just a mute display of white light against black night, blinking like guns from a battle beyond the range of sound. It seemed the work of Hecate—the dread Greek goddess of night, the goddess of the dark of the moon, the mother of witches and queen of ghosts, the keeper of the keys to hell, the three-headed stormbringer who left the netherworld nightly to terrify travelers, rising from a crossroads, her approach heralded by wolf-pack howls and screaming winds and the trembling of the earth, bearing aloft a sword and a torch, cloaked by the pale, writhing spirits of the dead she unleashed each night to haunt the dark world, invisible to all but the packs of hellhounds who attended her and who ascended into the sky in a terrifying vision that drove travelers mad. It didn't start fading until it was seventy miles old, just before I crossed the Red River into Texas. A misty near-full moon appeared in the jigsaw of open sky, backlighting the clouds and silhouetting their borders like the edges of continents.

Grounded, parked on the flight line at Carswell Air Force Base in Fort Worth, the B-52s were ominous and predatory beasts. Their straight, pipeline bodies, pushing back into the darkness, seemed as long as trains, and their great wings—185 feet tip-to-tip, longer than the 159-foot bodies, longer even than the Wright Brothers' first flight—swept back off the fuselage tops, not the middles, to give the planes the hunched-shoulders look of vultures. Their cockpit windows were tiny yellow eyes. Their color was an unbroken, featureless, thunderhead gray, camouflaging them against the night. They had names like *Master Blaster, Viper, City of Fort Worth* and *Texas Two-Step*. They could each carry twenty nuclear warheads—eight short-range attack missiles in the bomb-bay belly, twelve air-launched cruise missiles hanging under the wings like bats—with a total explosive yield more than 250 times that of the atomic bomb dropped on Hiroshima. They were deadly flying warehouses, and Carswell was home to twenty-seven of them, more than a tenth of the Strategic Air Command's total B-52 force. Air Force Technical Sergeant Otis Duffee piloted a van between them. "Go ahead, *Viper*," he said into his radio.

"You know those pins? Those bomb-door pit pins? I need one," came the request from a mechanic getting *Viper* ready for a morning takeoff.

Floodlight carts spotlit some of the planes like a movie shoot, focusing on engine cowls, noses, bomb bays. Duffee, the flight-line expeditor, drove up and down the line over and over again, orchestrating the eighty members of the Organizational Maintenance Squadron (his baseball cap shortened it to OMS) who were working the graveyard shift. Their night mission was recovery and preflight maintenance: patching the planes that had just landed, prepping the planes due to fly.

"He's got bomb navigation problems, oxygen problems, oil pressure problems," Duffee said to a mechanic. "It'll take a lot of time to turn that one."

The prehistoric look of a pterodactyl-winged B-52 is a reminder of its origins in the prehistory of modern weapons systems: The name refers to the year the first one flew, America's big gun at the start of the Cold War. Carswell's B-52s dated from 1960 and 1961. Designed to fly a total of five thousand hours, they had already logged an average of twelve thousand hours each. "It takes a long time to do one of the sixties. The sixty-ones do better," Duffee said. "If it flies every night, it starts to fly real good after three or four days. If it sits for three, four days, then flies, then sits three, four days, it doesn't seem to fly as good." *Iron Maiden*—the B-52, not the heavy metal band—had arrived from Hawaii at 11:30 P.M., and before it could leave again on another training mission at 6:15, the crew had to check, among other things, the oil, inlets, ejection-seat pins, hydraulic reservoirs, liquid oxygen and brakes; fix, among the other in-flight write-ups, the infrared camera, oxygen regulator, window defogger and electronic warfare units; and refuel it, pumping enough fuel from the underground lines into the wings to make their tips dip seven feet, bending as if to kiss the tarmac. "It sounds easy. It just takes a while to do it."

Duffee had spent twelve of his sixteen air-force years on graves, an unlikely shift for someone with his affection for light. "To be honest with you, I'm definitely afraid of the dark. I like to know what's goin' on. They say don't be afraid of what you can't see, but I am. At night it seems like you can hear all the little-bitty things. I've never been broken into or anything like that, but I just don't like the night." His fear hadn't stopped him from volunteering to stay on the shift year after year ("I spent a year on the day shift and I didn't like it a bit, no sirree bob"), nor from joining friends for an occasional night hunting coyotes. He had learned to sleep in the daytime, despite his two children and the three children, six to eighteen months old, his wife baby-sat at home ("I never wake up. If I do anything good, it's sleep"); he savored the cool relief from the one-hundred-degree, tarmac-frying Texas sun; and he enjoyed watching his night's work fly away. "When you see the airplane go, you know you did something that night. On the day shift you can work all day long and not see 'em leave. To me what it's all about is getting off the ground. That's the part I like."

Parked adjacent to the flight line Duffee worked were the ready-for-war planes—eight loaded B-52 Stratofortresses and five KC-135 Stratotankers, flying refueling stations, surrounded by barriers, razor wire and, in case that didn't get the this-is-for-real message across, the deadly force line, the red line beyond which, if you crossed it without authorization, the guards could shoot you. The crews were behind the line with the planes, standing by in the alert facility, a windowless building like a minimum-security prison. A piercing Klaxon would send them sprinting toward the skies. "When I'm on alert, I don't think it's really going to happen, but I'm certainly prepared to do it," said Captain Mark Millard, navigator for the crew designated S-01, the top-ranked B-52 crew at Carswell. He wore a dull-green flightsuit, zippers along his legs and arms and chest, and a yellow-and-black ascot. The crew, planning this morning for tomorrow's mission to Canada, was due back on alert next week, seven full days of waiting for the Klaxon. "It's in the back of my mind that, yeah, we're the first to go if anything happens."

The Klaxon could blare at any time—when the crews were watching TV in the alert facility's TV room, or shooting pool, or sleeping in the dormlike bedrooms—because war could come at any time. "Do you think the end of the world will come at nighttime?" Sal Mineo asked James Dean in *Rebel Without a Cause;* and it's also a question the American military has asked itself incessantly, because war, for America, has often come in the dark—in the Revolution (Washington crossing the Delaware to surprise the British), the Civil War (the Confederate bombardment of Fort Sumter), World War I (the Ninth Bomb Squadron, ancestor to the same squadron the Carswell B-52s belonged to, flew America's first night combat missions at the Battle of Saint-Mihiel), World War II (the Allied invasion of Normandy on D-Day), the Cold War (the first nuclear test blast in the New Mexico desert, and the first barbed-wire strands of the Berlin Wall), Korea (the North's invasion of the South) and Vietnam (the Tet Offensive). American forces in the Gulf War sighted their Iraqi enemies through a wide array of night-vision equipment that lent the dark landscape a ghostly glow of false daylight.

SAC went on twenty-four-hour alert in 1957—a term that used to mean loaded bombers always airborne, ready to continue on to their targets and fire but that, since 1968, had meant crews like S-01 stationed a dash away from their planes at bases like Carswell. About forty of its bombers were kept on ground alert, and each crew spent about one week out of every four on alert with them. "A lot of people stay up late, since there's no family responsibilities," said Major George Earnhart, the aircraft commander. "Ten years ago we'd run TV marathons, see who could watch TV the longest. Now we try to maximize alert week and try to get as much ground training done as possible. Now you have more free time when you're not on alert." Crews were no longer under house arrest in the alert facility during alert week, but they were confined to the base, and they had to stay within range of a Klaxon. The Cold War's demise hadn't meant unemployment for them: The B-52s can also carry conventional weapons. "When

Iran gets hot and heavy, or when terrorists get going, we stand up and listen. It's probably more likely for us to go conventional than to go into the nuclear threshold." Before long it was Iraq that heated up, and B-52s rained bombs on the desert.

Between alerts, flying a sortie or two a week, the crew saw a wider piece of the world ("You start measuring the world in flight time," Millard said, "Hawaii's not three thousand miles, it's eight hours, and it's eight hours to the North Pole"); but they saw it from an airborne workplace even more claustrophobic than the ground-alert facility. B-52s were built for the comfort of weapons, not humans. The bomb bay was as roomy as the two-level cockpit was cramped. The gunner and the electronic warfare officer sat downstairs, the commander, copilot, navigator and bombardier sat upstairs, the total space, all squeezed into the nose, wasn't much bigger than a train or truck cab, and the only place to stand up straight was on the ladder between the two squat floors. Night flights can be tedious and long—a B-52 can fly 8,800 miles, sixteen hours, without refueling—but the dark sky sometimes performed for them. "You can spot a storm one hundred fifty miles away," Earnhart said. "It's an absolutely beautiful light show." Night is also when you can see the Saint Elmo's fire brought by an electrical storm, a blue haze dancing all over the airplane like a possessing spirit. "It's the most peaceful time."

"There've been times when there was nobody in the world to talk to me but Alaska and Turkey," said Dale Freitag, the electronic warfare officer.

Carswell heard the first sound of war every morning at ten, when the Klaxon, like a small-town fire whistle, blew a test blast. It blew again once each week for an alert exercise. "Not a lot of guys sit and ponder, 'Is the Klaxon gonna go off?' but we're trained like Pavlov's dog to respond if it does," Earnhart said. "When it goes off, the first thing you do is look at your watch to see if it's a test. It's kind of an event, even if you're not on alert. It's fun to watch everybody running around." But once when it went off—after a June midnight in 1980, when he was on alert at another base—it was neither a test nor an exercise. A message from the NORAD early-warning center in Colorado said that Soviet sub-launched missiles had been fired at America. "The message decoded as real. It was a different feeling. Usually when you run out, you pretty much know it's an exercise. This was entirely different. People got real serious." There were no incoming missiles. The enemy was a defective forty-six-cent computer chip in a communications board. "They cleared the problem and stood us down. But when it decoded as real, everybody got a shot of adrenaline. It felt like after a mugger was in your bedroom. Your heart was pounding. Nobody went to sleep for a long time after that."

The day's first B-52 lumbered out Carswell's taxiway at 6:15, its fuel-heavy wings dipped low as if flapping. Seen from a distance it was a child's drawing of an airplane, all long, straight stick lines. It turned, tail gliding like a shark fin, then shot down the runway, eight engines burning, two full sets of wheels racing like a tractor trailer. It looked too ungainly to get airborne, rolling and rolling and rolling, but then it started to lift, not climbing steeply, but floating up, like a kite. It rose slowly in the southern sky.

A sign on base rated the SRO, the security response option, as IV: world tension, that meant, was low. Within two years the B-52s would finally be called off alert, and Carswell would be targeted by a shrinking Pentagon for closure. A sign leaving the base warned: YOU ARE NOW ENTERING THE MOST DANGEROUS AREA IN THE WORLD—A PUBLIC HIGHWAY. DRIVE CAREFULLY. South along I-35, along between Waco and Austin, a tornado had left its mark. A blown-through Dairy Queen sign looked like a jaw stuck open. Some people picked through twisted debris that had recently been a home.

◐

At dusk Mexicans gathered across the river from Laredo and waited for night to open the door to America. Just seventy-five murky yards of the Rio Grande—not so grand here, just sluggish brown water that looked solid enough to walk on, foul with raw sewage from Laredo's Mexican twin city, Nuevo Laredo, small out of all proportion to its stately role as an international boundary—separated them from their goal. When darkness came, they would enter the water. The river was over-your-head deep in spots here, but mostly it was shallow enough to wade, the rank and muddy baptism required for entry into the new land. Carrying dry clothes in plastic bags, they would push across at an angle, deferring to the current, and aim for a bare patch of riverbank worn smooth by many earlier landings. Up in the dense thicket of brush, tall carrizo cane and spiky mesquite leaves, they would put dry clothes on their wet backs, illegal aliens now, subject to immediate arrest and deportation. They would hike up a dirt path so well trafficked it might as well have been paved and hung over with a green interstate sign, TO LAREDO. It led up to the warehouse district, the rail yard, the highway, the United States. But now, as the evening sky dimmed, they waited on the other side, and Jesus Morin, a U.S. Border Patrol agent, watched. "They're not there just on a picnic," he said. "They're just waiting to come across. They're just waiting for nighttime. Once the sun starts going down, it's like you open a gate."

The Mexicans saw Morin, but they didn't try to hide. *"Joto,"* they taunted: Queer. To them he was *"La Migra,"* Immigration, *"La Pinche Migra,"* Fucking Immigration, a barrier in their path. If they could get past him and his fellow officers, they might find their way to a job, washing dishes maybe, that paid three dollars an hour, a lottery prize to someone who, even at one of the American manufacturing plants that have migrated south over the border, might early only fifty-five cents an hour back home. Every night along America's vulnerable southern frontier—two thousand miles from the Gulf of Mexico, along the Rio Grande, through the deserts of New Mexico, Arizona and California, to San Diego and the Pacific—all the big questions about politics, economics, sociology and immigration policy were reduced to hundreds of Border Patrol agents chasing thousands of illegals in the dark. "At night it can get kinda hairy," Morin said as he shouldered out through the brush, past the discarded clothes and plastic bags. At thirty-four he still had the build of the high school fullback he had been back in Falfurrias, his hometown ninety miles to the east. "They can see you with your big old flashlight, you might as well have a spotlight. You can't see them until you're right on top of them. If they're down here with any type of weapon, they've got the drop on you."

Laredo, with 173 miles of river and 430 agents to secure it, was the fourth-largest of the Border Patrol's nine sectors along the Mexican border (behind San Diego, El Paso and Del Rio, Texas) and it had caught 2,491 illegals in the last twelve days. The 1986 Immigration Reform and Control Act—which penalized employers who hired illegals and allowed many illegals already here to become legal—had cut traffic initially, but not dramatically, and the numbers seemed to be inching back up. "Every year a new group comes of age, and it's their turn to come," said Richard Marroquin, Jr., deputy chief patrol agent in Laredo. The Border Patrol, the law enforcement arm of the Immigration and Naturalization Service, is, like the FBI, part of the Department of Justice. "Civil liberties and humanitarian groups, farm growers, they're all for letting everybody in the world in. The other side, the labor unions, they say it brings wages down, you've got to protect the border. It can get pretty frustrating. I'm not here to defend it or bash it." But they did enforce it: He expected the Laredo section to apprehend between 80,000 and 90,000 illegals that year.

Laredo's founders were drawn to this spot two centuries ago for the same reason would-be immigrants were drawn now: The Rio Grande is easy to ford here. Morin drove his patrol car, a pale-green Chevy, through the warehouse district and down toward the city's riverfront heart. The streets of Laredo were narrow and stopped with traffic, faced by a dense wall of storefronts and Spanish signs. Walkers outnumbered drivers. The money exchange houses advertised the day's rates: 2,430 pesos to a dollar. Graceful oak and pecan trees shaded pockets of greenery. Cars, trucks and pedestrians streamed toward and from the clogged international bridge. "To me, we're in Mexico now," said Morin, whose grandparents were born there. This side of the river, the American half of *"los dos Laredos,"* looks little different from the other side, a living, history-breathing, Spanish-speaking reminder that Texas once belonged to Mexico; that Laredo itself, after the Texas Revolution and before the Mexican War, was capital of the short-lived Republic of the Rio Grande.

Morin drove north from the river on I-35—the main road out of Laredo, a piece of the Pan American Highway that runs from Chile to Alaska, and a direct but difficult route into America for immigrants. A billboard offered NICE BIG ROOMS . . . CLEAN AND QUIET at the Border Inn for thirty-four dollars. The city thinned through the outskirts strips until it was replaced entirely by the brushy void, one step up from desert, that continues almost unbroken for the next 150 miles, all the way to San Antonio, and that comprises a more formidable barrier than the river. Illegals must leave Laredo soon after they arrive: There is no nearby fieldwork—this is ranchland, not farmland—and the city is thick with Border Patrol agents. They must get to San Antonio, Houston, Dallas, any city away from the border, so they must cross this bitter, empty land. Some walk, drinking at cattle wells, packing their food, sometimes dehydrating and dying alone. "Sometimes they just give themselves up," Morin said. "They get tired of walking through the brush and they come out to the road and flag you down. 'Take me, take me.' " Some hop a freight train. Most pay a smuggler, a "coyote," for a ride; the fare to San Antonio might run $500, even $1,000.

Fifteen miles up 35 from Mexico was the checkpoint that tested a coyote's skills. A canopy shielded the road like a gas station, marking the spot where every vehicle—three thousand per eight-hour shift—was stopped by Border Patrol agents, surveyed, questioned, maybe searched.

"Somebody drives up and as soon as you see 'em, they act nervous, uptight, they're kinda squiggly in their seat, they hesitate to answer questions, they're sweating, gripping the steering wheel. With years of experience you develop what I call a sixth sense." Morin hit a wall of brick air when he got out of his car. The temperature had reached 108 degrees that day, making Laredo the hottest place on the TV weatherman's map of America, and the evening hadn't much cooled it. An oven wind blew across the low, dark brush. One of three first-line supervisors on the shift, he had twenty-seven agents under him, including those working their way through the line of traffic stopped at the checkpoint. Some vehicles passed with a question or two from the green-uniformed agents. Some were asked to show papers. Some were directed over to the side for further questioning, possibly a search. Illegals were the first target, drugs the second. A Greyhound bus, its destination sign reading simply AMERICA, continued north after an agent walked its aisle. A battered yellow Datsun pickup was pulled over, parked and waiting, a young woman and her mother sitting beside it under the canopy's pale fluorescent light. The daughter, crying and smoking, wore a Marlboro T-shirt. An agent questioned in Spanish a young Mexican man who claimed to be the daughter's husband but who had no documents besides a California marriage certificate that was, suspiciously, partly typed and partly handwritten. The trio were headed to Missouri, the woman's home state. The answers were still elusive after Morin joined the questioning, and the man was taken into the office. He didn't contest the decision to send him back across the border. The woman could, if she chose, petition for his later admission. "Small things just didn't add up," Morin said. "The guy didn't remember when they got married. I said, 'C'mon, you don't forget stuff like that.' "

Morin drove north past the checkpoint, toward San Antonio, toward Missouri. "It's like trying to empty the ocean with a teaspoon," he said. Some illegals—OTMs usually, "other than Mexicans"—request asylum and are taken to detention centers to await immigration hearings; most are just taken back to the bridge. Some deported Mexicans stay in Mexico only long enough to plan another trip across. "Sundays and Mondays are big. It almost seems like they go home or something and then they try again."

Three more checkpoints crouched on the three other roads that led north from the border, covering all the outbound motor traffic, but the spaces between the roads yawned wide from Texas horizon to horizon in a tempting, forbidding mirage of freedom. By day, to a thirsty walker under the hard sun, the austere land is a close approximation of hell. By night, the time of refugees forever, it is a concealing passage for flight. Policing the vastness requires strategies from both this century and last: Helicopters hover like traffic reporters, throwing searchlight beams through the darkness; sign-cutting teams track the brush in daylight like hunters trailing deer. Morin parked by a roadside fenceline and waited to meet two agents coming in from the brush. Two tall shadows approached, harrumphing softly—Lynda Gonzalez on George, a black mare, and Tim Coates on Jed, a sorrel mare. The agents wore chaps. The horses, imposing half-ton quarterhorses, wore BP brands. They stood together, silhouetted against the moonlight. "Sometimes they're so surprised, they stop dead in their tracks when they see us," Gonzalez said.

Horses are still the best-designed vehicles for off-road travel here, especially at night. "The horses can sense anything long before we do," Coates said. "They perk up their ears and turn their heads in the direction where people might be." Their job appears at first a futile phantom chase, so secure a shelter does the huge night seem to offer, but the brushwalkers have certain habits that shrink the blank, interplanetary terrain and shorten the odds. The walkers tend to follow established pathways: a rough trail worn by previous walkers, a bald swath above an underground cable. They gravitate toward landmarks: a radio tower, power lines. They leave clues, often found by sign-cutting teams and passed on to night patrols, that telegraph their routes. They travel more when the moon is bright. They travel in groups.

"Sometimes you can hear them from quite a ways," Gonzalez said. "Nine times out of ten we see them first. They usually respect authority pretty well. When they see us, they'll run sometimes, but when we catch them, they pretty much sit."

Morin's car continued north, until the radio told him that a sensor on a remote ranch road—so lightly trafficked that any activity on it, especially at this hour, was suspect—had detected a passing vehicle. He stationed himself beneath an overpass just beyond the ranch road's intersection with the highway. A second patrol car joined the stakeout. "He'll wait across the road to see what comes out. I'll be ready to stop them up the road." The radio reported that the vehicle, still approaching, had hit a second, nearer sensor.

"We got a vehicle coming," the watch car announced. "He's turning northbound."

Morin saw the lights first, rushing ahead along the roadside brush, and then the car, a brown Mercury Cougar riding low in the back. "If that doesn't look good, I don't know what does." He sped off in pursuit. The Cougar pulled over, and the driver, a long-haired man wearing a bandanna and a beard, opened the trunk: a cooler and a spare tire. "No such luck," Morin said, returning to his car. "Boy, I thought I had a good one. It was a classic smuggler profile."

Back at headquarters, his shift ended, Morin learned that the horse patrol had seized sixty pounds of marijuana, two duffel bags full, from some walking smugglers.

The train whistle blew at 1:30—a boarding call to the illegal commuters hidden away, waiting, in the sprawling rail yard. It was the second, and last, train of the night, a northbound freight, destination San Antonio. The engines swelled, the cars inched forward, and two men, shadows in the distance, sprinted out of the brush and past a warehouse and hopped aboard.

"They hear it and they come running," agent Roger Schofield said. He and his partner, Mel Rodriquez, were standing as close to the track as war brides to a troop train. "They'll jump on when it's moving pretty fast. I like to think that I'm pretty brave, but I sure wouldn't try it. If they fall, they're dead meat."

"They run right past us," Rodriquez said. "They've got more balls than I do. I've had them run past on my right side and run past on my left side to get on a train."

The agents' flashlights brushed the passing train with light, turning up two men, three, under a truck trailer on a piggyback car, five, seven, pressed against a ladder, nine altogether, widely spaced along its length, one old man among them, his worn face betraying a glimmer of fear in the swift beam, the rest young, all ignoring the agents' exhortations, shouted in Spanish over the din, to jump off.

"That old man there was thinking about getting off," Rodriquez said as the train faded into the distance.

"Those were the same two I caught earlier, down at the river," Schofield said of two of the young riders. "It's frustrating. You might catch the same guy four or five days in a row."

They drove down toward the river and walked through the cane to the water's edge. Schofield's flashlight beam crossed the border and hit the

Mexican shore, silhouetting nothing but brush. Festive music drifted back over in return, muted, like a bar band heard through a closing door. "When you're hungry and you're trying to make a better life, you take chances," he said. "One man said to me, 'My stomach is in the United States, but my heart is in Mexico.' I think a lot of people feel that way."

"I guess being poor is a lot worse than risking your life," Rodriquez said. They and their fellow agents had caught fifty illegals so far tonight on the trains and in the rail yard.

A shuttle van, carrying a dozen anxious Latino faces, was stopped up at the I-35 checkpoint. Friday night was turning into Saturday morning, and they were on their way, they hoped, to San Antonio, the opposite direction from the Border Patrol vans carrying illegals back to the bridge. Their papers passed, to their great relief, and their weekend trip proceeded.

"Hi, how're you doing today?" Keith Fukunaga, an agent who hailed from Hawaii, asked a tractor-trailer driver who followed. He opened the sleeper-cab door and found the driver's two young kids sprawled across the mattress. The truck was hauling glass auto parts, made in Mexico, addressed to Indianapolis, and the driver was planning a tourist detour.

"We're goin' to Memphis, Tennessee," he said, "to see Elvis Presley's house."

A skinny young man bounced out of a beaten old car the agents had pulled over, fidgety, hands jammed in his pockets as if the night had actually chilled the air enough to make him shiver. He pinched a cigarette with one hand, opened the rumble-seat-sized trunk with the other. It was deep and empty and—at 4 A.M., in a car whose driver claimed he was going to visit his grandmother in San Antonio—suspicious. "It looks like a load vehicle," said Jimmy Trevino, Jesus Morin's late-shift successor as first-line supervisor. Illegals sometimes walk through the brush to avoid the checkpoint, then meet their arranged rides along the road beyond. "He looks like he's in too much of a hurry just to visit his grandmother. He didn't say anything about an emergency."

Trevino tailed the car north on 35. The driver had said he was from Laredo, but a license-plate check found that the car was from Alice. "That car was bought just to smuggle," Trevino said as his quarry passed the most likely pickup spot and exited onto a local road that shadowed the interstate. "He knows it's us. He got off to see if we'd get off." Trevino did get off—to turn around and backtrack to a stakeout spot. "He pegged us right, he knew what he was doing. Now it's just a waiting game—does he come back or doesn't he?"

Trevino waited, lights off, on a small rise above the highway. "Our problem in America is that we can't feed our own people, and until we can take care of our people, we can't be inviting everybody in here," he said. He was a Brown Beret in the 1960s, active in the Chicano movement, and he had been a psychiatric social worker before joining the Border Patrol. "I'm not a Mexican American, I'm of Mexican descent. I'm American first and Mexican second. But I do sympathize because I know how bad things are there." A pair of southbound headlights approached on 35. The kid with the big trunk, if he had in fact gone to the next logical exit and turned around, should have been back by now. Trevino watched through binoculars: wrong car.

By 6 A.M. the graying Texas sky was easing shut the door to America. Back at the checkpoint Trevino told the agents, as he would tell his day-shift successor, to keep an eye on the pickup spot he had staked out. "He'll be back," he said. The traffic and the light grew together, another day of sorting out who belonged from who didn't. "When you ask if they're a citizen, some people answer, 'What do I look like?' " Trevino said. "So I say, 'Give me a good description of a United States citizen and we'll find out.' "

Beaumont Watkins was halfway through supper in the kitchen of his ranch house—steak he had raised himself, fried potatoes, beans, tortillas straight from the family cook's pan—when the phone rang. His wife and son were watching *L.A. Law* in the next room. He was the only lawman on duty tonight for all the vast stretches of Uvalde County that surround the couple of county towns big enough to have their own police, and he knew the phone meant supper was over. The dispatcher from the sheriff's department was calling with a report of a prowler. Watkins, a deputy sheriff, bolted a last few bites of steak and grabbed his white Stetson-style panama hat. He wore black boots, tan pants, a white shirt, a dark tie secured by a tiny spur, a gold Cross pen, a gold badge in the shape of Texas, and a Colt .45 with a special sterling-silver grip that came from Mexico. One of the peacocks he kept cried behind the house as he walked to his patrol car, a white Plymouth. He drove out the long gravel road through the ranch, just

1,000 acres, hardly a ranch at all in his eyes, especially when set against the 100,000 acres his father once ranched, but big enough for 30 cows, 400 Angora nannies (their long, silky hair was woven through the local agricultural economy), corn and winter oats. "I could run more cattle than that, but what I've got, I own, not me and the bank," he said. A jackrabbit dashed across his headlights. Two small, skittish deer foraged just beyond the roadside brush. He bumped over the cattle guard and out onto Route 83. "I think about it all the time," he said about the responsibility of sheriffing the county at night. "They're all asleep, and I'm protecting them."

Uvalde County is one of those blocky, four-right-angles, checkerboard rural counties that make up the bulk of the Texas landmass and the Texas myth, but only a slice of the Texas people: The state's population now is 80 percent urban, and half of all Texans live in the Dallas and Houston metropolitan areas. Rugged, upland hills and valleys cover the north half of Uvalde; flat, mesquite country covers the south; and a powerful emptiness covers it all. Uvalde, seventy-five miles west of San Antonio, doesn't have much oil, but it does have plenty of space and its attendant freedom. The cattle inspector is an important local lawman, checking brands and looking for rustlers. At night the frontier is doubly empty, the white spaces on the map all turned to black, and the sheriffs are left to keep order in it. Beaumont Watkins's piece of the Texas night was roughly forty miles wide and thirty-five miles tall.

Watkins had spent the early-evening part of his shift, the presupper part, in the city that gives the county its name and is home to its sheriff's department, its jail, its courthouse and, with fourteen thousand people, almost two-thirds of its population. Uvalde, the city, has its own police force; Watkins, the county, was serving civil papers. He cruised the pleasant, shady, dusk streets—stately live oaks grew down the middle of one street—checking addresses on the mostly one-story houses. "All I know is that he lives in this area and drives a yellow Chevy," he said. He found the right yellow Chevy, the right house and the right man, sitting shirtless at his kitchen table eating supper with his wife, and then ruined the young man's appetite by politely serving him with a paternity suit brought by an ex-girlfriend. He served divorce papers to a woman whose TV sprayed cop-show gunfire outside when she opened her front door. He rapped on an apartment door with his pocketknife ("Saves my knuckles") and was told that the man he had a small-claims citation for had moved; he checked the license of the car parked outside anyway. "If I find out it's his, we're going back, and I may not be as polite this time," he said, but it wasn't, and he soon went home for supper. "Sooner or later we'll get him."

The prowler report had come from a woman in a trailer just outside the west city limits and just into county land, the sheriff's jurisdiction. She came to the door in a green housecoat. Her dog, a yellow dog of indeterminate breed, barked wildly. "That dog's hair stood up on end," she told Watkins. "I didn't like the way she was acting." He checked the back, crossing the border where her outside light stopped and the brush beyond began. Her neighbor was the cemetery where lay buried Uvalde's most famous citizen, John Nance Garner, Franklin Roosevelt's vice president, best known for describing the vice presidency as "not worth a pitcher full of warm spit." "I don't see anything now, ma'am, but I'd be more than happy to come back," Watkins told her.

"I just thought there coulda been somebody there," she said. "I know the dog. She'll take off after a varmint."

Watkins crossed back east through town, stopping briefly at headquarters to file a report on his prowler check, and started patrolling out where the suburbs would be if there were any. Pastureland flanked the road, and an armadillo crossed it. "I want to tell you, a black animal at night is the hardest animal to see. You usually don't see 'em till they turn around to look at you, just before you hit 'em." Tonight was the night of the last day of school, and he thought he might find some celebratory beer parties. He checked the Pits: nothing. He checked an unbuilt subdivision site. "I roped cattle back here when it was a ranch. Now it's a popular spot with the kids. They come up here to drink beer and hug on their girlfriends." Again he found nothing, just a parking-romance view of the Uvalde lights below that illustrated the booster slogan ("a sparkle in the eyes of Texas") from a billboard on the highway into town. He paused to dip a pinch from the tin of Copenhagen in his right breast pocket. Southwest of town he pulled up behind an old blue Pontiac Grand Prix parked on the shoulder beside a cotton field.

Holding the licenses he had just taken from the two young men, brothers, in the Grand Prix, Watkins said into his radio, "I need a couple twenty-seven twenty-nines on Texas DLs." One was old enough to legally drink the beer in the ice chest they had, but the other wasn't. The license check found clean records for both.

"I'm gonna give you a citation for making alcohol available to a minor," he told the older brother, who stood, like the younger brother, in the patrol-car headlights in a tank top and jeans, right leg trembling slightly, arms crossed tightly over his chest, hands clasped against his bare biceps as if he were chilled.

"I bought the beer," the younger brother offered, already looking to plea-bargain. "I can tell you who I got it from. They didn't ask for no ID or nothing. I've bought it there lots of times."

"Would you be willing to buy it again there sometime?" Watkins asked, already looking to sting a liquor-law violator. "What if one of the ABC guys got in touch with you? Would you be willing to go buy it with him?"

The young man agreed. "I'll be talking to the ABC guy," Watkins said, giving the brothers the citation and a full-forearm soul shake. "I advise you all to go home, and don't be giving your younger brother any more beer." The brothers and the deputy sheriff drove off in opposite directions. "I'm sure he'll be willing to do something for them," he said about the state liquor agent, "if they do something for him."

At the plant that freeze-dried vegetables—irrigation has created some farmland here—he saw the parked cars of the late shift as he passed. At the end of a dark gravel road northwest of town, Hacienda Road, he expected to see the parked cars of some young drinkers. The road led out from the highway into the brush—mesquite, prickly pear, persimmon, sage. "Everything in South Texas either bites you, cuts you or stings you." Watkins spotted a lanky boy standing beside a pickup parked on a dry riverbed near a triple-arched railroad bridge.

"Didn't I stop you at a beer party a while ago?" Watkins asked the boy, whose name he knew before he looked at the license. The boy looked off toward the brush where his drinking buddies had escaped in their four-wheel drive. "Didn't I tell you if I caught you again, I'd give you a citation?"

The boy shuffled his feet, looked at the ground. "Now, who'd you say drove off?" Watkins prompted.

"Sir?" the boy said, avoiding the question.

"They have any beer with them still?"

"No, sir, it's all finished. We were just sitting out here now."

"What would your daddy think about this? You know I visit with him sometimes. I think the world of your daddy and your mom."

The boy was contrite, abashed. "You don't have any whiskey behind the seat?" Watkins asked.

A Day in the Night of America

"No, sir."

"If I go behind the seat, am I likely to find any alcohol?"

"Not that I know of."

"Let's go have a look." Behind the seat was dry. He let the boy off with a warning he wanted passed along. "Go on home, and don't let me catch you again. You tell them, 'Don't be running.' If they're big enough to do the crime, they're big enough to do the time."

At a truckstop bar on the other side of town the jukebox was playing a song Watkins had been whistling all night: "There's a Tear in My Beer," by Hank Williams, Jr. They were shooting pool here, and Watkins—small, fifty, a late-blooming lawman, just five years with the department but already a captain—strode through the crowd, straight up to a beefy biker in a Harley T-shirt and asked to see a license: He thought he had a warrant on him. It was the wrong man. He turned and strode back out. "They need to get shook up once in a while."

Back in the patrol car he sang the song's chorus: "There's a tear in my beer, 'cause I'm cryin' for you, dear." "I love that song," he said. "I like country music, I like history and I like guns." He called on another bar, where the dance floor was busy with two-stepping couples, then orbited the city limits again, finding nothing but quiet. "Law enforcement a lot of times is just basic horse sense and how would you like to be treated, unless POPO comes to visit," he said, using an acronym borrowed from a police-academy instructor: pissed-off peace officer. "To use a for instance, say I see a car pulled over and a guy drinking beer who I told to stop before. I go back up to him again and he says, 'Oh, fuck you.' Okay, what's gonna happen? I've got two options—one, I could ignore him, two, I can put the son of a bitch in jail. If he's pissed me off, you know what I'm gonna do? I'm gonna put him in jail. I firmly believe POPO puts a lot of people in jail."

The truckstop bar's night had ended, as the law required, when Watkins passed it again just past 2—"They did a pretty good job clearing them out"—and so had his. A budget squeeze had erased the full overnight shift the sheriff's department had maintained up until the year before: Night was the most expendable time. Watkins, on duty since 5 P.M., would now go home and stay on call until 5 A.M., when another deputy would take over and go on call until the full day shift started at 8. "I go to sleep and hope the phone doesn't ring." But first he had some paperwork waiting back at headquarters. He whistled his song again as he walked from his patrol car out through the still Uvalde night.

⬤

The slow, aching notes of taps, the military's good-night ode, drifted down like a blanket over Fort Sam Houston in San Antonio, sounding as mournful as if they were coming from a battlefield bugler and not from the recording in a small office in the fort's headquarters. "The army's day is done and you'd better be in bed," Chief Warrant Officer James Downer said as the final note faded, just a shade past 11 P.M. on Memorial Day. Ten thousand soldiers, officers and privates alike, had called it a night now. Downer and Sergeant James Randle, the other staff duty officer for the night, were among the few assigned to stay awake; they sat side-by-side at a pair of old, wooden, glass-topped teachers' desks facing a microwave oven, a small refrigerator and a TV tuned to CNN. Flags, folded for the night, were tucked away behind the doors of a glass case. Hanging on the wall was a Frederic Remington print of cavalry soldiers gathered around a campfire. The screen door opened out onto a wide, palm-shaded veranda that ran the courtyard length of the building, a single-story white-clapboard horseshoe, and gave it the look of a colonial outpost in the tropics.

Fort Sam was one of the bases where the new army lived in close quarters with the old. It sprawled along the eastern edge of the only major Texas city that dates back to the Mexican era, the city where the Alamo was lost. The pale stone Quadrangle, still the fort's historic heart, confined the Apache warrior Geronimo after his surrender, and outfitted Teddy Roosevelt's Rough Riders on their way to Cuba. Growing out from the Quadrangle in a century's worth of architectural styles, the fort now looked like a college campus. It was home to the Army Health Services Command, the Brooke Army Medical Center, the Fifth Army, and the Army's Academy of Health Sciences, which trained young soldiers as medics. It had no combat units, and few fences. The street in front of headquarters, empty now, ran along MacArthur Field, where soldiers reported for morning exercises, out through the open base and straight onto the city streets, quietly crossing, with no ceremony and no sentry post, the unmarked line where the military met, and blended into, the civilian.

Around and around the post's 3,160 acres, the military police, in their Plymouth Reliant cruisers, circled again and again all through the night.

A Day in the Night of America

"Sometimes you get dizzy," said E-4 Frank Gannon, a patrolman who might cover 120 all-too-familiar miles in a night. "The troopies are like children. We have to make sure they're in at night."

The patrol cars, six out tonight, were tethered to the MP station, an old brick building that was accustomed to staying up all night: It used to be a bakery. "If we get caught sleeping, it's like, big-time trouble," said E-4 Sheila Hammel, who sat in battle fatigues before the red and green lights of the radio-room console, answering calls, watching for tripped alarms and dispatching cars. A patrolman came in with a report of his last call—a young soldier, nineteen, who had taken an overdose of pills, an apparent suicide attempt. " 'How much did you take?' I asked him. He said, 'I don't know,' then he started cussing. 'I don't give a fuck about military bearing.' I took him to the hospital."

On slow nights some MPs went "breeder hunting," looking for young soldiers who—briefly, nocturnally and covetously AWOL from their barracks—had taken their girlfriends and blankets out into the dark woods. Sergeant Raul Sanchez, the patrol supervisor, was just looking for anything out of the ordinary. He passed a tall apartment tower popular with military retirees that was, because old habits die hard, completely dark but for one apartment. He passed a lone hooker still on duty on a street outside the post. He passed the dark privates' barracks, and he passed the quiet lane, gracious with shade trees and a gazebo, where the generals lived. "You don't get into those houses without a star on your shoulder," Sanchez said.

Back at headquarters, Sergeant Randle answered the phone. "I'll see what I can do for you. As long as he's been at Fort Sam for three weeks or more, I possibly can help you." Randle checked, but he couldn't find the name the 3:30 caller was looking for. "We don't have him on microfiche. You have any idea what school he came here for? . . . Combat medic?" He gave the number of a medical battalion. "They may give you another number because they have five companies."

Burt Reynolds was on the TV, in *Heat*, swaggering around Las Vegas in a flashy silver suit. "He's getting ready to mess up a coupla guys," Randle said, as Reynolds beat up a guy who had pulled a gun on him. "Now he's gonna get the girl." The night was closing in on the predawn hours when Randle, trying to beat the Texas sun, often ran: He was an ultramarathoner to whom 26 miles was a mere sprint—the races he ran were as long as 100 miles—and he logged between 90 and 110 training

miles each week. "I've never been here when the sun is up," Burt Reynolds was saying now, the neon Vegas night burning behind him. "I have
a feeling it turns into the real world then."

Chief Warrant Officer Downer's attention moved up and down between
the screen and his book. He had just finished one—David Hackworth's
About Face, the memoir of the highly decorated army colonel who publicly
decried the Vietnam War that he had, long and valiantly, helped fight—and
now he was working on a second, Thomas Merton's *New Seeds of Contem-
plation,* a collection of meditations by the famed Trappist monk. He was
preparing to give a talk at the Episcopal church he belonged to, and he was
reading Merton's thoughts on war:

> At the root of all war is fear: not so much the fear men have of one another
> as the fear they have of *everything.* It is not merely that they do not trust one
> another; they do not even trust themselves. If they are not sure when
> someone else may turn around and kill them, they are still less sure when they
> may turn around and kill themselves. They cannot trust anything, because
> they have ceased to believe in God.

"It's strange," said Downer, who served in Vietnam. "You're talking about
an old combat veteran here, but that's true, really true. That's what it is all
about. I've got a twenty-one-year-old who can't wait for the next war. I say,
'Wait. The longer we can stretch it between them, the better.' "

Reveille blew at 6, another recording, to wake the army up again.

The storm warning, in the stern prepare-for-war tone of the Emergency
Broadcast System, came over the car radio just after I had passed the
cemetery in Goodnight, Texas. Northern Armstrong and Carson counties
were told to brace for severe thunderstorms and hail. I checked the map,
driving northwest through the Texas Panhandle, and I saw that northern
Armstrong County was exactly where I was. The afternoon sky, huge and
heavy over the treeless land, grew late-dusk dark, dappled by smudgy
patches of light like a portrait photographer's backdrop. Sharp, bright
lightning split the granite clouds. A TV news crew from nearby Amarillo
parked on the shoulder and aimed their camera at the apocalyptic vista. The
hail started near Washburn, a million trucks dumping a million loads of
gravel. A county-seat bank thermometer a ways back had marked the
temperature at 89 degrees, but now iceballs were falling from the sky. The

hail hit with the force of angry stones from a street riot in the final revolution. I pulled over and waited for my windows to shatter. The hail bounced on the highway, splashed into a new brown river that was rising fast in a roadside ditch and battered my roof until I felt like I was inside a tin-can target at shotgun practice. The bombardment stopped, moving on to a new county, after twenty-five minutes. I drove on through Amarillo and into a sky that opened again to let in the slow, late sun. My car's hood carried evidence of the storm for long, long after—the pings imprinted by the hail, concave shadows that followed like a memory of a brief and violent early night in Texas.

10

At 4:30, in a mile-high alpine meadow in the ROCKIES, *a white-robed monk sat alone in a dim chapel, deep in silent prayer.*

The road switchbacked up Cheyenne Mountain for three and a half miles, slowly climbing toward a line of pale-orange lights near the peak that looked like torches in the ramparts of a dark-and-stormy-night castle. It reached a plateau, high above Colorado Springs, and then, floodlit and bordered by razor-wire-topped fence, continued into the mountain itself, swallowed by a half-moon tunnel mouth. The tunnel was eerily empty, like the Lincoln Tunnel vacated for an air-raid drill, and it curved at an angle that concealed its other end. About a third of a mile in, armed guards in battle fatigues stood beside a thirty-ton blast door. Through that door and, a little farther in, through its twin, both wide open now, was NORAD—the North American Aerospace Defense Command, the night watchman for war, a complex of fifteen steel buildings set in a grid of hollowed-out chambers like a village in a coal mine.

Inside one of the buildings was the Command Post, where the clocks hanging in a row on the wall were set to different times: Alaska, Pacific, Mountain (the local time, 3:30 now), Central, Eastern, Zulu and, marked in red, Moscow. Five officers were on duty, watching for any enemy fire directed at North America. "We learned our lesson well from Pearl Harbor," said air force brigadier general James McIntyre, the commander here tonight. "Our job is to continually answer the question, Is North America under attack?"

With a quarter-mile of granite mountain above it, a thirty-day food supply, 350 cots, a medical ward, a barber shop, a dining facility ("The Granite Inn"), self-contained fuel and water reservoirs, flexible walkways between the buildings and giant shock absorbers and steel springs beneath them (to smooth the bumpy ride through a nuclear blast), six diesel engines each turning 1,750-kilowatt generators, and enough space-age hardware to outfit the secret conquer-the-world lair of a James Bond villain, NORAD's Cheyenne Mountain Complex was the military installation that probably best embodied the millenarian, end-of-the-world-as-we-know-it character of The Bomb. The satellites and radars that shielded the continent sent their data to the eighty-seven computers here. It was NORAD's job to distinguish "events" that might constitute a real threat (an incoming Soviet SS-18 ICBM, say) from "events" that were more benign—a flight of Canada geese, an errant piece of orbiting space junk, a forest fire, an unusual weather phenomenon, a nonbelligerent rocket launch (1,500 worldwide this year, from the space shuttle to small Soviet test missiles). "We determine it immediately and make our assessment known immediately to the national command authority," McIntyre said. "The last thing in the world we want to do is think we've got something when we don't."

The Command Post was about the size of a small classroom, dimly lit and busy with screens and electronic consoles like a TV-station control room—deceptively matter-of-fact interim quarters until the new Command Post amphitheater, under construction at the time, was finished. "I might argue that it's busier at night because on the other side of the world it's daylight," McIntyre said. "Any R-and-D launch in the USSR, we're going to see it." A polar-view map up on a wide screen outlined North America in green, the Soviet Union and Cuba in red. To accommodate a civilian guest, me, the room was in "unclassified configuration," so the map was otherwise as blank as after the final war. Once I left, the battle staff could again call up full maps and displays on which to paint strategic murals of the world, complete with submarine locations, aircraft routes, satellite orbits, defensive positions and missile trajectories arcing like comet tails. There was a red trash can, classified waste only, and a red phone; the phone to the president was black.

Back out in the tunnel a bus was on duty now, ready to carry in the seven hundred people who worked the day shift and carry out the three hundred who had worked the night shift in the mountain where it always looked like night. According to the clock, the sun was rising outside. In Washington the chairman of the Joint Chiefs of Staff had recently returned from a visit to restricted Soviet military sites, during which he and his Soviet counterpart signed an unprecedented accord: Neither nation, they agreed, would use force against the other in response to any accidental military confrontation. The outbound bus rounded a bend, and there it was, you could see it plain as day, light at the end of the tunnel.

◗

The early-warning system bing-bonged like a doorbell, the familiar sound of a border crossing. Two women had opened the front door and passed the threshold of the 7-Eleven on Lake Avenue, breaking the light beam that tripped the signal, and they continued on into the hospital-bright store from the dark night outside.

"Your mountains sure are a lot different from ours," one of them told Dave Harper, the manager behind the counter. They were visitors from Virginia, the mother and grandmother of a cadet at the U.S. Air Force Academy, which makes its home up near the sky here on the high ground of Colorado Springs. They had come west for both his graduation and, since he was a second lieutenant now and finally permitted to marry, his wedding. The wedding party had just ended, one of the dozens that immediately followed graduation, and they were still dressed for the occasion and high on the pageantry they had seen. The grandmother was especially taken with what she called the "swords" the other cadets had raised for the bride and groom to pass under.

"Mother, those are sabers," the daughter corrected as they left with their two coffees and—since the city's altitude, taller than Virginia's tallest mountain, had not agreed with them—their two headaches.

A waiter in a tuxedo shirt had a headache, too. "I sleep only two hours a night, not that I don't try," he said. "The doctor says it's hormones or something." He bought aspirin.

A man in a blue World Wrestling Federation jumpsuit followed, in town for a show; he had spent the evening at ringside, ringing the bell. "The Brainbusters lost to the Bushwackers tonight," he said, relaying the result of a tag-team match.

"But all that wrestling stuff's phony, right?" Harper prodded. "C'mon, you can level with me."

"Yeah, it is pretty phony." Three packs of cigarettes.

The counter floated like an island at the east end of the store, washed on all sides by milk, soda, magazines, potato chips, motor oil, burritos, micro-waveable cheeseburgers, cigarettes, bread, canned beans and enough other stuff to make you wonder how much you really needed something if you couldn't find it here at 3 A.M.

"Excuse me, you got any fishing worms here?"

"Right here, ma'am," Harper said, pointing out a small refrigerator at the front of the store. "Where you going?"

"Pueblo," she said, bringing her worms up. "Night fishing."

7-Elevens, and all the similar enterprises they spawned, are the general stores of the new frontier—stocked not with the salt pork and axes of the western boom towns, but with sustenance for the inhabitants of the frontier of night. Most of America's seven thousand 7-Elevens, including this one on the southwest edge of Colorado Springs, were open twenty-four hours now, and their name was just a name, not the open-and-close schedule it was when the chain was first christened after World War II. They have altered America's shopping habits; helped settle the night; extended to the noncity populace the previously city-exclusive luxury of round-the-clock service; rendered almost obsolete the practice of borrowing a cup of sugar from a neighbor; and created in many consumers the impression that somewhere, everywhere, a store is always open and that therefore you can always get what you want.

A long-haired young man heated a chili burrito in the microwave, a midnight snack apparently intended to soak up some of the lonesome beer sloshing in his belly. Another man paid four dollars for gas. Three packs of Dorals. A king-sized Reese's peanut-butter cup. Cookies and bread. "Need any milk tonight?" Harper asked. "You can't have cookies and bread without milk." No milk.

"It's cold out there," said a high school boy new in town from Arkansas. He wore a T-shirt and shorts as he played a video game, Black Tiger, in the corner. "You got a curfew here?"

"How old are you?" Harper asked him.

"Seventeen."

"Seventeen? You shoulda been home three hours ago." The boy's mouth dropped. "I'm only kidding. How do you like it here?"

"It's a lot better than Arkansas," he said, and returned to his game.

Maybe one hundred people came into the 7-Eleven between 11 and 7 on an average night, and Harper greeted all of them tonight when they tripped the light beam, letting them know that he knew that they were here.

"You get more people trying to shoplift at night," he said. The cartons of soda displayed on the apron outside were stacked low, leaving an unobstructed view out through the store-length windows. A thin height chart ran up the inside doorframe, not to measure growing children but to gauge the size of any fleeing thieves. Signs pleaded poverty to potential robbers: STORE HAS LESS THAN $30 AFTER MIDNIGHT; TIME-LOCK SAFE—CLERK CANNOT OPEN. According to a study by the National Institute for Occupational Health and Safety, only cabdrivers were more at risk for being murdered on the job than convenience-store clerks; about 10 percent of Florida's death-row inmates were convicted of killing people in convenience stores. In his thirteen years with 7-Eleven, Harper had never been held up.

A can of V-8 juice. A turkey sandwich and potato chips. A boy in a Led Zeppelin jacket and a Pizza Hut hat, just off work, paying for gas. Two state baseball lottery cards. "I got a hundred and thirty-six of 'em so far, I should win something."

Harper wore glasses, a dark beard and a white, short-sleeved, pharmacist-style smock imprinted with hundreds of small red-and-green *7-Eleven*s, its wide green collar open to a tie pulled tight against a buttoned top button. He ran the 2,400-square-foot store, a $60,000-a-month business, and was boss to a staff of nine, eight of them full-time. Born in Los Angeles, he started with 7-Eleven up in Denver, planning to work just long enough to earn a down payment on a set of tools for auto mechanics' school. He was an assistant manager before he knew it, and the tools were soon forgotten. "I call it the janitor shift. Mostly what you've got to do is clean the store up and get it ready to go by five A.M. I like graveyard. I like doing everything. It gives you the satisfaction of the store looking real nice in the morning, and nobody helped you, you did it by yourself. When people come in in the morning, they compliment only you: 'The store looks great.' You're proud of yourself." He cleaned the popcorn popper between customers.

A Super Big Gulp Coke. A large cheeseburger. A package of flour tortillas. "That's still yesterday's," Harper told a guy picking up a newspaper. The Dolley Madison delivery man. Free coffee for a cab driver, thanks for checking up on the store occasionally through the night.

Harper filled bags from the ice machine out back. The graveyard shift had introduced him to his wife. "She was filling in as a field manager and came in at five A.M. to pick up some paperwork. She wasn't there five minutes and I asked her out." She said no. He asked again later. She said no again. "A week later I was promoted to manager. It was a new store and she and I stocked the whole store ourselves. That's when we got to know each other better. We got married three months later. That was twelve years ago." The ice machine emptied, forty fresh bags of ice finished.

The post-last-call minirush straggled in soon after 2. Friday, tonight, was usually the week's busiest, Saturday was second, Sunday last. A cowboy hat bought Fritos, a burrito, Nestlé's Quik. A pack of Marlboros, a ham-and-cheese sandwich, Hawaiian Punch. A plate of nachos, cheese pumped on them like ballpark mustard. A bundle of *Gazette Telegraph*s arrived. Two quarts of oil to the Hardees hat, who fed it to his Volaré outside. Ten dollars' worth of gas and five baseball lottery tickets. "Let me have all of these," the gambler asked after noticing that his tickets were near the end of the roll, the place where his intuition and folk wisdom told him that winners usually hid out.

"All of 'em?" Harper asked.

"Yes, sir," he answered with a high-roller's swagger. Thirty-five dollars.

"I remember when they were fifty cents for these things," said a Denny's waitress paying $1.50 for a pack of Virginia Slims menthols.

"Wanna buy a Mustang?" a kid asked proudly. "Top speed one-forty."

Between 3 and 4 the customers barely outnumbered the deliveries. A barbecued chicken sandwich for a fat guy in a camouflage vest. Fresh muffins and doughnuts to fill the Dunkin' Donuts case. A dozen eggs. The Hostess cakes truck. Coffee for a uniformed army MP. The Slurpee machine, Coke and orange-pineapple tonight, kicked on like a refrigerator in a night kitchen. The video games, unplayed, beeped sporadically like a slow respirator. The hot-dog grill rolled no hot dogs.

Skip Smith, who usually worked nights alone, swept the apron outside. He wore gray flannel pants, gray loafers, and a white shirt and tie under his smock. He grew up in the tiny California desert town of Essex, spent twenty-one and a half years in the army, was wounded in Vietnam, and was last posted to nearby Fort Carson. "Last week I had this drunk come in, about two A.M. There was this display of spray perfume that looked like cigarette lighters and he wanted one. I kept telling him it wasn't a cigarette lighter, it was perfume, but you know how a drunk is, you can't tell him anything. He got it anyway and he squirted it all over his damn face trying to get the damn thing to light. He finally turned around and bought himself a lighter." Other night visitors had included John Denver, Terry Bradshaw, Bobby Unser, Jr., and a man who had inadvertently driven off while his wife was still in the bathroom. "She came out five minutes later, white as a ghost. 'Where's my husband?' " Smith recalled; her husband eventually retrieved her, half an hour later.

Every room window in the motel next door was dark. Out past the four gas pumps and the tall 7-Eleven sign, Lake Avenue ran silently west toward the Broadmoor, a famed resort that sits at the base of Cheyenne Mountain's civilian side. Up on the other side of the mountain you could see the lights of NORAD. Smith broke for a beef-and-bean burrito lunch out back.

Traffic picked up after 4:30, and customers with early faces, for whom it was now morning, started displacing those with late ones. Coffee and doughnuts. Six-packs of Doral menthols. A six-pack of 7UP and nachos with cheese. Coffee. A bleary goateed man in a Corona shirt. A blue-uniformed off-to-work waitress, fresh makeup and nail polish. Harper spread his paperwork over the counter near the nachos. Smith finished cleaning up yesterday and started preparing tomorrow: He faced shelves, neatly pulling the merchandise up to the edges; stocked the cooler with Mountain Dew (a night person's secret elixir, more caffeinated than cola); set the ninety-nine-cent breakfast sausages on the hot-dog grill to brown; dumped old coffee grounds and ground new beans into the filters. By 5:15 five pots of coffee were going on the Beverage Bar.

"Pack of Marlboros," a man requested, and Smith reached up over the register where the best-selling brand was kept; the other 183 brands were arranged alphabetically around an overhead horseshoe. A full tank of gas for a Chevy Blazer. Pepsi and a hot ham-and-cheese sandwich. Gas and grape-fruit juice for a cowboy hat. More tens and twenties for the time-lock safe's tube.

"I ain't even been to sleep yet," said the regular coffee. Orange juice and Dr Pepper. A withdrawal from the automatic teller machine. A mother (coffee) and daughter (gum). Two men in uniform: a navy commander in white, wiping his shoes with a paper towel out at the gas pump; a Broad-moor waiter, bow tie and five-star lapel pin, buying cigarettes.

"Boy, I'm a hurtin' unit this morning," the bread man said, hauling in fresh loaves. "I had to get my wife out of bed to tie my shoes." Coffee. Coffee. Bread, orange juice and coffee. Directions and coffee for the staid blue-blazer and blue-dress motel couple. Smith had seven pots going now. A dozen pots vanish in just two hours here on a Monday morning, the busiest morning, a regular rush of cheap, quick fixes that help pull the store's average purchase down to about $3.50 a head.

A Day in the Night of America

By 6:15 the door was playing a rising chorus of bing-bongs, eight people were in the store, the assistant manager had arrived for the day shift and Harper and Smith were getting ready to leave, a garbage truck had breakfasted on the big Dumpster, and the sun was breaking through the clouds to the east. Cheyenne Mountain's rising slopes caught the first sun, glowing, a premonition of the morning light that would soon descend to replace the thin dawn shade now washing over the 7-Eleven. The summit was still invisible, shrouded by dark clouds.

Potatoes, bananas, mayonnaise, mustard and pickles, and a cookie for her sleepy young son riding in the cart. "I just woke him from his baby-sitter," the young mother told Jerry Miller, the checker at Register 6, the only register open at this hour at the King Soopers supermarket in the Austin Bluffs section of Colorado Springs, northeast across town from the 7-Eleven. She had just finished the evening shift at a plant that made microwave ovens.

"You can't go on the horsey. He's broken," she told her son. The mechanical pony was out to pasture with an out-of-order bag over its head. "Have a good morning," she said to Miller as she left.

"Most people say, 'Have a good night,'" Miller said when she was gone. "You get some weird ones, like 'Have a good day.' I think, 'Day? This sure is a strange-looking day.'"

The store, all 61,000 square feet of it, twenty-five times the size of the 7-Eleven, was a dream of plenty to anyone who had ever bumper-carred through a rush-hour supermarket aisle or languished in a long checkout line. The pharmacy had closed at 9, the meat and seafood departments and the bakery at 10, the deli at 11, the customer service counter at 12, but the rest of the store—the mountain range of groceries across its heartland, from the health and beauty aids foothills over the frozen food valley to the fields of produce—was wide open all through the night.

Most twenty-four-hour supermarkets, packed with staples too inconvenient for convenience stores to carry, stay open all night more by default than by design: Their main nocturnal mission is stocking, not selling. Every night, after every day's harvest by shoppers, the aisles are replenished with fresh goods. Since the night crew occupies the store anyway, the logic follows, and the electricity hums unbroken, it might as well open for business. A single night checker's salary is the sole added cost: Of the dozen or so people working tonight, Miller was the only one who wouldn't be here if the doors were locked to shoppers. This King Soopers, one of eight in the city and sixty-six in the state, went to twenty-four hours two years before, after an expansion and renovation, and after a similar schedule change by its nearby competitors. The number of open hours rose by 37 percent, business by 2 percent, much more than enough to pay Miller.

Seltzer and tortilla chips. Three boxes of White Castle microwave hamburgers and microwave french fries. "That oughta be easy to make," Miller said as he put the boxes in a plastic bag.

"Yeah, my girlfriend's coming over."

A home pregnancy test to a young man whose anxious face asked for a negative. "I remember one guy who ran all the way down and all the way back up for a pack of condoms," Miller said as the man went off toward his verdict. "I guess he was afraid she was gonna change her mind."

In Aisle 11, Danny Bustamento deftly razored open a case of canned sweet peas and reholstered his cutter in his belt. "In my opinion it's the most important job in the entire store," said the night-crew foreman. "We make the place presentable to the public. If it wasn't for these people filling the shelves, there wouldn't be any product for the customers to buy." He wore the official crew top, a yellow polo shirt, and the semiofficial bottom, blue jeans. The peas flew onto the shelf—throwing stock, they called it—subtract another case from the 600 that had to be thrown tonight, a slow night. Mondays, the busiest nights, might bring as many as 2,100 cases.

Bob Chacon, a nineteen-year King Soopers veteran, worked the high-end specialties. "I didn't even know we had this stuff. Ten dollars to eat salmon eggs? To me that's the stuff you go fishing with. Somebody said, 'Well, put it on a cracker, it'll taste better,' and I'm like, 'Right.' "

Pat Keegan painted a Michael Jordan mural with boxes of Wheaties on an Aisle 8 shelf. He was on his fourth skid of cases. "I'm always hungry anyway. It makes it more convenient at lunchtime—you've got the whole store to choose from. But sometimes you come off break with a full stomach and you won't even want to look at it, it's like 'Please, no more.' " He had two more skids, piled high with cases of Bran Chex, Raisin Bran and other cereals, to put up before breakfast.

Tuna, bananas and bread back at Register 6, another express-lane-sized load; full carts were uncommon after midnight, only a handful each week. "I keep the till low," said Jerry Miller, who had never been robbed. "If they don't see much money, they'll think it's not worth it, or at least I hope they think so."

Two bartenders paid in singles, almost twenty dollars' worth, their tip money. "I've had some give me thirty, forty dollars in singles." Miller was deep in the retail valley now, doing more stocking than checking. He worked nights by choice and had weekends off ("To get weekends off in the grocery business is quite a challenge"). He picked his two boys up from school each afternoon while his wife worked as a day checker. Off duty he played guitar and wrote songs, including one about working the night shift, "The Devils of a Midnight Moon." "At night I'm working out lyrics in my head. If I were a day checker, I couldn't do that—too many people, too much noise. One night an artist came in, and he was telling me that his best time for painting was three or four in the morning."

Two rental videos (*Coming to America* and *Iron Eagle II*) to a young couple, he in flannel shirt, jeans and workboots, she in red high heels, pink ankle socks and ruffled red miniskirt. "She looked pretty good for this time of the morning," Miller said.

In an aisle clear of both packing cases and shoppers, Fred Heedt swung slow arcs across the floor with a high-speed buffer, guiding it like a lawn mower. "Man, I remember my first night shift," said the maintenance manager, who had started on nights ten years before, not long after two shoulder operations had cost him his pitching ability and his baseball scholarship. "I got off work and I drove home and I saw all these cars with lights on coming to work and I thought, 'Man, this is weird.' But I never thought I'd be doing it ten years later. It's hard to explain to anybody who's never done it." He was the father of three now and a student again, studying accounting part-time at the University of Colorado, three years down and probably three years yet to go. "I used to have a lot of problems sleeping during the day. Since I've been in school, I've had no problems sleeping."

At 6 A.M. at Register 6 Jerry Miller rang up pantyhose, contact-lens solution and a single red rose for a young woman in a Sigma Kappa sweatshirt. "People buy flowers at weird times," he said. "I make a killing on those roses."

An empty cart, 7-Eleven coffee cup riding in the child's seat, set off into the aisles, the morning's inaugural big trip, piloted by a woman clutching a shopping list in one hand. "People do a lot of things just to get away from the crowds," Miller said. "I dunno. I wouldn't get up at five-thirty to go shopping. I'd have to really hate crowds."

The store was just about ready to supply the day now. The meat and bakery and produce trucks had made their deliveries out back, and the in-store bakers had scented the air with their ovens. Seven aisles had been waxed, and a fan blew down the last one to help it dry. The shelves were mostly filled, and the facing was now under way—"covering the wood," the final-touch work of pulling forward the groceries to cover the bare spots and form a line as straight and solid as a military parade.

"After you get finished, it looks really cool. Everything's all neat," said Danny Bustamento, drilling a troop of chili cans in Aisle 10. "I find myself when I go grocery shopping pulling things forward." He moved on to the Campbell's soup, building a red-and-white wall three cans high. Next was Aisle 9, where he stacked sugar like sandbags against a rising flood.

Soon after 7 all the wood was covered, the day shift, eighty or so, was on their way in, and Miller had taken in maybe $500, less than the 7-Eleven had. Bustamento and a colleague were off to celebrate their worknight's end with a beer at a nearby bar that had just opened. The empty parking lot was sharp with diamond light. The last traces of snow at the peak of Pikes Peak glinted in the morning sun.

The Rockies loom behind Colorado Springs like the petrified curl of an epic tidal wave, frozen in granite after racing across the West from the Pacific, poised to break on the wide strand of the High Plains. I crossed them by day, not night: I wanted to see the peaks, not guess at them; I had watched too many movie cars plunge off winding cliff roads; and I chose not to challenge two frontiers, of time and extreme geography both, at once. I drove up into them so high that I almost hit winter: It was June, and it was snowing. Up at Independence Pass—where the road topped out, at 12,095 feet, and crossed the Continental Divide—the snow still lay like a glacier blanket. When it melted, the snow on the east side of the line rolled down toward the Atlantic, the westside snow, the snow I followed, down toward the Pacific.

The mountains bumped slowly, slowly down, white replaced by gray replaced by green replaced by terra-cotta, southwestern-looking now, reddish scrubby with green, whispering out, fading into gaunt mesas and canyonlands, gouged and brown like a gnawed apple left out to the air. "The Western Slope's only talk radio," the station announced. I was passing Grand Junction, crossing into Utah, and hearing a voice, their network feed, that came from New York: "Talknet puts you in touch with the rest of the country." A lonely-hearted woman was in touch with Talknet now. "I'm in love with a talk-show host," she said. "I feel like I want to be part of him. I have a picture of him, and when I look at it, I just melt." It was the emptiest country I'd ever seen and it kept repeating itself, mile after interstate mile, like a Road Runner cartoon backdrop.

A ghostly Park Service message played over and over again on a travelers' information station like a phonograph in an abandoned house: "To the south of you lies one of the most varied and scenic landscapes on earth," the disembodied federal voice said about Arches and Canyonlands National Parks. One hundred and two miles on I-70 out of Grand Junction came the first sign that the human species had staked any claim here: GREEN RIVER, a billboard announced, ALL SERVICES 24 HOURS. If you were weary, or hungry, or your car even slightly thirsty, there was another message that subtly counseled the wisdom of stopping now: NEXT SERVICES 110 MILES.

Green River, an interstate whistlestop of one thousand or so people, was the only place to buy a night's sleep, the only real settlement of any kind at all, for 212 miles along I-70, a blasted expanse of open space that refutes century-old obituaries for the American frontier. The Census Department defined the frontier as anywhere with fewer than two people per square mile, and in 1890 declared it closed; but you would be hard-pressed to find a better word to describe this swath of Utah. About 45 percent of the American landmass—including the counties around Green River, and most of the rest of the territory between the Coast Mountains that bisect the Pacific states and the Ninety-eighth Meridian the freight train had crossed back in Nebraska—still has fewer than six people per square mile, and is classified by some geographers as a contemporary frontier. People across this expanse collect into towns like Green River much the way people across the night collect into pools of light: Company provides some comfort against the void.

Irrigation from the river that named the town had raised some melon fields here, but Green River drew its sustenance mostly from its interstate locale. Main Street, a business spur off I-70, was a two-mile stretch of motels, gas stations and restaurants, an incongruous strip of suburban America. River rafters and wilderness trekkers made base camp here. Vegas-bound gamblers from Denver stopped, halfway to the casinos. Interstate nomads ate, filled up, slept. The economy was based on one-night stands and less. Just outside town the night was black as a coal mine. Laid straight through Green River was a bright, reassuring line of lights.

The Motel 6, my chain of choice across the country, marked the eastern terminus of the strip, neighbor to the battered screen of a defunct, brushy drive-in theater. A historical marker out front honored MAJOR POWELL, COLORADO RIVER EXPLORER: THE FIRST ORGANIZED ATTEMPT TO CONQUER THE SWIRLING RAPIDS AND PRECIPITOUS WALLED CANYONS OF THE GREEN AND COLORADO RIVERS—they meet south of here in Canyonlands—WAS MADE BY MAJOR JOHN WESLEY POWELL, CIVIL WAR HERO AND EXPLORER. Another sign read, SORRY. The motel, like most of the others in town, was full.

"Where's the next motel," asked a young woman.

"Salina," said Doris Schumacher, who managed the motel with her husband.

"How far is that?"

"110 miles." The sign hadn't been lying.

All 103 rooms, in two balconied stories wrapped around a pool, were spoken for by travelers who expected nothing beyond a phone and a free TV (no more $1.49 rental fee) in a clean, cheap (not the $6 it was when Motel 6 was named, but $23.95 for one person, $29.95 for two) room from the chain that institutionalized and popularized spartan accommodations. The staff consisted of just ten maids, three desk clerks and, after 11, when the office closed, one Doris Schumacher. "You keep answering the night bell. You just hope the stupid thing doesn't ring. Usually around four A.M. the traffic stops." Bookkeeping duties usually kept her busy until the last reservations arrived. Answering the night bell was her husband's duty after that. "I'm one of those people, when I go to sleep I die."

The Schumachers had, like military personnel, come to Green River on somebody else's marching orders: Motel 6's. Their children were grown, they were short of retirement age, the trucking line he worked for had been squeezed out of business by deregulation, so they signed up with the company, were trained in Scottsdale, Arizona, and were deployed here. "Some people really like this country," she said, especially French and German tourists. "They come for the open spaces." She did not. "I like trees. I like mountains." They had lived for many years in Steamboat Springs, Colorado, and, later, in Grand Junction. "UPS only comes twice a week. We drive fifty miles to Moab to shop. It'd be nice if you could go to a grocery store." They had asked for a transfer.

By 10 the next morning the motel was almost a ghost town. Jack Schumacher was at the front desk, taking room keys from the last stragglers. His wife had been up until 3:30, when the last reservation had arrived from

California. "People from California don't realize how big the desert is, they just keep going," he said. "They're the only people we have that trouble with."

The narrow road east out of Ogden cut into the mountains like a driveway into a private, timeless kingdom. It shared a steep-walled canyon with a river and then opened up into a high, green, paradisical valley, ringed all around by snow peaks of the Wasatch Range, a western flank of the Rockies. A lake fanned out behind a dam on the river, the town of Eden on its north shore. (The town of Paradise was a couple of mountains farther north.) On the south shore was Huntsville, home to thirty-two Trappist monks who rose daily at 3:15 and, in a ritual transported almost whole from the twelfth century, prayed together in the deep, silent mountain night.

The monk's sanctuary, 1,850 mile-high acres and the heavens above, spread across the flat greens and up the hillsides at one end of the Ogden Valley in northern Utah. The entrance was arched by the kind of gate you might see at a Texas ranch, except that it read ABBEY OF OUR LADY OF THE HOLY TRINITY, and displayed a cross, not a brand symbol. The drive curved gently in for two-thirds of a mile through fields of alfalfa, wheat, barley and pasture grass. Cattle lowed in the distance. Siberian elms rose to shelter the drive as it approached the monastery compound—barns, coops and other farm outbuildings where the monks worked on one side, the abbey where they lived and prayed on the other. Holy Trinity's abbey, "unique in the history of monastic architecture" according to the monks, looked more like a lushly overgrown army camp than a catacomby, Gothic, Dark Ages cloister—a quadrangle of light-gray three-story quonset huts, punctuated by green-trimmed windows and sprayed thick with foam insulation that made it look like a concrete bunker reinforced against the enemy outside.

The buildings, military surplus left over from World War II, intended as temporary, had grown into permanence, softened and shaded all around by trees and greenery, embodying the community's functional simplicity. Heavy snow piles on in winter until the abbey resembles an Arctic research station, collecting data from Earth's farthest reaches. One side of the quadrangle, the chapel, rose a little taller than the others, crowned by a graceful parabolic bell tower. Beside the chapel was a small cemetery with one large white cross and twelve small ones, a daily reminder that just as the monks' lives were tied here—they rarely ventured past the gate—so, too, were their deaths.

Seven times a day, every day, the monks filed into the spare, white, tunnellike interior of the chapel to celebrate the Divine Office—the daily schedule of psalms, readings, prayers and hymns that comprises the official prayer of the Roman Catholic church—and the seventh time today was at 7:30 for Compline, the closing prayer before sleep. A beam from the setting sun shot through the rear balcony window and hit the tabernacle on the altar like a celestial spotlight. The last few monks arrived singly, hands folded and invisible in the cavernous sleeves of their white, floor-length robes. They bowed from the waist, slowly, deeply, before taking their places among the other monks in the narrow choir stalls that faced each other, two rows on each side, across the chapel's middle. Many wore over their robes a black scapular like a blacksmith's apron. The calls of the evening birds outside were clear in the silence inside. They stood as one and began intoning the Compline psalms:

> I will lie down in peace and sleep comes at once for you alone, Lord, make
> me dwell in safety.

Their voices merged in the ancient, droning, haunting rhythms of Gregorian chant, the unaccompanied and unharmonized liturgical plain-song that dates to the sixth century. The sole apparent concession to the modern church was the language: English, not Latin.

> You will not fear the terror of the night
> nor the arrow that flies by day,
> nor the plague that prowls in the darkness
> nor the scourge that lays waste at noon.

Many of the monks chanted from years of chanting before, scarcely glancing at the hymnals laid out on the long easel-slanted desks before them. Their average age was sixty-one. Their hair was cropped boot-camp short.

> Lift up your hands to the holy place
> and bless the Lord through the night.

A Day in the Night of America

May the Lord bless you from Zion,
he who made both heaven and earth.

The psalms finished, the abbot blessed the monks with holy water. One went off to ring the bell. It was 7:45 and their day was officially done.

The dying sun outside was climbing the mountains, draping the valley in shadow. Most of the monks retired to their rooms, but one stood out in the small parking lot with a curious family of Mormon visitors to whom he appeared doubly out of place—both in this century and in this state. He explained about the practical side of monastic life—they supported themselves mainly by raising beef cattle and selling eggs and creamed honey— and the spiritual. "I wanted my life to say something about my relationship with the Lord," he said. When they left, he walked down the drive with another visitor, a Salt Lake City radio deejay who was, though he had been raised Lutheran and was now a divorced father of two, considering joining. He returned after the departure of the alpenglow, the last memory of sun that lingers on the highest peaks, and then he, too, went in for sleep.

The front wing of the abbey quadrangle was the guest wing, open to any men, Catholic or not (women were welcome in the chapel, but not as overnight retreat guests), who wished to share the monks' routine for a day or two. I was still on night-shift, not liturgical, time, so I browsed the reading room there. The shelves were labeled by subject: Hagiography, Theology, Prayer, Christ, Our Lady, Church History. One shelf, labeled simply MERTON, was reserved for the eloquent Trappist whose writings (especially his best-selling spiritual autobiography, *The Seven Storey Mountain*) introduced the secular world to the order and gave it an intellectual cachet that filled the abbey with would-be monks in the 1950s. Holy Trinity's population peaked at eighty-five back then, fifty-two of them novices. A handful stayed to take their final vows; some lasted but a single day.

The Holy Trinity monks stood at the end of an austere, contemplative line that reached back a millennium and a half, an almost incomprehensible span in instant America, to the Rule of Saint Benedict, the fifth-century Italian monk who sketched the blueprint for Western monasticism. The white robes came in the twelfth century, when some monks, thinking the life had grown too soft, founded the Order of Cistercians and returned to the ascetic poverty of the original Benedictines. The Trappist name came in the seventeenth century, the result of another back-to-basics reform movement, a split that originated in La Trappe, France.

"Many people, even among Catholics, don't understand our life," Abbot Malachy Flaherty said the next day. He had entered the Trappist monastery at Gethsemani, Kentucky, in 1943, and was a novice under Merton. "Maybe they think it's a waste of time, a waste of life, because there's no tangible fruit you can point to as being useful to the church. We're not teachers, we don't care for the poor, we don't preach retreats. We feel our contribution is not direct, but indirect. It's to pray for world problems. Usually we have enough awareness of what's going on in the world and of what needs prayer. Every prayer is heard, but it may not be heard the way you want. He has his own reasons. We have to just bow our heads when things are not the way we pray for. Our life is based on faith and the value of prayer."

"We come here to pray," Father Baldwin Shea said. "It's really a life of prayer and sacrifice and penance for the whole world."

"It's an effort to unite ourselves to the prayer of Christ on behalf of the whole church, the whole world," said Father Charles Cummings. "I consider it a ministry to pray for the world within Christ. It's the prayer of Christ we're organized for continuing."

The reading-room walls were hung with photos charting Holy Trinity's passage since it was founded here in 1947 to handle the overflow from a crowded Gethsemani—the abbey in lush, blooming summer, and in deep white winter; the monks tilling the fields, making hay, eating at the communal tables in the refectory; one monk in the music room listening through headphones to a record, *Don't Go in the Lion's Cage Tonight,* by Julie Andrews; a line of nine monks, seen from behind and shrouded like hobbits in dark hooded robes, walking up a treeless dirt lane in their heavy boots. "When we came, there was not one tree here," said Father Baldwin, one of the original thirty-four settlers. "I can remember getting off the bus, coming from Kentucky where there were beautiful forests and trees, and we just made a sign to each other, 'No trees.' " For the first two years they lived in barracks salvaged from a wartime prison camp that had held German POWs. The Trappists had survived Henry VIII, the French Revolution, Bismarck and, more recently, Vietnam, China and the Eastern bloc, and they had now, prodded in part by the churchwide Vatican II reforms, negotiated some accommodations with yet another potential foe: the shrinking, sprinting modern world. They still avoided unnecessary conversation, but they had exchanged sign language for spoken. They were still vegetarians—the beef they raised was strictly for profit, not sustenance—but they now ate eggs twice a week and fish on Sunday. For their work outside the chapel they now mostly wore donated odd-lot civilian clothes (a flannel shirt here, a Denver Broncos cap there) rather than the long, rough, entangling robes. Some devotions had been shortened, simplified (night vigils could once last as long as three hours) and English had replaced Latin, although fitting it to the Gregorian chant took some work. They read outside periodicals now (sprinkled among the religious publications in their library were the Ogden *Standard-Examiner, The Christian Science Monitor, U.S. News & World Report, National Geographic, The National Review,* and *Popular Science*) but they watched no TV. Back at Gethsemani, according to Father Baldwin, the monks' knowledge of World War II was limited to three announcements from the abbot, who kept track of what needed praying for outside. The United States is at war, he told them after Pearl Harbor: Pray. The war with Germany is over, the war with Japan continues, he said after V-E Day: Pray. The war with Japan is over, he finally said after V-J Day. "That was it, nothing else. He never said another word about it." They voted now, more conservatively than you might expect. They saw movies on rare occasions: *The Sound of Music* was a special favorite. "When we saw *Patton,* the monks' eyes bugged out of their heads because of all the cursing." Their music room was well used, their collection mostly classical. They had John Deere tractors, Honda ATVs, pickups, old cars and bicycles to get around with, a well-equipped exercise room, a Xerox machine, a computer for the honey business. Their solemn perpetual vows remained fixed as the mountains: poverty, chastity, obedience, stability, and conversion of manners. "You never say you're holy enough," Father Baldwin explained.

I took Room 12, the Saint Peter room, upstairs along a dormitory hall. A lone ceiling bulb illuminated a spare, clean cell beside which a Motel 6 room was a Ritz suite—narrow bed, dresser, table, two chairs, coatrack, Bible, psalmbook, crucifix. A liturgical schedule was posted on the inside of the door: Rise 3:15; Chant Office of Vigils 3:30–4:05; 6 A.M. Office of Lauds; 6:20 Community Mass (again at 11 on Sundays and Holy Days); 7:45 Office of Terce; 12:15 Office of Sext; 2:15 Office of None; 5:30 Office of Vespers; 7:30 Compline. The label on the bed's rough gray-wool blanket said it had been made in Australia. In 1943.

* * *

Kevin Coyne

The four white-cowled monks sat still as statuary in the choir stalls' tiny flip-down seats, bent forward slightly at the angle that signals reverence or weariness, or both. The light from above shone down on them as on a stage, leaving the rest of the chapel in cavern darkness. The stained-glass Christ set in the half-moon wall behind the altar was a shadow, no light from outside to animate it. The illuminated clock up on the right marked the time at 3:20. Five minutes before, just as the schedule warned, a wake-up bell had bing-bonged out in the hallway, leaving me with the groggy, unsettling impression, as it sounded again and again, that somebody was at the front door and nobody was answering.

A red-velvet rope cordoned the rear third of the chapel, the section reserved for the public, from the front two-thirds, the enclosure (the choir stalls back through the altar) reserved for the monks, a reversal of the usual congregation-to-clergy architectural proportions of most churches. The gate down at the end of the drive was locked, and I sat alone up in the dark balcony. The four became six became twelve became twenty-four—the others, some older and sick, prayed alone in their rooms—and at 3:30 they stood together: "Praise be the Father, the Son and the Holy Spirit, both now and forever; the God who is, who was, and is to come at the end of the ages." First they sang, then they chanted Psalm 17. The voice was eerily familiar: It was the same voice, the same cadence, given to old movie ghosts.

Then the earth reeled and rocked;
the mountains were shaken to their base:
they reeled at his terrible anger.
Smoke came forth from his nostrils
and scorching fire from his mouth:
coals were set ablaze by its heat.

Their individual voices submerged into the larger voice, as their individual lives submerged into the communal spiritual life of the monastery. It was a solemn voice, hypnotic and otherworldly, but it was also tender. It didn't try to shout God out; it gently coaxed.

He lowered the heavens and came down,
a black cloud under his feet.
He came enthroned on the cherubim,
he flew on the wings of the wind.

He made the darkness his covering,
the dark waters of the clouds, his tent.
A brightness shone out before him
with hailstones and flashes of fire.

The Lord thundered in the heavens;
the Most High let his voice be heard.
He shot his arrows, scattered the foe,
flashed his lightnings, and put them to flight. . . .

You, O Lord, are my lamp,
my God who lightens my darkness.
With you I can break through any barrier,
with my God I can scale any wall. . . .

A reading from the Book of Daniel followed. Daniel, read the monk with the faint Irish brogue, was cast into a lions' den for the night, but the dawn found him whole and unharmed, preserved by his faith. The monks sat in a marble hush when the reading was done, meditative, demonstrating the geometric progression of silence: The more who share it, the louder it grows. A red handkerchief appeared from the voluminous sleeve of one monk, and he blew his nose, a rifle shot. A cough resounded with a canyon echo. They rose again to chant Psalm 18.

The heavens proclaim the glory of God
and the firmament shows forth the work of his hands.
Day unto day takes up his story
and night unto night makes known the message.

No speech, no word, no voice is heard
yet their span extends through all the earth,
their words to the utmost bounds of the world.

I heard the voice filling with light, vanquishing the cold, dark, damp ecclesiastical stone my unaccustomed ears had initially heard ringing in it. It rose like the hum of the universe, the sound you might hear if you could amplify the unheard spinning of the spheres through space. The chapel, already a mile high, seemed to levitate even higher, uprooted and floating over the dark meadow.

There he has placed a tent for the sun;
it comes forth like a bridegroom coming from his tent,
rejoices like a champion to run its course.

At the end of the sky is the rising of the sun;
to the furthest end of the sky is its course.
There is nothing concealed from its burning heat. . . .

Standing and chanting in apparitional white, absorbed in their elemental communion with God, the monks seemed almost to lose their corporeality, becoming more spirit than flesh. They continued on into Psalm 26.

The Lord is my light and my help;
whom shall I fear?
The Lord is the stronghold of my life;
before whom shall I shrink?

They bowed deeply at psalm's end and sat for another reading, from a letter of exhortation by Saint Boniface, eighth-century missionary, monk, bishop and martyr. "Our duty is to not abandon ship," Father Charles said in his preface to the reading. He switched off the lectern lamp when he was finished, and the monks sat again in stone silence for several minutes. They stood and faced the altar and sang, and at 4:05, with a final "Thanks be to God," they finished. The bell rang three times, paused, three times again, paused, three times a third time, paused to complete the trinity, then unleashed a long, joyous, pealing chorus that, confined though it was to a remote and sheltered valley, sounded as if it were meant to wake an entire city.

The universe of stars hovered against the moonless sky outside like a soft flurry of mountain snow. The chapel windows, five tall rectangles aglow with golden hearth light, made a lone, faint stand against the conquering darkness.

"What you saw from outside is a very good image of why we're up at that hour doing what we're doing," Father Charles said later. "It's because of the contrast of the world all asleep, all enveloped in darkness, and here at one point, in this valley, in these mountains, there's a bright center of light. Our praise of God kind of counterbalances the rest of the darkness around."

"At night, when you first get up, you really are better able to pray then," Father Baldwin said. "It's the quietest time. We're farmers, so we're busy during the day, but at that time of night, no. We're not bothered by any visitors or guests. It's a very precious time."

"We watch because it is characteristic of lovers to watch for the return of the beloved," Father Charles wrote in his 1986 book, *Monastic Practices*. He devoted a full chapter to the custom of the night watch, from the Gospels through the early Christians (the Acemetes, a fifth-century order of monks dedicated to perpetual recitation of the Divine Office, slept in shifts so that their community prayer could continue unbroken) to his own experience: "By quietly watching and praying through the night, I learn to live with the slow process of my own spiritual growth. I have no control over the future and I do not know exactly what will happen. I am asked only to stay awake and be ready because the light will surely come and will claim its victory over every form of darkness, despair, suffering, and death."

"It is of the nature of vigils that they be a test of the power of spirit against the power of flesh," Father Charles wrote. "Watching promotes and symbolizes the ascendancy of spirit over flesh in our life, and the final victory of life over death in our physical body, for the oblivion of sleep is the image of death. Watching strengthens and prepares us for the time of testing. The great adversary of night watching is not sleep so much as Satan, ruler of the night. The person who watches and prays at night challenges Satan at the height of his power, for the night belongs to him."

"There is nothing so feared, even by Satan, as prayer which is offered during vigils," Saint Isaac of Nineveh wrote in the seventh century.

"And there shall be no night there," the Book of Revelation promises about the kingdom of heaven.

The starry night sky—immense beyond knowledge, an invitation to faith—illustrated the monks' name for this predawn time: The great silence, they called it, the contemplative summit of the contemplative day, the two hours between Vigils, the first office, and Lauds, the second, the time when the earth, wrapped in darkness and peace, most nearly approximates the basic condition of the universe. The monks had dispersed, the communal devotions replaced by solitary. "It's like a spiritual meal to start your day," Abbot Malachy said later. From behind one closed door I heard a typewriter; from another a voice reciting the Beatitudes: "Happy are the poor in spirit, for theirs is the kingdom of heaven. . . ." Some meditated silently in their cells. Some said Mass privately. Some read sacred texts. Some said the rosary. Many drank coffee. At 4:30 one monk still sat alone in the shadowy chapel, deep in silent prayer. "It's really a form of conversation," Abbot Malachy said about the monks' prayers. "For some it's more a vocal process, for others it's more a mental process to experience contact with God. We can't see God, but faith tells us he's present, not just in the Eucharist but in his word. If you and I were in a room talking, and it was night and the lights went out, I'd still know you were here. It's something intangible, but real. Basically it's a form of friendship, a real conversation."

By 4:45 the eastern sky was bluing behind the mountains, and the undertone of birdsong was ascending toward them. The chapel lights seemed to weaken like a dying candle. By the Muslim definition—the time when you can discern the difference between a black thread and a white— dawn had arrived. The bells rang at 5:45, prefatory to Lauds. As the world returned, the night shift at the prayer factory was ending.

Abbot Malachy lapped the chapel slowly, stopping in prayer at each of the Stations of the Cross, while the monks trickled back into the choir stalls. At 6, the hour of ringing alarm clocks across America, they stood for the Office of Lauds and chanted, among other psalms, Psalm 8.

> When I see the heavens, the work of your hands,
> The moon and the stars which you arranged,
> what is man that you should keep him in mind,
> mortal man that you care for him?

Ten monks repaired offstage to the sacristy when Lauds ended at 6:20, returning in vestments for the concelebrated community Mass. Father Charles, in red vestments, led. The reading was from the Book of Tobit; the Gospel from Mark, the parable of the tenant farmers who killed their landlord's son. The Mass shared the form of any parish Mass, but not the sound: All the prayers were sung. The monks skipped the sign of peace, the moment in Mass when neighbor turns to neighbor in greeting. They formed a horseshoe around the altar for the consecration of the bread and wine. All but one received communion.

The chapel floor was speckled now with a stained-glass mosaic of light. The Christ window had risen out of the shadows, backlit by the morning. The rest of America was waking, starting a day of deeds that would soon need praying for. The prodigal sun had climbed up over the mountains and returned to the valley.

For the remaining day—after Mass and breakfast and the next office, Terce, at 7:45—the monks mostly shed their cowls for work clothes and took up the jobs that sustained the community: egg washer, tractor driver, janitor, cook, electrician, boiler operator, tailor, beekeeper, bookkeeper, launderer, woodworker, mechanic and the rest. Hay needed cutting today, some broken irrigation pipe needed fixing, eight thousand chickens and three hundred head of beef cattle needed tending to, and the farming tradition of their monastic ancestors—the Cistercians had led medieval Europe in the development of new agricultural techniques—needed upholding. A monk under a cowboy hat drove a pickup out into the fields. Father Charles, the guest-quarters cook, hoped to do some thinking and writing on a subject that had interested him of late, the links between ecology and spirituality, but he had to make a meat loaf first—for the guests, not the monks—and then cut the grass down at the gatehouse, where the monks' relatives stayed when they visited. "That's the greatest sacrifice," Abbot Malachy said of the monks' separation from their families. "At the same time you have spiritual compensation and the grace to live a celibate life. We leave one family and we find another. In a way it's more intense than in the world, where your children grow up and go away. We kind of grow up and stay."

Their family had now grown up to an age that required, back among the small dormlike cells, an infirmary with its own chapel. The monks all looked younger than their years, but only a handful were under fifty, and few were arriving to replenish the ranks: Just two young men were now in the long process of becoming Trappists. The abbey's dairy had closed recently, the daily milking chores too much of a drain on the dwindling work force. The Catholic church had enough trouble recruiting priests, let alone finding men whose faith called them to leave behind their lives—Holy Trinity's monks included a navy pilot, an electrician, a truck driver, a motel manager and many who had come as young seminarians—and exile themselves to the Utah mountains. For every five men who entered the abbey to try the life, maybe one was left, five and a half years later, to take his final vows. "I feel that if God wants it here, he'll provide for it," Abbot Malachy said. "You can't give grace to people to come here, only God can do that."

The monks returned to the chapel at 12:15 and again at 2:15 and at 5:30

and at 7:30 and again the next morning at 3:30 and 6 and 7:45 and again and again seven times each day, every day, as they had for forty years here at Holy Trinity, as they did at the eleven other Trappist monasteries in America, at the remaining seventy-nine worldwide, as they have for century on century, almost a millennium now—a continuum of public prayer that derives its ritual power from its granite stability and military discipline. "It seems like yesterday," Father Baldwin said of his arrival here in 1947. "If time begins to hang heavy for somebody, that means he's not going to make it. He's not really losing himself in prayer. If you are, you hardly know time is passing."

"The time goes very fast," Abbot Malachy said. His Holy Trinity years could be measured by the trees he tended when he could get away from his administrative work—poplars, pines, maples, elms, cottonwoods, rising along the drive, in the guest garden, in the tree patch, the little arboretum behind the abbey, up out of the middle of the quadrangle and over the verdant cloister garden. The trees reminded him of his native Kentucky. They looked as if they had come with the valley, immemorially attached to the landscape, but they had actually come with the monastery, each one planted and nurtured and raised by monks they will likely outlive. "You wonder where all the years have gone."

11

At 5:00, in a LAS VEGAS casino, a bow-tied craps dealer, pattering at auctioneer speed, pushed the dice across the green-felt table toward a new shooter.

"Robert and Dorothy, we are gathered here together in the sight of God to join you together in holy marriage. Let us pray. Father, we love you and we thank you . . . "

Charlotte Richards—owner of the Little White Chapel, minister of the Grace Calvary Church of Faith, clad in a black tuxedolike pants suit, hands clasped before her at reverent ecclesiastical height—stood at the head of the small, low-ceilinged, lavender-carpeted chapel and commenced the five-minute ceremony that would legally unite Robert and Dorothy forever. She spoke in the whispery, consoling tones of a confessional priest. To her left stood a golden candelabra, flickering with fifteen electric flames. Long purple drapes hung on the windows, and purple ribbons festooned the six tiny white pews whose purple seat cushions held no witnesses. Garlands of artificial flowers brocaded the room. Two stained-glass doves kissed in the side window. Robert and Dorothy stood facing each other, holding hands.

"Robert, do you take Dorothy to be your wedded wife?"

"I do."

"Do you promise to love and honor her, to respect and cherish her, for the rest of your life?"

"I do."

"Dorothy, do you take Robert for your husband?"

"I do."

"Do you promise to love and honor him, respect and cherish him, for the rest of your life?"

"I do."

Richards excused herself briefly to shut the chapel door against the dull hum of Strip traffic that was seeping in through the waiting room beyond. A pair of red neon hearts shone within the run of flashing lights that bordered the Little White Chapel sign outside, and flashing white neon tubes outlined the small steeple. A second, louder sign—the one that first seduces your eye as you drive down Las Vegas Boulevard—announced in red letters, JOAN COLLINS WAS MARRIED HERE. The chapel's white bricks were incandescent under the floodlights. An olive tree and a palm tree rose from a vestpocket Astroturf lawn that glowed green.

"Robert and Dorothy, this is the day the Lord made, and he just started bright and early for you this morning, didn't he? . . . I pray that you will always be kind and be gentle to each other, forgive each other like our heavenly father forgives you. . . . Don't look back at any problems of yesterday, but straight ahead with God, hand in hand with him. . . . I, Robert, take thee, Dorothy . . ."

"I, Robert, take thee, Dorothy . . ."

The video camera atop the tripod to Richards's right was pointed down and away from the bride and groom: They had opted for the Economy package ("$125 complete") rather than the Joan Collins Special ($500, including video, wedding cake and French lace handkerchief). They had picked their flowers from the refrigerated case out by the front door, a red rose boutonniere for Robert's gray pinstriped lapel, a corsage for Dorothy to hold as she stood in her office-length white dress and white heels. Their mirroring smiles were wide and bright. Her eyes glistened.

"Robert and Dorothy, by the power invested in me by the state of Nevada it is indeed my pleasure and my honor, here in the Little White Wedding Chapel, at twelve forty-five A.M., to pronounce you husband and wife, together forever. You may now kiss your wife, Robert."

As they celebrated their first minute of marriage with a long, close kiss, Richards turned back to switch on the cassette player that hid behind the flowers on the gold-trimmed white altar, unleashing a soapy piano arrangement of "Evergreen," the love theme from *A Star Is Born*. The night clerk at the front desk snapped the official newlywed photos (the package included one 8-by-10, two 5-by-7s and four wallet-size) after she finished answering the anxious phone questions of a next-day bride ("How old are you? . . . I don't think you'll have any problem. . . . That's all right, at the age of thirty-five you don't have to have your father with you. . . . If you're thirty-five, don't worry about it. They're pretty tight around eighteen or twenty. . . . It's not how old you look, just tell them how old you are.'').

"Always remember that Jesus loves you, and so do I," Richards said, and with that they left the chapel alone together, out through the paparazzi floodlights and into the limo that would carry them back up the Strip to their hotel, invested members now of a club that included Joan Crawford, Kirk Douglas, Rita Hayworth, Betty Grable, Mickey Rooney, Judy Garland, Jane Fonda, Ann-Margret, Wayne Newton, Mary Tyler Moore, Michael Jordan, Elizabeth Taylor and Richard Burton, Debbie Reynolds and Eddie Fisher, Frank Sinatra and Mia Farrow, Paul Newman and Joanne Woodward, Xavier Cugat and Charo, Elvis and Priscilla Presley, and the seventy thousand or so mere mortals who get married each year in Las Vegas, home of the no-waiting, no-blood-test, just-sign-here, $27-please marriage license and of wedding chapels that keep the same hours as convenience stores.

If you drive into the capital of the American night from the east, as I did, and if you arrive after dark (as everyone should), you will see the city long before you reach it—a pale-orange fog over the black horizon, incongruous and unaccountably wide out here in the desert void. I had descended through clouds from the monks' heavenly mountain and had left the sun flaming out behind the Black Rock Desert as I streaked southwest toward Nevada's hot and tempting valley. On a country station Faron Young sang "It's Four in the Morning." A Los Angeles station reported on freeway conditions four hundred miles away. A caffeine-pill commercial on Talknet shouted "Wake up, you sleepy nighttime people!" Frank Zappa talked to Larry King about his autobiography, much of which he had written late, late at night. Past the bordertown casinos of Mesquite, the Vegas stations reported on a musicians'-union strike sparked by casino plans to replace some live players with tapes. Cresting a hill at milepost 60 on I-15, I saw Las Vegas spread out below me in the distance, a vast reservoir of light, aglow like a uranium mine, rippling with gentle waves like heat.

The Vegas night, seen from within at street level, is a Fourth of July sky drifted down to the ground intact. The city has a signline, like a boardwalk, rather than a skyline, like Manhattan. The earthly competition washes out the stars above. The Little White Chapel, and several other chapels, shone in the lower-wattage gap between the Strip casinos and downtown, neighbor to a small hotel-casino, a motel that advertised in-room adult movies, a Chinese restaurant, a law office and an antiques store that offered, among its other wares, old, emptied slot machines.

*   *   *

"John and Marci, I'm sure that when you first met, you never dreamed this moment would come to pass. . . . Our heavenly father tells us, in his holy word he says, 'Husband, love your wife as Christ Jesus loves each of us.' That's just a big bunch of love. . . . One time somebody made me realize that I couldn't have a mountaintop unless I went through a valley. You get strength in that valley. So when you have times of difficulty, realize that God's gonna be right there. . . ."

John and Marci, California natives now living in Alaska, had brought along two friends to serve as best man and maid of honor and stand beside them on this particular mountaintop, presumably the highest yet in their young lives. Marci fidgeted nervously, giggling like a girl caught passing a note in biology class. She was shoehorned into a tight white dress and wore a frothy garland in her big hair.

"Take this ring and place it on his left hand, look into his eyes and say, 'I, Marci, take thee, John . . .' "

"I, Marci, take thee, John . . ."

"For my husband . . ."

"For my husband . . ."

"And with this ring . . ."

"And with this ring . . ."

"I thee wed."

"I thee wed." His ring slipped on easier than hers had.

" . . . What God hath joined together let no man put asunder. John and Marci, by the power invested in me by the state of Nevada, here in the Little White Wedding Chapel, at about one minute after one o'clock in the morning, I pronounce you husband and wife." Their taped piano music was the theme from *The Rose.*

Joan Collins's taped music—according to the framed *Star* clipping that memorialized the night the Little White Chapel became a cathedral of celebrity and that was displayed now as proudly as a four-star restaurant review out among the scores of happy-couple photos lining the front room's walls—was "Here Comes the Bride." She wore, the *Star* reported, a $15,000 wedding ring. Her daughter, her sister and her father were not invited to her secret wedding to Peter Holm, who had just negotiated a $90,000-per-episode *Dynasty* contract for her. "I think Joan has made a big mistake," her father was quoted as saying. "I don't think it will last. It is not a marriage made in heaven."

"Since then it seems like God has just blessed my life, and I thank him for it," Richards said. "It just keeps getting better and better, it really does." The Joan Collins name outside was the equivalent of a *Good House-keeping* seal of approval to many potential customers—stargazers, star wannabes, moon-eyed out-of-towners, connoisseurs of the cheesy local shtick who figure that if you're marrying Vegas, you might as well go all the way. Richards owned three other wedding chapels, but the Little White Chapel, her only all-night chapel, was where the tour buses stopped: A group of Germans had visited earlier in the evening, followed by a French group, and the two English words they all knew were *Joan Collins.* "Let's face it, there's something special about somebody with so much notoreity." Hung in another place of honor was a framed certificate from a wedding Richards performed by request one night at the Golden Nugget: Walter Bruce Willis, the groom, Demi Gene Moore, the bride, both of Malibu, California.

"When do you wanna get married?" the night clerk asked the caller. "The minister is here, the limo driver is here, I can send the limo right out to get you now. Do you have a license? . . . We'll take you to the courthouse and back to your hotel."

They needed a half hour, they said, to dress for the occasion, so half an hour later the limo was waiting outside the Travelodge up near the Holiday Inn and the Flamingo. The smoked-glass privacy wall closed on the backseat stereo's music (The Spinners' "Then Came You") as they settled in for the ten-minute ride down the Strip to the Clark County Courthouse downtown, a block behind the Four Queens (Frank Sinatra, Jr., tonight, last show 12:30 A.M.), where the Marriage Bureau that closed at midnight during the week stayed open round-the-clock on Fridays and Saturdays: Love, the local officialdom understands, stays up late on weekends. They walked hand-in-hand up the steps. Six other couples were on line, filling in the information forms ("Mother's Maiden Name _____ Number Of This Marriage [1st, 2nd, etc.] _____") with the county's pencil stubs. The graffiti on the courthouse wall outside asked, "Have you suffered enough? Is your life a mess? Is it hell? Are you hurting? Lonely? Empty? Sad? Try Jesus (God's Son)." Within twenty minutes they were back in the limo with their license, going to the chapel.

"Some people let me know right away, 'Make it short and sweet and no religion,' " Richards said. "But there's not a wedding I do that I don't personally put God in it. He is always here. You have to understand, this is a wedding chapel, not a parish. People come here because they don't go to church. This might be the only church they ever set foot in.''

People come here to get married because they're young, or old, or one is young and the other old, or their parents disapprove, or their parents don't care, or it's their second or third or seventh time around (40 percent are first marriages, Richards estimated, 40 percent are second, and the rest are leaps of faith taken by unbowed veterans of three or more), or they wearied of arguing with the caterer, or they want a miniaturized white-lace-and-promises facsimile of the big church wedding they can't afford, or they have no use for tuxedos ("People get married in shorts, no problem"), or they want their dog as best man ("One dog actually walked down the aisle with them"), or they're due back at their military base Monday, or they have more love than money (the basic chapel fee was forty-five dollars), or their guest list wouldn't pass church muster ("One night a motorcycle gang took up the whole front of the place, there must have been twenty motorcycles. They came in with their chains hanging, but they were really nice, they put their arms around you and hugged you"), or they're gay and have misinterpreted Vegas's reputation for tolerance ("That happens a lot. I have to be tactful and tell them I sympathize with them, that their problem isn't with the chapel, it's with Clark County"), or they want a private validation before their public ceremony (" 'This isn't the real thing,' they say. 'We're gonna get married in a month or two' ''), or, this being Vegas after all, they have a fondness for certain lucky number combinations (at 7 on the eleventh, say, or 11 on the seventh, or 3:45 on 6/7/89). People come here at night because they prefer the shield of darkness ("On graveyards we usually get people who don't want to get noticed by the public"), or they just got into town and can't wait another minute, or they're afraid the morning light will change their minds, or they're pregnant ("We had one bride in here at three A.M. who was in labor. She could barely say, 'I do.' They carried her out and called back an hour later to say she'd had a little boy. She just managed to get married before the baby was born"), or they believe in love at first sight, or they consider marriage just another species of dating, or they defer to the wisdom of their astrological charts, or they defer to the call of their loins.

"There are some that you have a hard time doing because you just know, you have a feeling inside, it's not for real," said Richards, who claimed to have performed 500,000 weddings in the last thirty years. "But it's not my place to judge them. You feel sorry for them. You can almost feel their pain." She had that bad feeling inside earlier today—a laughing bride, thirty, and her straight-man groom, sixty-two. "My spirit was grieved because I didn't want to perform the ceremony." Her fifth chapel was on wheels, a motor home that took her out to marry couples wherever they chose—atop nearby Mount Charleston, on a boat in Lake Mead, on horseback, on motorcycles, in a hot-air balloon.

"I really attribute all of my success to God," she said. "I witness to a lot of prostitutes and I've seen a lot of miracles happen here in Las Vegas, just telling them that Jesus loves them. There's nothing more important in life than knowing who God is."

"Now, we want you to stand on this side of him. You know why? Because you're closest to his heart, and that's where we want you to stay always. Take him by the arm." The limo was back from the courthouse with Stan and Maria, and Richards was setting them in place. "Now, the man comes on this side, I don't know why."

"Closer to the door," Maria suggested. She wore a white blouse and white heels with a red print skirt. The collar of Stan's white shirt was open under his dark gray suit. He wore no tie and carried no wedding rings.

"You left them?" Richards asked.

"We didn't buy them," he said. They had just flown in from Texas, where they were both students—she an undergraduate computer-science major, he in medical school. She was Catholic, he was Baptist.

"Oh, you don't need them anyway. She's gonna put a ring around your heart that'll never come loose, right?" Their music was a taped organ "Here Comes the Bride."

". . . through sickness and health"

"through sickness and health . . ."

"Rich or poor . . ."

"Rich or poor . . ."

"Till death do us part . . ."

"Till death do us part . . ."

". . . By the power invested in me by the state of Nevada, it is my pleasure and honor, here in the Little White Wedding Chapel in Las Vegas, Nevada, at three-twenty A.M. to pronounce you husband and wife, together forever. You can kiss your wife." He did, and then he put the wedding on his credit card, $87.10. The limo had the new couple back at their hotel by 3:35.

ThePointerSistersCAESARSPALACE"NudesOnIce"ASexsationalRe
viewUNIONPLAZAWorld'sLargestBuffetCIRCUSCIRCUS$2.9
9DinnerYourChoiceOf12DeliciousFavoritesLADYLUCK"CityLite

You could stand at a slot machine at Binion's Horseshoe downtown for unmarked falling hours as the night spins out, listening for the flat and hollow silver ring of a payoff, or sit in a poker game, listening to the sharp snap of turning cards and the soft click of stacked chips, or lean over a craps table's field of green, listening to the raindrop thud of tumbling dice, and then, with no clock around but your own internal tally of wins and losses, look out through the wide arcadelike entrance to see a slice of noon-bright sidewalk that pedestrians share with palm trees and be persuaded that it's morning already, another of the 320 sunny days Las Vegas gets each year. But walk out into what you think is tomorrow and you'll find that it's really still tonight, the sky 3 A.M. black up beyond the neon. This is Fremont Street, maybe the brightest block in the American night, a floodlit midway walled in by the dense cluster of casinos downtown here in Glitter Gulch. It was 69 degrees Fahrenheit out on Fremont now, down from 97 this afternoon, low enough that you didn't notice the change when you left the air-conditioned casino caverns. The earth's temperature, like the body's, cools at night, and nowhere on earth does sundown release more creatures from their burrows than in the desert: coyotes, geckos, Gila monsters, scorpions, jackrabbits, tarantulas, kangaroo rats, night-flying moths that pollinate night-opening yucca flowers, batlike Stealth fighters from Nellis Air Force Base, gamblers.

"All the passions produce prodigies," Simone Weil, the French philosopher, wrote. "A gambler is capable of watching and fasting, almost like a saint."

"The greatest experience in life is winning a bet," Nick the Greek, the Vegas gambler, said, "and the second greatest is losing one."

Just outside the brightest lights was a pawn shop. DIAMONDS GOLD SILVER, it advertised, BOUGHT AND SOLD 24 HOURS.

"Coming out again, coming out, coming right out, folks."

Tony Anton mixed the six translucent red dice with his slender, whippy stick, sautéing them like shrimp in the center of the craps table, asking for fresh bets on a fresh roll. Some craps dealers bark like carnival pitchmen, or call like racetrack announcers: Anton's vocal style was the monotone patter of an auctioneer, accented like a speeding Gregorian chant. "Coming right out."

Eight players, plus their several trailing kibitzers and mates, stood beside him around the table, one of four still going at 5 A.M. here at the Flamingo Hilton out on the Strip. The chips were mostly red, five dollars apiece. The new shooter, a fading rock-star type with Rod Stewart hair, picked two dice from the six Anton offered, shook them and tossed, opening his palm as if throwing dust.

"Seven, a fast winner," Anton said, and the two dealers on the other side of the table, behind the velvet ropes, paid out the winning bets. The shooter was five dollars richer as he took up the dice again and hoped, along with every other player, that a hot hand was on the way. The band in the casino lounge played "Honky Tonk Women." "I like listening to all this music," he told his friend, whose hair was a darker version of his own. Anton shouldered his stick like an on-deck batter and watched the dice fly.

Craps is the casino game that better than any other embodies the Vegas allure: the illicit, Guys-and-Dolls, back-alley thrill of throwing dice; the excited, spontaneous communities that collect around hot tables like pedestrians around a street performer or a fight; complex rules that adhere to an arcane internal logic only gamblers could have devised and that scare away the amateurs; odds that, if you know what you're doing, narrow the house's cold, inevitable edge. "It's the hardest game to learn," Anton said.

The narrative of a craps game is not fixed and repetitive, like blackjack, but unpredictable and shifting, like desert sands. You can't always root for the same number because the numbers that win and the numbers that lose change from roll to roll, bettor to bettor: 7 wins now, loses later, wins for one bettor, loses for another. "A lot of people are intimidated because they don't know how to play," Anton added. "It's tough to try to explain. Most of the time they don't know where the money goes." The money can go on any of the dozens of possible bets, marked on the outfield-green table layout by an irregular pattern of boxes and symbols mystifying to the uninitiated, but most of it goes on the Pass Line, where it multiplies when the shooter is hot and vanishes when the shooter is cold. All the players with bets on the Pass Line won when the rock star threw a 7 on his first roll, the "come-out roll" Anton had announced, and now, watching the dice fall, they hoped the temperature would rise and bring them another win. A 7 or an 11 always wins on a come-out roll; a 2, a 3 or a 12 loses; any other number leads to another roll.

"Nine is the point," Anton said after the dice had bounced off the knobby rubber pyramids along the table's far sidewall and come to rest, a 5 and a 4. Nine was the ally now, 7 the enemy: They would all win if the rock star threw a 9 again, but would lose if he threw a 7 first. They all increased their bets by "taking odds," betting he would make his point before he sevened-out. The dealers slid the pucks over into the "9" boxes, one on each end of the table, to mark the point.

"Hard eight, hard eight," Anton said after the next roll, a pair of 4s, a "hardway" 8 (a 5 and a 3 would have been an "easyway"). The dealers collected the bets that had lost—the field bets, the proposition bets—and paid the one winner who had made a place bet on the 8. The Pass Line bets sat and awaited a decisive roll.

A hot hand—pass after winning pass, blocked by no errant 7s—can turn $5 into $500 in twenty minutes. "The dice do get hot and cold, they really do," Anton said. The hottest player he had ever seen had won $250,000; the coldest had lost $100,000. "Once in a while I can feel a hand coming on. As the dice roll, I can sense it."

The rock star's last twenty minutes had seen his original twenty-dollar stake wax and wane as the dice passed around the table, from cold hand to tepid to cold to warm, long enough to get him a free drink from a cocktail waitress in a little penguin-tail tux outfit, but not long enough to put him ahead. All he had left was on the line now. He rolled a 5, reprieved, then a 4, still hoping, then a killing 7, finished. "Hey, at least we got drinks out of it," he said to his friend, leaving the table.

"It's a very fast game," Anton said. "Every roll of the dice, somebody wins, somebody loses."

The Flamingo Hilton is the descendant of the resort hotel that inaugurated the flush postwar era in Las Vegas, a metropolis whose population has grown almost a hundredfold over the last fifty years and whose lights have attracted to this unlikely setting—a remote desert in a state Mark Twain once described as "the most rocky, wintry, repulsive wastes that our country or any other can exhibit"—possibly the greatest concentration anywhere of the ten million citizens of the American night. In 1855, according to a Mormon settler, Las Vegas consisted of little more than "a nice patch of grass about a half a mile wide and two or three miles long," the original Strip, a green rest stop on the Old Spanish Trail between Sante Fe and Southern California. A mining boom brought some gold and silver prospectors, and the railroad brought the first real hotel in 1905 (the thirty-room, canvas-roofed Hotel Las Vegas), but not much else disturbed that strip of grass until 1931, the local equivalent of 1776: Gambling was legalized in Nevada that year, and construction started on the Hoover Dam on the nearby Colorado River, bringing workers and, later, electricity to power all the neon signs.

The new casinos mostly shouldered close together along Fremont Street downtown, until Bugsy Siegel looked out into the desert and saw the future. Siegel is remembered now, with a lot of wink-and-nudge euphemisms, as a dapper and glamorous gangster who cut a Runyonesque figure, one of the Good Bad Guys ("We only kill each other," he is said to have said), but his career actually included murder a dozen times over, bookmaking, rape, drug trafficking, prostitution and most of the other pursuits of a ranking racketeer. He built the Flamingo several miles out of town on Highway 91, the barren road to Los Angeles, not the first on what became the Strip, but the most lavish and the farthest out from Glitter Gulch. He spent $6 million, four times the original estimate, and trucked in palm trees, and when it was finished, it was a green island in a dry sea. Jimmy Durante headlined on opening night, the night after Christmas 1946. George Raft drove three hundred miles through storms from Los Angeles to be there that night and help his old pal celebrate his dream. Even the janitors wore tuxedos. But the Flamingo flopped at first: The casino lost $100,000 in the first two weeks, angering the heavy money behind Siegel. "Class is for suckers if there's no dough in it," Lucky Luciano is said to have told him. There was plenty of dough in it eventually—as a newly mobile and affluent nation, having already pushed out to the Pacific, doubled back to seek some modern frontier thrills in the desert it had bypassed on its swift way west—and the Strip rose around the Flamingo, linking it to downtown and then spilling beyond it farther out into the dusty void. Siegel's hotel had grown from the original 98 rooms to 3,500 now, but he never saw his vision vindicated. One June night in 1947, just six months after the Flamingo opened, he was sitting on a chintz-covered sofa in the Beverly Hills mansion he had bought for his girlfriend, wearing a gray plaid suit and reading the *Los Angeles Times,* when bullets pierced the living-room window. One slug shattered a marble Bacchus statue on the grand piano, another punctured a painting of a nude holding a wineglass. Siegel fell dead, shot in the face. They found his right eye fifteen feet away, come to rest on the dining room floor like an errant die.

*   *   *

"Four is the point," the new stickman called, and Anton, on the other side of the table now, moved the puck to the "4" box. Four dealers work a craps game, three on the table and one on break, and every twenty minutes they rotate like baserunners. Anton was at first base now. He shifted his weight from his right leg to his left, an exchange he made regularly to help relieve the pressure that standing all night put on his back. It was 5:30, the lounge band had finished their last set, night workers all over America were thinking about home, and Anton wasn't even halfway through his shift. The typical shift cycle in Las Vegas, a city where more than half the employees work at night, is divorced from the routine rhythms of the rest of the nation and tied instead to the playnight beat of gamblers: To avoid shift changes at the height of the night, the Flamingo's graveyard shift started not at 11 or 12 or even at 1 but at 2:30 A.M.

"A lot of people can't adapt to the hours, they can't adjust to getting up so early," said Anton, who grew up in another round-the-clock place, Aliquippa, a western Pennsylvania steel town. He usually supplemented a good evening's sleep with a short after-work nap. "I've gotten used to five, five and a half hours. I wake up before the alarm. We're all creatures of habit."

A creature of a different habit dropped seven hundred-dollar bills on the table: Unless you're a bank teller or a drug trafficker, nowhere else are you likely to see so many portraits of Benjamin Franklin as you are in Vegas. The shooter had sevened-out before he could throw a 4, and a new roll was coming out. The boxman, business-suited and seated between the two dealers, slipped the seven hundred dollars through a slit in the table into the drop box: Actual money disappears fast here; you don't get to see how much legal tender you're losing. The bettor took his chips and set a green one, twenty-five dollars in disguise, on the Pass Line.

"Adult Disneyland, I call it," Anton said. He was compact and fit in his uniform—bow tie, black pants, his name stitched in script on his white shirt—and the gray flecks in his thick black hair were the only sign that he was old enough to have gone to high school with Mike Ditka. He broke in as a dealer at the Horseshoe, then worked at the International (Elvis's Vegas base, now the Las Vegas Hilton) and the Dunes (where Adnan Khashoggi was among the high-rollers to visit his table) before the Flamingo. His oldest son, fresh out of law school, was working late now too—studying for the California bar exam.

"Yo-leven, it's a winner," the stickman called when the dice came out, a 6 and a 5. Anton paid the players at his end of the table, chips dropping from his fingers like quarters from a change dispenser. The $700 man set his new green chip neatly atop his first one.

"The point is six," the stickman called after the next come-out roll, and Anton moved the puck again. The ON imprinted on it was, from certain angles, easy to misread as NO.

"I don't know what's goin' on," said a man who stopped to watch on his way back from the blackjack tables, "and I don't wanna know."

"If you live here and you gamble, you're gonna get busted, you're not gonna get ahead," Rick Bartlett, the pit boss, said. "I don't even see a paycheck. It goes straight to the bank."

With his gray suit, gray paisley tie and white shirt, Bartlett looked like a loan officer. He patrolled behind the ropes, circulating among the floormen, the boxmen and the dealers, reporting to the manager when he passed by, his official conversations conducted as discreetly as a funeral director. Hidden behind the mirrored ceiling above him was the eye-in-the-sky surveillance network—a sophisticated version of the postal inspectors' catwalk back in Memphis—that watched him as he watched them as they watched the players as everybody watched the dice and the tens of thousands of dollars' worth of chips stacked on each active table. "To a guy looking from the outside it looks glamorous, but it definitely becomes a business after a while," he said. Opposite shifts hadn't helped his first marriage, so he made sure he and his second wife both worked the same hours: She was across the room dealing blackjack, a game that interested him less than his own. "It's just a better game," he said of craps, which he dealt before he worked up to pit boss. "If I'm watching twenty-one and I don't know the guy playing, I'm bored to death."

"Bet 'em up while they're hot, comin' out, comin' out."

Anton was at third base now, and the dice were warming up. The come-out roll was 10, and the $700 man backed his $50 Pass Line bet with $100 on odds.

"Ten is a winner."

"Yeah," $700 said, punching down into the air with his fist. "I needed that one."

A hand was on, the passes kept coming, the $700 man's bets climbed to

$100 backed by $200 (it was a $2–$2,000 table with double odds), loud exclamations and exhortations and exultations rose to overwhelm the silent dice, and the dealers were busy keeping track of whose bets were whose where, making computer-quick calculations (different numbers pay different odds; "it's like learning multiplication tables"), and paying out from the colorful skyline of house chips to the winners who built little chip suburban villages on the table before them. On the twelfth pass the shooter finally rolled craps, a 12, and the summer weather broke. The 7s started coming at the wrong times. A predawn cold front moved toward the table.

"I can't win no money unless I throw some points," the $700 man said when the dice came around to him, and he didn't. "I wouldn't bet a dime on myself."

One man left before his village had completely depopulated. "Good night, sir," Anton said, collecting the chip the player had left as a tip, a "toke" in the local language. "For the dealers, sir? Thank you." A fresh wave of dealers walked into the casino like a baseball team taking the field for a new inning. Anton clapped his hands and opened them over the table with the nothing-up-my-sleeves motion of a magician, then left for the breakroom.

By 6 the players had coalesced around the two tables still open, and a hand vacuum was mowing over the green lawn of the one table Bartlett had just shut down. Brief downpours of metal rain trailed the coin collectors as they emptied the rows of slot machines. Atlantic City's casinos close for a few hours around dawn, but in Vegas the cleanup crews move among the hard core, the insomniacs, the early risers, the speed freaks, the first-nighters just in and caught up in the schoolkid excitement of staying up past bedtime and trying to win it all. "You can tell if it's the start or the end of the day for them," Anton said. "It seems like most of the serious gamblers come out after two or three A.M., when most of the tourists are gone. The players are a little looser then. I don't know if it's because they've had a few more drinks or if it's just that time of the morning, but it's quite a big contrast."

It is easier at night, when the neon tempts you in from the dark, to convince yourself that the dice will come up your way, because just as the night lifts inhibitions, so too does it lift hopes. It is easier then, in the absence of reason, to believe that the next roll will solve everything, and to forget that the house, day in and night out, always wins in the end. "You don't see the house walking down the street with its hands in its pockets early in the morning looking for a ninety-nine-cent breakfast," a Flamingo craps instructor had told the audience around his table earlier today.

"The only time I play now," Anton said, "is when friends are in town."

Outside the Flamingo the Strip was as empty as it ever gets, the pale morning light erasing the bright, shining vision of the night before. Never is Vegas so clearly revealed as a city of the night than at daybreak. The signs had all faded, losing the pattern and meaning the darkness had lent them, as discordant now as any suburban strip. Outside of town, out where the Strip appeared only as a wavy mirage in the distance, the landscape was harsh and lonesome, blasted, seemingly reduced to naked atoms strewn over the baked earth. The broiler heat was climbing through the eighties. The mountains to the west looked parched and brittle, as if they would crumble to powder at the touch. The unsparing sun, you could see, had the same effect on the desert as the casino darkness had on the worn and weary face of an all-night gambler: It bleached it of color, of life. It is the light that is heavy and desolate here, not the night. Twilight is a promise, not an end, and dawn smells of failure.

TheLittleCasinoWithTheBigPayoffs!SLOTS-A-FUNSexiestGirls!Ho
ttestDancers!TheGreatestAcro-HandBalancingTeam!"Dan'SinDirdy"MA
RINAWinAPorscheOnOurQuarterMachinesTROPICANANau

The Nevada desert is so vast and unpopulated that the Atomic Energy Commission, back in the 1950s, actually exploded nuclear bombs in the sky over its test site just about an hour northwest of Las Vegas. Picknickers lined the highway to watch the spectacle. You could see the mushroom clouds billowing up beyond the signs of Glitter Gulch. But despite the implications of all this free space (if it's big enough for the Big Bomb, it's big enough for anything), Las Vegas is tamer than its frontier image, reined in all around by limits (law, sublimation, control, salvation) that check the natural impulses of its main industry (greed, lust, license, sin) and prevent it from degenerating into the kind of brawling, Wild West chaos that would scare off many of its twenty million annual visitors. The gambling tables bracket their minimum-bet floors with maximum-bet ceilings. Most of the entertainers could safely play Peoria: Elvis flopped here when he was young and wild and on the edge, triumphed when he was older and mainstream and preserved in rhinestones. Bare breasts are bountiful on the show stages, but so are G-strings. *Nudes on Ice* at the Union Plaza wasn't a tableau of snowbunny Playmates but a revue featuring topless skaters gliding through scenes with titles like "Western Jamboree" and "A Russian Palace Fantasy," interspersed by a husband-and-wife juggling act, a fire-wielding magician and a balloon-twisting comedian. The government still tested nuclear weapons out at Yucca Flat—the most recent was just the week before—but the explosions now were all deep underground.

You can buy sex in Vegas—"food for the animal," is how one local described the trade—but you have to break the law to do it. You can dial one of the "entertainment bureaus" and "escort services" whose ads fill twenty-five Yellow Pages; you can buy from a corner box the kind of newspaper that reports phone numbers, not sports scores; you can hear plenty of stories about couples sitting at dark bars, and women ducking down as if to retrieve their purses, and ecstatic expressions crossing men's faces; you can find someone who can find you a hooker or you can find one yourself ("When you said you had a better job," I heard a man say to a nightwalking woman of his acquaintance on a downtown street, "I thought you meant a traditional job"); but Clark County is not among the counties in Nevada, the only state with any such counties at all, where prostitution is legal. You have to drive sixty miles up to Nye County, the county where the nuclear tests were, to find the nearest legal brothel, or all the way up to Storey County to find the most famous.

"Welcome to the Mustang Ranch. These are the girls available to you tonight."

A dozen women, their outfits streetcorner brief and bright or bedroom filmy and frilly, stood shoulder to shoulder in the entrance parlor, snapped up to attention from their plush red lounging couches by the buzzer that had sounded when the customer came in through the iron gate outside. They could see him as he walked up the floodlit Astroturf path and in through the front door, and he could see them through the door's window as they arranged themselves for inspection like an after-hours beauty pageant, or a police lineup.

He looked about forty, wearing jeans, a baseball cap, a black mustache and a smirk of anticipation. The manager's welcoming introduction produced no apparent sparks of lust at first sight. The buyer went back to the dim bar to browse from over a beer, and the women fell out of formation. The garish decor was heavy with red, purple, black, orange, pink and other spotlight colors that echoed the employees' uniforms, and the walls were hung with the kind of fleshy nudes that hang in movie versions of western brothels. Among the songs on the thumping jukebox were "Whip Appeal" and "Make You Sweat." One woman sidled back to hustle him as he drank, no sale; then another, no again; before he finally struck a deal with the next and headed off with her to a room somewhere back along the maze of red-carpeted hallways.

About ten miles east of Reno (a dry town, like Vegas, for prostitution), the official green sign at Exit 23 on I-80 read simply, MUSTANG, and if you got off there and drove past the SLOW—CATTLE CROSSING sign and the scrap dealer and the auto wrecker and then crossed the small bridge over a moatlike river, you would arrive at the oldest, largest and best-known of the three dozen or so legal brothels in Nevada. Set among 330 acres of scrubby hills and sagebrush, the Mustang Ranch was a sprawling, one-story, 105-room complex that, with a tall black iron fence surrounding it and a watch tower rising from within above it, looked like a cross between a motel and a minimum-security prison. Maybe two dozen cars and a pair of trucks waited in the floodlit parking lot. A bug zapper sizzled with fresh victims. Christmasy red, green and white lights were strung outside. The moon was full in the east, haloed by three rings: blue-purple, yellow-green and orange-red.

"The bottom line is, you're never gonna eliminate this business, you're never gonna get rid of it, and any fool that tells you otherwise is nothing but a fool," said Joe Conforte, founder and owner, referring to the entire industry of sexual commerce, not just his franchise. He was just back from a Giants game in San Francisco, standing in the cafeteria-style dining room where the evening meal for the women had been cream of broccoli soup, baked chicken and rice. "So since you can't get rid of it, let's clean it up. Let's control it, let's keep the drugs out, let's keep the pimps out, let's keep it as clean as possible. Any logical person can tell you that's the best way." His inspiration, he said, came when he was driving a cab in Oakland. "All the guys were coming back from Korea after the war and the first thing they all asked was, 'How can we get a girl?' I thought, 'It's gotta be easier than this.' "

The buzzer sounded again, another customer coming up the walk. Summers were busier than winters ("It's only because there are more tourists then, it's not because people want to make love more"), nights busier than days, and the hours between 10 P.M. and 2 A.M., when the prospect of going to bed alone can drive a man to desperate acts, the busiest of all, the climax of the daily business cycle. The ranch was always open, the women always available, because the urge was always lying in wait somewhere.

"And this is our Orgy Room," Suzy the manager said, as casually as a real estate agent showing the kitchen in a subdivision split-level. The Orgy Room, vacant and chaste at the moment, was a Hugh Hefner pleasure suite—life-raft-round bed, Jacuzzi, porn movies for the TV, mirrors that multiplied both the purple color scheme and the population of the orgies. Doors all up and down the other hallways were shut, whether for sleep or for work. A bulletin board outlined several maxims for the women:

Girls—please do not flush any more rubbers down the toilets
Overhustling is self-defeating. All you do is lose the customer
Treat every customer the same no matter how much they spend

The Mustang Ranch was both home and office for its working girls, "a licensed boarding house," according to a prospectus for an unsuccessful public stock offering, "at which the Independent Contractors, as female prostitutes, make available their services for the performance of sexual acts with male customers." Women packed their things and checked into the dormlike rooms for anywhere from several days to several weeks. "The longest we like to see it go is twenty-one days," Suzy said. "After that it's time for a rest." How much money they left with depended on how many men picked them out of the lineups, and how much each man's desires were worth to him: "The price negotiated by an Independent Contractor," the prospectus had continued, "for any particular sexual act with a customer will be entirely within the control of the Independent Contractor." The minimum price, Conforte said, was thirty dollars; the maximum was limited only by the measure of your bankroll and your stamina. The proceeds from each sale, major credit cards accepted, were split evenly between the women and the house.

The Mustang women had several advantages over their professional colleagues elsewhere, the sanction of law chief among them, but they worked shifts longer and less glamorous than at most factories—twelve hours at a stretch, fourteen hours on weekends. About seventy women were in residence now, and they spent their slack hours hanging around together, playing cards, knitting baby booties, watching soap operas (*General Hospi-*

tal was a favorite) and generally giving the place the air of a sorority house gone to seed. "This is a job for the ladies. They're not into this for enjoyment," Suzy said. "We don't allow no kissing, we don't allow penetration without a condom. Their emotions come out with their loved ones. Most of the girls understand why they're here, and they keep in perspective what they're here to do." The Ranch had managed to reduce sex to little more than plumbing and friction.

Two women, their hitch up, hauled their luggage out to a cab. "We'd like to see you again," Suzy told them. "The door is always open." The phone rang, a prospective recruit. "You have to come in for a personal interview, sweetheart, I don't hire over the phone," Suzy told her. "You have a current AIDS test at the house you're working at? . . . Don't be fucked up or drunk, or I won't even interview you. And no track marks. I know the difference between a working girl having monthly blood tests and track marks, believe me."

"I just like the night, it's something about me," said Desiree, wrapped tight in a fluorescent-lime miniskirt. "You might come in at three A.M. and see a lot of tired girls, but I'm always boppin' around, dancin' in front of the jukebox.

"I used to work for an escort service, but a few of my girlfriends got beat up by guys, so I thought, before this happens to me, I'm getting out." She was twenty-five, a mother since eighteen, but she acted as if she still spent her nights cruising, as she said she had as a teenager, in the lowrider muscle cars of the older boys. She left her two kids at home with her boyfriend when she came to the Ranch for her usual three-day stints. She was small and thin, part Apache, she said, and part Spanish. Her long black hair matched her spike heels. "My parents both know what I do. They look at it like, I'm a big girl, as long as I'm happy. Hey, I'm a happy person, I enjoy my life, so they can say, 'Hey, my daughter's happy.'

"If they start getting too attached to me, I tell 'em straightup, I'm married, more or less, so don't look to get affection from me," she said of her customers. "It's not fair. Put yourself in my place. I'll be your friend, but I can't return the affection." Some men asked not for affection, but for punishment. "They come here to get what they can't get at home. Some want their ass beat with a belt. The rainy weather brings the freaks out. You can bet on the freaks coming out on a rainy night in Reno. Sometimes I do get some real goofballs. Very rarely do I get a virgin. The oldest virgin

I had was twenty-eight and had never seen a pussy in his life. I said, 'You gotta be kidding.' He said, 'Can I look at it?' and I said, 'Go for it.' Then he said, 'Where do you put it?' That was the icing on the cake. I fell right off the bed laughing."

Her room looked disconcertingly like the fluffy sanctuary of a high school girl, decorated around a theme of unicorns—unicorn posters, unicorn figurines, stuffed unicorns and assorted other unicorn notions. "I'm infatuated with unicorns," she said.

"My philosophy is that I'd rather have quality than quantity," said Shannon, who, with her sedate manner and coiffed blond hair, could have passed as a schoolteacher had she been wearing something other than a short black skirt, black stockings and white heels. At thirty-four she was one of the oldest women here. "I've built up a good clientele. It's better to find somebody you know and get along with and are comfortable with."

She grew up in Minnesota, switched from Catholic school to public in sixth grade and had worked, starting in New York fifteen years before, "everywhere and every way you can" in the profession. She had been coming here for the last five years. "I like my freedom. I'm an indoor person—I sew and clean and cook.

"I do well," she said, dodging the question, as everyone here did, of how much she made, or even how many jobs (dates or parties, she called them) she did in a night. "After twelve hours all I really want to do is take a hot bath.

"We have a very good understanding," she said of her relationship with her longtime boyfriend. "I don't take what I do here home to him and lay it on the table, and I don't ask him what he does when I'm here." She hoped to retire from the business next year to have a baby. Tonight was the last night of a four-week stay—her veteran status at the Ranch allowed her to push the three-week limit—and tomorrow she was flying home to Las Vegas, where she did some freelancing on her off weeks. The prospect of disease, she said, didn't worry her. "I'm a very clean person, most of my customers are very clean, and I clean up after every party."

On her off-duty hours she didn't bother much with the weight room, where many of the women worked out. Her job, she figured, was a sufficient fitness program for her. "I exercise all night long."

"I've always been a night person," said May, whose gun-shy demeanor and protective shell kept her eyes averted during conversation. Her hair was straight and blond, her white knit dress was short and tight around a body that still carried a trace of baby fat. "I've always had graveyard jobs. I was a truckstop waitress, I worked in a greenhouse trimming bushes, I was a grocery shelf stocker. During the day it's too nice to be working.

"One of the main reasons I'm doing this is so I can take months off at a time." She lived near Lake Tahoe, where she taught windsurfing, and she spent several winter months camped on the beach in Mexico. If she felt her body running down during her two-to-three-week stays here, she sometimes took a B-12 shot. She read health and sports magazines, and she tracked her investments (penny stocks, commodities) in *The Wall Street Journal.* "I don't expect to do this for more than five more years. If I'm out by the time I'm thirty, it'll be okay with me."

On the drive back to Reno the early news reported that at 2:09 A.M., while the Mustang women were at work in their small rooms, the state of Nevada, working in a small beige room of its own at the state prison in Carson City, had executed a murderer. William Paul "Bud" Thompson, fifty-one now and forever, had been convicted of three murders and had admitted to three more. Before walking the thirteen feet from the holding cell to the death chamber, where he was strapped to a heavy wooden table and injected with lethal chemicals, he had eaten a last meal of four double bacon cheeseburgers, two large orders of french fries and a large soda. The radio said his last words were, "Thank you for letting me die with dignity."

On a gray and chilly November morning in 1990, hundreds of people, men and women both, gathered here under an orange-and-white-striped tent to peruse and bid on the merchandise—on everything, the land and the buildings and the items inside, except the working girls themselves—as the Internal Revenue Service auctioned off the bankrupt Mustang Ranch. Conforte watched as his brothel was dismantled piece by piece, towel by sheet by champagne bottle (forty-three bottles) by condom box (sixty-one boxes), to pay his back taxes. "You make a mistake in dealing with the IRS, you gotta pay for it," he told reporters. (The women he called independent contractors and maintained were not subject to withholding, the IRS called employees, and the bill had mounted to $13 million.) He had taken the business into Chapter 11, put it up for sale and tried several times to take it public. After the last stock offering failed ($20 a share, a print of a LeRoy Neiman painting for big investors), the government finally seized the Ranch and padlocked the gate. A federal bankruptcy judge nixed a short-lived plan by a court-appointed trustee to reopen the business (which would have lent new meaning to the phrase "getting screwed by the government"), and Storey County revoked its brothel permit, so the IRS sold it as just another fenced-in, 105-room, red and purple and black and orange and pink complex. There was talk by some prospective buyers of converting it into a nursing home, a religious retreat, a halfway house or a home for wayward girls; but the winning bid ($1.49 million) came from Mustang Properties, a newly formed corporation whose sole officer was Conforte's longtime lawyer. By December, just in time for the Christmas rush, the Mustang Ranch was open again, and the brothel permit, still in Conforte's name, was reinstated. Conforte said he was just the general manager now. He denied having any financial interest in the business, or having outsmarted the IRS.

Playboy'sGirlsOfRock&RollMAXIMGirls!Girls!Girls!TotallyNude!B
urlesqueAtItsBestCANCANRoom$9.95CompletePrimeRibDinnerA
nd"CrazyGirls"ShowRIVIERAHilariousOutrageousLaffternoonR

"How you doin', cupcake?" asked a lanky, graying man who sounded as if he hailed from the same state, Texas, as the bartender he was addressing.

"I'm doin' just fine," said Drew Clark, leaning forward, arms outstretched and ear cocked, in the familiar what'll-it-be? stance. The Discus Bar—round as its name, at the edge of the main casino, the Roman Forum Casino, at Caesars Palace—encircled her like a shiny black atoll, washed all around by steady waves of sound: the singsong of the dealers, the churning slots, the lounge band's last-set reprise of "My Prerogative."

"I would like a double C.C., water on the side."

The graceful motion of a skilled bartender free-pouring exactly a shot's worth of liquor, guided by a practiced eye, had largely been stilled in Vegas, where the drinks, like the bets, were now subject to certain limits. Bottom-line concerns about portion control had imposed a rule of shot glasses and measured pouring spouts. Clark poured, one, two, shots of Canadian Club in a glass and squirted a second, ice-packed glass full with water. "I need six fifty please."

Her shift had started at 2, closing time or beyond in most places. Round-the-clock drinking was a tradition in Vegas well before the Strip's taps opened: ALL NIGHT LONG, boasted the sign on the Black Cat, a speakeasy popular with the workers who built the Hoover Dam. "I call it the 'gravy-yard,' " she said of her shift. "I make as much on graveyard as other bartenders make on swing (the busy evening shift), and I work half as hard. They spend all of swing getting people loosened up enough for graves. The more you drink, the more you seem to shovel it out."

Two dozen maroon padded stools surrounded the bar, and at 3:30, after the music had stopped and some lounge drinkers had drifted over here, half of them were occupied. On busy nights Clark might face a six-deep wall of customers and make several thousand drinks. On a slow weeknight like tonight she might make a few hundred. "You get people who lose their money and they're angry at anybody, and then you get guys who are winners and are happy with everybody. You don't get too many people crying on your shoulder about their personal life. In a local bar you get to know your clientele better, but in a casino it's mostly tourists, just here for a visit." She was a visitor herself when she came to Vegas in 1966, as a flight attendant working a Valentine's Day charter. Weary of winter weather and enticed by a sunny, 70-degree February, she quit her job and stayed.

"I like to laugh and to have funny people around. When they're drinking, they don't realize what they're saying." Her uniform was yet another variation of the prevailing Vegas tuxedo theme: red bow tie and cummerbund, white tux shirt, navy pants with a light-blue stripe, short, waiter-length, light-blue jacket with epaulets. "If you work in this business and you let the customers get to you, you're not gonna last. When somebody gives me a bad time, I think, 'Who's giving them a bad time and making their life miserable?' "

"This Scotch tastes like bubblegum," said a young man whose drink Clark had just poured.

"You know what it is?" his date informed him. "You just drank sambuca."

On Thanksgiving Day, 1966, Howard Hughes, who was accumulating a casino empire here, moved himself and his reclusive-billionaire eccentricities into the penthouse of the Desert Inn—a move that, despite its deep weirdness, was in some ways just an extreme and perverse adaptation to the local environment. Las Vegas, a night city and a desert city, is also, by natural extension, an indoor city. You could go for days here without seeing the sun or breathing fresh air. The action is concentrated at night, and the Strip resorts are sovereign corporate kingdoms, built so that you can go from room to restaurant to bar to shops to pool to health club to showroom to lounge to windowless casino and never have to cross the border if you don't want to. This expanse of always-open, always-lit interior space, spread across a city whose incessant schedule is unbeholden to the sun's rhythms, amounts to an Eden for night people. Being awake at 3 A.M. here does not make you a suspect, and being asleep at 3 P.M. does not make you a misfit. (A small army of Southern Baptist door-to-door canvassers, in town this week for a convention, had been instructed not to ring or knock more than once at any door, in deference to the many local day sleepers.) Vegas has overthrown, more successfully than any other American metropolis, the tyranny of the daytimers whose small-minded assumptions—that their time-table was the world's—I had grown to resent. "When you're used to a life-style like ours you're used to being able to eat at ten, eleven, twelve, anytime you want," Drew Clark said. "I remember being in L.A. and being terribly sick one night and not being able to get cold medicine."

Vegas often has the same effect on visitors as windowless rooms have on the subjects of human-isolation experiments: It makes them stay up later than usual. The body's natural circadian cycle actually runs about twenty-five hours, not twenty-four, and when people are shut away from the sun, the clock, the calendar, the newspaper, the TV, the radio and all the other signposts of time's passage—whether in a casino or in a scientist's lab—their cycles stretch out beyond the shorter package imposed by the day. A woman in a recent experiment, a twenty-seven-year-old Italian interior decorator, had just spent 130 days alone in a small plastic cubicle in a sealed cave thirty feet below the hills near Carlsbad, New Mexico, never seeing sunlight or hearing a human voice that wasn't her own. Her new cycle stretched so far that she stayed awake twenty to twenty-five hours at a time and slept about ten. Monitored by Italian and American scientists, including NASA researchers interested in how astronauts might be affected by the long solitude of interplanetary travel, she broke the previous women's cave-dwelling record of 103 days; lost her menstrual cycle, seventeen pounds, bone calcium and muscle tone; increased her powers of concentration; and learned a little English. "Wow, man," she said as she emerged into the 97-degree day from the constant 74-degree cave-cool night. "I feel great." One hundred and thirty days in a casino, also windowless and clockless and cut off from the world, would not, of course, have produced the same results: In a casino, after all, you can see the hours passing in the faces of the gamblers.

Vegas residents, unlike the visitors, are usually better adapted to the rhythms of their upside-down city, and better able to avoid the trap of staying up later and later each night. "I think it's all a matter of mind," Clark said. "Most people tell you they can't work graveyards, but when I get up, I just think of it as morning. When I come in at two, it's nine A.M. and when I get off at ten, it's five. I get home, eat dinner, go to bed at three P.M., get up at ten and I'm ready to go."

"Screwdriver, rum and Coke, one coffee," Deborah Kelly said to Clark, setting her tray down on the bar and adjusting her headpiece, a braid coiled like a snake around a tall hidden cone and trailing a ponytail in back. Caesars' cocktail waitresses were called "goddesses" and their outfits were styled like centurion tunics—short white pleated dress trimmed with gold, gold belt, small cape tossed back over a shoulder. Kelly was six months pregnant with her first child. "Hopefully by child number two I'll be on the day shift."

It was past 6, and the morning drinks—Bloody Marys, mimosas, jump-start shots of bourbon—were starting to mingle with the night drinks. Some of the coffee orders now were to wake up, not just to stay up. "Cocktail? Cocktail?" Kelly asked as she patrolled the casino floor, distributing the free drinks that all gamblers were entitled to and taking orders for more. "I have to see that they're actually playing," she said. "Even if they're sitting and playing one nickel at a time."

The slot machines were mostly silent, the casual gamblers they attracted all sensibly sleeping. "There might be nobody at the slots, but there's always people at twenty-one and craps," Kelly said. A man with alligator boots, a concrete pompadour and a hard wildcatter's look leaned over a craps table, clutching a fistful of hundred-dollar bills and hoping on an 8. A man with a big gold pinky ring, playing twenty-one *mano a mano* with a dealer, stood at 16. The dealer's third card brought him to 16, too, but the rules said he had to keep going. He drew a 5.

The unofficial end of the night came at 7:45 A.M., when, for the first and last time on her shift, Drew Clark was alone at the bar, surrounded by twenty-four unoccupied stools. By 7:55 she had another customer, and morning had arrived.

TheFourTopsFrankieValli&TheFourSeasonsLASVEGASHILTONT heShermanHemsleyShowSAHARA"105CastMembers4,000CostumeP ieces14,000ShimmeringLights"TheWorldFamousFoliesBergereTRO

Kevin Coyne

"You're gonna need an ocean," David St. David sang, "of calamine lotion," bobbing and weaving on the small stage of the Casbar Lounge at the Sahara, his low-buttoned white suit and scoop-necked white T-shirt bright in the spotlight, "You'll be scratchin' like a hound, the minute you start to mess around," his four-man backing band (guitar, bass, drums, keyboard) kicked in for the chorus, "Poison Ivee-ee-ee-ee-ee, Poison Ivee-ee-ee-ee-ee," he took it back alone, "Late at night while you're a-sleepin' Poison Ivy comes a-creepin' arow-ow-ow-ound," the band wound down the Coasters' song with a few lada-dada-dadas and segued straight into Chuck Berry, "Nadine," St. David stopping just long enough to pick up a guitar and play the lead, "Nadine, why can't you be true?" . . .

He was forty-seven and a grandfather, a contemporary of the songs that comprised his show, born in Philadelphia, schooled professionally on band-stands along the Jersey Shore and throughout the Northeast before coming twenty years earlier to Vegas, a company town that employs musicians and other entertainers the way Detroit employs autoworkers. "I spent a couple of semesters at Duquesne University, but I wanted to go back on the road. The music was so hot then, that early-sixties period, and I thought this was my shot at becoming a star, naturally. I lose no sleep over stardom now. I know my age, and I know what the music world is looking for." He looked a little like Tom Jones, dark curly hair and well-toned muscles, and he sounded a little like Tom Jones, a powerful voice that could span four octaves, "a cultured baritone with a tenor range," as he described it. He had averaged forty-seven weeks of lounge work annually over the last couple of years. "I know I can kick butt against the youngest people in town."

. . . and three couples were up dancing in the dim and forgiving light of the lounge, two steps down from the casino floor, and two dozen or so other people watched from the cushiony loveseats and sofas and armchairs set around the cocktail tables their drinks rested on as St. David traded his guitar for congas, standing and drumming with his hands through Santana's "Oye Como Va" . . .

"We weren't born as nocturnal creatures and we never will be. When you take on the task of working late into the night, it automatically does something with your body, your physique. It's definitely something I've had to battle in the night life. Roughly ten years ago I used to hit the pool with a couple of chicks and go without sleep, and people weren't saying to me, 'Thirty-seven? You don't look that,' they were saying, 'You look your age.' " He started working out, "I cleansed myself," quit smoking, "eliminated all chemicals and drugs.'' ''I look at it this way—it's up to the individual. How good do you want to feel? Do you want to be Jack La Lanne or do you want to pass on to the ages at fifty with a heart attack? I want to kick up my heels like George Burns. I'm trying to defy the breakdown of genes and chromosomes. My shows are very physical, and what's kept me in business is that I'm in very good physical shape.'' He was headed to the gym to lift weights after his final set, soon after midnight. Tomorrow he planned to work at his hobby, restoring classic muscle cars. His next two bookings were graveyards, ''third trick,'' he called them. ''The people I meet in the late hours, their random conversation never gets past B. I'm not talking A to Z, it's just B—'Where's the party? Who's got the drugs?' I have very little in common with people who hang out in the wee hours and who stay out until the sun comes up. You won't find a multitude of serious people out there. I'd say if you're looking for a better quality of person, you're not gonna find it in the wee hours.''

. . . ''We're gonna slow up the pace a little now,'' and the bass started a loping doo-wop stroll, ''something from Johnny Maestro and the Crests, for anybody celebrating a birthday tonight, 'Siiiiixteeeen candles,' '' and the band chimed in with ooohs and aaahs and echo harmonies of the accent phrases, ''only sixteeeen'' and ''I've ever seeen'' and the rest, and St. David's voice rose with the final declaration, ''for I love you soooo,'' taking it high on that soooo . . .

''Usually it's three to four years here and then you die. You can't put up with the aches and pains anymore. But I'm callused. When I get a job on the phone I yell like a pro basketball player, I smack my fist and slam the phone down and go, 'Yeah!' You get these prima donnas who come to town and they think they know how to entertain, they think they know how to sing. They say, 'I paid my dues, I shouldn't have to do this.' They're not Vega-tized yet. Only a handful of us have survived. It's like being a pro football or basketball player. You do the best you can and try to be the winner. I just get up there and kick myself in the butt and then people come to me after the show and say, 'You're the best lounge show in Vegas,' and I just might be one of the best around, not the best, but one of the best. You go to a showroom and you ain't gonna touch Wayne Newton or Diana Ross, but I met a guy tonight, he's from Pennsylvania, and we started talking. People come up to me and say, 'David, remember us? We're from New Jersey, or Ohio.' I've worked every city in America and I say to them 'I know where that crossroads is.' Maybe to all the people out there I don't have the name, but I know I'm gonna go out having touched millions of lives, all those people who know me, maybe became my friend, went out to dinner with me, enjoyed my company."

. . . and he strapped the guitar on again, "Here's a little one before we say good night," and the band shifted into the fast lane, "See you later, alligator," and then, after a few rave-ups, they braked to a final stop, "Thank you so much, we'll be back tomorrow night, seven to twelve, the Rock 'n' Roll All-Star Band, the Henry Shed Trio will be here to entertain you next, have a wonderful morning here at the Sahara."

In Las Vegas, where every night is meant to feel like Saturday night, you need never wait to be entertained. The cultural calendar here is continuous, unaffected by the seasons, the traditional workweek schedule, the touring habits of shows and stars, or even the full moon, a factor that, in the age before outdoor lighting made it safer and easier for carriages to negotiate the darkness, determined the dates of society balls. Vegas is built on and sustained by the diaphanous promise of a never-ending weekend, and in order to produce its contracted quota of assembly-line Saturday nights it employs legions of singers, dancers, comedians, magicians, trapeze artists, stunt cyclists, contortionists, ventriloquists, hypnotists, ice skaters, synchronized swimmers, high divers, jugglers, puppeteers, impressionists, animal trainers, motorcycle daredevils, acrobats, jazz trumpeters, rock drummers, country guitar pickers, Elvis impersonators, Marilyn Monroe impersonators, drag-show female impersonators with no particular specialty, high-kicking chorus lines, showgirls in sequins and feathered headdresses and little else, and assorted other novelty acts of the sort that have found work in precious few other venues since the demise of the vaudeville circuit. Maybe thirty thousand people fill the showrooms each evening for the celebrities and the revues, but most of the marquee talent is offstage not long past midnight; even the aerialists who twirl above the gamblers at Circus Circus return to earth by twelve. In the deep, deep hours of the night, responsibility for keeping the endless soundtrack playing is handed over to the lounges.

"On the road again," Henry Shed sang, sitting at the piano that had taken St. David's place at center stage, a red spotlight shining on him, trim and natty in a light tan suit, white shirt, red tie and matching red pocket handkerchief, drums and synthesizer playing beside him to help load and carry his elegant, understated piano stylings, "Just can't wait to get on the road again."

In the wee small hours in a lounge in Las Vegas—a town whose basic style was forged in the fifties, and where you can sometimes still hear women described as "broads," gays as "swishy" and Mob figures as "bandits"—you might expect to be haunted by the drown-your-sorrows, broken-tryst melancholy of "One for My Baby" ("It's quarter to three/ There's no one in the place, except you and me/So set 'em up, Joe . . ."), the saloon standard sung by Frank Sinatra; but the songbook in Henry Shed's head was bigger than that. Between midnight and 5, when the lounge finally fell silent, he might play fifty songs, none of them off a prepared set list. "The bartenders and waitresses in some places say they can set their watches by what the band is playing. I hate that. I just play what pops into my head." His selection widened as the night lengthened. "With this shift you can do more. On the early shift [7 to midnight] you get people coming in from the dinner shows and they wanna hear more 'New York, New York' type of things, and it's hard to mix it up for them."

Billy Preston's "Will It Go Round in Circles" popped in next. A big guy in white shoes drummed along on his table. "Sometimes people say to me, 'Man, you know everything,' " Shed said. "It's because I've done so many kinds of gigs." His first in Vegas was a two-week booking at the Aladdin in 1974, "and I've been here ever since." He was a minister's son from Arkansas and a former high school teacher, and he had spent a few years acting in Los Angeles. He had started piano lessons when he was six. "There's a few generations running through it," he said of his piano style, colored by jazz, rhythm-and-blues and, his prime influence, Ray Charles. The oldest of his four children—Henry, Jr., who had recently earned a degree in organizational behavior from Stanford and was making a run at a music career—was the synthesizer player. "Lately I've been playing more of their music."

People drifted in and out of the lounge, no cover no minimum, staying for a few songs, "You Are So Beautiful," or for a whole set until a break, "Sloop John B," maybe dancing, "Just the Way You Are," twelve people now, then ten, then six, "With or Without You," then eleven, then fifteen, an audience as fluid as a craps table's. "You have to deal with it," he said about playing to small late crowds, and sometimes to no crowd at all but the gamblers out in the casino, to whom he furnished living background music. "They know nobody's gonna be here, nobody expects you to have the house full, but it's your job. You play for the floorman and the pit boss and the dealers, just to have something going, like something's going on. I know a lot of entertainers couldn't do it and probably wouldn't do it. I'm a family man, I've got to have the checks rolling in. I can't sell shoes, I can't sell cars, I don't want to teach school. I still love what I do."

A fortyish couple breezed into the lounge, straight onto the dance floor. "We've been looking all over for a place to dance," they announced to Shed as they swung past to George Michael's "I Want Your Sex." The Casbar was one of the few casino lounges where you could hear live music after 3 A.M. "Las Vegas has changed," Shed said. "People are going to bed earlier, they really are. They don't stay out like they used to. It used to be you could go to a place like this at three or four A.M. and it'd be full of people." He slowed the nomadic dancers into a clinch with "Lean on Me."

It was 4:15 in the morning, nineteen people were in the lounge, and one of the five young guys with Coors cans had a request: "Speed it up," he called. Shed did, with Billy Ocean's "Caribbean Queen," and the floor filled with dancers, including one guy in chinos who was so far off the beat that he had almost lapped it and caught up again. The party wound down from there, and Shed said good night by 4:45—late compared with most lounges, early compared with a 2-to-8 shift he had once played at Caesars Palace: "That was weird." No closing-time lights came up, sparing any new couples from a harsh unmasking of whatever flaws in one the hopeful shadows had concealed from the other. The lounge's silence was filled by the casino sound track: "I'm gonna kiss your head if you roll an eight," one craps player told another, but the 8 didn't come and the relationship remained unconsummated.

Shed was due back at the piano in nineteen hours. The eastern sky outside wore just the barest touch of blue, and the towering 222-foot Sahara sign still glowed against the darkness, flashing the time (5:05) and temperature (73) and marking the northern end, the end nearest downtown, of the Strip—longer now, at three and a half miles, than the original grass strip the Mormons found, and, save for the gaming tables and the cash, far less green. "When you're part of the night life," Shed said, "you never feel quite like you're part of the real world, the day world, even in Vegas."

12

*At 5:30, on a LOS ANGELES freeway, a repair crew
poured and smoothed another fresh panel of concrete, making the road whole again.*

Tommy Chong and his wife, Shelby, were walking down the leafy concrete
steps into MacArthur Park near downtown Los Angeles when they heard
a shout, "Motherfucker," in the dark distance and started running toward
it. CUT. "Shelby," director William Lustig instructed, "when Tommy
takes off, why don't you hold a couple of beats on the stairs and then pursue
him."

"Quiet, folks, rehearsing," an assistant told the mingling, murmuring,
watching crowd of extras waiting in the shadowy park beyond the bright
star lights.

"As soon as Tommy goes out of frame, we're gonna cut," Lustig said.

Tommy Chong and his wife, Shelby, were walking down the leafy
concrete steps into MacArthur Park when they heard a shout, "Motherfucker," in the dark distance. He took off, dreadlocks flopping. She paused,
then skittered after him as fast as her high heels and her second-skin black
minidress would allow. CUT.

"If you holler 'motherfucker' here, he'll probably be down here when he
stops," Lustig told the person who was shouting the cue. A hair stylist
sprayed the blond curls that frothed out from under Shelby's little black
garrison cap.

"Okay, folks, the next one's picture, we will be rolling sound, so keep
it quiet. Stand by for picture, roll sound." The slate clapped in front of the
camera, marking the first take. "Action."

Tommy Chong (best known as the tall, slow-witted, zonked-out half of Cheech and Chong, the drug generation's answer to Abbott and Costello, starring now as "Far Out Man" in the movie of the same name) and his wife, Shelby ("Tree," his long-lost and now-found wife) were walking down the steps into MacArthur Park and talking—exactly what they were saying was audible only to them, the sound man and the audience who would eventually see this movie—when they heard a shout, "Motherfucker." He took off. She paused, then followed. CUT.

Tommy Chong and his wife, Shelby, were walking down the steps into MacArthur Park when they heard a shout, "Motherfucker." He took off. She paused, then followed, running with one hand holding her cap this time. CUT.

Tommy Chong and his wife, Shelby, were walking down the steps into MacArthur Park when they heard a shout, "Motherfucker." He ran off into the darkness and she followed. CUT. "Do it again," Lustig said after the third take. "After this we'll break for lunch."

Tommy Chong and his wife, Shelby, were walking down the steps into MacArthur Park when they heard a shout, "Motherfucker." He ran toward it, and she followed. CUT. Once they were out of the frame, pulled up short in the shadows by the line of directors' chairs, they stayed out of the frame, spared another trip up the steps for another take. "That was it," Lustig said at 9:15 P.M. "That's lunch, half an hour."

The caterers were up on the yawning stage of the park bandshell, dishing out chicken, pasta and vegetables to a line, maybe one hundred long, of grips, best boys, gaffers, assistant directors, costumers, prop assistants, camera assistants, set decorators, makeup artists and extras (who got thirty-five dollars, plus this evening lunch, to serve as human wallpaper for the camera). The Chongs took their plates off into a parked black BMW. Outside the temporary movie encampment the park's nightly routines proceeded uninterrupted—the fountains splashing in the lake a reminder of an elegant past of fashionable strolls and afternoon concerts, the homeless men and the drug dealers doing business up on the corner a reminder of a harder present. Wilshire Boulevard bisected the park on its way west, a wide boulevard that runs sixteen miles from downtown to the Pacific, past Hollywood through Beverly Hills closing credits in Santa Monica, and that inscribes a Main Street through this fanned-out freeway city.

All over the city tonight crews were out on location shooting movies—*Darkman* on East Sixth Street, *Backstreet Strays* on Hollywood Boulevard,

A Day in the Night of America

Internal Affairs on Mountaingate Drive, *Bride of Reanimator* on North Figueroa, *Dad* on South St. Louis, *Vital Signs* on North LaCienga, *California Casanova* on Wilshire, and a marqueeful of others, the latest in a line that reached back to 1913, when Cecil B. DeMille rented a barn at the corner of Vine and Selma and made *The Squaw Man,* the first feature-length movie shot entirely in Hollywood. The L.A. landscape has been filmed so often that even if you've never been here, it feels as if you have. It unreels, when you finally do drive through it, like a nagging case of low-grade déjà vu. You have probably visited MacArthur Park, without ever knowing its name, through scores of scenes that called for a green and landscaped city park. The Industry, as the business of movie and television production is known in the local shorthand, is not the biggest industry in town—about 7 percent of the metro area's jobs, if you count all the indirect and part-time workers—but it is the most visible from a distance; and although it had dispersed a substantial portion of its location shooting to locations beyond southern California, it still turned frequently to the streets of Los Angeles for the kinds of scenes a studio or backlot just can't fake. *Far Out Man,* a dopey farce about a leftover hippie's improbable reunion with his wife and son, was one of 162 movies made this year in L.A., where film crews were such a common, and often unwelcome, sight that some jaded locals had taken to extorting cash payments in exchange for promises not to disrupt the quiet-please shoots with loud music or revving lawnmowers.

The night tonight was needed as a curtain behind the movie's climactic fight scene, the source of the "Motherfucker" the Chongs ran down the steps toward in the last shot. The lights, camera and action had moved now and reconvened behind the bandshell, facing the extras and motorcycles gathered before its brightly muraled rear wall. "Night is night, you can't cheat it," said Lustig, who had directed many nights of location shoots in his career. His credits included *Vigilante, Relentless, Maniac, Maniac Cop* and *Maniac Cop II.* "You can cheat daylight better than you can cheat night. There's nothing like shooting in New York at night. You really have the run of the town, you don't have to worry about people walking into the shot, and there's something spiritual that happens around two, three, four A.M., something spiritual that takes place. You become light-headed and your adrenaline gets going."

"You can't get the depth you want to get, the city lights in the background," cinematographer Jim Lemmo said about trying to catch the night in a studio. "There's also something about being out at night. It gives an energy to the scene and the picture that you can't get in the studio. If you're doing an action picture, you want to be out here in the elements."

"I'd rather work nights than get up for those six A.M. days," Tommy Chong said.

"Here we go, folks, lots of energy now," Lustig told the extras. "You're having a good time, you're partying down." The bandshell wall acted as the exterior of a rock club, and the extras acted, with the exaggerated naturalism of amateurs, as the young crowd milling outside it. Paris Chong ("Kyle") and Peggy Sands ("Misty") emerged from a smoky open door, exiting a concert scene that had already been shot in another place at another time. His day-glo green hair was molded into tall porcupine spikes. He stopped cold, open-mouthed in shock, when he saw the bikers who had chased him with murderous intent after he accidentally knocked over their Harleys earlier in the movie. He fell backward, toppled by his own surprise, and knocked over the Harleys again.

"What the fuck?!" said Buddy Daniels ("Gang Leader"), clad all in black, wearing a studded dog collar around his neck and a skull-and-crossbones tattoo on his brow. "Back off, guys, I'll handle this, man." He shouldered past the other gang members—the guy with the coyote-pelt hat, the guy with the red headband, the guy with the bushy gray walrus mustache, real bikers all, not actors like him, the owners of the real tumbling bikes—and stalked toward Paris.

"Hey, he didn't mean it," Sands said, trying to intervene.

"Bitch, move," Daniels said, tossing her aside.

"Cut, no good," Lustig said. "Misty, you've gotta get away from him quicker. Let's do it again."

Tommy Chong wrote and directed *Far Out Man*—Lustig had been called in to help reshoot some final scenes—and he cast it like a home movie: In addition to Shelby and Paris, his teenage son, it also featured his daughter, Rae Dawn Chong, and his son-in-law, C. Thomas Howell. It was his first solo movie since his breakup with Cheech Marin. "You know how it says 'A film by so-and-so'? I'm gonna put down 'A Tommy Chong Attempt,' " he said. It included cameos by Martin Mull, Judd Nelson and even Cheech himself, who popped into a truck cab just in time to keep Chong from falling asleep at the wheel, but not in time to keep him from making a dumb movie; and its humor (centered around, in the best Cheech and Chong tradition, drugs and sex and other bodily functions) was generally as low as its budget (about two million dollars, a five-and-dime price by Hollywood standards).

"I think this film is going to be like *Naked Gun*," said producer Paul Hertzberg, referring to the off-the-wall police comedy hit. He was president of CineTel Films, an independent production company, and he was on location tonight, wearing a black leather jacket, to watch the final night of shooting. "I wouldn't miss the wrap on this for anything."

"Buddy, you're gonna be stepping into the shot," Lustig said. "Take it from the point where the bikes went down. Let's see how it plays."

As Daniels moved in on the fallen Paris, Tommy Chong ran into the frame and stepped between them. Almost two hours in real time had passed in the few seconds of eventual screen time it had taken him to get here from the earlier down-the-park-steps scene. "Hey, man, mellow out, dude," he told Daniels, speaking with a loopy pothead drawl. Ragged in his ripped jeans and khaki tank top, he could have easily swapped places with the homeless man who was watching the action from a nearby park bench.

"Get outta my face, asshole, I'm gonna kick that dork's ass, man."

"Hey, you're really tense, man. You gotta change your diet. I bet you eat meat." Daniels grunted angrily. "I knew it, man, look at your eyes, man. You need calcium, man." As Chong pulled a bottle of pills from his pocket, Shelby ran up behind him and embraced Paris. "Listen, man, I've got these . . ." Daniels knocked them from his hand. CUT.

"I didn't get my grunt," Lustig said to Daniels.

"When do you want the second grunt? After 'calcium'?"

Daniels grunted, again and again and again, and threw a punch at Paris that hit Shelby instead, over and over and over, and Paris responded by knocking Daniels out cold, once twice thrice. CUT. CUT. CUT.

"Give me a little more snap of the neck," Lustig told Shelby, and then, when she had, they did it all over again from the opposite angle.

"We got it," Lustig finally said at 1:30. The fight scene was finished, several miles of film and several hours of work for 90 seconds of eventual screen time. The big 10,000-watt tungsten lights went out slowly, fading through gold like a Pacific sunset.

"One shot to go and this movie's history," Hertzberg said.

The camera was reloaded and moved up into the wings of the bandshell stage, which was standing in tonight as the interior of a Fresno bar. "A little more smoke, please," Lustig requested of the smoke machine operator. Paris dialed a number on a pay phone, tried to make a collect call, then hung up. CUT. CUT.

"That's it, that's a wrap, folks, that's a wrap." The crew's location permit didn't expire until 6 A.M., but Lustig pronounced the movie done at 2:05.

"It ended up with a phone call, 'Yeah, hello, good-bye,' that's it," Chong said. "We could get that shot anytime, and it ended up being the last one."

The wrap celebration up on the bandshell stage consisted of Pepperidge Farm cookies and champagne in red plastic cups. The crew packed the trucks, returning the park to its usual nocturnal tenants. The film was on its way to Burbank for overnight processing. The bikers came up to shake Chong's hand and say good night. "Nice meeting you, man," the last one said, and they roared off on their Harleys.

Chong looked around and surveyed the folding scene. "When it's really done, you get sad. It's like, 'Don't tell me it's over.' "

When *Far Out Man* was finally released, it was billed, as Chong said it would be, as "A Tommy Chong Attempt," but his humility won him little mercy from the critics. Some were generous—"a certain goofy charm," "good-natured low humor," "an amiable nonchalance," "its silliness is somehow agreeable"—but more were not. "Unless fate and Hollywood take some very peculiar turns, a Judd Nelson cameo should never be the highlight of any movie," *The New York Times* said. "Just say no," *Daily Variety* advised. The *Hollywood Reporter* even rendered a direct judgment on the night in MacArthur Park: "The scene where Tree gets hit by a biker is not funny." It made just $82,000 in its first three days in the theaters, vanished soon thereafter, and reappeared in video stores a few months later—its passage through the public consciousness as invisible as most things that happen at night.

●

Los Angeles is walled off from the desert behind it by the San Gabriel Mountains, peaks reaching to 10,000 feet, far higher than anything east of the Mississippi but almost commonplace out here in the West, and to drive up them at dusk, up to the top of Mount Wilson, winding and switchbacking up past 2,000 feet, 3,000 feet, 4,000 feet of tan brushed with evergreen, up to 5,700 feet, where the TV transmission towers stand against the dimming sky like the skeletons of great trees after a forest fire, is like climbing to the uppermost seats in the Hollywood Bowl, the natural amphitheater nestled down in the Hollywood Hills. The Los Angeles basin spreads out below like a vast stage, stopped only by its opposite barrier, the Pacific Ocean.

A Day in the Night of America

Tonight the stage was shrouded like the set of a foggy mystery movie, covered by smog as thick as clouds beneath an airplane: The mountains that wall in the city also wall in its bad air, the inversion effect that was noticed as far back as 1542, when Juan Rodríquez Cabrillo, the first European to see this coastal plain, sailed past and named it Bahía de los Humos, Bay of the Smokes, after the trapped smoky haze that hung over the Indian campfires. As night deepened, lights punched up through the smog, painting it pale orange and outlining the contours of L.A. It was a breathtaking view, from an angle that in New York or Chicago is obtainable only by aircraft, looking out over the first American city entirely lit by electricity, the city where MGM once boasted of having "more stars than there are in heaven." But when night was complete, the view down took second billing to the view up. From up here, through the searching telescopes of Mount Wilson Observatory, astronomers discovered that the universe revealed by the night sky was far, far larger than had ever been dreamed.

Mule teams started hauling equipment up the rough dirt roads to the crest of Mount Wilson at the dawn of this century, and by the eve of World War I it had become the astronomy capital of the world, a position it would hold until after the end of World War II. The mountain offered distance from the dust and turbulence below—raw height alone was not important, because even a mile-high peak is barely a step on the trillions-of-miles journey out to the stars—and the Southern California climate provided the kind of clear, cloudless nights that offered what astronomers call "good seeing." Before the eyes of Mount Wilson opened, astronomers believed our home galaxy, the Milky Way, was the only galaxy in the universe; after Mount Wilson, and Edwin Hubble's work here, they saw that our galaxy is but one of billions.

The two observatory domes sat among the dark trees atop the mountain like extraterrestrial landing craft, bright and unearthly in the moonglow. The two solar telescopes, aimed by day at the nearest star to Earth, towered like oil derricks. Mount Wilson was still an active astronomical center, but it had been upstaged now by other mountains with bigger telescopes—by Palomar, its sister observatory down near San Diego; by others in Arizona, Chile and Hawaii; by the Hubble Space Telescope, in orbit above Earth, higher than any mountain.

The eyeslit in the bigger dome was shut tight, sleeping soundly, the hundred-inch telescope inside, once the world's most powerful, mothballed at least temporarily. The eye in the smaller dome was awake and open. Up the inside stairs and under the dome, lined with cork and riveted like a battleship, the air was as cool as the air outside: Unequal temperatures diminish the quality of seeing. The darkened chamber under the dome was of ecclesiastical shape and dimension, and the telescope, a tall octagonal erector-set cylinder with a sixty-inch mirror at its base, stood at attention in the shadows at the center of the floor, at the axis where the altar would be. Red darkroom lights shone dimly up along the track the dome rotates on. A radio played the Temptations' "Just My Imagination." Lit by a single desk lamp, Jim Frazer and Walter Bennett bent over an electronic control console that was hooked up to a vintage-1908 telescope, elegant with brass gears and wheels, and that, along with several computer terminals and video screens, added a stark modern accent to a space with the venerable archival look of an old movie-scientist's lab. "We can't do quasars and black holes here," Frazer said, "but there's more to the universe than quasars and black holes."

The telescope was pointed into Boötes, a northern constellation southeast of the Big Dipper, and focused on a cool yellow star of the type classified as a G8, smaller and cooler than our star, a G2 better known as the sun. The star's light was collected by the telescope's reflector, recorded and analyzed by a detecting instrument, and eventually added to the mountain of data Mount Wilson had been accumulating since 1966 for a long-term stellar research project. After they finished with this star, Frazer and Bennett would aim the telescope at the next star on the night's itinerary. Their explorations stayed close to home, by universe standards, confined to our neighborhood, the Milky Way, and were designed to help learn more about the nearest star by watching other farther stars that resembled it—their temperature, brightness, chemical composition, starspot activity cycles; how they evolve, age and die; their fate, and maybe ours. "Then we'll know more about where the sun's coming from and where it's going," said Frazer, whose title was "observer," and who, like his fellow observer, held no Ph.D. ("You don't need a Ph.D. just to push the buttons to run the telescope"). The data went to a Harvard astrophysicist. The project list included about one thousand stars, some observed weekly or more, some monthly. Some stars took as long as thirty minutes, some as few as four; the average was around ten. They might get to eighty stars on a long winter night, just thirty on a short summer night. In the starlight they captured they could see back only as far as the Dark Ages; all of the project stars were within one thousand light-years of Earth.

The telescope turned as it watched—floating on mercury, guided by computer-controlled drive gears like a giant Swiss watch, turning too slowly to notice but fast enough, at the same one-revolution-per-day pace as Earth itself, to track the stars. If it stood still and did nothing to compensate for Earth's daily rotation, the stars, once found, would soon sweep out of view of its mirror. "At night—excuse me, in the daytime—we turn it off," Bennett said about the drive mechanism. He had two engineering degrees, had worked in the telephone industry and had quit at thirty-nine to return to college to study astronomy, aiming toward a new career, "teaching science to nonscientists." He was nearing the end of a nine-month hitch up on the mountain. On his late-night lunchbreaks he often toured the universe beyond the project stars. "I've never seen anything unexplainable. But if we knew everything, we wouldn't be studying it. If we had any idea how big it is and what's happening out there, we'd probably all be frightened."

The star sitting for its portrait now was HD 131156B, classified as a K4, an orange main-sequence star of middling temperature. "Pictures in books look a lot better than what we see," Frazer said. "It's just dots when we look at the TV screen." A native of the basin below, he had come to work at Mount Wilson, "my first and only job," fifteen years before as a night assistant, and he lived now in one of the eight houses, fitted with light-tight bedroom window shades, up here on the grounds. He worked from dusk to dawn. Summer nights were shorter but generally clearer; winter was the rainy season in L.A., bringing clouds that shut the telescope down as firmly as a metal grate on a city storefront, snow that sent him up to the dome with a shovel and cold that forced him to wear a parka inside. Humidity, frost, forest-fire smoke and mechanical problems occasionally meant useless nights. He could sometimes hear deer foraging outside, or a bear raiding the Dumpster. He was listening now to the detector measuring the star's light, emitting a Geiger-counter click-click loud enough to rouse the drowsy. "Just think, the light from that star travels all that way through outer space, bounces off the mirror and dies on the detector. That one photon must be pretty happy to be recorded for posterity. But what about that photon next to it? It must be upset that it traveled all that way and then died just half an inch from the detector, half an inch from posterity."

"Okay, we're ready to go to the moon," Bennett said, detouring from the project to give me a quick ride through the solar system. He steered the telescope over a moonscape that looked like a floodlit Utah, over craters and deserts and mountains as high as the Himalayas, finding the Bay of Rainbows, Plato, the Lake of Dreams, the Sea of Tranquillity (where the Apollo

11 footprints are), Copernicus, the Sea of Clouds, Clavius and, finally, the Terminator, the sharp line between the light of the lunar day and the dark of the lunar night. When it is full, the moon showers Earth with a thousand times more light than all the stars together, enough to wake sleeping day birds, but the light it reflects by night is still 400,000 times less bright than the light the sun generated by day.

Bennett left the moon and soared out to Saturn, the solar system's signature planet, its rings apparently as solid around its middle as a race-track, its black-and-white image on the video screen tilted at an angle that made it look like the CBS eye logo. Next stop was Pluto, the smallest of the nine known planets (a frozen snowball of methane and water smaller even than the moon) and the farthest (it takes 248 years to orbit the sun), but still seven thousand times closer than the next nearest star. It was just a tiny white dot on the screen—about the same size Earth is in the group portrait of the planets snapped by Voyager 2, the unmanned spacecraft that is soaring out toward interstellar space, our farthest emissary into the universe's lasting night.

"Watch out for that Klingon vessel," Frazer said, a joking reference to *Star Trek*.

In a nearby clearing, in a trailer that looked more like a construction-site office than an astronomical facility, Craig Denison and Tom Armstrong sat watching a parade of numbers on a computer screen. The lights were on, and the narrow space was stuffed with banks of electronic equipment. Nothing resembling a telescope was anywhere to be found. "It's a different way of looking at stars," Denison said of this optical interferometry project. The trailer's eyes were a pair of ten-inch rotating mirrors outside, sidero-stats, separated by a twenty-seven-meter gap that enabled them to see one star from two angles at once. The light they collected was reflected through vacuum tubes and combined, a technique that reduced atmospheric distor-tion and yielded a more accurate picture of a star than just one mirror alone could obtain. "It's the next generation of interferometry." Astrometry was one aim of the project, to better map the stars most of us see—if we see them at all—as simply nameless night ornaments; another was to measure the diameters of stars and to determine how long it took binary stars (two stars that orbit a common center of gravity) to revolve around each other. Tonight's list included thirty-two stars, each to be visited, they hoped, five times or more before morning. In breaks between stars, Denison read a paperback copy of Bram Stoker's *Dracula*. "I really don't get into L.A.

much," the Colorado native said, "and after looking down at the air, I'm glad I don't."

Armstrong left the trailer and walked out into the moonlight to check on the mirror. It sounded like a distant police siren, far down the mountain road and climbing, as it faintly whirred into a new position. It moved just a few inches down here on Earth, but its view out in space swept across light-years. "These stars are quite nearby compared with radio astronomy," said Armstrong, whose Ph.D. work was in radio astronomy, which studies celestial bodies by their radio waves rather than their light. "People are amazed by the high numbers, but it gets to be commonplace. I don't experience the immensity of this, except when I start explaining it." All above him was a laboratory rich with almost unimaginable challenges. "We get to think about things and try to figure out things no one else has figured out."

At the KTLA tower atop Mount Wilson the signals were not incoming but outgoing—electromagnetic waves that any TV set down under the inversion layer could, if tuned to Channel 5 between midnight and 12:30, translate into *The Honeymooners*. Tonight it was the episode where Ralph and Ed are stuck on the fire escape outside the kitchen window of the Kramden apartment in their Raccoon Lodge outfits. Mike Welte, sitting alone in a darkened glassed-in control room at KTLA's studio on Sunset Boulevard in Hollywood, watched their predicament unfold on one of the twenty-nine screens that rose above his wide electronic console. Although *The Honeymooners* have been floating through the atmosphere for decades, they are not, unlike a quasar, a naturally occurring signal. Nobody in L.A. would see Ralph and Ed, or Alice and Trixie, tonight if not for Welte and his two co-workers, whose job it was to keep the station broadcasting through the deep night. "Looks like about a minute to break two," Welte said into a microphone that carried his voice out to his fellow graveyarders, back in the bright rooms where the tapes and films were, and a minute later, right on schedule, Ralph and Ed were spelled by a commercial.

KTLA, the first commercial TV station west of Chicago, started broadcasting from a small building on the Paramount Pictures lot in 1947, when the estimated TV-receiver population of L.A. was all of 350. Its debut program, emceed by Bob Hope, featured Cecil B. DeMille, Dorothy Lamour, William Bendix, Ann Rutherford and the Rhythmaires. Two years later it offered on-the-scene through-the-night continuous news coverage, twenty-eight hours' worth, of the unsuccessful attempt to rescue a three-year-old girl who had fallen into a deep abandoned well. As the L.A. TV population grew, so did the station, moving in 1955 to its present home on the old Warner Bros. Studio lot, a Hollywood landmark: It was on Stage 6 here that Al Jolson sang his way through *The Jazz Singer,* the talking picture that broke the sound barrier. *Gunsmoke*'s Dodge City street was here, and Esther Williams's pool. The building Welte worked in had, on the inside, hosted the *Looney Tunes* cartoon gang, and, on the outside, appeared in *Get Smart* chase scenes. Ralph and Ed had since come in off the fire escape and, at 12:30, been replaced on Channel 5 screens by *Carson's Comedy Classics.* Tina Turner was sitting in the guest chair beside Johnny. "When I was ten years old, I decided I wanted to stay up all night watching movies. I wanted my own TV station," Welte said. "It's a nice change getting paid now for doing what I wanted to do then. Working graveyards is kind of like sitting up all night and playing with your own TV station." Until the mid-1970s KTLA usually signed off with a star-spangled flourish at 1 or so; Welte was among the first on the shift when it started staying on the air through the night. "It was the new kid on the new shift, which made it easier," he said. "It used to be that nobody wanted it. Now I have to protect it jealously. I would retire from this job if it's still here when I'm ready to retire."

USA Tonight followed Carson, George Bush instead of Tina Turner. "I watch the shows if they're good, I watch the commercials if they're not." He also watched the seconds on the clock. Television time is—despite the neat illusion of the daily listings, with their orderly procession of tightly wrapped half-hour packages—an often messy assemblage of shows that sometimes run too short, movies that sometimes run too long, commercials (a Hacienda Chrysler spot was up now), station identifications and promos, and public-service announcements; and Welte's job as technical director was, whether by stretching or squeezing, to fit it all into the allotted hours on his shift. "They expect from the graveyard T.D. that no matter what goes wrong, you're running on time at six A.M."

USA Tonight ran a little long, leaving Welte eighteen seconds behind schedule for "Movies 'Til Dawn." To compensate, he could cut some of the credits at the end of the night's first feature, *Storm Boy,* a 1976 Australian movie about a boy and his pelican. "There's one minute and four seconds of closing credits, and I don't figure anybody in the movie is sitting up and watching it." Welte wasn't watching too closely either as the camera sweeps across the isolated South Australian coastline where Mike, the Storm Boy, lives in a tumbledown beach shack with his gruff, reclusive father, Hideaway Tom; but he was listening. "If there's a pause in the audio or the screen goes black, I notice that right away, even if I'm not paying attention." *Storm Boy* had won several Australian film awards and been rated four stars by most Australian newspapers, but the acclaim hadn't been echoed on this side of the Pacific Rim: The *Los Angeles Times* TV listings for the day gave it two checks, one more than its competition on HBO *(The Hidden)*, one less than its competition on Channel 13 *(The Male Animal)*. It was the kind of movie Welte usually read through—science fiction novels, police procedurals, computer magazines and news magazines. "It's annoying to be in the middle of something you can't put down and then have to put it down every nine minutes." In the morning the ratings would show that 81,600 people were watching *Storm Boy* now, second only to a rerun of the late news.

On the screen, roaming through lyrical shots of sunsets and windswept shores, the Storm Boy has befriended a wise aborigine, Fingerbone Bill, and adopted an orphan pelican, Mr. Percival. "Looks like about a minute to break four," Welte said. A commercial for a waterbed store appears at 2:16:44, followed at 2:17:14 by Sy Sperling and the Hair Club for Men. How many people were watching now was unknown: The overnight ratings stopped at 2.

"If I worked half as good as these things, I'd be in great shape," Jim Crear said as he rewound Reel 1 of *Storm Boy,* finished now, on projector A after the next commercial break. It was a real film, 16mm, not a videotape, and it was playing, Reel 2 now, on a real projector, Projector B, a sturdy and venerable RCA. The image was a tiny box, smaller than all the TVs it was appearing on. The room sounded like a theater projectionist's booth as the film clicked along. If the bulb burns out, it's time for an impromptu commercial break, or the Technical Difficulties tape and some music. "It hasn't gone out on me in a couple of years."

After Reel 1 of *Storm Boy* was rewound, Crear threaded Reel 1 of the next movie, *The Heiress,* into Projector A, preparing for the 3:30 showing. "It isn't hectic on this shift. The drive in is easy, and when I come in, the executives are gone, the office people are gone, the phone has stopped ringing. It's a very mellow atmosphere. The only problem we have is just trying to stay awake, to stay alert and not let the computers lull us into a false sense of security. I can make it till two, no problem, but after two A.M. it gets rough, it really does. There's a Hostess Twinkie then with my name on it." He averaged three cups of coffee a shift, down from the six or seven he used to drink. "The idea is to stay out of black"—that is, to keep the station broadcasting—"and make the money."

The screen now is gray and blue, not unprofitable out-of-order black, as the pelican flies out into a storm with a lifesaving line to rescue a sinking ship. "For two and a half years I had no TV set, and here I was working at a TV station," Crear said. "Honestly, there's nothing on TV I really like. If you work days, you can veg out in front of the TV at night, but during the day there's nothing worthwhile on." He studied for his real estate exam instead, and practiced karate to stay in shape, and worked toward his goal of becoming a screenwriter. "Especially when I see stuff like this," he said, pointing toward the pelican, "I say, 'Hey, I can do better than this.' Somebody was well paid for this. You look at the writers driving out of the lot with their Mercedeses and Porsches."

The pelican is dead now, shot by hunters and buried in a sand grave by Storm Boy, who, older now and wiser to the ways of the world, moves to a nearby town to go to school THE END, and *The Heiress* begins. Olivia de Havilland, laced tightly into a corset, is dressing for an evening party. "In three to five years I'll be active during the day and sleeping during the night," Crear said.

At 2 A.M. each night, according to A. C. Nielsen Co., 12 percent of American households are watching TV, a surprisingly high number, given the usual viewing choices at that hour. "The graveyard shift ends up as a dumping ground for programs that are paid for already and don't get ratings," Welte said. *Wonder Woman* had been a frequent visitor lately. "You can tell when a contract's gonna run out on a show because they stick it on graveyards." It was 4 A.M. now, hard into the dry hours when television, like the body, sinks to its lowest depths, a bleak and dismal desert of Dark Ages reruns, Veg-O-Matics, half-star movies, "AND THAT'S NOT ALL," pleading preachers, "ORDER NOW," 800-numbers, stale news, 900-numbers and, worst of all, half-hour informercials (unleashed when the Reagan administration lifted limits on the length of TV ads) peddling miracle solvents, impotence cures, hair replacements, weight-loss schemes, get-rich-quick real estate courses, car wax and other your-life-will-never-be-the-same-again products that prey on the audience at the ripe, weary time when the mind is most ready to believe the world can change; but KTLA's insomniac viewers were treated to the best movie of the night. *The Heiress,* the 1949 Paramount version of Henry James's novel *Washington Square,* starred de Havilland as a wealthy and lovesick young woman wooed by a golddigging cad (Montgomery Clift) in nineteenth-century New York—a four-star, and five-Oscar, classic of the sort that, before VCRs, could keep a bleary-eyed movie buff up until dawn.

De Havilland, her dark hair pulled back in a tight Emily Dickinson center-parted bun, gazes moonily at Clift as he sits playing her harpsichord and singing, in French, a song that sounds a lot like Elvis Presley's "Can't Help Falling in Love." They met at the party the night before, and he, aware of her inheritance and her availability, has promptly come calling. "You know what it means?" he asks, and then he translates. "The joys of love, they last but a short time."

"I was born in time to catch *Howdy Doody*—my life was planned for me," said Welte, who was about the same age as this movie. "One of my earliest passions was TV. As a kid I'd buy broken TVs and fix them. I had the only TV in the house and I'd charge my sister to watch it. I have the TV on all the time now, even when I'm sleeping. I probably know the plots of several soap operas because they're imprinted on my brain while I'm sleeping."

De Havilland and Ralph Richardson—her widowed father, a stern and proper doctor who disapproves of Clift as a "selfish idler"—are boarding a ship bound for Europe. Richardson opposes the young couple's plans to marry, and he has proposed this trip, which will keep them apart for six months, as a test of their love. Clift is there to see them off. The "Can't Help Falling in Love" music swells in the background. He kisses de Havilland's hand. "I will be thinking of you, Catherine."

"I used to love it," Welte said of nights at sea when he was a navy electronics technician. "The stars were big as golf balls, the moon was like a basketball. In the middle of the night in the middle of the ocean, no lights around anywhere, you could lie on your back and look up at the sky and immerse yourself in it. You could lose yourself in the sky. The boat rocking gently could put you to sleep. It was so peaceful, like what some people go to the desert or the mountains for." He later became a Buddhist. "I was the only hippie in the world with a crew cut."

De Havilland, home from Europe now, rushes out into the rainy night to embrace Clift. He tells her of the plans he has made for them to elope the next evening. She is impatient. "Morris, take me tonight," she pleads. "In another hour everyone will be asleep. We can get away quietly and no one will know." He agrees. "It's almost ten-thirty," he says, checking his watch. "I can be back here at twelve-thirty on the dot, in front of the house." He is anxious that her father not take offense. She tells him of their estrangement, of his threat to disinherit her. Clift looks crestfallen, envisioning a future without her wealth. "Till twelve-thirty, then," he says, without conviction. "Hurry, my darling," she says.

Welte wore a dark beard now, and his hair, fading on top, was pulled back into a small ponytail. "This is the flag that says, 'I hate authority.' "

De Havilland waits in the front parlor, bags packed, giddy with anticipation. The appointed hour passes. The clatter of an approaching carriage brings her rushing outside, but it is not Clift, and it does not stop. The clock strikes. "He must come, he must take me away, he must love me, he must," she implores. "Morris must love me, for all those who didn't." The next morning she wearily carries her bags back up to her room, alone, haggard and disheveled and looking ten years older, a girlish bride no more, transformed forever by her heartbreaking night watch for the suitor who never came.

"I hit my peak at three," Welte said. "At night I have the freedom to do it my way, rather than the daytimers' way. When I do get an occasional day shift, I'm bored in here."

One night several years later de Havilland sits in the parlor at her embroidery frame, switching an alphabet pattern. Clift, having heard of her father's death, has returned from California with a pencil mustache and a new marriage proposal. They have again arranged to elope, and he is on his way over. He knocks on the door just as she finishes the *Z* and cuts her thread. A servant goes to answer. "Bolt the door, Maria," de Havilland says, her voice hard and cold. Clift's knocking becomes banging as he calls out her name, "Catherine! Catherine!" She turns off the lights. His cries fill with anguish and desperation, "Catherine! Catherine! Catherine!" She climbs the stairs through her dark house, ignoring his pleas, abandoning him as he once abandoned her. THE END appears over a parting shot of Clift locked out on the doorstep, still banging, still begging, "Catherine! Catherine!"

"I'm happy they're long long, because I'm way early," Welte said as the credits slowly faded to black. He had killed an out-of-date station promo earlier, and now he had to stretch a little to make up for it. A Three Stooges or Little Rascals short could fill a big gap; an overrun, on the other hand, could be shortened by dropping an ad (local ads went before nationals) or even—as was necessary for him once when a 140-minute movie was mistakenly logged in as 1:40 (one hour and forty minutes)—an entire show. "I'm adding a thirty-second promo on the next break," he said into his mike. "That'll do it."

That's Incredible!, the 5:30 program, featured a singing parrot, followed at 6 by *The 700 Club*. By the time Pat Robertson had finished his hour of prayer, Welte would be on his way home. "The traffic's always on the other side of the freeway," he said.

Down on Santa Monica Beach at midnight you could gauge the size of the surf only by listening, not by looking. The damp and misty night had thrown a fuzzy halo around the three-quarters moon, and the sea and the sky had melted together to drop a wide, swallowing black wall over the horizon. Waves swelled and curled out there, but you couldn't see them until they broke, a line of white foam blinking suddenly on, like a rip in the darkness. A car echoed like low, distant thunder as it rolled over the wooden boards of the pier. To the south, along the shore's long, slow curve into the distance, a pale glow rose up from Los Angeles like smog, halted from rolling any farther west by the great black Pacific—the border where the light of the continental night gave out.

The lifeguard towers along the beach were all vacant, but the lifeguard headquarters next to the pier was not. Six lifeguards were on duty in L.A. County now, two for each sector of the seventy-two-mile coastline, waiting, like firefighters, to respond to calls of trouble on the beach. The two guards here in Santa Monica—headquarters for the central sector, from Malibu to Marina del Ray—were asleep now.

The news on the radio was of the trial of Richard Ramirez, a devil-worshipping drifter accused as the "Night Stalker"—the killer who had terrorized Southern California with a vicious crime spree, beating, robbing, raping and murdering random victims in their beds. "You don't understand, and you are not expected to," he said later, after he was convicted of thirteen murders and thirty other felonies and sentenced to die in the gas chamber. "You are not capable of it. I am beyond your experience. I am beyond doing evil. Legions of the night, night breed. Repeat not the errors of the Night Stalker and show no mercy. I will be avenged."

Out past the breakers a green light flashed on a buoy, but otherwise there was nothing but black—as uniformly the color of hell in the world's religions as brilliant day-shaming light is the color of heaven. The line of darkness that trailed the setting sun was racing west across the Pacific at almost twice the speed of sound, nearing the far side now, delivering the night to Asia.

At 6:30, just as at midnight, the sea was still the same color as the sky, pale gray now, not black. The lifeguards were awake. "This is the time you sometimes come across a body that's rolled in," lifeguard Ralph Lee said, but this morning he didn't. The night had passed with no calls. "I didn't hear anybody screaming."

A truck was unloading generic black-and-white police cars for the location shoot a film crew was setting up alongside Palisades Park, the slender green palm-shaded ribbon that parallels the beach. The clouds were expected to lift by eleven, the temperature expected to reach the low 70s. The water was 62 degrees.

Just after midnight downtown at the venerable Pacific Dining Car, a party of four walked through the long, narrow front room—mahogany, brass, dim clubby yellow lamps, a reproduction of a plush old railroad car—back to a table clothed with white linen. They ordered lamb chops, shrimp diavolo, a filet mignon sandwich, steak and eggs. Just after 1 downtown at the Pantry—where the steak-sauce bottle declared, "Never Closed, Never Without Customers Since 1924," and the cashier sat in a booth like a subway-token clerk's, and the only specials left now up on the blackboard between the erasure marks were roast pork ($6.05) and chef's salad ($4.00)—a stoolbound man at the counter waited as the grillman fitted his T-bone to a plate. "You want green beans with that?" All through the night all over town Angelenos were eating—hamburgers at Fatburgers, Belgian waffles with ice cream at Ben Frank's, even dialing friends between sips of coffee in the phone-equipped booths at Larry Parker's Beverly Hills Diner. Just after 2 at Uncle John's in Santa Monica waitress Kim Swaney walked back to pick up her order when she heard the cook call her number,

A Day in the Night of America

eight. "It's mostly breakfast items on graveyards," she said. Waiting for her up on the kitchen shelf were two plates: a Denver omelet and buttermilk pancakes.

America's nocturnal menu is utilitarian both in its origins—the horse-drawn lunch wagons that parked outside late-shift mills in nineteenth-century New England—and its present, a practical victory of substance over style, fuel over frills. The wine-list restaurants (the Pacific Dining Car was a rare exception) and the big fast-food chains, knowing there's not enough money in it, have largely ceded the night to the caffeinated specialists: diners, coffee shops, pancake houses, roadside service plazas. At Uncle John's, on Wilshire Boulevard just over the line from West L.A., you could order the same food at 5 A.M. as you could at 5 P.M.—veal melt, Hawaiian chicken, cheese steak, tostada salad, stuffed shrimp, lasagna, barbecued ribs, hot fudge sundae, everything but the dinner special, which had been erased from the board. Burgers were popular after midnight here, and club sandwiches, quesadillas and chicken sandwiches, but breakfast was the star. Eggs are the sustenance of the world after midnight—which is, after all, officially morning—and BREAKFAST SERVED ANYTIME signs were the flags I followed cross-country. To feed its graveyard customers, three hundred to four hundred people between 11 P.M. and 6 A.M., Uncle John's needed twelve pounds of coffee and fifteen dozen eggs.

"Since I got to this country twenty years ago, only for two years did I work in the daytime, it's always nights," said Augie Reynoso, Uncle John's assistant manager. "I wish I worked in the daytime so I could be together with my wife, but I tell her, 'What am I gonna do? It's life, it's life.' If you wanna live well, you have to go to work." He was born in Mexico, one of fifteen children, and worked his way up at Uncle John's from busboy through cook to his present job. He wore a jacket and tie. He had learned English from the waitresses, and now he taught the cooks to read the order checks. His brother was the general manager. "It's not my place, but in my mind it's my place, and it's my responsibility. I can't say, 'It's not my place, what the hell, I'm off.' I like to see the place do good all the time. If the place is gonna do good business, if it's gonna take care of the customers, I'm always gonna have a job." On busy nights he returned to the kitchen to help cook. "Believe it or not, every time I go in the kitchen, I feel beautiful. A lot of managers think they're just the boss, but I consider myself a worker, too." On visits to his Mexican hometown, where he hoped to retire, he carried bagfuls of clothes for family and friends.

On weeknights Uncle John's often served as a coffee-pouring study hall for a couple dozen or more students from UCLA and other nearby colleges. "It was a very beautiful idea," Reynoso said of the signs the restaurant posted on campus bulletin boards inviting students over. "It used to be really slow, and everybody would see the parking lot empty. Now the students stay, and people see all the cars and think, 'Something good must be going on in that place, we better stop.' " Tonight was Saturday, the students off pursuing nonacademic interests, and the parking lot was naturally full. Reynoso's night was over: He worked until midnight on weeknights, 2 on Fridays and Saturdays. He left for home, over the hills into the Valley. "I never in my mind thought I'd have a house in the United States, and guess what, I even have a swimming pool. I'm very happy, my wife's very happy, what else can we ask for?"

Two cops left, too—the border location drew coffee-breaking cops from both L.A. and Santa Monica—and a coed party of five arrived, part of the wave that washed out of the bars at closing time every night in search of solid food to soak up the liquid. "I make better money on this shift," Kim Swaney said, meaning sixty to a hundred dollars a night, four to five nights a week. Days she was a student at Santa Monica College, hoping to become a pediatrician. She brought out a basket of fried chicken. "Some people feel sorry for you because you have to work this late."

At 4 A.M. four tables were occupied, and Number 5 was arriving. "Sir, how many? Two?" graveyard manager Pete Martinez asked a young couple who looked to be at the back end of a date. "I remember my first two months, people would talk to me at eight A.M. and I wouldn't remember a word they said." His tie and pants were black, his shirt white. "If I'm sitting down and I start falling asleep, I get up, help the bus boys cleaning, help the cooks, help the waitresses. It keeps me awake. I go outside and walk around the parking lot and I feel like you can actually see people sleeping, you're like looking at everybody asleep. You can walk outside and look at every dark window and picture the people all with their heads down on their pillows and big smiles on their faces." He rang up a check for $11.29 and the table count was back to four.

Entering stage right were two young women—one in hot pink, one in black, both showing yards of leg—who looked as if they had just finished shooting a ZZ Top video. One young diner, instantly calculating that they were way out of his league, stared without shame, his eyes wide, frozen with wonder, and his jaw slack, heavy with lust. A waitress squirted whipped cream onto the strawberry pound cake the woman in pink ordered. A bus boy ran a vacuum over the floor. Kim Swaney served two sandwiches, a french dip and a chicken fillet, then returned to her sidework: refilling the salts, the sugars and the pancake syrups. Seven tables were taken now, and Sunday morning was nearing, the busiest morning of the week—a fifty-dozen-egg morning. ("By Monday," Augie Reynoso had said, "not even the chickens wanna have eggs.")

Another waitress took an order back to the kitchen. "Two poached eggs, poached kinda hard, and hash browns," she requested. "Did you hear me?"

"Assholes! Get to work!" called the shotgun passenger in an old Chrysler northbound on the Long Beach Freeway. The fast lane, the far left passing lane he was creeping along in, was the slow lane tonight, the only lane that was open. His anger was aimed at the road repair crew occupying the other three lanes.

"As long as they keep going and don't throw anything, it's all right with me," said Norman Suydam, a resident engineer with Caltrans, the state transportation department. A stomper, a great beast of a pulverizing machine, was smashing a concrete road panel into small pieces that would be removed and replaced before morning. The stomping spread into your chest like angina, a premonition of the heart attack Los Angeles would suffer if all its freeways were similarly blocked at once. "If we work at night, people ask, 'Why can't you do this work in the daytime?' If we do it during the day, they say, 'Why not do it at night?' If we do it during the week, it's 'Why not on the weekend?' In other words it's 'Why can't you do it at a time when I'm not on the freeway?' "

In Los Angeles there is no time when nobody is on the freeway, as in Manhattan there is no time when somebody isn't committing a crime, and to block the traffic here, like blocking the traffic in Manhattan's criminal courts, is to risk overloading a system already so overloaded that only round-the-clock perpetual motion keeps it from collapsing under its own weight. There is no good time to shut down for needed repairs, but nighttime is less bad than daytime. L.A.'s freeways—740 miles' worth in L.A., Orange and Ventura counties, enough road to get you to Salt Lake City—are often likened to rivers, sinuous concrete streams that, instead of merging and widening and rolling out to the sea, knot themselves into a dense spaghetti delta; but what they more resemble is a ganglion of nerve cells, messages pulsing through their circuitry, often gridlocked by the excess stimuli of modern life. Unlike the tenement cities of the east, Los Angeles was from the start a roomy, far-flung metropolis, a sprinkling of distinct communities interspersed with orange groves (L.A. was, until 1920, America's richest agricultural county) and roped together by the Red Cars, an interurban streetcar network that could take you, say, from Pasadena to Santa Monica. But Angelenos found the rails confining, and early and quickly embraced the freedom offered by the automobile. By the mid-1920s, when one of every seven Americans had a car, one of every two Angelenos did, the highest ratio in the nation; the *Los Angeles Times* was reporting that "all night long, long strings of trucks can be seen on any of the local boulevards carrying supplies to every town in the south"; and the L.A. Traffic Commission was fretting "that the onward march of Los Angeles toward its place of destiny will be made immeasurably slower unless a solution is found for the traffic problem." By 1940 the first freeway had opened, the Arroyo Seco Parkway between Pasadena and downtown, later renamed the Pasadena Freeway. By the 1970s, when the city unbalanced its decentralized design by building a downtown skyscraper center, the freeways were chronically jammed. The average speed was thirty-five miles per hour now—for junk Chevys and vanity-plated BMWs alike—and was expected to slow to fifteen miles per hour by 2007. In a single day Angelenos drive nearly 100 million vehicle-miles and waste 100,000 hours in traffic jams. It cost more in dollars to fix the freeways at night (with time-and-a-half wages, maybe $300 per yard of concrete, instead of $250 or $275 during the day), but it cost less in societal aggravation.

A backhoe pried up and lifted out shattered shards of concrete with the same motion as an elephant grazing for breakfast with its trunk. It reared up off its front wheels, stabilized by its outriggers, in an effort to dislodge the biggest pieces. It dumped the old road into a waiting truck. Portable floodlights lit the scene as starkly as a state trooper's headlamps in your rearview mirror. "It's like a dentist's job," Suydam said. "You've got to do the drilling before the filling." The backhoe exposed a neat doorway-shaped plot, twelve feet wide by fifteen feet long by one foot deep, exposing to light for the first time in decades loamy roadbed soil the ocher color of a spring infield. Between backhoe grunts you could hear, and feel, the stomper at work up ahead on the next panel. Freeway neighbors sometimes mistook the stompers' shudders for gunshots or, more ominously—especially after an earthquake—for deeper, wider tremors.

A Day in the Night of America

The repair crew hopscotched up the freeway like a slow parade—stomper, backhoe, trucks, lights, white-jumpsuited Caltrans inspectors, orange-vested contractors. The closed three-quarter-mile route had twenty-four stops, the panels already marked by an earlier crew that had walked lanes three and four (the official numbers go 1234 from center to shoulder) in search of cracks, holes and general decrepitude. Concrete is the surface of choice in dry southerly climes like L.A., away from the abrasive wear of salt and tire chains in the icy north. It is more expensive than asphalt, but it lasts up to twice as long, twenty years or more. It can also be effectively replaced tooth by tooth, panel by panel or even by half-panel, instead of a whole mouthful at once. The cars in Lane 1 drove past, watching, at slower speeds than they could have. "They wanna get a look at what they've waited for," Suydam said.

Down in the shallow cavity one of the contractor's men was compacting the treated base soil by running a machine like a floor waxer over it, a wacker. "It looks good," said Joe Kapono, a Caltrans principal assistant who was inspecting the work. He had spent thirty-seven years with Caltrans, and two-thirds of the last decade working nights. "I watched it be built, now I'm watching it be torn up." The Long Beach Freeway—named, like all L.A. freeways, for its destination away from the city, and built in the freeway binge of the late 1950s—runs from East Los Angeles down to the ocean in Long Beach and echoes, in both its route and its appearance, the Los Angeles River, a concrete channel that sits dry most of the year. Tonight's stretch was in Bell Gardens, one of the sprawlcities that reach south down to Orange County. The southbound lanes, clear of repair-crew dams, streamed with vehicles on this weekend-opening Friday night; the northbound lanes, stagnant and studded with trucks hauling containerized cargo from the giant Long Beach port, backed up with bile.

"Fuckin' bullshit!" observed one car, and the next chimed in with a long horn blast.

"The other day somebody threw an apple from a car, hit a guy and knocked him right out," Kapono said. Freeways are meant to be traversed by tires, not feet, to be seen by drivers, from the angle of motion, not pedestrians, from the angle of stasis. To step out onto the roadbed from the protective steel shell of a vehicle is to instantly cross the wide distance between a familiar neighborhood, comparatively safe, and a foreign, hostile territory. "One night, how he missed me I'll never know," Kapono said about a close call with a driver. "He just brushed my trousers, going fifty miles an hour. I was fortunate. I jumped the right way." When a rash of shootings plagued the freeways, a new level of menace was added. "That was very much on everybody's mind. We thought, 'My God, who is there to be more mad at than us?' "

Driving on the authorized-vehicles-only side of the reflective cones and squeezing up past the RAMP CLOSED sign on an exit ramp, Norman Suydam swung up and around and back onto the southbound freeway to check on two other worksites. Lanes 3 and 4 over here had already gotten the rehab treatment Lanes 3 and 4 over there were getting tonight, and they bumped gently along underwheel, fifteen feet by fifteen feet, with the steady, comforting rhythm that lulls babies to sleep in their carseats. Less-healthy roads unfold with a jagged rock 'n' roll backbeat. "When I'm driving along with my wife sometimes, I'll point out things and say, 'I did that.' "

The road was clear enough to let Suydam choose his own speed, rather than have it chosen for him by the traffic patterns, and it offered a sharp side-by-side picture—speedy southbound cars, stalled northbound cars— of the uneasy marriage on the freeways, as in the night itself, between freedom and claustrophobia. It also offered a picture of L.A.'s transportation future. Many remedies have been suggested for the chronic traffic and smog woes here—a new commuter-rail network and a double-decker highway, both under construction now, electric vehicles, methanol and other cleaner-burning fuels, rush-hour truck bans, carpooling, staggered work hours—and among them is one that dates to first-century Rome, where daytime snarls were relieved by restricting chariot traffic to nighttime. Already 28 percent of the region's commuters tried to beat the morning traffic by leaving home at dawn and getting to work by 7; and L.A., like a factory with costly machinery adding a third shift, might eventually have to push even more drivers even farther into the night, when the freeways most nearly realize the promise embodied in their name.

The road shrank and slowed again as it approached a bridge repair. "It's a small job, but with a big problem," engineer Peggy Yu told Suydam, shouting over the jackhammers. Some kind of unfamiliar old epoxy in the joints, unexpectedly troublesome to remove, was fast revising the night's goal of one hundred feet down to fifty, maybe seventy-five. "We thought it was gonna come right out, but it definitely isn't." Clear south, then around and behind the cones and back on the north side, Suydam stopped at another bridge, northbound over Del Amo Boulevard. The roadbed lay open like an anesthetized patient, a skeleton of green-coated steel reinforcing rods waiting to be covered by concrete.

A Day in the Night of America

"Hey, you got that fucking traffic backed up to the other side of Long Beach!" a passing driver informed the repair crew. Traffic was backed up not only on the Long Beach Freeway but also for several miles on the intersecting San Diego Freeway.

After idling and creeping and seething for so many miles, the cars burst out of the single open chute on the bridge and fanned out like birdshot across the wide, unobstructed expanse beyond. Suydam joined them, knowing, as they mostly did not, that this freedom was illusory, that they would be trapped again in another six miles or so by the worksite he had started from. He passed a too-common 3 A.M. scene—bent Buick, crunched Toyota, black-and-white cruiser, a man in handcuffs, apparently for drunken driving. The freeway tapered as it led to the next repair closure, first one lane blocked, then the second, then the third, squeezing the cars into a reluctant reunion. Traffic was still bottlenecked, still a ways from achieving "free-flow." "Usually where all the action goes on is right at the end of the queue," Suydam said. "People are driving fast, not paying attention, then 'Boom!' " He slipped behind the cones at the first taper.

The new road sat waiting in a queue of its own, in the mixer trucks idling behind like a line of circus elephants. The filling crew, trailing the digging crew, had started pouring concrete at about 2, making the road whole again, and by 6 they had poured the last of the night's 150 yards into the last of the night's twenty-four holes. The last marshy-gray panel moved like a Jell-O mold under the wide broomlike bullfloat the concrete finishers used to smooth its surface. Lane 2, the buffer lane for the workers, was reopened, but Lanes 3 and 4 would stay closed for four more hours, to allow the concrete time to cure; a new road, by contrast, gets ten full days. The crew would reconvene tonight to dig and fill the next stretch, conditions permitting: Rain or sub-50 temperatures meant no pouring.

Traffic was thin enough now that you could probably drive from one end of L.A. to the other in record time, well under two hours. As the lights went on in the sky, the lights went out on the cars: For astronomers, darkness ends when the approaching sun is still 18 degrees below the horizon; on the road, morning arrives when you see more cars driving with their headlights off than on. The news on the car radios informed all the drivers that today in L.A.—the destination city of a destination nation, the American capital of the rising Pacific Rim—would be another day of "unhealthful air quality."

*　　*　　*

"How do you find your way back in the dark?" Marilyn Monroe asked, driving into the night with Clark Gable, the last lines she spoke in the last film she finished before she died.

"Just head for that big star straight on," Gable said, in his final screen lines, the closing lines in *The Misfits*. "The highway's under it. It'll take us right home."

13

At 6:00, at the Port of TACOMA, *a tugboat guided a five-hundred-foot ship out of the harbor and into the dock, where it would load up with Japan-bound logs.*

The color of the night over Seattle was gray, not black, the sky lightened by leaky clouds that polished the streets with a fine drizzle. Bob Richardson, parked curbside downtown near Pioneer Square and the Kingdome, started up his darkened bus again at 12:20. Its inside lights flickered on like a fluorescent tube in an emptied night office. The tall wipers squeegeed flat against the windshield, set wide and flush as a display case. He began another circuit of the city by driving north among the thick trunks of an office-tower forest larger than downtown L.A.'s. "I love the rain," said Richardson, who didn't see any in the first three months after he moved here almost two decades before. "I suppose it depresses some people, but it doesn't have that effect on me." He picked up twelve passengers before Eastlake Avenue took him north away from downtown. Looking back, you could see the spindly Jetsons-era Space Needle rising along the fast-sprouted skyline like the upstretched arm of a cocktail waitress balancing a drink tray on her fingers as she threaded through a crowd. It was still lit up, but its observation deck had closed at midnight. Farther south loomed the signature of the slow-grown natural skyline, Mount Rainier, a 14,410-foot snowcapped, glacier-embroidered volcano, silent and invisible now, hidden by the night. Richardson crossed the drawbridge into the University District, in the city's northeast section, with nine passengers, three having already hit the signal bell, a bing like a department store, and gotten off.

The rain had started for me, as if on cue, on the interstate bridge over the Columbia River between Oregon and Washington, and all evening long, as I drove north to Seattle, it had alternated between actual thudding drops and the illusory, diffuse sponginess of an animated fog. I followed the same route north that many migrating Californians, weary of freeways and smog and unaffordable real estate, had followed in recent years, to a city that in barely a century had bloomed from a scruffy lumber camp on the outer fringe of the frontier into a mecca metropolis regularly hailed as America's "most livable." Seattle was, like Vegas, a boomtown, growing at twice the national clip. Its natural setting is a collection of basic scenic elements (mountains, trees, ocean) that meet as neighbors more often in children's ideal drawings than in the nation's landscape. It also has rain, a persistent shade of torpor gray: Indian legend attributed it to Ocean, who kept his children, Cloud and Rain, near home by digging a great trough (Puget Sound) and packing the dirt into a pair of barrier mountain walls (the Cascades on the east, the Olympics on the west). "This is the first night it's rained in quite a while," Richardson said. "Usually it's just a real fine mist. Every time it's kinda gray out, people think it's raining, but it isn't." Seattle actually gets less rain than any East Coast city—parceled out lightly and slowly here, not unleashed in brief bursts—but some locals are content to let the eternal-April-showers image stand: It might, they reason, slow the incoming tide of paradise-seekers.

Metro Bus 3060, on Run 90C, followed Route 71 through the neighborhoods of northeast Seattle, a forty-foot shoebox of light gliding along wet, sleeping streets. Richardson deposited a rider at a stop near the University of Washington. "At night I'm like alive. I just figure I'm a natural night person," he said. He spun the steering wheel, chest-high and big as a basketball hoop, and took a right onto Northeast Sixty-fifth Street. His wavy hair was the rust color of metal left out in the rain. His uniform, yellow shirt and brown pants, echoed the color scheme of the bus. He made more stops in Ravenna, and then in View Ridge, over near Lake Washington, all offs at this hour in this direction, no ons. "All my life I thought I'd always work nights if I had the chance. I can't imagine getting up in the daytime and going to work. I get along better with night people. I fit right in." The last outbound rider exited in Wedgwood at 1:10, and Richardson turned around to retrace the route, inbound now, collecting new passengers for the downhill trip back downtown.

"Hey, how're you doin?" he asked one of his regulars, a woman in a denim jacket who got on at University Way and Forty-fifth.

A Day in the Night of America

In the centuries before buses and streetlights and late-shift cops, night travelers wary of lurking night creatures carried protective charms (walking staffs of mountain ash, daisies, St.-John's-wort) and left offerings at crossroads (ewes, fish and eggs, milk and honey, garlic cloves). Richardson carried only the confident lesson of his nocturnal experience—that there was less to fear in the night than most daytimers imagined. "It's all in their head, something they conjure up for themselves, and it becomes true for them." He had seen violence erupt on his bus—a drunken fight that turned into a stabbing ("One guy pulled a knife and stuck the other guy four or five times. I saw the guy wipe the knifeblade off inside his coat, but everybody's attention went to the guy he knifed and he disappeared. I would recognize him today if I saw him"), a fight that turned into a police-heavy brawl ("It was an amazing thing. They were fighting everywhere, all the way from the back of the bus to the front. It took twenty minutes and eight or ten cops to get these two Samoans off the bus, so I figured the Samoans won")—but he often managed to defuse it first.

"A lot of times people will apologize, but sometimes they want to instigate things. It's funny about people—I don't know what the answers are as to why people do what they do. It seems like they'd get up and knock you out, or whatever, but they don't. Most times they get up and leave. You have to outthink the thinkers. A little reverse psychology trips people out, they don't know what to do. You say, 'Hey, you, stay right there, don't move,' and most get right off. If you approach things sideways instead of right straight on, you get the result you want." Back downtown he passed an empty bus shelter. "I know the passengers are mostly on my side. If they like you, they protect you. Then nobody will mess with me."

By 2 the bus had changed its name—ROUTE 7, its sign now said—and was parked at the stop at Fourth Avenue and Union Street downtown. "How long you gonna be here?" a man asked Richardson, who had stepped out to stretch his legs among the knot of waiting riders.

"Fifteen minutes."

"Good, I'll sit here and rest my bones."

"In the White House, there are black shadows everywhere," a young man in a knit cap declaimed, "and dark secrets in primitive sacred places, like moles burrow holes in sacred places." His voice trailed off with a low, slow, whispery tone. "I call it 'Black Shadows,'" he said. "I haven't finished it yet."

Two men discussed the possibility of other universes. Two women in black veils brought their homes onto the bus with them, each wheeling a stuffed box strapped to a little suitcase cart. "Hey, my buddy," Richardson greeted a young man who said he had just been released from juvenile detention. Before he became a bus driver, Richardson had worked with a prerelease program for state prison inmates. "I meet people, they get on the bus, and they say, 'Man, where do I know you from?' " he said. "It's the same kind of work. This is actually more productive. You get to really touch people's lives. They get to know you, and they know you're different, they know you care. They're looking for somebody to talk to. I figure if I stay on this route long enough, I will know everybody."

At 2:15, the time designated on the schedule, Richardson pulled away with thirty passengers, two-thirds full, west on Union, south on First. Most of Seattle's Metro buses—like Boston's subways, San Francisco's cable cars and many other city transit systems—shut down soon after midnight; his was one of just seven Metro "Night Owl" runs. A drunken woman at the back of the bus was laughing insensibly, a running cackle that sounded like an infant crying. The front of the bus was not amused.

"She's S.O.S.," one man said, "Stuck On Stupid."

An attempt by her drunken male companion to quiet her degenerated into an exchange of obscene insults and fuck-yous. "They pay to go to the zoo, they may pay to go see you," he told her.

"Go eat your bananas," she told him.

The veiled women fidgeted with silent annoyance, unable to sleep for the noise. "Man, they let anybody ride Metro," one rider said as he disembarked on Rainier Avenue.

"Hey, you know we try to screen 'em, but some get through," Richardson said.

"All right, man, thanks for the ride."

The woman's laugh gradually trailed off like a wound-down toy, and the veiled women fell asleep. Richardson stopped to pick up a man with a cane, a machinist who had worked overtime tonight on his usual 4-to-midnight shift—at a workshop for the blind that made parts for Boeing, Seattle's anchor industry. The cackle erupted briefly again, apparently triggered by some private joke nobody else could hear.

"This is the coolest bus driver," one rider offered. "Some drivers, you're a penny short and they make you get off."

"This is you," Richardson said at the blind man's stop. "See you probably Thursday."

"I'll be here," he said, feeling his way out into the dark with his cane.

Richardson still had nine sleeping riders at 2:50, when he reached the end of the line, Sixty-second Avenue South and South Prentice Street, and turned around, the bus pointed north again, for the ten-mile trek back downtown. "This is more sleepers than usual." They were going nowhere except where they were right now, at rest in a mobile temporary homeless shelter, the seats their warm beds for a couple of hours. The night was chilly as well as wet, the temperature down in the forties. "If they have a pass and they're cool, then I treat them like passengers. I let it be their home for a while." The laughing woman was gone.

At Fourth and Union his bus became Route 83, its third name since midnight, before heading over the bridge again into the northern reaches of the city. He picked up half a dozen people after turning around and driving south on University Way, back toward downtown and the last stop of his night, but the sleepers still outnumbered the travelers when he recrossed the bridge. It was only 4:15, but the clearing sky was already lightening to a royal blue: The night had been shrinking through the months I'd been traveling—both physically, as the daylight lengthened toward summer, and conceptually, as I watched a restless nation invade dark late hours once reserved mainly for sleep. Above the Space Needle, its lights off now, a cloud sailed in front of the almost-full moon. "Man, you see so many changes working like this. Isn't that beautiful? I love it."

Barbara Cunningham, Dianne Peterson and Janice Crawford, striding crisply together, navigated through the late-evening stragglers at the airport terminal—the tentative arrivals looking for the right way in, the uncertain departures looking for the right way out—steering a straight, sure course toward their plane. They each wore a blue blazer and blue skirt and trailed a brown suitcase on wheels. They stopped at the United Airlines screen to check that the plane was where it was supposed to be. It had arrived from San Francisco at 11:22 and was waiting at Gate N7. It was scheduled to depart for Chicago, with them aboard, at five minutes past midnight, 00:05 in airline time. "I think about my family at home all nestled into bed," Crawford said. They walked down the jetway into the empty Boeing 737 and started readying for the trip east.

"If they have a blanket and a pillow, they're happy," Peterson said of late-night passengers on red-eye flights. She and the two other attendants removed the blankets and pillows from the overhead compartments before the burying avalanche of carry-on luggage arrived. "We get a lot more requests for aspirin at night."

"Usually the person who sits up all night wants to talk to somebody," said Cunningham, who had once been a preview audience for a eulogy a funeral-bound man had written for his brother. "He read the whole thing. I told him it sounded like his brother was quite a character."

"Children have a rough time on all-nighters," Peterson said. "Adults tend to make the best of things, but children, if they feel tired, they show it, and usually Mom's too tired to take care of them."

The three cleaners had filled their trash bags and gone, and the three flight attendants were making their checks—oxygen supply, emergency flashlight, fire extinguisher. They would, once airborne, make a single pass with the service cart and then turn off the lights. On their frequent cabin checks they would be careful not to trip over the feet of stretched-out sleepers. The aisles would be cramped tonight: Four of the eight first-class seats were filled, and 103 of the 120 in coach. Before landing in Chicago, at 5:51 local time, they would serve morning juices.

Cunningham, who was working first-class tonight, stood greeting the first of the boarding passengers. "This is the only time I drink coffee," she said. In Chicago she would go to sleep at a layover hotel; she was not scheduled to continue working on a morning flight, as sometimes happened after a red-eye. "The people getting on all just woke up and they seem so fresh, you can smell the aftershave lotion. You serve them breakfast and you're half-asleep and you want to throw up when you serve the eggs, ugh."

"Oxygen?"
"Check."
"Hydraulic pump?"
"On."
"Fuel?"
"32.5 and we need 31.6."

The instrument panel in the cockpit stared back at the two pilots—Skip Wood, captain, and Bill Smith, first officer—like watch faces in a jeweler's display case. They had taken off from San Francisco at 9:25 and now, as their forty-three scheduled ground minutes ticked down, they worked through their preflight check. "Parking brake?"

A Day in the Night of America

"Pressure normal."

"It's quieter," Smith said of night flying. "There's not much talk on the radio, so we talk to each other a lot to stay alert. There are few visual cues at night. You lose depth perception, it's just nothing, so you try to compensate by being more mentally alert in other areas."

The passage over the dark, sleeping continent can be as lulling in the cockpit as it is in the cabin: The entire crew of a 707 fell asleep one night in 1978, overshooting Los Angeles and getting one hundred miles out over the Pacific before they woke up and turned around. "You try to sleep more than you ordinarily would," Wood said of days before red-eyes, "but it doesn't always work out that way."

The night sky they cruised through staged regular shows that relieved the hours of blanketing weary blackness—twinkling cities, expansive electrical storms, curtains of northern lights (a display just last week near Vancouver was, Smith said, "the best I've ever seen, and I've seen the Arctic"), and, sometimes, the elusive green flash you can see when the sun enters or exits the horizon. "It's best to see it with someone," Smith said, "because you're not sure you really saw it."

"Even after thirty-five years it's still gorgeous," Wood said of his pilot's-eye view of the world. "Every day we see things most people only fantasize about."

The road to O'Hare tonight was straight and empty, blocked by no traffic detours. "We take off from here, make a right turn after fifty, sixty miles, and we're cleared all the way to Chicago," Wood said. "In the daytime you could never do anything like that." In the daytime tomorrow they would sleep. Tomorrow night they would fly from Chicago to Omaha to Sioux Falls, South Dakota. They would return home to San Francisco at 11 P.M. two nights after that, ending a four-day trip.

"We'll see the sunrise on our way over there," Smith said of tonight's flight. "Then we'll descend into the grunge and crud of Chicago."

Down on the loud ground, mechanic R. C. Walker watched an electric tug push back Flight 328 onto the taxiway. "It came in with no write-ups," he said. "It didn't need anything done." He had done a walkaround of the plane as it sat at the gate—checked the tires, checked the leading edge for bird damage, checked the wheel wells for hydraulic leaks. "What's harder at night is that you can't see as well. You use a flashlight instead of the sun, and that's a big difference," he said. "It all looked like it should." His shift—late swing, which he had worked by choice for twenty-three years—

ended at 1:30. Three maintenance crews would work overnight to fix deferred items. Flight 328 taxied out into the night toward Chicago.

Inside the terminal the United ticket counters were empty. The next flight didn't leave until 6 A.M.

"TWA Twenty-three, Seattle departure, radar contact, climb and maintain flight level two-five-zero."

From his seat in a dark, windowless room just below the air tower at Seattle-Tacoma International Airport—better known by its racehorselike moniker, Sea-Tac—all Dick Bobb could see of the planes he was guiding were the green blips on his radar scope and the corresponding paper I.D. strips laid out before him. The blips told him how high and how fast the planes were flying; the strips told him who they were and where they were headed. He in turn told them all where to go, and when. He wore a headset like a telephone operator's, using a foot switch to speak.

". . . turn left, heading one-eight-zero, maintain three thousand . . ."

". . . resume normal speed, climb and maintain flight level three-seven-zero . . ."

It was past 12:30 now, and the sky, thick with traffic since dawn, was finally clearing. At midnight fifteen planes had speckled Bobb's screen ("I was shucking and jiving, pumping and banging to get it all done"); three blipped across it now. By 1 most of the commercial flights that were coming or going tonight would have come or gone. His authority, as an air traffic controller in the terminal radar approach control office (Tracon), extended up to thirteen thousand feet for a fifty-mile radius around the airport. The regional center, forty miles away, covered the wide spaces above and beyond; the glass-walled tower directly overhead covered the nearer territory, five miles around, from the taxiways up to two thousand feet.

". . . past Boeing field at about two thousand . . ."

"Seattle Center one-two-six-point-six. Have a good flight."

"One-two-six-point-six," the pilot echoed. "Thank you."

Bobb's voice was crisp, swift and calm as he spoke to the pilots, giving compass headings, altitudes, speeds, radio frequencies. He steered the roaring planes away from sleeping neighborhoods. "You don't put jets over Mercer Island," he said, referring to the affluent island suburb in Lake Washington east of downtown. "We try to keep 'em high over the water." Controllers handled nine hundred to one thousand arrivals and departures each day at Sea-Tac, six hundred to seven hundred each evening, and ninety-five to one hundred on each midnight shift. They worked an unusual rotating schedule, rotating within the week itself, usually two evening shifts, two days and a week-ending midnight. "Every week for thirty years, and I'm tired. It's a young man's schedule—guys under thirty-five love it, guys over thirty-five hate it."

". . . maintain eight thousand . . ."

". . . Seattle Center one-two-zero-point-three, have a good flight."

"TWA One-eighty, Seattle departure, radar control, climb and maintain flight level two-niner-zero."

The blips, each representing a plane traveling at speeds up to 450 miles per hour or more, moved with a deceptive slowness across Bobb's screen, the only one of the seven in the room occupied at this hour. As he was watching the flat two-dimensional image, he was thinking in four dimensions. He first added a third dimension of space, picturing how the planes stacked up in relation to each other, and then added the fourth dimension of time, picturing where they would be in the near future—in thirty seconds, in two minutes, in five minutes, until they safely left his jurisdiction. He had to keep them separated by a minimum of one thousand feet vertically and three miles horizontally. His commands imposed order on the trackless night outside, paving highways in the black sky.

"Southern Air nine-one-niner," he said to a CIA plane flying under cover of darkness between McChord Air Force Base, south of Tacoma, and Travis Air Force Base in California, "Seattle departure, radar control, climb and maintain flight level one-niner-zero."

"One-niner-zero for nine-nineteen," the pilot echoed. Even the CIA needed some guidance through the night.

An American Airlines flight from Chicago—making the opposite run from the United flight Wood and Smith had piloted, evening the exchange between the two cities—dropped toward Sea-Tac for a 2:10 landing. "Runway one-six left, clear to land, wind one-eight-zero at seven," Cara Park, from her perch in the control tower, told the pilot. The tower's wide glass walls angled up to the flat roof as from an eye to its brow. She had switched the inside lights off, erasing the reflective glare and opening a clear vista of the night. The Seattle skyline was a faint nebula in the north distance. The plane's lights descended toward the runway like the headlights of a car coasting down an invisible mountain. The fuselage itself appeared then, landing, braking to a long stop. "Turn left at the first taxiway," she instructed.

"We're going to the gate," the pilot said.

Park switched the lights back on and sat in a barstool-height chair before a central bank of screens and consoles. "I try to bring something to read, otherwise it seems like the night goes on forever." In her territory, the ground and five miles around, the midnight shift meant fewer clearances to issue, fewer planes to vector to their proper route. "As long as I've got two or three to keep it interesting—if I get a slack period, I'll start to fade. You think about these airplanes, how many people they've got on board, and that wakes you right up."

Traffic moved at wide intervals, cargo planes outnumbering passenger planes. "Taxi cross runway one-six left, runway one-six right clear for takeoff," she told a departure. "Seattle tower, runway one-six right or left, your choice, clear to land, wind one-eight-zero at seven," she told a later arrival.

"I'll just take the right," a female pilot's voice decided.

A pair of binoculars sat on the console. "You don't use them at night much," Park said. A plane lumbered out of the Alaska Airlines gate and into the darkness. "Alaska seven-eighty-one is cleared to Anchorage," she told it. ". . . maintain flight level three-one-zero, departure frequency will be one-two-zero-point-four . . ." After it floated up and away, absorbed into the night, about the only movement left down on the field was the truck out checking runway lights.

"This is Boeing, I have a Lifeguard jet, you have anything moving?" the radio asked. A burn victim in Juneau, Alaska, needed a medical evacuation flight out.

"I've got no departures," she said, but she did have another arrival soon after—an America West flight from Las Vegas. "Turn left when able," she told the pilot after he had set it down. "Taxi to the gate."

At 4 A.M., down in the wide, bright empty caverns of the terminal, the shops were dark and closed, the long rows of ticket counters vacant of both buyers and sellers. Travelers trapped between connecting flights, briefly homeless, sprawled asleep across the benches waiting for morning. The disembarked passengers from the last plane Park had cleared to land stood in a loose knot in the baggage-claim area—bleary gamblers waiting to collect whatever possessions Vegas hadn't already collected.

"I just took off southbound at Tacoma Narrows," radioed the pilot of a small plane departing a small airport, "I'd like to climb up through this lower overcast, which appears to be about a three-thousand-foot base and, uh, I don't know what the tops are . . ."

"Thank you for the history of aviation," Tracon controller Larry Brennis said off-mike, impatient with a narrative paragraph where a telegram phrase would do. "I'll tell you what, the tops are seventy-five hundred . . ."

Traffic was thickening in the early sky, real travelers replacing the mythical travelers of night whose passage had left no imprint on the radar screens— Nyx, Hecate, the owl of Minerva (the Roman goddess of wisdom), Elijah (the heavenly messenger who, traveling by night, can reach any corner of the globe with just four beats of his wings), Nott (the Scandinavian goddess of night who rode across the sky in a chariot until her son, Day, forced her down beyond the horizon, the froth from her horse's mouth falling to earth as morning dew), assorted other spirits and creatures and the wandering souls of all sleeping dreamers. Fresh controllers were arriving to work beside Brennis and Bobb.

"Evergreen Ninety-eight, heading two-five-zero, vector for the bay approach, maintain one-zero-thousand."

"Turn left, heading one-four-zero, I'm gonna run you right in."

"Okay, there's about three people transmitting—say again."

Nine planes were on the screen. "We're still trying to recover," Brennis said, referring to Ronald Reagan's wholesale firing of 11,400 striking controllers in 1981. The volume of air traffic had grown by almost 50 percent since then, and the Federal Aviation Administration estimated it was still short three thousand to five thousand fully qualified controllers. "Reagan's biggest mistake in firing all those controllers was in thinking, 'They're just a bunch of mechanics.' But we're not. We do a very important job and we do it extraordinarily well. We don't see ourselves as government workers, like the Post Office."

"Traffic twelve o'clock, three miles, northwestbound, twin Cessna, twenty-six hundred."

"Descend and maintain five thousand," a controller told a pilot, but he got no answer. "Descend and maintain five thousand," he repeated. "Listen up, asshole," he said off-mike.

"Descend and maintain five thousand," the pilot finally acknowledged.

"We're just skimming along the base," another pilot reported, "and we oughta be able to see the field in another coupla miles."

"United Nine-forty-five, descend and maintain twenty-one hundred."

"Horizon Seventeen, descend and maintain four thousand."

"Evergreen Ninety-eight, reduce speed to one-eight-zero."

Eleven planes were on the screen. "It's a question of concentrating," Brennis said. "You sit there with fifteen, eighteen, twenty planes and you think, 'What'd I forget? What'd I forget?' You're constantly worrying you're gonna lose the picture. You're actually navigating the airplane for the pilot." He had forgotten a plane once, in a storm more than twenty years before, but he never forgot the feeling that accompanied it. "A bolt of fear went through me because I forgot this guy—stark fear. 'Where the fuck is he?' I forgot about him. I got so involved in a crossover that I forgot about him. It scared the living shit out of me." He soon found it safely aloft. "You get about three or four shots of adrenaline. I don't know what other occupation's like that. There's no excuse for failure."

"Turn right three-one-zero."

"Horizon Forty-three, I'm sorry, that's not gonna work, maintain three thousand, three thousand."

"Alaska Two-oh-six, report the airport or report sighting an Evergreen Seven-twenty-seven one o'clock at five miles."

"Horizon Forty-three, you following an Alaska jet there at twelve o'clock at three miles? . . . Just leave him three."

"Horizon Seventeen, if you can see company there at ten o'clock and four miles eastbound, he's going to the left runway, and you can follow him to the right."

"Horizon Forty-three, the Alaska jet's going to the right, you're cleared visual approach one-six left . . ."

Flocks of blips entered the screens, homing toward the center, each representing at least one human life and perhaps hundreds more. "Shit, here they come, goddamnit," one controller said.

"There's assholes all over the sky, aren't there."

"Here comes a swarm."

"You ready?" Dick Bobb asked. "Here they come."

Down in the terminal at 6:30, baggage-heavy lines were already snaking up to the ticket counters. Alaska and United drew the biggest crowds. The ground traffic outside was mostly inbound—the travelers who would fill the radar screens all morning long.

A Day in the Night of America

The Pacific Ocean steals past Cape Flattery and leaks into America's northwest corner through the Strait of Juan de Fuca, washing around lush, smoky green islands where bald eagles fly and killer whales and harbor seals swim, flooding into Puget Sound, a crevasse that was carved by glaciers in the last ice age and that now reaches down like a grasping arm into the state's populous core, ebbing past Seattle and down to Tacoma, where at midnight a tugboat sat silently waiting, docked along one of the slender waterways that extend like fingers from Commencement Bay into the city's port area. The side of the white-and-green boat carried the tug company's name, Foss Maritime, and motto, "Always Ready." The windows up in the darkened wheelhouse sloped up and wrapped all the way around, like the windows up in the Sea-Tac control tower. Dave Corrie, first mate, sat listening to the radio say nothing, fulfilling one of a first mate's traditional duties—the "hoot owl" watch, from midnight to 6. To starboard glowed a giant paper mill. "We're not downwind of it, so you just smell the sweet sawdust, not the acrid mill smell," Corrie said. Straight ahead, out in Commencement Bay, where the glacial melt from Mount Rainier is carried by the Puyallup River, the lights of two big ships were strung like the lights of two small villages. The *Wedell Foss,* named for one of the founder's sons and pronounced "wheedle," would guide one of the ships from anchor to dock at dawn.

At 2 A.M. Corrie climbed down to the galley directly below the wheelhouse and fixed himself a meat-loaf sandwich. A photo on the wall showed a tug towing a towering drill rig. He sat at a counter stool and gestured toward a small denlike alcove equipped with a TV and VCR. "That's the crying room—where everybody pisses and moans about how they want to go home," he said. He and the other four crew members were in their fifth day on the tug where they lived and worked for fifteen days at a stretch—six hours on, six hours off, six on, six off. Their link to home now was the pair of phone booths down on the dock. Corrie spent his fifteen-day off-duty stretches home on San Juan Island, up on the Canadian border, where his boat of choice was a kayak. "When I go home, I can't keep my eyes open after dinner for days, but around midnight I get perky."

In the last century, in the era of the great sailing ships—majestic on the open sea, awkward in cramped inland waters—rival tugs waited off Cape Flattery for days at a time, racing each other out toward the first masts they spied, offering their towlines, at competitive and quickly negotiable prices, to captains wary of challenging the treacherous strait and sound unaided.

Modern tugs generally wait dockside until called upon—to tow barges, escort tankers, assist large vessels through small spaces, maneuver ships into and out of dock. The *Wedell Foss* was designed to work mainly "inside," east of Cape Flattery; other tugs worked "outside," towing barges out in the open ocean. It had docked oil tankers, log ships, container ships, refrigerated fruit ships and every other kind of ship at Seattle, Everett, Port Angeles and every other Puget Sound port, but lately it had spent a lot of time among the grain ships, lumber ships and car ships in Tacoma, the city that was chosen over Seattle a century ago as the western terminus of the Northern Pacific Railway (an ancestor of the Burlington Northern) and that had grown into a major shipping, distribution and industrial center. The crew averaged seventy-five ship jobs on each fifteen-day tour; five were on today's schedule.

Corrie stepped out onto the neat gray deck, a long oval shaped like a life raft. The afterdeck, in the rear, was the main work space, where the towline, thick as a firehose, was spooled around a drum. DC-10 tires cushioned the tug's sides. The *Wedell Foss* was of an unusual design—a Foss-conceived tractor tug that looked and moved something like a bumper car. Instead of a rear propeller and rudder it had a "cycloidal propulsion system"—blades that hung from a pair of rotating tables beneath the hull, up near the bow, like the twin beaters hanging down from an electric food mixer. The tug was sturdy like a whale, displacing 450 tons, and nimble like a dolphin: It had direct thrust in any direction, 360 degrees around; it could do 12 knots forward or backward, and could walk sideways at 4 knots; it could stop within its own length, 100 feet; it could spin on its own axis like a top; and it could maneuver easily, sure and strong, around the biggest ships.

Jeff McPherson, mate on the tug docked next door, the *Sandra Foss,* came aboard the *Wedell* to discuss the job the two tugs were scheduled to team up for at 3:30—moving a three-story, five-hundred-foot-long barge out of its dock. After the barge was clear, the *Wedell* would cut loose and the *Sandra* would tow it north to Seattle. It was a short walk in the park compared with some of the outside trips McPherson had made on ocean tugs: Manila, Venezuela, Prudhoe Bay on the Arctic Coast of Alaska. "After working ferryboats I had a romantic notion about traveling and seeing the world," he said. Much of what he saw, he saw by night. "I love it," he said of the night watch. "You have solitude and privacy in a world where there's little of either. If I get home and I don't adjust, I'm on the twelve-to-six TV watch on cable." He was tall, with paint-spattered jeans and long graying hair, and he stooped under a low ceiling on his way out. "If I shaved my head, it would look like a road map." He made his way back to the Sandra without adding a new bump to his topography.

Back up in the wheelhouse, where Corrie sat alone again, the radio mouthpiece hung silently down from the ceiling like a ring announcer's microphone. Coming in off the harbor now was another Foss tug, the *Iver Foss,* returning to dock with a bunker barge that had been refueling a ship. Its lights approached like a car through a dark field, startling the gulls on a parked barge up into flight. Corrie shone the *Wedell*'s spotlight on the *Iver*'s target. "He hit the nail on the head with that one," he said after the barge was docked. The night was approaching its last two hours—the tenuous floating hours when the clock seems disconnected from the actual passage of time; the sluggish, suspended between-time hours that are rarely savored by those people still awake to see them, but are instead endured the way the homestretch miles of a marathon are endured by long-distance runners. "If I'm rested and I haven't worked overtime, I'm okay, but if my rest is affected at all, the toughest time for me is from four to six." Before working nights on tugs, Corrie had ridden many nights on ferries with his father, who had captained on the boats that connect Puget Sound's islands with the mainland. He had learned to sleep anywhere and anytime he wasn't standing watch. "I can close my eyes and be out like that."

The two diesel engines below awoke just before 3:30, starting up with a 3,000-horsepower rumble, and the *Wedell Foss* churned out into breezy, black Commencement Bay. The captain, Duane Crowley, had returned to the wheelhouse he had left just a few hours earlier. His hair was pillow-tousled, his voice gravelly with sleep. He sipped black coffee from a Foss cup. "When you come up to do a job, you try to remember what you ate last so you know what time of day it is," he said. "You look at your watch and it says five o'clock and you think, 'Is that five A.M. or five P.M.?' " He stood at the helm, turning a flat wheel like a bus driver's, pushing a lever like a stick shift; the twin set of controls, on the other side of the wheelhouse, mimicked his movements, as if in the invisible hands of a phantom. The tug passed the Sealand docks, where the hoot-owl shift was still stirring, and got downwind of the paper mill, where the smell was of a refrigerator gone bad. The barge loomed in the *Wedell*'s spotlight like a great white warehouse caught in the beam of a night watchman's flashlight.

"How you gonna want to do this, Duane?" the *Sandra Foss*'s captain asked over the radio. His tug nuzzled against the barge's side like a dog with its nose against its owner's leg.

"There's a line back here on the corner I can get hold of."

Crowley faced backward in the wheelhouse as the *Wedell* and the barge met, stern to stern. Corrie's job now was to board the barge, untie it from the dock and hook it up to the tug's bargeline. "You go in there and it's black," he said. "It's just like going in a room with no windows and the lights out." Jeff McPherson did the same down at the other end, boarding the barge's bow from the *Sandra*. Crowley maneuvered the spotlight by turning a wheel up on the ceiling.

"Okay, we're ready to fly," McPherson radioed the two captains when all the lines were clear on one side and secure on the other.

"I'll just nurse it out," Crowley explained. "I don't want to get up any speed."

Working together with a taut, delicate choreography, applying the practical lessons of physics and geometry, the two tugs—the *Wedell* at one end, the *Sandra* at the other—eased the barge out. It moved like an iceberg, silent and slow and heavy with potential hazard.

"The corner's touching right now and we're coming away nicely," McPherson reported through the radio. "The port bow is still touching. . . . The corner's coming away now. . . . Okay, the bow's all clear here."

"Let me know when you feel comfortable with it, Duane," the *Sandra*'s captain said.

"Let's get a little farther away, then I'll swing around in front," Crowley said. He was on his second cup of coffee. The barge slid out into the open harbor, where the *Wedell* unhooked and left it with the *Sandra*; its ultimate destination was Valdez, Alaska, where it would be used for living-quarter modules for crews cleaning up the Exxon oil spill.

Crowley faced forward again—the *Wedell* had two sets of navigational lights, one for each direction—as the barge sat behind in the pale silvery-blue light that veiled the predawn harbor. "My dad was a towboater," he said, using the term preferred within the tug industry, "and I wanted to be a towboater." His father had been a Foss captain, towing log rafts with single-propeller tugs; his grandfather had worked on the waterfront, too, as a boom man on log rafts; and he had spent seven years towing log rafts himself—as many as forty-eight eighty-foot-square sections at once. "That's seven acres of wood back there," he said. "It's still an art. You don't have many guys who know how to tow logs." He bent low over the *Wedell*'s log now, flashlight in one hand, and recorded the barge job. "I'll go and catch my half hour now," he said at 4:30 and, coffee in hand, climbed back down to his cabin.

Corrie took the wheel, watching for deadhead logs (one end low and waterlogged, the other floating high like a hull-thudding mine) as the *Wedell Foss* plowed back across Commencement Bay on its way to pick up a harbor pilot. The water and the sky had drained of black to equal shades of gray. At Pier 4 the pilot climbed down onto the deck and up into the wheelhouse for a ride out to the *Green Master,* a five-hundred-foot ship of Panamanian registry that was headed into dock. It was familiar duty to a Foss craft: The company had started one hundred years before as a rowboat launch service, ferrying people between anchored ships and shore. Out in the harbor the parked *Green Master* lowered a ladder to the *Wedell,* and the harbor pilot—carrying in his head the memorized charts of all of Puget Sound, and the skill and experience to negotiate any corner of it—climbed up to take control.

The *Green Master* hauled up its anchor chain, ready to shove off. It was empty now, riding high in the water, exposing the red paint of the lower half of its hull. "It will sink down below the red when it's filled," Corrie said. Once docked by the *Wedell,* it would spend the next five days or more being loaded with raw logs—6 million board-feet of fir and hemlock bound for Japan.

A pair of tugs bracketed the *Green Master* now—the *Wedell* in front, towline sloping up to its high looming bow; the *Claudia* behind, pushing its stern. "We're kinda like the flies around the buffalo," Duane Crowley said, back at the wheel at 5:15. "We just keep out of the way." The big ship wasn't dead weight: Its own engines moved it forward, but it was too unwieldy to maneuver with the accuracy demanded by the tight terrain, the currents and the wind. The tugs were not its tow truck, but its guidance system, steering it the way the air traffic controllers steered the big jets.

"Docks are expensive, ships are expensive, bridges are irreplaceable, so it's just not worth it to try," Corrie said.

The three vessels, yoked together and traveling as a unit, rumbled toward land at a prudent five knots. "We just got under way from anchor with *Green Master,*" Crowley radioed ahead to the drawbridge tender on the Blair Bridge.

"Do you know the length and height on *Green Master?*" the bridge tender asked.

"I'm gonna have to have a full opening. Her length is four hundred ninety-nine feet, her height is one hundred twenty feet."

Crowley's attention swiveled from front to back, trying to encompass two directions at once, looking ahead to the bridge, then behind at the ship that filled the wheelhouse's rear windows like the biggest truck that ever tailgated you. His forearms were illustrated with a pair of tattoos from his navy days—Popeye on the left, a hula dancer on the right. "I wanted Olive Oyl, but he didn't have that, so I got a hula girl," he said. As he neared the bridge he blew the tug's air horn, one long blast and one short.

The bridge opened slowly, welcoming the entourage into the Blair waterway and blocking the dawn drivers. "He's one of the best they've got," Crowley said of the harbor pilot, "but it always makes me nervous when they come zipping through like this." They all squeezed through the bridge, one, two, three, intact. In the narrow waterway, its mountainous bulk juxtaposed against the close and shrunken land, the *Green Master* seemed to grow even larger. "There are times when you go to bed at night and there's a job coming up that you know is gonna be tight, no room for error, and you think the job through," he said. "You start to visualize different ways to do it."

They reached the turning basin, a wide cul-de-sac at the end of the waterway, and made a sweeping collective U-turn. The morning was blessedly free of fog. "Fog is my worst enemy," Crowley said. "I'll fight wind and bounce around, but I don't like fog." He could see the whole length of the *Green Master* and the whole length of its destined dock at the Blair Terminal. The harbor pilot directed the tugs as they set to the painstaking job of parallel-parking a five hundred-foot ship.

"Stop the *Claudia*," the pilot said.

"*Claudia* stopped," the *Claudia*'s captain said.

"Stop *Wedell* . . . easy, *Claudia* . . . stop, *Claudia* . . . Okay, Duane, let me know how much room I've got between the bow and the stern of the guy in front."

"You've got one hundred eighty feet."

"Easy two, *Wedell* . . . easy one, *Wedell*."

"One hundred and twenty feet."

"Easy two, *Wedell* . . . easy one, *Wedell* . . . stop the *Wedell*."

"*Wedell* stopped, eighty feet to the next ship."

Landing time was 6:25, as the first line was tied between the *Green Master* and the dock. The *Wedell*'s afterdeck was drenched by a brief waterfall from the big ship's hawse pipe. "We just finished tying up *Green Master*," Crowley radioed ahead to the *Toyokaze* as the *Wedell* cut loose. "We put him in to just like we're gonna take you out of."

To get to the *Toyokaze*, a tanker waiting dockside in a parallel waterway, the *Wedell* and the *Claudia* first had to navigate past some rush-hour water traffic and get back out through the bridge: A lumber ship was heading in, threatening to block their way. "The race is on," Crowley said as the tugs sped down the straight lane. The big ship was no match, still plodding in as the tugs slipped out. They turned and swept back in under another bridge, maneuvered around a log raft and a gravel barge, and found the *Toyokaze* standing ready for takeoff, harbor pilot already aboard. It was carrying tallow to Japan, but first it was going north through the sound to Bellingham to fill its other empty compartments with chemicals. The *Wedell* hooked up to the rear this time, the *Claudia* to the front, and they pulled it away from the dock like pulling a couch away from a wall, moving it in a direction it was never designed to move—sideways.

"She's kinda light up there, isn't she?" the *Claudia*'s captain said. "She just popped right out."

"Could you take the stern back toward the dock?" the pilot asked the *Wedell*. "I don't want to get any closer to that ship."

The *Toyokaze*'s engines were roiling the water now, and the *Wedell* pulled straight back on it like a dog pulling back on a leash, checking its forward motion, preventing it from gathering too much speed. The trio eased away from the dock, out into the waterway.

"Okay, just the weight of the boat on the *Wedell* back there so we don't pick up any speed," the pilot requested.

The *Toyokaze* lumbered toward the open bridge at three knots, the *Wedell* dragging behind like a dinghy. "Now all the people running just a minute late are getting caught by the bridge," Crowley said. At 8:25, the big ship safely out in the open harbor, the *Wedell*'s worknight was done.

"Okay, Duane, I'm sure you're getting tired of looking at my stern, so we'll go ahead and turn you loose," the pilot said. "Thanks a lot. By god, you made us look good."

"*Wedell Foss* clear," Crowley radioed.

As the *Wedell* turned and started in toward its dock, the *Toyokaze* started out on a journey that would eventually take it west across the Pacific to Japan, and west across the international dateline into the next day. In Tacoma it was, to Crowley's relief, another gray Northwest day, leaving the precious store of sunlight untouched, safe for a better time. "If we have a sunshiny day when we're working, we feel like we're wasting it," he said. "It's kind of a sad situation. You think, 'God, that's just one more day you're not gonna have when you go home.' " In the distance you could see that the horizon had returned again, like a drowning swimmer surfacing for air.

14

Through all the hours past midnight, on the Arctic Coast of ALASKA, *the sun circled the sky, never setting, and the night was as bright as the day.*

"WAAAAAOOOW!" the recorded voice of James Brown shrieked from a radio station loudspeaker, echoing across an Anchorage park like the death cry of a grizzly victim, "I feel good, I knew that I would now." Several hundred runners, clustered on a green field, bounced and stretched to the music, limbering up for the race that was about to start. The chill wind off Cook Inlet raised goosebumps on the legs of anyone wearing shorts. The sky was gray with clouds and dusk. Mountains blocked the horizon all around, across the water and behind the city. My watch, which had nothing wrong with it, said the time was just before midnight. Tonight was the night of the summer solstice—the shortest night of the year everywhere in America, especially in Alaska, where it was no more than the sweet length of a poem—and the sun had just set, at 11:42 P.M.

"We are thirty seconds from the start of the Summer Solstice Midnight Run in the Country in the beautiful scenic Kincaid Park," said the announcer from the radio stations sponsoring it, KYAK-AM and KGOT-FM. He counted down toward midnight as the runners waited at the starting line. "Ten, nine, eight, seven, six, five, four, three, two, one," and they were off, 450 of them, down and around through the woods of this arrowhead peninsula at the far western edge of Anchorage.

It is hard to discuss Alaska, a state where American citizens hunt whales for food, without using the word *beyond*—as in beyond big (it constitutes one-sixth of America's landmass) beyond civilization (it has more square miles than it has people); beyond the map (you need a globe to fix its proper location, so far is it from the rest of America that it is usually exiled to an out-of-scale box alongside Hawaii); beyond cold (it was minus 80 degrees Fahrenheit once at Prospect Creek, up along the Pipeline, the lowest temperature ever recorded in the United States); beyond wild (it has 70 percent of all the nation's parkland, 90 percent of all the wildlife refuge-land), beyond private property (the government controls 60 percent of all the land in the state); beyond law (until just two decades ago you could still homestead land, and until 1991 you could possess small amounts of marijuana for personal use); beyond prosperous (the state collects no income tax, but instead disburses, to anyone who has lived in Alaska for at least a year, an annual dividend check, $873 per person in 1989, from an oil royalties trust fund); beyond beautiful (rivers, forests, glaciers, fjords, islands, volcanoes, valleys, seventeen of America's twenty highest mountains, immemorial expanses barely explored and never named, their wonder magnified by their splendid anonymity); and beyond history (the antediluvian landscape is a reminder of what the rest of America, even Manhattan, once looked like). And in the winter, when the sun hardly rises, Alaska is beyond the day; in the summer, when the sun hardly sets, it is beyond the night. Because Earth is tilted in its orbit, the night's length varies by geography—a phenomenon first widely noticed during the Crusades, when Europeans marched south to the Holy Land. If you travel due north from the equator in spring or summer, your nights will progressively shorten until you finally reach the North Pole, where the sun shines continuously from the spring equinox to the fall equinox, the world's longest day; if you travel in fall or winter, your nights will lengthen until you reach the Pole again, home also of the world's longest night, where the sun sets on the fall equinox and doesn't rise again until the spring, six months of darkness later. Anchorage—several hundred miles below the Arctic Circle, the southernmost line at which you can see the sun circle the sky without setting on the night of the summer solstice—had nineteen hours and twenty-one minutes of daylight today, and four hours and thirty-nine minutes of something you couldn't quite call night. The sun would rise again at 4:21 A.M. to punch in for another long day at its summer job.

Most of Alaska is beyond roads, too, and earlier in the day I had driven to the end of one and near the end of another. The state road network, with fewer miles than Vermont, is a giant blowup of the closed-circuit street grid in a remote Plains town: The roads, having nowhere else to go here at the end of the continent, connect only among themselves before they finally die, like salmon that have returned to their upstream spawning grounds. You can't drive to Juneau, the state capital; a mountain range that tops eighteen thousand feet and a glacier bigger than Rhode Island separate it from the rest of the state. Except for a couple of roads that dead-end in the Southeast Panhandle, only two roads—both into Canada's Yukon, one of them gravel and closed in winter—connect Alaska to the Outside, a word that is always capitalized here. Prudhoe Bay is the ultimate end of the road, way up on the Arctic Coast, but Homer is also the end of the road, and Hope, and Knik, and Talkeetna, and Petersville, and Kantishna in Denali National Park, and Manley Hot Springs, and Cheena Hot Springs, and Circle, and Eagle, and Nabesna, and Skagway, and Haines, and McCarthy, and Valdez, and Seward, where the Alaska railroad ends its run south from Fairbanks and where I landed after driving south from Anchorage through a white-tipped green world of snow peaks, alpine meadows, wildflowers, waterfalls, glacial streams and thick stands of spruce, birch and aspen. Down by the ferry dock on Resurrection Bay, downstream of the big oil spill, some trailers were marked by a sign, OTTER RESCUE CENTER. I turned around and drove back to the fork in the road, thirty-seven miles north, turning west there to cross the Kenai Peninsula. Minute rock particles, glacier flour, gave Kenai Lake its distinctive color, a milky Caribbean green. The radio picked up Sly and the Family Stone's "Hot Fun in the Summertime." A message inscribed in the dust on the back of a trailer with California plates declared, I SURVIVED THE TRIP TO ALASKA. The city of Kenai—Alaska's original oil boomtown, predating the Prudhoe Bay strike—was equipped with a twenty-four-hour 7-Eleven. I turned around again at the Russian Orthodox church, a small, brightly painted old wooden building crowned by a blue onion dome, and started back toward Anchorage, home to almost half the state's population. A white-bearded priest stood silhouetted against the day-bright evening sky, the wind billowing his long black robe.

The sun had come out from behind the clouds at about 7, and all the way back I kept waiting for it to finally set. It lingered instead with an afternoon sluggishness. When it did leave, it only went under the clouds, not under the horizon. Looking up the long sweep of Turnagain Arm, an inlet walled in by mountains that sloped down into the water from a flat gray cloudroof, I could see a patch of bright sky at its far end, blue and yellow and white, like a door open into a room beyond. At 10:25, just fourteen miles out of Anchorage, a rainbow ascended from one mountain's foot into the incandescent edge of a backlit cloud.

A Day in the Night of America

Anchorage was closed—the gas stations, the malls that had advertised solstice sales in the day's papers, the brief boxy office buildings in a skyline that looked imported from a small Sun Belt city—and at first I couldn't help but wonder why. It was 11 P.M., I tried to keep reminding myself. Plenty of people were still out jogging, bicycling, strolling, dog walking or drinking. Long, dark memories of slow winters spurred Alaskans to spend their summers in overdrive; they regarded the sun with the affection desert dwellers had for water. The solstice was the summit of the light season, and it was widely celebrated. The Midnight Sun Festival in Nome featured a blanket toss; the festival in Moose Pass included a moose-calling contest. In Fairbanks the night before, 2,250 baseball fans had watched the Alaska Goldpanners beat San Diego Sea World, 7–3, in the 84th Midnight Sun game, which started at 10:35 P.M., ended at 1:17 A.M. and was played in its entirety on a field illuminated only by the white night sky. (Up over the Pole, today's papers had reported, a Norwegian ship broke through ice floes to rescue almost 1,000 passengers from a Soviet liner that, while on a midnight sun cruise above the Arctic Circle, had struck an iceberg.) Here in Anchorage tonight, many people whose ideas about celebration didn't include a midnight run had driven up to Flat Top Mountain behind the city for a wide look at the year's latest sunset, the birthday of the infant night.

In Kincaid Park the first runner returned from the five-kilometer loop through the woods and crossed the finish line at fifteen minutes and fifty-seven seconds past midnight. David Shaul crossed about five minutes later, followed soon after by Kathleen Bedner. "We were looking for something to do at midnight," she said. Her T-shirt said, ALASKA—LAND OF THE INDIVIDUAL AND OTHER ENDANGERED SPECIES.

"It looked like fun," he said. "I've never run at midnight before."

She was a French teacher, originally from Wisconsin, twelve years in Alaska. "I don't think anyone ever gets used to the darkness. I sleep with the curtains open. If I have three or four hours with the curtains open and the sun coming in, I'm regenerated. What's worst is that now the days are getting shorter. I'll start getting depressed in the next couple of weeks because winter's coming."

The light was pale and inconclusive now as the runners filtered out of the park, a spot accustomed to nocturnal activity: It had once been home to a battery of Nike and Hercules missiles. Crews from the Fourth Missile Battalion Forty-third Artillery had stood alert round-the-clock here for almost two decades.

"Is it out?" they ask in Alaska, like rain-weary Seattleites asking after the sun. "Is it out yet?" they ask again, like eager fans outside the dressing room of a reclusive star. Mount McKinley is the one thing big enough here to carry its name in no more than a pronoun—a looming ice-age remnant frozen by time and temperature, visible clear to downtown Anchorage, the tallest mountain in North America and the tallest-seeming anywhere (its vertical relief, 18,000 feet from base to summit, is the world's highest), rising more lordly over its domain than even Mount Everest (which is shouldered all around by giant Himalayan attendants)—and Alaska is the one state big enough to hide it from view. The native language named it Denali, "the high one," and it stands so cold and tall that it catches all the wet wind from the Pacific, turning moisture into clouds and rain and snow, making its own weather. McKinley was visible only one day out of three in the summertime, and tonight was one of the blind two. It was not, to answer the question, out tonight. The only people who could see it now were the 273 climbers who were actually encamped on it, creeping toward the 20,320-foot summit.

Down in the park that surrounds the mountain, Denali National Park, ranger Charlie Strickfaden was looking around, not up. He made a brief pass through the narrow bar in the park hotel. "I like to go into the bar early and see they're not too smashed," he said. He wore the green uniform and the broad mountie hat of the National Park Service. "We wear the hat everywhere. Some people have to be urged to, but I love wearing it. It's so rangerish. I don't go anywhere without it." He walked out through the lobby to his car, a white Chevy with a green stripe, and drove toward the campground—the only law enforcement ranger on patrol duty tonight in a park the size of Massachusetts.

The campground was filled, the curtains on the windows of the sleeping trailers and RVs drawn tight against the stubborn twilight. Strickfaden watched for errant animals as well as errant humans. Last night at 2:30 some bears had killed a moose calf by the railroad depot near the hotel and dragged the carcass across the road. Bears are high on the things-to-see list of most of Denali's 600,000 annual visitors—a count that had risen from 20 in 1921 and now represented almost three-quarters of all the people who visited Alaska in a year, making the park as central to the state's tourism industry as the North Slope fields are to the oil industry—but not high enough that they wished to meet one on such intimate terms. "We don't make any attempt to move any animals unless they're aggressive or fearless of humans," he said. "That's the biggest danger, when they lose their fear. We try to make it unpleasant for them to be around humans." He saw no sign of interspecies contact.

The mountain's gray gloom spilled down its icy slopes, over its glaciers and across its foothills, all the way down to the park entrance. Strickfaden was driving west toward the wild heart of the park, windshield wipers slapping at the drizzle. "This is about as dark as it gets," he said. "Last night was incredible. I don't know if you'd call it a sunset or not, but it was dusk for five hours." He had worked at seven national parks in the last five years, arriving at Denali six weeks ago for the start of the summer season. He came with a tan: His last job was at the opposite end of America, as a naturalist at Biscayne National Park, south of Miami, a place of coral reefs, dolphins, sea turtles, glass-bottomed boats and winter sunshine. Alaska provided less heat, but more light. "Only in Alaska has the solstice ever meant much to me," he said. He worked days his first few weeks, and the lingering light had kept him up late, hiking, bicycling, playing volleyball until midnight, trying to wring the most out of evenings that never seemed to end. "In the back of my mind I'm still roughly thinking of the normal parameters, like I should be in bed by a certain hour." His home for the summer was a cabin in what had originally been a New Deal–era Civilian Conservation Corps camp. He had hung beach towels over its curtainless windows and made cardboard shutters to help darken his sleeping hours. "Last night I saw a guy walking along the road at one, one-fifteen. I stopped to talk to him and he said he just got in and he had to get out and around. People take advantage of the light out here."

The park road, still below the timberline here, cut silently through stunted taiga forest that let you delude yourself into thinking you had some height on this land. Long winters mean short trees—*taiga* is Russian for "land of little sticks"—and the stands of spruce, slender and spiky as pipe cleaners, looked less like a forest than they did the timber ruins of old settlements; brush grew lush and green where the foundations would have been. Clouds prevented the hidden mountain from restoring perspective and shrinking you back toward nothingness. Strickfaden's only company was a rabbit that exploded from one side of the road and disappeared into the other, and a trailer camped illegally on the shoulder. He gave the retired

Texas couple in the trailer a written warning and instructions to find a proper campsite come morning. The road he was patrolling was about halfway between Anchorage and the Arctic Circle, halfway nearer the latitude of no night, but the overcast painted Denali's sky the same dull shade as the city's. You could see just a hint of the night's true color in the sliver of pale cream light that had opened over the jagged western horizon.

Strickfaden's territory was the small populated corner around the park entrance, and he reached the end of it at the Savage River checkpoint, twelve miles in. Beyond here the road continued as a seventy-nine-mile dead-end gravel street into a high realm of tundra, glaciers, mountains, grizzlies, caribou, moose, wolves, backcountry rangers who travel by dogsled in winter, and wilderness campers—all of them on their own now against the night. Ranger Chris Mabey sat in the shadows in the log-walled booth, responsible for turning away anything but tour buses and registered campers. "I'd turn the light on, but I'm playing a little game," he said. "I want to do as much as I can at one A.M. without turning the light on." He came from Vermont, had worked for the park service in New Hampshire and had hung maps of Alaska in his bedroom. "I've had Alaska set in my mind for four years." His first month here had already fulfilled the maps' promises. He had slept in an alpine meadow at 4,500 feet ("There were Dall sheep all around us—we heard rocks tumbling down the talus slope") and hiked across tundra tussocks ("It's like standing on top of a basketball"). Just tonight, working what was known here as the Z-shift, he had seen a fox chasing an arctic ground squirrel. A sightline through the trees from the booth opened a view to the mountain you still couldn't see. "I've stayed up for incredible amounts of hours," he said. "I stayed up for twenty-four hours, then I finally realized, 'Oh, wow, that's right, I forgot to sleep.'"

Backtracking east, Strickfaden found that three more campers had arrived and parked themselves by the side of the road for the night. "It's really rampant tonight," he said after sending them to campgrounds outside the park. "They were just getting in and they had no clue where to go. It's that Outside mentality. They all looked fairly perky. I don't think they were really aware of what time it is." Back at the hotel bar it was 1 A.M., and closing time was uneventful. "It's a more comforting night. When I'm out all by myself and I'm the only one in the park, it sure helps to have plenty of light. If I pull a car over, I have an edge."

Half an hour after closing time a hotel security guard spotted some potential trouble brewing. "We just had a report of bears being sighted by the railroad tracks," Strickfaden radioed his dispatcher. "I'm gonna go check it out. He said he saw them headed for the airstrip."

"What size bears are those reported?" asked the dispatcher, who was already contacting one of the park's bear specialists.

"The information's sketchy, but they appear to be the same bears as last night."

Strickfaden drove slowly from the hotel toward the airstrip on the other side of the railroad tracks, scanning the wooded roadside for any sign of the bears, a sow and her cub. "I haven't seen any this close myself, so I might start seeing things or hearing things," he said. A brown sock sheathed the barrel of the patrol car's shotgun. A clearer, lighter night would have been welcome now. He saw or heard nothing of them at the airstrip. "They're in the woods headed up toward the post office," the radio told him.

Back on the main road Strickfaden met the guard who had first seen the bears and who had just spotted them again from his car. "They went from the train tracks up the hill toward the hotel and the employee housing," the guard told him. "They acted the same as the two last night. Instead of running away they just stopped and looked."

"I'd definitely stay around your vehicle," Strickfaden said. "I'd avoid walking." The guard drove up toward the hotel from one direction—it was on a loop road on the other side of the wooded area, its one hundred rooms filled with safely dreaming tourists—and Strickfaden drove up from the other. He didn't get far before he saw something that stopped him: Two moose, a cow and her calf, were chomping on the greenery just beyond the road's shoulder. "This is a dangerous situation. This is escalating now. If a bear happens to be passing through, fine. If a moose happens to be passing through, fine. But both, that's not fine." The most dangerous moose is a cow who thinks her calf is threatened; the most dangerous bear is a sow who thinks her cub is threatened; and a moose calf is a prime target for a hungry bear, who will then defend its kill as vigorously as it defends its cub. Nature had set the stage for a confrontation better suited to the wild places beyond the checkpoint. "Okay, we've got a moose and a calf in the area," Strickfaden radioed. "Still haven't seen the bears."

"Keep those moose in sight and we'll be down in five minutes," the bear specialist said.

The moose continued their late-night meal, paying no heed to either the bears who might be stalking them or the human who sat in his car watching them. "Something about the vehicle just doesn't register in their Rolodex,"

Strickfaden said. "As soon as you stand up and break that silhouette, then they know just exactly who you are."

The bear experts drove up and joined the vigil. "If those bears keep going right up the mountain, it's cool," one of them said, "but if there's a bloody fight in the middle of the road and Wilma and Elmer Fudd come and take pictures, we're gonna have serious problems."

"They're off in the woods somewhere, but we don't know where," Strickfaden said.

The moose ambled across the road and started munching their next course. Strickfaden's shift had officially ended at 2—no rangers patrolled between 2 and 7—but he stayed on for baby-sitting duty. "Sometimes I'll feel burned out and somebody will come up to me and say, 'You mean you live here?!'" By 2:45 the moose had moved on, the bears hadn't shown, and everybody went to bed. Signs were posted near the hotel the next morning, CAUTION—DANGEROUS BEARS IN AREA, and the waking tourists buzzed among themselves about what the wild things were doing the night before.

The bears I finally did see—from a shuttle bus on the road into Denali, home to more than two hundred grizzlies—were not the pair from the hotel. Three of them crossed the broad, open valley of the Toklat River, far enough that you could see them only as dark, bulky specks moving against the gray; four others strolled up across green tundra, near enough that you could make out the rippling of their golden fur. The road wound and crept through the Alaska you see in PBS nature specials, an unworked landscape that is, like the starry night sky, raw evidence of Creation. It didn't lead into the big mountains, as the road in Colorado had, but just skirted them at a respectful distance. The dim day hid McKinley as completely as the night had, leaving it alone still with its climbers. Many Japanese hike up their national mountain, Mount Fuji, by night, timing their climb to reach the peak by dawn; ascending our national mountain is a two-to-three-week journey of Himalayan proportions, subject even in summer to instant blizzards, gales and windchills of minus 100 degrees Fahrenheit and below. The bus driver told us that six climbers had already died on McKinley this season, but that a Siberian husky, lost for eighteen days from a French dogsled expedition to the summit, had just turned up alive at a camp at 14,200 feet. He stopped the bus at his turnaround point, a visitor center that had a postcard angle on the mountain. Where you should have seen a wall of craggy white, thirty miles away but bearing down like a glacial tidal wave, you saw instead only a close gray curtain of fog and cloud, drawn as if across a stage.

Outside the windows of the 727, the clouds parted long enough to open a view to Mount McKinley. It was finally out now, at least from up here, and it was whiter than the whitest summer night, its granite bulk encased by ice, hundreds of feet thick in spots, and permanent snowfields. It seemed massive enough to exert its own gravitational pull, and I wondered briefly if it might suck the plane in. It looked like something that had punched violently up through Earth's sealing crust—emerging not from the planet's living core, like a lava-spouting volcano, but from some older, frozen place, some geological vault of history. Looking at it was like looking at time. Had I seen a woolly mammoth traversing it, I would not have blinked. The plane continued over the Interior, past Fairbanks, across the Arctic Circle and over the Brooks Range—the northernmost mountain range in the world, the farthest annex of the Rockies, and the extension of the continental divide I had crossed back in Colorado, except that here the split was between the Pacific Ocean and the Arctic Ocean. The mountains sketched the border beyond which the land settled down for the long, flat run to the Pole. They marched six hundred miles across the roof of Alaska, from Canada to the western shore—unnamed, unclimbed, uninhabited, the vast polar negative of the Manhattan skyline—and they faded through their northern foothills into a wide, treeless tundra, the North Slope, under which lay North America's largest oil field. The 727, leased from Alaska Airlines by the ARCO oil company, landed on a gravel airstrip in Prudhoe Bay, 125 miles north of the Brooks Range, 250 miles north of the Arctic Circle, 400 miles north of Fairbanks, 640 miles north of Anchorage, and 1,500 miles south of the North Pole. The temperature was 40, the windchill was 20. If you went by the clock, the time was mid-afternoon. If you went by the sky, it was just past noon on a day that had started when the sun rose at 12:09 A.M. on May 20 and that wouldn't end until the sun finally set at 11:48 P.M. on July 22, almost sixty-four calendar pages later. I had outrun the night completely now.

Alaska's population, like the night's, is distributed in small clusters across a wide space, and the ARCO employees disembarking at Prudhoe Bay were among its outermost settlers. A bus took them and their bags to the Operations Center and the Main Construction Camp, the downtown of this remote private village. The day was a November gray. The tundra was a flat, endless plain of damp brown grass, like a salt marsh with a crew cut, its treasures secreted deep below and its surface emptiness broken only by scattered bits of Cleveland—the pipelines and drill sites and industrial plants, some as big as Ford factories, that extract the oil and send it out to the rest of America. The nearest tree was 150 miles south, a lone spruce beside the Trans-Alaska Pipeline. The snow had just melted last week—97 percent of Alaska is snowfree in summer—and the land was slow to green-up after an especially harsh winter. Several of the caribou who summer here were grazing in the distance, their antlers big as tree limbs. Tundra swans, newly arrived from their Chesapeake Bay winter homes, paddled in one of the pothole lakes that pockmark the surface like puddles on a road after a rainstorm. The oil workers migrated into sprawling dorms, built on gravel pads and stilts that kept the inside heat from melting the permafrost below. Prudhoe Bay's human population traveled more frequently than its wildlife: They came for a week, most of them, then went home for a week (taking the return flight to Anchorage, which was referred to here as "in town," a phrase often accompanied by a backward-nodding head or a gesturing thumb, as if the town in question were just a mile or two down the road), repeating the on-off cycle week after week throughout the year.

A predawn hush filled the corridors of the dorm wings. QUIET AREA, PLEASE, a sign advised, OUR NIGHT WORKERS NEED THEIR REST. Many of the doorknobs wore hanging messages of the type that in hotels say, DO NOT DISTURB. DAYSLEEPER, they said here, illustrated by a cartoon sun, eyes shut, emitting a string of snoozing *Z*s. ARCO's North Slope employees worked a shift schedule from the past—seven days, or seven nights, of twelve-hour shifts, like the workers in the first round-the-clock factories in the nineteenth century—but they lived in an incessant community of the future, a place more hospitable to the upside-down needs of night people than any other I had seen. The 126-seat theater screened movies four evenings and four mornings each week, at 8 P.M. for the day shift and 8 A.M. for the night shift; now showing were *True Believer* and *Heartbreak Hotel*. Available to all was an array of diversions and facilities meant to ease the harsh isolation of the Arctic weeks—sauna, running track, basketball court, weight room, billiard room, cross-country skiing machines (the tundra was too fragile and the air too cold to do much real skiing), HBO,

Cinemax, CNN and other cable stations. They made upward of $60,000 a year, but they need bring none of it north with them: Everything was on the house. Those off the afternoon plane who were working tonight took their rooms, ate supper in the cafeteria (Dungeness crab was among the evening's choices; Sundays brought prime rib and strawberry shortcake), made their lunches from the bounteous larder in the Spark Room and reported to their stations in the Last Frontier (the night) of the Last Frontier (the North Slope) of the Last Frontier (Alaska, as the legend on every license plate declared).

The wellhouses stood on the tundra like a line of overgrown beach cabanas, each one marking the site of an oil well and sheltering a single "Christmas tree"—a wellhead that resembled a tall fireplug. Gary Douglas, a drill-site operator, opened the door to Well 9-3. "It makes your job a lot easier," he said of the constant summer day, a welcome change from the constant winter night. "Everyone's attitude changes, particularly on the night shift, when you get to see the sun. In the fall you get on the night shift and you won't see the sun all week. It's almost like somebody pulled the plug or turned the juice down or something." The oil was rising through the thick pipe—because the Prudhoe Bay reservoir has enough pressure to force up the oil without pumps, the wells here are not topped by the rocker arms that dip and rise all over Texas like drinking pterodactyls—and you could feel its heat by holding your hands near the steel surface, as if warming them over a radiator. Douglas checked all the valves, found everything in good order and moved on to the next wellhouse.

Flowing silently and invisibly through the pipes Douglas monitored were the headwaters of a river of oil that reaches deep into the Lower 48. The North Slope oil fields—Prudhoe Bay, by far the largest, has several nearby neighbors—provide 25 percent of America's domestic oil, almost one-eighth of all the oil the nation consumes, an immense source of heat and light buried in a place that is cold and dark most of the year. It took twenty years to find, and when the discovery well finally hit in 1968, it set off the biggest gold rush of all in a state with a rich gold-rush history. The Pipeline—eight hundred miles long, forty-eight inches in diameter, half underground and half raised on trestles—was built to carry the oil south to Valdez, where it is loaded into supertankers the length of six football fields. The oil under the North Slope is, like the Pipeline, owned by a number of oil companies; ARCO is paid to operate the east half of the field, BP the west. About six hundred wells had been drilled already, and ARCO expected to drill four hundred more before all the recoverable oil, estimated at eleven billion barrels, was tapped out. Five drilling rigs were out in the field now.

Back in the control room for Drill Site 9, Douglas opened wide a door to the outside. Birds were chirping like morning. "There aren't many days when you can keep it open," he said. "I try to keep it open until I'm almost shivering." Much of his night was spent watching the oil electronically—on the consoles that displayed its progress up through the drill site's thirty-seven wells and into the pipeline-thick manifold building—but when the chill air wasn't enough to ward off grogginess, he got up and went out to watch it personally. "To stay awake, you have to keep physically active, not mentally active," he said. There were neither dams nor leaks in the river tonight: The wells were producing at a 75,000-barrel-a-day clip. "This place'll fuck up your mind. You'll be sitting here when it's fifty below outside and the wind's blowing and this well's not flowing. You go, 'Oh, fuck,' and you put all your gear on and find out why it's not flowing. First you check the warm stuff inside the building, then it's usually the hydraulics, something got too cold. Fortunately when we do work outside, it's a short time exposure. The longest exposure is when we do the standard check of the wells."

His boom box played a Def Leppard tape in the background. "There are a lot of rockers up here," he said; his other favorites were Bob Seger and the Rolling Stones. "The hardest part of this job at night isn't the job and it isn't here, it's when you go home." He had come from Colorado, and he lived now down on the Kenai Peninsula with his wife and three teenage children. "She's a very understanding woman, well educated, and she has a lot of variety in her life. We're not joiners—the only thing we belong to is the National Geographic Society." He walked over to the door that opened out into the light. He wore a small earring in his left ear. "Around three A.M. you get really tired and you start pacing. You stand here and look at the sun and you think, 'What in the fuck am I doing here? There's gotta be a better way to make a living.' "

What came up from underground—a puddinglike emulsion of oil, gas and water ("Oil with a lot of water looks like coffee with a little bit of cream in it," Douglas said)—next traveled through small pipelines from the drill sites to the flow stations that rendered it fit to travel in the big Pipeline. "If I had the opportunity to pick, I'd probably take steady nights—I think you get more done on nights," said Kenny Kimler, lead operator at Flow Station 2. A lot needed doing these nights, because the field wasn't what it used to be. In the first years the oil came up almost straight; but now, with almost half the original recoverable reserve gone, it came up as diluted with water as a cheap drink. To get 250,000 barrels of oil, Flow Station 2 now had to separate out 250,000 barrels of water, which was then injected back underground, and 500 million cubic feet of gas. "This whole year is gonna be terrible," Kimler predicted, and he was right: Prudhoe Bay oil production would fall this year for the first time ever; and by the year 2000 it was expected to plummet to less than a third of its current level.

The sun, still hidden behind the milky clouds, had dipped nearer the horizon, taking the light down with it. "Myself, I've grown real accustomed to the daylight and darkness," Kimler said. A Texas native, he had first come to Prudhoe Bay in 1976, nine months before start-up. "I don't pay a whole lot of attention to it now, whether it's two A.M. and it's daylight, or if it's winter and it's nine A.M. and still dark. But it's some kind of beautiful at one A.M., when the sun's sitting low on the horizon. I took a picture of a swan once at one A.M., and the sky and the water were the same color. It was an exact reflection." The concise summer brought mosquito plagues, wildflower blooms, enough warmth to make "you sweat like you've been digging fenceposts," and even some winter (snow had fallen on each of the two previous July Fourths), though nothing to match the genuine article. "I was trapped in the building for twenty-four hours this winter," he said. The temperature was minus 54, the windchill minus 135, and the relief crew couldn't get to the flow station. "I couldn't see the first step when I opened the door, and I came back in."

Not much snow actually falls here—the North Slope is classified as a desert, with less than seven inches of annual precipitation and air so dry it flakes the skin—but the epochal cold locks what does fall into place, keeping the tundra blanketed by white most of the year. In deepest winter hot coffee flung from a cup out a door will appear to vanish before it can hit the ground, instantly freezing, crackling and shattering as it goes, into tiny ice crystals. "It just goes away, like a magic trick," said Doug Terry, a sergeant with the security force. "The elements keep you inside. You don't go out unless you really have to go." Thick electrical cords dangled from a tall rail, the "bull rail," in the area outside the Main Construction Camp where his patrol truck was parked. In winter they plugged into heaters that kept engine blocks from freezing up; now they swung slack and unused, like ropes from a saloon hitching rail in an old Western. The parked vehicles were covered with the khaki road-dust of summer, looking prematurely aged: The odometer on one grizzled four-wheel drive showed it had traveled just fifty-seven miles. "Every once in a while I'll be driving around and I'll look out and I'll think, 'Wow, where am I?' " he said. "It is strange, it is different, and I think you have to be a special person to work here. You have to be mature, number one, and you have to have some experience."

It was Terry's job to help ensure that the work force maintained its maturity, and to prevent this mostly male encampment at the edge of the world from degenerating into a brawling frontier outpost. His ally was a strict ban on alcohol. "You don't have too much room for error. You're up here to do a job. People here know fighting is a one-way ticket home, and one whiff of alcohol and you're gone." A Tennessee native, he had come to Alaska with the military, serving with the security police at Elmendorf Air Force Base outside Anchorage. His work hitches lasted two weeks, longer than the one-week hitch most people worked, but shorter than the year-long remote tours you might be assigned in the military. "That's what you're here for—to work."

The ice had melted by now in the smaller pothole lakes, and in the larger ones it had shrunk to lone central islands, surrounded by open water like the last cube floating in a glass. Some lakes were marked by signs that named them in honor of wives and girlfriends, and one featured a summer tableau of a model boat pulling a water-skiing Barbie doll; small models of offshore oil rigs stood in the waters behind here. The warmth was better for the humans than it was for the oil field. "When the temperature's cooler, you produce more oil, because there's more room for the gas," said K. C. Kilty, a production technician at Flow Station 1. The gas, which was injected back underground, declined in volume as the temperature dropped. "Winter's great. It's cold all the time and we give them as much as they can handle." Like Kimler, he had been here for the start-up, coming to Alaska from a job as a computer operator in New York. "I was in a nine-to-five rut," he said. "They said, 'Come up here and work twenty-four weeks of the year on the coast of the Arctic Ocean,' and I said, 'Sure, why not?' "

The wide control board Kilty sat at caught some of the white light that fell in through an unshaded window. The flow station's exterior doors were as thick as the doors on meat lockers. "Everybody knows what their personal cold record is," he said. His was minus 57, when he was working at a drill site and had to go out to tighten a fitting on a hydraulic panel for a wellhead. "It was like working on the moon. I was seriously dressed—the only thing you could see was my eyes." Tonight was his first night back after an eighteen-day vacation on Maui.

"I've never seen a polar bear, but I've seen a lot of caribou," said Jack Bradford, an operator at the Central Compressor Plant, where the gas went after it was separated from the oil. "I love watching them." His huge building had enough horsepower to fly two 747s, and it handled enough gas each day (3.8 billion cubic feet) to heat a typical American home for twelve thousand years. Nine low-stage compressors, each driven by a giant turbine, first compressed the gas from six hundred pounds per square inch to 2,200 psi, then four high-stage compressors compressed it further, from 2,200 psi to 4,000 psi. The compressed gas, tighter now than when it came out of the ground, was injected back into the reservoir's gas cap—to maintain the pressure and help push the oil out, and to await some future moment when it became valuable enough to justify the cost of moving it south across Alaska. ARCO's compressor plant served the BP side of the field, too. "The whole North Slope passes their gas here," Bradford said.

Bradford came to Alaska from Texas as a boy—his father was in the air force—and had worked on an oil platform in Cook Inlet before coming to Prudhoe Bay. "I'm as far as I can go," he said. "What worries me most is that something happens at home and I can't get there for a day because the weather's bad—if my wife's hurt or my boy's hurt and I've gotta wait until the next flight out. That's my only drawback." He had taken readings at the turbines and the compressors at midnight, and he would take them again at 4. He stopped briefly in a break room where, a few years earlier, a window had been installed in a previously solid wall. "If it's nice and sunny, I make an attempt to stand and look out," he said. "That sunlight coming in in the summer makes a difference. I can see it. I can see it in people's personalities."

As the oil went out to the nearby Pump Station 1, the start of the Pipeline, the numbers came into the Eastern Outtake Center, a computer-stuffed room in the Operations Center building. Oil was coming out of the Prudhoe Bay field at the rate of 1.5 million barrels a day—650,000 barrels from the ARCO side, 850,000 from the BP side. When the smaller fields were added in, the North Slope's total contribution to the Pipeline today was 1.78 million barrels, all of them rolling south toward Valdez, slightly less than usual. "The field's coming up after some maintenance," explained Jeff Tinnaro, whose job it was to "optimize field offtake" and "maintain the highest amount of oil flow." Five screens along a console showed him what was going on in all the facilities. The oil field was like a big sponge, and if you squeezed it the right way, you could get more out of it. "When I see an opportunity to make a little more oil, I suggest changes," he said. "Toward the end of the week they're a little less inclined to listen."

Tinnaro had come to Alaska in 1976 from Los Angeles, the city where much of the North Slope's oil wound up, fueling the cars that jammed the freeways. "The first couple of summers up here I wasn't sure whether to stay up or go to sleep," he said. Engineers and supervisors came and went through the Outtake Center all day long; at night Tinnaro worked alone. "Given a choice, I'd rather fly with eagles than do it with owls," he said. A shade was drawn over the window to cut the glare on his computer screens. "It's pleasant to have that view now, because when it gets dark up here, it stays dark for a long time. When you look out, your horizon's not very far. It's very black out there."

At 3 A.M., the exact center of the true night, I stepped off a rock on the shore and across a rivulet of open water onto one of the small floes of pack ice that still cluttered the Arctic Ocean. The sun had finally emerged, higher now than two hours earlier, climbing back up from its brief nightly trough. It hung in a swath of blue sky, bordered by a bank of peach clouds with lavender bottoms. The northern horizon was concealed by a wall of a single color, proving just as elusive as all the other horizons in America were at this hour—except that here the wall was not black but white, the white ice merging with the low, distant white clouds. The emptiness was deafening. I felt farther from the world than anyplace I'd ever been: Even in the deepest Rockies you know that Denver is eventually on the other side, that the wild is encircled by civilization; but here the civilization was encircled by the wild. I looked north and saw nothing but light and ice, and beyond where I could see was nothing but more light and ice, and more and more and still more, all the way over the Pole and clear unto the next landfall, Murmansk in the Soviet Union. In the huge and strange light of this huge and strange place—at the northern edge of Alaska, a state that is to the Lower 48 as the nation of night is to the nation of day; at the far opposite side of a continent that Columbus's night lookout first spotted soon after an October midnight in 1492—floated the fact that I had found in my journey here: The world doesn't die at midnight; it is conscious when you are not. I had finally found physical evidence of the light within the night.

A Day in the Night of America

Before I started west into the darkness, I had perceived the night as too long to measure, much the way a young schoolchild perceives the nearing endless summer, but as I traveled through it, in real time not dream time, I learned, as every schoolchild learns come every September, that it wasn't so long as it seemed. It had distinct borders, and its hours held no more minutes than the day's did. I saw that the night was many of the things I had imagined, and that it was not many others. It had no monopoly on either good or evil: Churchill worked nights, but so did Stalin; the Berlin Wall went up at night, but exultant Germans danced on it through the night when it was finally opened. Through all these many nights I had not been robbed, beaten, stabbed or shot. I had not been attacked by any of the mythical night monsters who were said to prey on night travelers. My mouth sometimes grew cottony and my vision spidery when I stayed up too long at a stretch, and my skin had acquired a fish-belly pallor from all the sickly fluorescent light it absorbed, but I had not, like a cave animal too long in the darkness, gone blind. I had seen no ghosts, aliens, UFOs or any other unexplainable phenomena. I had taken no coffee or speed or No Doz, relying instead on Coca-Cola and Hershey bars. I had learned to accept the melancholy kept-after-school feeling that comes with working while everyone else is sleeping; and I had learned to treasure the victorious finish-line feeling that comes with watching the night turn into dawn, and seeing then that you have beaten the sun into the new day. The night, I had seen, was by necessity the black to the day's white, the yin that enables you to recognize the yang in the familiar Chinese symbol, but within its broad territory were located its own twin poles of darkness and light, scattered in patterns like the Benday dots in the shadows of a newspaper photograph. Even here, in its outermost precincts, the night was neither all black nor all white.

The same oblique angle that erased the night here would soon erase the day instead. Each night now, on its circuit around the sky, the sun would dip nearer and nearer Earth before climbing again, as if teasing the horizon to lunge and swallow, until finally the horizon obliged, holding its bright catch only briefly at first but then detaining it longer and longer with each passing day. Once the sun set at 12:27 P.M. on November 24, it wouldn't rise again until 11:18 A.M. on January 18, almost fifty-five nights later. The only light through the deepest winter would be the starlight that fell on the reflective tundra; the few hours of twilight from the sun that was creeping up behind the horizon, but not breaking it; the angelic northern lights that, some people claimed, you could almost hear, rustling like sheets; and the oil companies' tiaras of artificial lights. It might appear then that, astronomically speaking, the day had been eliminated entirely, but, practically, it was only an illusion, just as it was only an illusion now, under the everlasting sun, that the night had been eliminated entirely. The world is incessant, but humans are not. It was light now, but not everyone was awake. In six months it would be dark, but not everyone would be asleep.

The ice-covered ocean that stretched north of me was breaking up now into a dense, frozen archipelago. The pack ice would soon recede far enough from shore to permit tugs from Seattle to haul in their equipment-laden barges. Some natives would take to their skiffs to hunt whales in the open water. Some oil workers would fish for Arctic char; the hardiest would venture a Polar Bear Club dip. The sun kept climbing: The universe had again neglected, at least in this far latitude, to withdraw the light and issue its daily reminder of who was in charge. If I returned to this same spot in winter, the sun would be lighting the opposite side of the globe and I would be standing in the shadow of night that stretches into space behind Earth like a sideways ice-cream cone. The darkness would improve my view. Instead of looking into a white sky cloaked by the captive light of a single planet, I would look into black sky filled with the free light of Creation—the light you can only see at night. I would see the stars that are but a tiny fraction of the real population of the universe, just as the faces you see in the darkness are but a tiny fraction of the real population of the night. I stepped from the ice back onto the shore. Deep under my feet lay the fuel that helped light the night in the bulk of America that was covered by darkness now. I crouched and ran my hand through the water, far colder than the winter ocean the *Barnegat* had fished off Massachusetts, cold enough to wake the dead. I turned and left then, and sometime later—whether it was day or night, the sky couldn't tell me—I went to sleep.

ACKNOWLEDGMENTS

Traveling across America by night, I counted on finding enough lights on to guide me along the way—and, at each turn, I did. Many of the people I met weren't sure what to make of a stranger appearing after dark asking questions, but they answered graciously anyway, and I owe them all a great debt—first to those whose names and stories are in the previous pages, and then to those who aren't: Renee Acoffi, Larainea Allen, Arnulfo Alonzo, Frank Alvillar, Patsy Andersen, Susan Andrews, Richard Athey, Jim Baltas, Larry Baum, Keith Benton, Randy Berridge, Carroll Bledsoe, Jim Blosser, Jim Bowersox, Joseph Brazile, Jr., Mark Breen, Bill Brennan, Peter Brooks, Bob Brown, Diane Brown, Keith Brown, Myra Brown, John Brune, Floyd Buckhalter, Mike Buffington, Daisy Cajugal, Lisa Campbell, John Canter, Manny Carco, Jill Carey, Marla Carey, Ron Celnar, John Chapla, Ronnie Chappell, Neil Clark, Reid Collins, Bill Cook, Jacob Cook, Ralph Coon, Allan Cramer, Bill Csak, Rick Daughtry, Robert Davies, Gary Davis, Steven Davis, Jay DeFrank, Alan Dockery, Gordon Dorff, Vincent Dougan, Dave Duff, Nancy Duncan, Jo English, Bob Erlandson, Phil Exum, Carole Feldman, Ralph Fie, John Fiegener, Kin Floyd, Betsy Fredericks, Greg Frigault, Pat Fulton, Mickey Gallagher, Gloria Gasior, Frank Geraty, Darnell Gibson, Tom Griffiths, Mike Groothousen, Lisa Hansen, Eric Harold, Lawrence Harris, Ed Harrison, Ernest Hartmann, Bob Harvey, Tariq Hassan, Lloyd Hastings, William Headline, Sean Heraty, Ken Hillenbrand, Bob Hoffman, Edwin Holahan, Mel Holder, Don Holmes, Theodore Holmes, Marcine Hughes, Rich Jarden, Troy Jordan, Dan Kapono, Rus Karlov,

Robert Keating, Seth Kemball, Pat Kines, Larry Koch, Dale Kremer, Marie LaFontant, David Lantry, George Lee, Howard Lee, Rich Lee, Alyssa Levy, Jim Lindsay, Bud Littin, Jeff Lockamy, Andy Lohman, Mike Lopez, Jerry Loughman, Thomas Lozano, Mike Lumpe, Dick Lusetti, Frank Mac-Anulty, Richard MacArthur, Bob Maines, Rick Mardis, Joann Marrinan, Rick Martin, Phil Marx, Joel Matthis, Lyn McAfee, Donald McCoy, Gerald McKelvey, Butch McMichael, Todd McQueen, Mike Medus, Aaron Meecham, Dennis Mehr, Jay Meisenhelder, Murray Melbin, Richard Meyer, Julie Miller, Joe Misner, Sandy Monroe, James Moore, Juni Moore, Richard Morrison, Rodney Morrison, Jim Mosher, Jay Motyl, Stephen Myers, Darlene Nabinett, George Newcomer, Thomas Niemann, Charlie Olson, Mario Ortiz, Sung Won Park, Wiley Patterson, John Payne, Sheila Pedone, Michael Perez, Jeff Pfeiffer, Meredith Phillips, Jim Preston, Vince Price, John Quinley, Don Quinto, Lina Ramos, Sue Randall, Larry Reilly, Eric Rigot, Wanda Robertson, Becky Robison, Pat Rogers, Frank Romero, Linda Rucins, Preston Schleinkofer, Tim Schneider, Brad Schuldt, Robert Schuman, Lila Sebastian, Matthew Sexton, Steve Sharp, Glenn Simpson, Thomas Sims, Louise Sloan, Aubrey Smith, Kevin Smith, Charlie Solomon, Lisa Solomon, Joe Spinelli, Don Spitler, Bob Squires, Dennis Stanton, Ray Steiner, Neal Strodtbeck, Linda Sundvall, John Sutherland, Roy Synk, Danny Tice, Ralph Tingy, Steve Titunik, Mark Tomasch, Martin Turner, Zeke Varga, Carmello Vargas, Tony Verga, Jose Viola, Don Wallace, Phil Ward, Jay Welshouse, Michael Wenninger, Owen Wentworth, Susan Whitaker, Steve White, Albert Williams, Dan Williams, Alva Wilson, Kenny Wilson, Terry Wilson, Jon Wolman, Joan Young and Mark Zales.

I am also grateful to Taylor Armerding, Jennifer Ash, Karl Baer, Gary Belowich, Tom Benner, Myles Berkowitz, Rebecca Beuchler, Jill Bilzi, Dan Breen, Brian Coyne, Doreen Coyne, Johanna Coyne, Marc Darisse, Donald Feeney, Joe and Jan Feldman, Joseph Fili, Patricia and Dan Finkelman, Kate Frank, Helen Gifford, Annie Gottlieb, Mary Grasberger, Paul and Myrtle Grasberger, Howard Iverson, Jezra Kaye, Reni Kaye, Michael Kennedy, Sally Kerans, Andrew and Bliss Miga, John Muresianu, Jim Neidinger, Steve and Cathy O'Connell, Mary Peters, Phil Primack, Ken Rosenberg, Patti Satterthwaite, David Spink, Sydne Squire, Joe and Jackie Tabacsko, Michael Tabacsko, Craig Tomashoff and Mary Wright; to Paul Grasberger, Richard Kaye and Dorothy Tabacsko, who would have liked to see it, but who couldn't; and finally to Anne and Budd Coyne, who started me out right; Reid Boates, who pulled me into the light; David Rosenthal, who could see in the dark; and Jane Kaye, to whom I owe my best days and nights both, *sine* Jane *non*.

About the Author

KEVIN COYNE is a journalist living in Freehold,
New Jersey, with his wife and daughter. He is
a graduate of the University of Pennsylvania.
This is his first book.

About the Type

This book was set in Galliard, a typeface designed by
Matthew Carter for the Mergenthaler Linotype
Company in 1978. Galliard is based on the sixteenth-
century typefaces of Robert Granjon, which give it
classic lines yet interject a contemporary look.